A Language of

Sense and Meaning in the Maki
Weste

A Language of Its Own

Sense and Meaning
in the Making of Western Art Music

RUTH KATZ

The University of Chicago Press | Chicago and London

RUTH KATZ is the Emanuel Alexandre Professor Emerita of musicology at Hebrew University, Jerusalem, where she taught from 1966 to 1995 and founded, with Dalia Cohen, the Electronic Laboratory for Musicological Research. This is her eleventh book.

The University of Chicago Press, Chicago 60637
The University of Chicago Press, Ltd., London
© 2009 by The University of Chicago
All rights reserved. Published 2009
Printed in the United States of America

18 17 16 15 14 13 12 11 10 09   1 2 3 4 5

ISBN-13: 978-0-226-42596-2 (cloth)
ISBN-13: 978-0-226-42597-9 (paper)
ISBN-10: 0-226-42596-7 (cloth)
ISBN-10: 0-226-42597-5 (paper)

Library of Congress Cataloging-in-Publication Data

Katz, Ruth, 1927–
    A language of its own : sense and meaning in the making of Western art music / Ruth Katz.
        p. cm.
    Includes bibliographical references and index.
    ISBN-13: 978-0-226-42596-2   (cloth : alk. paper)
    ISBN-13: 978-0-226-42597-9   (pbk. : alk. paper)
    ISBN-10: 0-226-42596-7   (cloth : alk. paper)
    ISBN-10: 0-226-42597-5   (pbk. : alk. paper)
    1. Music. 2. Music—History and criticism. 3. Music—Social aspects. 4. Music—Philosophy and aesthetics. I. Title.
    ML60.K18 2009
    781.6'8117—dc22

                                                        2008055137

♾ The paper used in this publication meets the minimum requirements of the American National Standard for Information Sciences—Permanence of Paper for Printed Library Materials, ANSI Z39.48–1992.

In memory of Carl Dahlhaus
And for
Ruth HaCohen and Elisheva Rigbi

CONTENTS

PART III
The Retreat from the "Shared Understanding"

$\mathcal{T}$he following essay traces some of the key ideas that affected the development of music in the West. Although it deals with an extended historical process, it is not conceived of as a general history of the art. Although musical periods and their changing styles are touched upon, and names of composers and theorists are occasionally mentioned, they do not occupy center stage. The essay, rather, examines major theoretical issues—as they emerged historically—in an attempt to disclose and highlight the *rational base* that underlies the development of music in the West, in particular that of Western art music.

Music does not happen in a vacuum; it invariably contributes to and reflects the culture of which it is part. As such it must be viewed from the perspective of those who both shape the art and circumscribe its meaning, determining the ways in which it is to be understood. Many ideas go into the making of music; some emerge from the exigencies of the art, while others emanate from its social and cultural surroundings. These ideas, regardless of their origin, interact with one another in significant ways, lending musical traditions their distinctness and modes of continuity.

The arts in general and music in particular, may often be treated—depending on the tradition examined—as cultural subsystems. In societies where art and science, myth and social practice are inextricably intertwined—enveloped, as it were, by an ever present "cosmological" outlook—it is hard to sever subsystems from what seems to function as a unified whole. It is considerably less complicated to focus on cultural subsystems in societies that have undergone social and cultural differentiation in the course of their development. All societies, to be sure, undergo certain processes or procedures of differentiation, yet the dividing lines they create do not necessarily create subsystems with a marked dynamic of their own. The more diffuse the dividing lines between seemingly different issues, the more difficult it is to consider the separate realms to which they might belong. Yet the more differentiated the realms, the more they tend to conceal the shared social and cultural forces that affect their development.

Western art music emerged as a distinct subsystem in the centuries of its uninterrupted development. Each stage in this development was informed by the achievements of the antecedent stage and introduced refinements, changes, and novelties—as it saw fit—into their common heritage. While this continuous process gave rise to a great number of different musical styles, it also attests to an accumulation of basic theoretical presuppositions that built on one another progressively. In retrospect, it seems as though music was striving persistently toward a coherence of its own, anchored in musically meaningful elements and devices. This extended process culminated in what is generally known as "absolute music"—music that "makes sense" unto itself, though it does not articulate what it is about. In other words, music evolved a grammar of its own without a declarative semantics, a "language" of sounds communicative to those who have imbibed it, whether consciously or not. There is no denying, however, that the systematic marriage of words and music—over extended periods—branded music with verbal meanings, to which music lent affective specificity. This had consequences, naturally, for "pure" instrumental music as well, affecting its treatment, import, and reception.

However coherent this music may sound to a Western ear, it is not so perceived by one whose ears are attuned to music of another kind, guided by *its* indicators and signifiers. Nonetheless, the fact that Western music created a world of sounds that relate and refer to one another in significant ways—seemingly *independent* of the "extramusical factors" that affected their development—also made it possible for non-Westerners to acquire an appreciation for the art, if they are willing to make the effort to acquaint themselves with its language. Indeed, Western art music did cut across cultural boundaries and has long been identified—alongside other cultural products that gained universal standing—with so-called high culture.

In sum, the success of Western art music mainly resides in the way it went about establishing *internal references*—musical schemes of various kinds that could relate diverse musical elements to one another in meaningful ways. It did not happen all at once. Rather, it evolved in an extended process that kept providing answers to problems as they emerged, satisfying compositional needs and contemporaneous aesthetic expectations. Yet these solutions were constrained by previous ones, by those that had by then been acclaimed—by participants in that particular musical tradition—as part of an understanding regarding the ways in which music, qua music, functions. To unveil the logic whereby Western music constructed its internal references and crafted its understandings is the object of the present essay.

Although many ideas influence the making of music (e.g., social, economic, political), this discussion will consider only those ideas that can be shown to have had a *direct* impact on the ways in which music was constructed and understood by composers and their respective audiences. Thus, the essay, essentially, addresses two sets of ideas: one pertains to the development of those internal musical references that guided composers and listeners alike, while the other relates to various transformations in the understanding of symbols and the way they function in the arts. It is these two strands of "reasoning" that became inextricably intertwined in the construction of music as a subsystem in the West.

All of the above roughly coincides with the thousand years of the millennium just past, which might well be called the "European Millennium." This millennium, however, also generated processes whereby music's hard-earned coherence has gradually disintegrated—paradoxically, through pushing its limits. Having treated music's hard-earned achievements for an extended period as though they were an *intrinsic* part of 'music,' rather than an idiosyncratic cultural construction of the art, composers kept relying on the manner in which it functioned while increasingly challenging its dictates, thereby precipitating changes in the construction of music and in the ways in which it functions. The second millennium, thus, contains a story about *A World in Sound* that was slow in the making and, in a dawdling fashion, led to a fundamentally new conception of music, to radically new musical practices, and, above all, to novel ways in which music is heard and understood. Although I will also deal with this later phase in the development of Western art music, including its aftermath, the major thrust of the essay concerns the presumed steady "logic" on which *A World in Sound* was built, a world that for centuries commanded respect as a universally acclaimed cultural achievement.

As is well known, however, the whole approach to cultural achievements, including that of Western art music, has undergone drastic changes over the last few decades. The study of music, including that of its producers and consumers, has become more conscious of the multiple functions that 'music' serves and ever more attentive to the unspecified "meanings" that music imparts, making it increasingly difficult to evaluate and assess the accomplishments from a single reified perspective. World music, it seems, is gradually replacing Western art music, owing to an ever-growing endorsement of the music of "remote" cultures. Musical styles of different periods, including different musical traditions, are also adjoined at times in one and the same composition, challenging entrenched theories concerning the functions of art, the role of the artist, and the integrity of the work of art. And while sections with Western classical music are being removed from reputable record stores—from those that, paradoxically, once abounded in overlooked composers and neglected works by famous ones—rock music is steadfastly conquering the ears of the young and, for that matter, most of the public soundtracks, the world over. Much of the success of these compositions, moreover, rests on the orchestrations, arrangements, sound designs, and so forth provided by people other than the ones to whom the musical works are attributed, adding further confusion as to the significance of the contribution of each. The third millennium is obviously bound to redefine not only "worlds of sounds" but all that was hitherto believed to explain their value and import.[1]

It is too early to fully assess the impact that the steadily accelerating developments in the technological, economic, political, and social spheres must have exerted on mental attitudes and frames of mind, as well as the new issues and dilemmas to which they gave rise. Yet, this perspective, however ephemeral and complex, allows for a better appraisal of what, in retrospect and by comparison, seems to have followed a relatively slow and steady course. The second millennium, at any rate, harbors an interesting story that delineates Western art music in its *entirety*, highlighting the ways in which it acquired its uniqueness and distinction. This essay is an attempt to tell this story.

---

1. Based on astute observations concerning present-day trends, Lewis Rowell made an interesting attempt in the spirit of an insightful *musica speculativa* to envisage the development of music in the twenty-first century and to think about its implications for all of those who think and write about music. See Lewis Rowell, "New Temporal Horizons and the Theory of Music," in *Music in the Mirror: Reflections on the History of Music Theory and Literature for the 21st Century*, ed. Andreas Giger and Thomas J. Mathiesen (Nebraska, 2002), 295–312.

The essay consists of six chapters divided into three parts. Part 1 highlights the processes whereby music devised its self-referential world. Part 2 focuses on the transformation of major ideas that had a direct bearing on the essence of what came to be understood as music in the West, including its import. Part 3 attempts to capture the trends that irrevocably altered the "understandings" that came to the fore in the previous two parts. The first part is thus more instructive in nature, elucidating those aspects of music that are unique to the West; the second is more reflective and closely related to the history of ideas; the third abounds in social-political "overtones." Despite their seemingly separate concerns, the three parts closely follow—with minor overlaps—the historical unfolding of Western art music in the second millennium. In addition to familiarity with the history of that music and the composers that exemplify its diverse styles, the effort to trace the major "decisions" that had a bearing on the development of music requires, ipso facto, some acquaintance with seminal treatises, theoretical debates, aesthetic deliberations, and so forth, circumscribed by their own historical contexts. Adhering to the dictum that evidence must be brought to bear on claims (whatever their nature), the following essay tries to substantiate its claims by providing the relevant evidence, even at the cost of enlisting the reader's close scrutiny. For the benefit of the nonprofessional music lover, the text elucidates technical matters as much as possible, relegating the "cues" expected by the experts to the footnotes accompanying the text. Indeed, it is hard to strike a middle course that would both please those who wish to know more and lure the more knowledgeable to entertain a "new look." The reader, hence, should feel free to skip technical explanations that may seem oversimplified to the expert or too complicated for the amateur, in the hope that he or she will try nonetheless to follow the unfolding of the main arguments.

In order to prevent misunderstandings, it is necessary to state unambiguously that this essay is not a story about the "rise and fall" of Western art music. Nor does it represent the musical preferences of its author. Rather, the essay attempts to unveil the "turns of mind" that affected the making and understanding of Western art music in the course of its extended development. It rests on the axiom that music is man-made, that it invariably reflects its creators, and that it can never attain an ideal or final form. The essay, thus, deals with the interdependence of "sound" and "thought" in the construction of music in the West, and with the ways in which the balance between the ostensibly "rational" and "irrational" was continually negotiated. The processes of "balancing" clearly involved modes of rationalization; it is their underlying "logic" that the essay attempts to make salient. Thus, what seems rational in one context undergoes changes in another socio-intellectual context, redefined in light of both tradition and altered aesthetic desiderata. It is the outcome of these negotiations that constitute the self-portrait of Western art music at each of several points in time.

The essay, in fact, tries to show that the principal product of the Western musical tradition has not been music alone, but music cum writings about music and the indispensable interrelationship between them. Western music is the result of evolving ideas, ideas that often carried conflicting messages about what music essentially encompasses and how it should be understood and employed. Yet as a man-made "world in sound," music also rested for a long time on accrued assumptions about "music, qua music," that is, what came to be understood by 'music' in the West. In fact, the reification of musical works in the form of a canon and the inauguration of a "science" of music came into being only in the late nineteenth century, once some of these assumptions were challenged.

In his extensive introduction to *Text and Act: Essays on Music and Performance,* Richard Taruskin seized the opportunity to dispute some of the assumptions that underlie the study of music. He reminds us that it is "conventional to assert about music that while its style and structure are facts, its sense is merely subjective without any decent epistemological footing." This view, claims Taruskin, "fairly circumscribed the field of musicology" until recently: "style and structure were its objects of study (the former being the province of music history, the latter of theory), whereas musical meaning was off-limits to properly musicological investigation (though it kept a little toehold on the margins of philosophy)."[2] Indeed, although one can name some notable exceptions who transgressed the "off-limits" and also claim that the "toehold" constituted a significant "foothold," Taruskin's bifurcated picture of musicology can hardly be denied.

Quoting Manfred Bukofzer, Taruskin reminds us that Bukofzer claimed that "if the history of music is to have more than an antiquarian interest and significance, it must be seen as a history of musical styles and the history of *styles* in turn as a history of *Ideas*." Bukofzer actually suggested that via stylistic analysis it might be possible to extract the ideas whereby the musical elements of a given style are combined and the ways in which they achieve their specific effect.[3] Taruskin cites Bukofzer as an example of how historical studies of music managed to *evade* "extramusical" ideas by focus-

---

2. See Richard Taruskin, *Text and Act: Essays on Music and Performance* (Oxford, 1995), 42.
3. Ibid. See also note 76 on the same page.

ing on "the music itself." It can be argued, however, that extracting the "logic" that underlies musical styles may constitute a procedure whereby the incommensurability of the physical and metaphysical is resolved via a meaningful common denominator that bridges sound and idea, including extramusical ones. Interestingly, it may be said of the new musicology that it employs many such "common denominators" that relate music and ideas in ways that "give voice" to hitherto "concealed" meanings.

The present essay does not attempt to unveil hitherto concealed ideas, nor does it present new ideas that enrich our present-day understanding of the past. Rather, this essay is an attempt to trace the ways in which music in the West *construed itself* in light of changing social and cultural circumstances. It tries to show that the Western conception of 'music,' in and of itself, emerged from the fundamental relationship between ideas and musical construction, between spiritual aspirations and musical import, a relationship that jointly produced the *self-portrait,* as it were, of Western art music.

To be sure, self-portraits are not exempt from assessments and interpretations, yet they involve narratives of a different kind. Such narratives tend to focus on objects of art so as to unveil their hidden—unvoiced or silenced—meanings and artistic messages, as the new musicology well exemplifies. The new musicology obviously represents a contemporary "turn of mind" that can no longer accept uncritically some of the entrenched ideas about Western art music, even if they seemed sensible in "the world of yesterday." We must nevertheless remember that no period in the history of Western art music was as diligently engaged with the "rethinking of music" as the period we live in, an era whose "vision" improved as the world shrunk in size. Indeed, the Eurocentric biases of much of Western historical writing became more discernible once those who were excluded from the "progressive features" of the West came into sight.[4] Modern

---

4. In *The Theft of History* (Cambridge, 2006), Jack Goody endeavors to show that many of the central ideas attributed to the West actually emerged in cultures and geographic regions other than Europe. He also shows how and in what way Europe managed to set itself apart from the rest of the world. The perspective of those who study prehistoric times that stressed the unity of Bronze Age civilizations across Europe and Asia was fractured, we learn from Goody, by the notion of an "independent European Antiquity" that identified a phase in the history of the world unique to Europe, a phase that also prefigured its subsequent development. "The problem of Antiquity, " argues Goody, "becomes especially acute, both for the present and for the past, when European scholars attribute the prestigious origin of a form of government (democracy), of values like freedom, of individualism, even of 'rationality', to this historical period, and hence to Europe rather than elsewhere" (290). Goody believes that a valid comparison

technology clearly changed our forms of attention. Yet by subjecting our daily lives—more than ever before—to dramatic and rapid changes, it also seems to have affected our sense of continuity and tradition, harboring both threats and promise. This being said, the present essay tries to portray the expanded development of a particular musical tradition and the unique ways in which it acquired its credibility and significance.

Given this trajectory, it must be clear that the present essay could not have been written without standing on the shoulders of the scholars cited in my bibliography. Obviously, I am also in debt to all those who labored to unveil the seminal writings that accompanied the development of music in the West. I am grateful to all of them.

In a sense, this essay summarizes what I managed to learn in the decades that began at Columbia University in the '50s. At Columbia, I had fallen under the spell of Paul Henry Lang and the rigorous demands of Erich Hertzmann. Lang instilled in his students an awareness that music does not transpire in a vacuum, while Hertzmann's intimate familiarity with theoretical treatises and musical tractates left no room for unsubstantiated claims, however tempting. That the artistic expression of non-Western civilizations deserves serious attention was impressed on us by the delightful Curt Sachs, who traveled uptown from New York University to deliver his Columbia lectures. Oliver Strunk made it across the river from Princeton to lead a seminar on Byzantine music, and Nino Pirrotta made it across the Atlantic before securing a permanent position at Harvard. There was no shortage of great scholars at Columbia in those days, yet some acquired special fame for their efforts to contextualize—in effect, to substantiate Lang's claim that nothing transpires in a vacuum. Nobody could afford to overlook the legendary lectures on art by the great Meyer Shapiro. A sample of one made you come back for more, and back I came. The same held true for Lionel Trilling, the scholar of literature. There were many renowned figures, but it was difficult to fit them all in. Eventually, on the shoulders of D. P. Walker, Claude Palisca, Pirrotta, and others in diverse fields, I attempted in *Divining the Powers of Music* to show

---

among cultures must abandon predetermined categories and construct a sociological grid "laying out the possible variations of what is being compared," instead of pointing to the "progressive features" that preoccupied Western historians. The historians, argues Goody, "have stolen history by imposing their categories and sequences on the rest of the world" (304).

that the rise of opera was embedded in the Scientific Revolution of the late sixteenth and early seventeenth centuries.

While I was preparing for my doctoral exams, my husband, Elihu Katz, joined the sociology department at the University of Chicago. At the time, the most prominent members of Chicago's music department were Howard Brown, Leonard Meyer, and the "mighty" Edward Lewinsky. Attending some departmental seminars, I got to know all of its members, but, in particular, I befriended Leonard Meyer, whose highly influential early work—*Emotion and Meaning in Music*—had just been published. We remained in touch even after I returned to Israel and became a member of the musicology department that Alex Ringer helped to establish at the Hebrew University of Jerusalem.

Born in Germany, raised in Palestine, and having completed university studies in the United States, I returned to an Israel that held a prominent place on the map of conductors and performers who appreciated the country's Philharmonic Orchestra and its music-loving public. I somehow expected the cosmopolitan Hebrew University and its National Library to reflect this musical activity in a scholarly way, but the library could hardly take pride in its music division. Teaching Western art music constituted a lesser problem than did research, which became heavily dependent on journeys abroad. This situation, however, gradually changed. Once musicology became firmly established in the University, the library kept adapting itself to the needs of faculty and students. At the same time, it was hard to overlook that Israel, with its diverse ethnic groups, presented an ideal laboratory for ethnomusicological studies. My research activity divided, therefore, between ethnomusicological and musicological studies that continued in this way throughout my career. I soon realized that these seemingly divided concerns affect each other in significant ways. Yet, while working on *The Lachmann Problem: An Unsung Chapter in the History of Comparative Musicology,* I could better understand why the University opted for Lachmann—given his interest in Arabic music—in preference to Curt Sachs, who was the more established scholar when they were both ousted from the country of their birth. Eventually, the thinking of Lachmann, Sachs, and a host of other eminent ethnomusicologists influenced my and Dalia Cohen's study of *Palestinian-Arab Music: A Maqām Tradition in Practice.*

I have been intrigued by music since early childhood. Although I had practiced the piano for many years, I invariably preferred listening to accomplished performances. In retrospect, it seems that my interest in music is closely related to my overall interest in processes, transformations of all kinds, and in the ideas that lurk behind them. As human beings, we invariably employ strategies to guide our understanding; that is, we use ideas to *think with* about ideas, though we are mostly unaware of their origin. My interest in ideas explains my fascination with philosophical deliberations and, in recent years, with cognitive studies. Nothing, however, vexes me more than the empty ritual of substantiating a claim by flaunting the name of a famous philosopher inappropriately. This dissatisfaction of mine resulted eventually in the four volumes of *Contemplating Music,* compiled, edited, and annotated by myself and Carl Dahlhaus, the whole of which is structured around central musical issues that were addressed by philosophers, taking account of the state of the art during the time. The experience of exchanging ideas with Dahlhaus was more than I allowed myself to fantasize about when I first encountered his writings. My admiration for his broad horizons and vast knowledge did not frighten me, since I had no reason to pretend that I was his equal. More than I owe to those already mentioned I feel indebted to Carl Dahlhaus, my idea of the consummate musicologist.

While working on *Contemplating Music,* I enlisted Ruth HaCohen as our assistant. Ruth came to my attention during the first year of her studies at the University. I was struck by how much her interests coincided with mine. From that time on, Ruth and I became sounding boards for each other. This mutuality led to our joint works *Tuning the Mind: Connecting Aesthetics to Cognitive Science* and *The Arts in Mind.* Elisheva Rigbi, by contrast, was no novice when she enrolled as a doctoral student. She had been a practicing musician with a master's degree from Indiana University's School of Music, and she had served for several years as a music critic. In view of her initial skepticism about musicology, Elisheva presented an opportunity to observe a person in the process of "shifting gears." As it turned out, her brilliant research broadened my own understanding of the transformations that took place at the turn of the nineteenth century. Ruth and Elisheva are echoed in my essay and are explicitly credited. Indeed, good students improve the mind of their teachers!

The list of people who impacted this work would be incomplete without Nelson Goodman. My essay, as will become clear, enlists a goodly number of philosophers because of their relevance to historical "turns of mind" that affected the structuring and understanding of music. Nelson Goodman, by comparison, improved *my* understanding of an important stage in the development of music, that is, the committing of sound to script. Having taught notation, I naturally had some ideas as to what had taken place, but Goodman's uncanny rigor and mastery of symbolic logic put order into my diffused thoughts, and not only those concerning notation. I was lucky to be able to test my understanding of Goodman with Goodman himself during his visit to Jerusalem as a guest of the department of philosophy. He expressed genuine interest in my presentation of the historical development of notation as "compliance" to his theory. Had I knocked on his door at Harvard, I was told, I would have had to wait for several weeks to be received.

To recapitulate, I am grateful to those who charted my course in musicology, to those who helped steer my way within the discipline, and to all those whose thinking had a direct impact on this attempt to render a reliable portrait of a venerable musical tradition. Last but not least, I want to thank the readers of my manuscript whose observations, comments, and criticisms I addressed with utmost care, and to offer special thanks to Kathleen Hansell, music editor at the University of Chicago Press, who shepherded my manuscript on its journey with great care and devotion.

The Guiding Conception of Western Art Music

*W*estern art music was identified for a long time with what is commonly called "high culture," though the distinction between high and low was already seriously challenged, on social and political grounds, during the French Revolution and, subsequently, by other ideological movements.[1] In the last few decades, however, in light of the rapid changes that have occurred in the political, ideological, and technological spheres, affecting all societies as well as their awareness of one another, distinctions of this sort have undergone more careful scrutiny. Thus, historians of culture, anthro-

---

1. The French Revolution, as is well known, declared that art must not be the privilege of the rich and the leisured, or an idle pastime, but that it must teach and improve and contribute to the happiness of the general public and be the possession of every man. By creating a correspondence between the idea of artistic truth and that of social justice, the revolution challenged the dictatorship of the academies and the monopolization of the art market by the court and the aristocracy. The period that followed denied that there existed objective rules of any kind to govern the production or consumption of art. It enshrined the uniqueness of individual expression and the struggle against the very principle of authority and rule. Whereas the prerevolutionary middle class saw art as one means of expressing identification with the aristocracy and aloofness from the lower classes, in the postrevolutionary period it began to think of art as a "matter of taste" that might vary among different people, at different times, and in different places. For a suggestive discussion of this turn, see Arnold Hauser, *The Social History of Art* (London, 1951), vol. 2, 622–710.

pologists, students of folklore, and ethnomusicologists, among others, have helped divert our attention from a distinction that no longer seemed unequivocal and to redirect us toward differences among diverse cultures and subcultures.

Without enlisting the roles of minority claims, the diffusion of popular culture, and economic constraints, it is abundantly clear that Western art music has lost much of the standing it once enjoyed, though the number of its adherents was always relatively small. Although the same holds true for many other cultural products that had been previously universally acclaimed, an uncanny atmosphere hovers over Western art music as the new millennium begins. This includes, paradoxically, the ostensible blessings that inhere in the steadfast expansion of the so-called authenticity movement, as well as the renewed interest in opera.[2] Those familiar with the art and its historical development may sense that a world of sound, articulate and meaningful unto itself and on its own terms, may be nearing its end.

More than any other kind of music, Western art music has been extensively studied, and more is in the offing. Yet it has never been looked at as an *entirety.* Interestingly, the systematic study of music, which evolved in the West, often addressed remote cultures as "wholes" in the attempt to delineate their uniqueness, even while aware that such comprehensive pictures manifest themselves in different ways and degrees. Paradoxically, the universal standing of Western art music defied delineation of this kind, by having eclipsed the distance necessary for doing so. As long as

2. It has been pointed out that the growing diffusion of performances of early music did not necessarily rest, from the start, on authenticity claims, but rather on the "novelty" of the music and the "persuasiveness" of its performance. However, the immense strides of instrument builders, music editors, and performers tended more and more in the direction of historical faithfulness, contributing, thereby, toward more so-called authentic renditions (see the articles by Howard M. Brown, Nicholas Kenyon, and Philip Brett in *Authenticity and Early Music,* ed. Nicholas Kenyon, Oxford, 1988). While scholars, instrument builders, and performers of old music were refining their knowledge of the past, it also became increasingly clear that their dedication created a kind of "distancing" from the present. The preoccupation with the past introduced, in fact, new queries concerning the present. One of the key questions raised by the success of the authentic performance movement concerns the *ways* and the *extent* to which the present still constitutes a continuation of the past, that is, the extent to which tradition still animates and informs the present (see Richard Taruskin's and Robert P. Morgan's articles in ibid.). Unlike the issue of 'authenticity,' the renewed interest in opera, and its increased "popularity" in recent years, has not been studied systematically. A large segment of its audience consists of people who do not attend symphonic or chamber music concerts. The search for more "accessible meaning"—meanings that one can readily recognize and identify with—may explain, at least in part, this interesting sociological shift.

Western art music retained its privileged position among the music of the world, its students could linger on stylistic changes of all sorts, indulging in the refinements of their details, experiencing no need to make salient what their variety holds in common. However, as the "remote" increasingly draws nearer and the "near" increasingly recedes,[3] the time has come to examine the whole of this particular music as a unique "world making" in sound.[4] Its uniqueness can be revealed through the *processes* of its unfolding and its conceivable disintegration.[5]

From the perspective of "world making" we need to identify the phases that appear to have been crucial to its construction—those that allowed it, in the first place, to become a "possible world"[6] with an intelligibility of its own—as well as the later phases that appear to have threatened its existence. Indeed, an overriding curve connects the particular stages in the development of what is commonly called "classical music," commencing with music's attempt to detach itself from language, trying to create

3. One need no longer go to India to hear Indian music, nor does one have to reach other parts of the world to hear indigenous music. It can be heard everywhere in the "global village" that the various means of communication have helped to create. Forgoing "context" contributed, no doubt, to paving the road toward what is known nowadays as "world music."

4. The phrase "world making" is borrowed from Nelson Goodman who examined the ways in which the actual worlds we live in are made, claiming that knowing or understanding is no more a matter of finding than of making. See his *Ways of World-Making* (Indianapolis, 1978).

5. The kind of observation I have in mind is expected to cut below the surface—beneath specific descriptions of music-theoretical aspects and musical realizations, and below observations pertaining to obvious ties between social elements and musical practice—so as to unveil the overriding guiding force whereby Western music differs from that of music belonging to other civilizations. Max Weber, as is well known, claimed in his many studies that an ever-growing preponderance of rational social action runs through the development of the Western world. What is less known is that Weber also applied his thesis to Occidental art in general and, in particular, to music. In his essay *The Rational and Social Foundation of Music* (Munich, 1921), he examined some of the building blocks of Western music—for example, scale and tone systems, temperament and tonality—in order to reveal the rational properties of Western music that were produced by social factors in Occidental development. Unlike Weber, though aware of his thesis, I intend to trace the *historical* development of Western music in order to characterize its striving toward a coherence of its own (i.e., seemingly independent of external references) and its departure from this objective toward new goals.

6. The phrase "possible world" is borrowed from Gottfried Wilhelm Leibniz who viewed this world as the best of all "possible worlds," for it was freely created by a rational God who always chooses the best for a good reason. This best of all possible worlds, Leibniz maintained, is "the one which is at the same time the simplest in hypotheses and the richest in phenomena" (*Discourse on Metaphysics* § 6).

a "communicative language" of its own, and terminating with a "self-absorbed kind of music" that was no longer understood by those for whom it was intended. In retrospect, it seems as though music strove for centuries, irrespective of different styles, functions, and meaning, toward a "coherence of its own," which, once fully achieved, succumbed to a probing of its limits. It must be remembered, however, that the self-referential systems that music developed (including their procedures), rather than annulling the quest for meaning, were ingeniously used. They were employed in ways that helped to elucidate not only dispositions of many kinds but also narrative allusions of various sorts. In due time, however, composers also developed expressive means at the expense of music's own internal reasoning; thus, from a desire to tell the listener what the music was about, the "what about" often lent coherence to the music that it employed.

A mistrust in music's categorical systems eventually led to a devolution of music into individualized musical expressions that expected to thrive on the technical innovations they engendered. Whether its purpose was to promote new outlooks on music or to abandon habitual ones, this led—in one form or another, using different pretexts—to the dissolution not only of a world in sound that was intelligible unto itself but also to a forgoing of the *spiritual signification* that music represented to its respective audiences. Though well entrenched, music yielded nonetheless to other guidelines with objectives of their own, affirming once more that nothing stands still in history. The art music that was identified as "Western" evolved over a drawn-out period, corresponding roughly to the millennium that has just ended. As time goes on, the second millennium may yet come to be known as the European Millennium with Western art music as one of its major representatives.

The time has now come to look at Western art music from the perspective delineated so far, seeking to encompass the processes that underlie its *entirety*. Accordingly, the five chapters that follow address the conceptions that guided Western art music, drawing special attention to five fundamental issues that, sequentially and together, had a major bearing on the development of music in the West. These issues comprise both the phases relevant to its emergence and those relevant to its conceivable disintegration. A sixth chapter will conjecture about the future, based on present-day trends. The issues that require special scrutiny involve the following topics:

1. The "building blocks" of Western music and the *ideas* that guided their making and choice;

2. The codification of "musical laws" that paved the way for music's manifold constructions;

3. The development in theory and thought that led to a distinction between 'sense' and 'meaning,' granting "absolute music" a significant position among the arts;

4. The "probing of the limits" of music's achieved coherence;

5. The cultural and social climate that induced a *paradigmatic* shift in music theory and composition (including its aftermath);

6. Speculations concerning the future, based on present-day trends.

These chapters are hardly arbitrary, for each one addresses an issue whose clarification time corresponded, more or less, to a specific "time-span" in the historical development of music in the West. The clarification of each issue constituted, in fact, a necessary step toward the subsequent ones that raised new queries that needed to be addressed. The first chapter, accordingly, covers a period that spans the tenth through the fourteenth centuries; the second (with some overlap) covers mainly the fifteenth and sixteenth centuries; the third focuses primarily on the seventeenth and eighteenth centuries; the fourth centers on the nineteenth century, while the fifth concerns the twentieth century. Together they cover the entire millennium. The sixth chapter uses the emergent picture as a background to detect new vistas.

Before proceeding, a brief discussion is in order to reassure those who might wonder about the legitimacy of delineating the dominant features of a musical tradition as varied in styles, genres, and aims as Western art music. Let us begin, therefore, with some general observations about "stocktaking." As is well known, taking stock is a standard procedure in organizations and institutions that wish to evaluate their activities in light of objectives that constitute their original raison d'être. Such procedures rest on the belief that there is something to be gained from looking back that might be of relevance to the present and, possibly, to the future as well. It seems obvious that such a belief extends to a much wider range of activities, all of which relate, in one form or another, to *appraisals guided by spelled-out objectives.* This, needless to say, holds equally true for individuals, as it does for groups, as they attempt to assess each other's or their own achievements.

Historical research also entails a kind of looking back that yields assessments with implications for subsequent developments, yet it must itself often explain the very objectives that guide the assessments. The two seem linked to each other (albeit in intricate and convoluted ways) in our attempts to *judge* or *comprehend* man's aspirations, activities, and achievements. Judgment, we learn from philosophy, is invariably dependent on "framing."[7] This alone would suffice to explain why histories are rewritten time and again, though it is by no means the sole reason for this entrenched phenomenon. While social and political events supersede each other in a linear, seemingly progressive fashion, leaving scant apparent traces of earlier times (however important to the historical development as a whole), the arts, by contrast, abound in artifacts that survive their times as autonomous works. It is therefore no coincidence that the history of art chose to focus on styles and their changes, employing the artifacts *themselves* as evidence that discloses the objectives that guided their specific developments. Once it turned into a bona fide discipline, musicology too based its historical narrative largely on the musical works that exemplify its unfolding. If the study of music focused on styles, as did the other arts, it did so with an awareness that diverse styles, however dissimilar, may equally contribute to what might be termed *"the sum 'cultural capital' of a society."*[8] While works of art enjoy individual positions in such an admixture of cultural assets, their relative standing within it can vary over time.

In their attempt to unveil the forces that propel stylistic change, histories of art saw fit to enlist the broader contexts in which they occur, attentive to ideas and thoughts that seem to have affected changes in these larger historical frames. General ideas, not necessarily artistic ones, were thus presumed to manifest themselves in artistic desiderata. Interestingly, to unveil the desiderata that found expression in the various styles, it was deemed necessary to de-compose, as it were, the various styles into their constitutive elements and modes of construction, so as to be able to retrace the *thoughts* that guided their composition in the first place. It is these thoughts that became commensurable with nonartistic ideas, singling out those that became manifest in particular aesthetic preferences. Although the analysis of styles is expected to unveil their distinctiveness, that is, the ideas that distinguish them, it also enables us to gauge each

7. Even the field of ethics had a hard time conceiving of 'virtue' as moral goodness for its own sake. In recent times, however, the impact of "framing" has been investigated empirically, primarily in fields such as perception and decision making. We are all of course aware of the persuasive powers of "framing" and the role it plays in advertising and in the various image projections of public figures.

8. "Cultural capital" is a concept coined by Pierre Bourdieu in his investigations of the role played by cultural assets in society. See, for example, his "Artists Taste and Cultural Capital," in *Culture and Society,* ed. Jeffrey Alexander and Steven Seidman (Cambridge, 1991), 205–15.

individual work against the style to which it belongs and to the crystallization of which it may have contributed. The general and the particular,
thus, become two sides of the same coin, that is, the common features are
derived from individual works and the evaluation of each of them is assessed in light of the features they hold in common.[9]

To enable a comparison among different cultural traditions, so as to
be able to gauge the uniqueness of each, the history of art, interestingly,
uses the very same method that it employs for different styles within the
same tradition. But whereas the characteristics of a specific style, which
belongs to a given cultural tradition, are derived from individual *works* that
contribute to its formation (allowing for the uniqueness of the individual
work to emerge in light of these characteristics), the starting point for the
comparison among different traditions is their individual *styles,* that is, the
various styles that make up the tradition. What the different styles of a
given tradition have in common may thus serve a double function: to establish the uniqueness of each style within the tradition as well as the idiosyncrasies of the tradition (as a whole) in comparison with other cultural
traditions, whose characteristics have been established in a similar way. In
sum, the unit one looks at, large or small, invariably incorporates artifacts
that survived their time. Although such cultural repositories allow us to
unveil their *historical* unfolding only in varying degrees, depending on the
tradition examined (e.g., living or extinct, written or oral), it is invariably
possible to characterize them in their entireties. The Western musical tradition lends itself to both of these procedures.

Although styles come and go, replacing one another in ways that highlight the differences among them, overshadowing what they have in common, it is possible at times (depending on the tradition examined) to discern not only their connecting threads but even the direction in which
they lead.[10] At any rate, it can be shown that music in the West, despite
its variety of styles and genres, retained in a *cumulative* fashion those aspects that enabled it to "make sense" even without 'predication,'[11] as well

9. For the logic that underlies the assessments of individual works against the style
they hold in common, see Nelson Goodman's illuminating article "The Status of Style,"
in *Critical Inquiry* 1, no. 4 (1975): 799–812.

10. The development of harmonic tonality, for example, may serve to illustrate this
point.

11. The term 'predication' refers to expressions that can be used to say something
about objects picked out. It may refer, however, either to the activity of predication or to
what is predicated. By combining logic and grammar, the term came to occupy a venerable place in the philosophy of language.

as the aspects that in a cumulative fashion caused the pendulum to swing in the opposite direction. Rather than linger on stylistic details, however important, this book aims to expose the connecting threads among the various styles and the eventual weakening of their stitches, for in them reside the features that granted Western art music its "physiognomy" and uniqueness.

PART I

The Structuring of a Self-Referential World

ONE

The Making of Musical Building Blocks

PRELIMINARY CLARIFICATIONS

There are two basic axioms that require reaffirmation before launching a discussion of the musical building blocks that evolved in the West. The first pertains to the simple fact that music is man-made. The second pertains to a less evident verity, namely, that music is *not* a language spontaneously appreciated by every listener, irrespective of cultural background or hard-earned understanding.[1] The two axioms, moreover, are related to each other. Given that music is man-made and that cultures differ from one another, musical traditions are bound to differ from one another. Consequently, what may seem natural—that is, familiar and readily understood in one culture—may sound strange and unintelligible in another. Unless a special effort is made to discern the sonic and ideational elements that a particular culture has chosen for its musical organizations and their uses, an outsider will fail to relate to their *import*—to what is indicated, implied, or signified by the music. In short, being privy to the basic communicative/expressive aspects

---

1. Music, unlike speech, is mostly claimed to be the international language of mood and of feeling. Moods and feelings, however, also require some kind of decoding.

of a musical tradition, however obtained, is a prerequisite for its appreciation.

It should be stated explicitly, though it has already been intimated, that musical traditions differ not only in their organization of sounds and their import but also in the raw materials that they employ. These are not selected from a ready-made stock, as it were, but are likewise created. By harboring both possibilities, *as well as* additional constraints, such rudimentary creations already reflect cultural preferences, which will manifest themselves fully in the music once developed. Such creations, however, may undergo changes in the course of the musical development, for the two are reciprocally related to each other.

In dealing with the great variety of musical systems and modes of expression one can proceed in a number of ways. One may proceed, for example, from specific musical traditions in order to establish regional traits, or the other way round. One may try to characterize the music of whole civilizations, from "primitive" to highly developed ones, in an attempt to unveil some kind of developmental scheme for the very phenomenon of music-making. Geography, civilization, culture, and, of course, the musical systems themselves may constitute what one wishes to illuminate.

Music the world over has some kind of organization that lends each tradition its distinctness, and different musical traditions may also reveal certain relationships among themselves. Yet it can be shown, for example, that European music, although it has inherited quite a number of features from the East, is fundamentally different from Eastern music. Eastern music, to be sure, comprises a great variety of systems and modes of expression, yet when contrasted with European music it reveals certain common features that set the two apart. More than they reveal apparent differences in the music, such features reveal conceptual differences in the attitude toward music and its understanding. For example, the Eastern conception of the *identity* of a given melody is markedly different from the European one, since it does not conceive of the melody as a series of fixed "immovable" notes, but rather as a characteristic musical gesture that can be performed in a number of ways. Different renditions of a melody, therefore, may be considered identical as long as the character of the specific gesture is maintained. The gestures, in turn, entail *typified motives* and the manner in which they are employed. These may vary a great deal from one country, or group of countries, to another, yet they all seem to share a technique of composition whereby every piece, vocal and instrumental, is interspersed with typified motives. Thus the different versions of a melody in these musical traditions do not change its substance—as a European might think—but are left to the discretion of the performer, who is well versed in the gestures and the manner in which they are used.

In fact, European music has come to be fundamentally different from the music of the rest of the world because of the growth of harmony and the development of staff notation. Yet neither harmony nor the invention of written music is peculiar to Europe. Part singing is found elsewhere in the world and the unsophisticated forms of polyphony have a great deal in common with the earliest European forms. Likewise, various kinds of notation have been invented throughout the Eastern civilizations, but they have never been used as prescriptive signs for singing and playing, nor could they, given their nature.[2] What secures the European musician against taking "wrong steps" is staff notation, which developed only gradually. The more complicated the harmonic texture became, the more it had to rely on written music. Indeed, complicated musical textures are inconceivable without writing them down. It is the ever mounting desire to control the concurrence of different voices that precipitated the development of a special kind of notation—a notational *system* that leaves no room for ambiguity. It is this development that gave rise to the European conception of identity, and to the notion of an *authoritative version* of a musical composition. Naturally, this kind of "reasoning" harbors implications not only for the role of the composer versus that of the performer but also for the definition of what constitutes a musical work.

THE DEVELOPMENT OF WESTERN NOTATION AND ITS SIGNIFICANCE

The shift from an oral musical tradition to a written one, from devices that aid memory to visual devices that "conserve" the music—thereby enabling certain musical complexities that are inconceivable without them—is far from simple. Though promoted by specific musical developments that called for some kind of visual aid, such a shift necessarily rests on a process that ipso facto discloses a growing awareness of what was previously taken for granted. It was a drawn-out process, since it entailed the gradual emergence of agreed-upon means and ways that guide—and even enable—the observation itself. Tools, methods, and predispositions, as we have learned from science, affect the conception of the objects observed.[3] Although

2. See Walter Kaufman, *Musical Notations of the Orient: Notational Systems of Continental East, South, and Central Asia* (Indiana, 1967).

3. The biblical story of Balaam (who was summoned by Balak, the king of Moab, to

such conceptions may or may not affect the classification of objects, they invariably affect the developments of those objects that are, to start with, man-made. However complicated it might seem, this is precisely what happened in the historical development of music in the West.

The significance of such a development may be fully grasped when compared to the emergence of letter script. Considering its relative simplicity and economic aspects, the advent of letter script in the second half of the thirteenth century BC was undoubtedly a momentous event. Yet, its overwhelming aspect surely resides in the miracle of revealing the power of letters by unveiling their "reality," that is, their sound. Letter script must have become part of myth not only because it conveyed the sense of words[4] but also because it rendered their sounds.[5] To the extent that their sound was realized, the words, of course, preceded the script. Yet it is fair to claim that the magic of inscription, like the wonders of Pythagorean numbers, affected our thinking by providing a basis for further formulations and inferences. By analogy, the notational system developed in the West is another miraculous script related to sound, which, like the alphabet, included and affected musical thought. Moreover, as it evolved in the centuries bridging the early Middle Ages and the Renaissance, musical notation incorporated a basic understanding of Western music. Via selection, circumscription, and the opening up of possibilities, it took part in the making of a world of sounds with its own meaning and coherence.

Like letter script, the notation that concerns us here, if it is to fulfill a

---

curse the enemy—the Children of Israel—before engaging in actual fighting) suggests that Balak entertained the thought that "points of view" may affect the perception of the object observed and, consequently, the action it might elicit (see Numbers 23:11–13). In a less "literal" fashion, the query about the feasibility of "objective" observations has preoccupied not only physicists dealing with quantum mechanics but also many others—anthropologists, historians, not to mention philosophers—who also wished to supply "objective views" of the subjects, issues, or processes they had chosen to study.

4. The shape and structure of the twenty-two Hebrew letters, for example, were thought to have a share in the creation and re-creation of God's world. Indeed, cosmology, magic, and religion are replete with the special kinds of signs in which 'sign' and 'proof,' 'script' and 'fact' are one and the same thing. We need not travel far in time or space, nor need we turn to ancient civilizations or primitive societies, to become aware of the fact that inscriptions of one sort or another were supposed to have contained, in themselves, that which they denoted. The holy sign of Nostradamus's book of secrets, I presume, must have struck Faust in a manner not unlike the way the *Mene Tekel* inscription struck the Babylonian king.

5. If God himself inscribed the tablets at Sinai, those gathered at the foot of the mountain could not withstand the impact of Moses's reading of God's own words, for it practically amounted to "hearing" God himself speak to them.

similar function, must leave no room for ambiguity. Yet the development
of notation was primarily prompted by musical needs as they emerged,
those that required *immediate* solutions. Indeed, it is only in retrospect
that one can clearly discern how writing and the reduction of ambiguity
went hand in hand in the historical development of notation in the West.
In the prehistory of written music in the West, music had no independent
existence (it was certainly unaware of itself). Thus, the earliest musical
writing—which arose as expediency—contained only a fraction of what
was sung. Only gradually was the notation able to convey more and more
of what was actually sung, thereby revealing the ever growing independence of music from extramusical elements. It pays to retrace some of the
highlights of this development in order to fully grasp its significance.[6]

Gregorian Chant Revisited

As is well known, the early writing of music in the West is connected with
the tradition of Gregorian chant. For many years it was believed that the
Gregorian chant that developed in different parts of Europe had a common origin in the East—in the church of Jerusalem and its environs and
possibly in even earlier Jewish practice—having diffused geographically
along with the liturgy. Many a scholar has searched after the oldest sources,
repertoires, or traditions that might have preserved or could have been
related to the original chant melodies. Philological methods and paleographical acumen were invested in comparisons among early manuscripts
in the attempt to retrieve whatever was possible of the "authentic" versions. The effort was accompanied by detailed suggestions concerning the
historical development and diffusion of this tradition, not least because it
constituted an important base for the subsequent development of music
in the West. If this pursuit had remained unchallenged, one would have
had to conclude, according to Leo Treitler, that the neumes[7] "have always
been systematic, that their origin is to be traced to antiquity, that their
task was to always record the *pitches* of the plainchant, that chant melo-

6. The following discussion uses large portions (with only minor changes) of an article
I wrote honoring Nelson Goodman, "History as 'Compliance': The Development of
Western Musical Notation in the Light of Goodman's Requirements," in *How Classification Works: Nelson Goodman among the Social Sciences*, ed. Mary Douglas and David Hull
(Edinburgh, 1992), 99–128. While my understanding of the development of notation has
not changed since, this particular development gains in significance in the context of an
essay that proposes to address the overriding conception that guided Western art music.

7. Medieval notational signs used for writing down plainsong.

dies were conceived as sequences of individual pitches, and that they had always been written down."[8]

The argument was not without its loopholes, however, leaving some questions unanswered and plenty of room for doubt. How could the Ambrosian melodies, for example, be pronounced the oldest source still preserving an older common practice—the Latin chant before St. Gregory—in the absence of Ambrosian sources from before the twelfth century? Likewise, how seriously should we consider a comparison between the Gregorian, Ambrosian, and Byzantine melodies in the attempt to detect a common origin if the earliest available Western melodies are those notated in the tenth century and the deciphered Byzantine material is based on sources no earlier than the end of the twelfth century? How central, if at all, was the role of Gregory the Great and his Schola Cantorum in the organization and codification of the chant, given that the chant predates music writing? How should one understand the paleographical differences already present among the scanty early examples of neumatic notation? What was *their* common origin? Even more important, what was the *true* function of the neumes, given their erratic appearances in some manuscripts and their pervasive appearances throughout others?[9]

Though it produced works of lasting importance, the main paradigm of Gregorian studies has been seriously challenged. According to Kenneth Levy, it was the inability to establish an association between Gregory and the neumed plainchant that gave rise to the notion of an unwritten transmission—"between the melodies' conception and their writing-down"—which set aside "oral-improvisational issues." Gregorian versions were analyzed, he says, "for their modal behavior and melodic structure, pondering the origin of neumes, and debating the nature of rhythmic and microtonal nuances."[10] The *manner* of early plainchant transmission surfaced nonetheless, and has been reexamined in the light of "mechanisms" that emerge from the study of oral traditions in which processes of learning and recall are carefully scrutinized.[11] This perspective hoped to throw

8. See Leo Treitler, "Reading and Singing: On the Genesis of Occidental Music-Writing," in *Early Music History* 4 (1984): 186.

9. For additional queries and an elaboration of those mentioned above, see Helmut Hucke, "Toward a New Historical View of Gregorian Chant," in *Journal of the American Musicological Society* 33, no. 3 (1980).

10. See Kenneth Levy, "On Gregorian Orality," in *Journal of the American Musicological Society* 43, no. 2 (1990): 186.

11. See Leo Treitler, "Homer and Gregory: The Transmission of Epic Poetry and Plainchant," *Musical Quarterly* 60, no. 3 (1974).

light not only on chant transmission but also on chant "creation." However, if processes of learning and recall are now expected to be considered
important cornerstones in a theory of chant transmission, with all of the
implications they might entail, should not one challenge the "universality"
of the chant? If it is limited to specific cultures and purposes, we should be
asking which traditions of oral transmission harbor the greatest promise,
given the repertoire and the documents at hand. What, if at all, is the distinction between poetry and music conceived and transmitted orally and
poetry and music belonging to a written tradition? What, if at all, is the
distinction between an oral and literate mentality? Are there, then, oral
compositions that may be considered like written compositions though
they have not been committed to writing?

One can readily see how questions of this sort initiated a chain reaction whereby many of the interrelated claims concerning plainchant were
affected. What is most interesting, of course, is that the musical materials
themselves were now subjected to a new look and were redescribed. To be
sure, the formulaic construction that appears at every level of the chant,
from the small motive through phrases to the entire piece, had not passed
unnoticed even before. Now, however, through analogies with formulaic
procedures in other oral traditions, the interpretation concerning their
function has undergone a total revision and with it the status of the chants
as *intact* compositions. As a result, it was suggested that the division of
the text into units defined by sense was the basic principle underlying the
composition of Gregorian chant, and that melodic phrases corresponded
to units of text.[12] Moreover, melodies that were hitherto viewed as different melodies, each possessing its own individuality, were no longer considered as such, but rather as "documentations"[13] or exemplifications of
a performance practice entailing certain ready-made formulae. Regarding the formulae themselves, it has been argued that general constraints
produced general uniformities, resulting in standard passages that were
employed in structurally similar contexts. Thus, starting with the text,
suggested Treitler, the singer's task was to exploit the resources of melodic
functions (for example, initial and cadential formulae, recitation tones,
the intonational relationship between the recitation tone and the *finalis*)
in "rendering his understanding of the proper declamation and elocu-
tion of the text." The melodic constraints, in turn, should be viewed as a

---

12. Hucke, "Gregorian Chant," 452. Also see Treitler, "The Early History of Music
Writing," in *Journal of the Musicological Society* 35, no. 2 (1982): 243–44.

13. Hucke, "Gregorian Chant," 453.

formulaic system in which standard formulae corresponded to standard passages. Certain formulae, so the argument proceeds, apparently have become "stereotyped through practice under the control of a formulaic system." This, it is claimed, both resulted from and was instrumental for "a tradition of *oral performance-composition*."[14]

Levy, on the other hand, rejects the "oral performance-composition" theory. To begin with, he rejects the theory that neumes were signs that were used as "text-punctuations," since the shapes of the punctuation-neumes differ from region to region, so that "local correspondences can scarcely reflect a common origin." The whole notion of linking the overall phenomenon of neume origin to the usage of text and language, he claims, has found little support in scientific studies. It derived, argues Levy, from the Byzantine theory of origins, and from "the ekphonetic notations used in Byzantium between the ninth and fifteenth centuries to regulate the delivery of scriptural lections and ceremonial texts."[15] Levy also reminds us that "the improvisatory flights of Gregorian plainchant" took place in the medium of music, and those of the epic bards in the "medium of words," and that what Milman Parry and Albert Lord dealt with were the verbal texts.[16] For plainchant, says Levy, the texts "come verbatim from Scripture (or sometimes Patristic literature), and are not results of improvisatory elaboration." Moreover, the improvisations that produced the bardic texts, Levy tells us, also differ in character from those of the "plainchant melos." Whereas "epic continuities are built up in a succession of short repeated formations . . . freer melismatic improvisational elaborations, of the sort that may have contributed to the shaping of florid Gregorian chants, have no counterpart in epic at all."[17] To reinforce his arguments, he employs Bruno Nettl's findings (which are based on his own ethnomusicological studies of improvisation and traditional types of transmission) that revealed "improvisatory practice" to be located between "unpremeditated decisions" and "fixed, memorized melos." Though the neumes clearly

14. Treitler, "Homer and Gregory," 352–53.

15. Kenneth Levy, *Gregorian Chant and the Carolingians* (Princeton, 1998), 13.

16. Much of Treitler's claims rested on the interesting work of Milman Parry and Albert Lord. Their work transformed the field of Homeric studies and other oral poetry by pointing to the consistencies within their forms, that is, their use of formulaic language (repeated phrases and other formations) that helped poets to construct and remember their poems.

17. See Levy, "On Gregorian Orality," 190–91. Treitler introduced an analogy between Gregorian chant and the works of Balkan epic bards, which were studied by Parry and Lord. Plainchant, accordingly, was to be illuminated by the practice of Homer and the Serbian-Macedonian singers of tales.

"rendered the fixing of melodic shapes a practicality," some of the chants, argues Levy, must have gone, nonetheless, "from the freely improvisatory toward more calculated methods of melodic production" during the chant's oral stage.[18] Levy agrees that it is futile to look for a "single written original from which all Latin neumes organically descended"; he suggests instead three branches that coexisted during a period of some centuries. The oldest branch, accordingly, is not written at all, "it is memory: a melodic tradition of the Gregorian proper that was 'concretized' in professional memories at the time written processes began. This remembered reified melodic tradition went on to nourish two written branches during the early centuries of neumatic transmission."[19]

That debates of this kind should have challenged the dominant paradigm is self-evident—it had profound consequences for the understanding of the neumes, their origin, and their function. The theory that the neumes were derived from the prosodic accents, that is, from the upward and downward motion of the voice described by the Roman grammarians, was called into question. According to the old theory, the neumes were not only derived from the accents but also were viewed as the accents themselves "with but their names changed."[20] The compound neumes were seen as resulting from various combinations of these simple upward and downward signs. Though the theory suggests a unified conception of music and language, it sees in the accents the germ of music *independent* of text. This long-held theory was challenged not only because it did not correspond to the realities of the nature and origins of the neumes but also because it did not correspond to other aspects of the relationship between music and language-writing and between music-writing and the chant tradition itself.[21]

At any rate, it became increasingly clear that the chant tradition, which was previously considered Roman, was largely of Carolingian origin, a part of Charlemagne's decision to reform and unify the Frankish church in accordance with Roman practice. Charlemagne's broader plan, however, entailed the creation of an educated class "for the secular and ecclesiastical

18. See Levy, "On Gregorian Orality," 187. Also see Bruno Nettl, "Thoughts on Improvisation: A Comparative Approach," *Musical Quarterly* 60 (1974), and Nettl's "Types of Tradition and Transmission," in *Cross-Cultural Perspectives on Music,* ed. Robert Falck and Timothy Rice (Toronto, 1982).

19. Levy, *Gregorian Chant,* 116.

20. For a summary of the accent theory and its main representatives, see Treitler, "Reading and Singing," section IV.

21. Ibid., 186.

administration of the increasingly vast and heterogeneous domain over
which Charlemagne claimed hegemony." It is agreed that his educational
program, though it brought about a general revival of learning, was mainly
aimed at literacy.[22] Thus the value of classical texts "lay less in their contents than in the models they provided for a uniform language." Writing
itself was now supposed to gain in uniformity in order to turn reading into
a relatively easy task. The punctuation system that had developed was expected to contribute to the comprehensibility of the texts. It is these principles about word grouping, Hucke and Treitler argue, that are supposed
to have entered through analogy into medieval music theory as a "basic
concept for the structure of melody and as the foundation for a theory of
text-setting."[23] The primary task of the early neumes, accordingly, was not
that of indicating pitch patterns, but of providing the "technical means
of contact between language in the form of ecclesiastical and poetic texts
and the reservoir of melodic resources—more or less concrete—that the
readers of notation carried in their memories."[24]

Although this is hardly the place to discuss in great detail Kenneth
Levy's impressive and thorough investigations of the Gregorian corpus,
Levy challenged not only the theory of the "oral-improvisational practices" (which Treitler and Hucke claim continued after the introduction of
neumes) but also the date of the "conversion" to neumes of the Gregorian
corpus and the use of the Carolingian punctuation practice as the "rationale" of the early neuming technique. Based on his careful investigation of
chant multiples, he was able to show that the oral melos became stable and
memorized, and that even after the neumes were introduced they revealed
"considerable input from memory." Given that the neumes provide details
of duration and delivery but show less well information about pitch, "it can
scarcely be," says Levy, "that just the pitch choices were left to the vaga-
ries of re-improvisational or reconstructive performers." It must rather be
"that the musicians who devised the economical neumatic system of graph-
ing melodic events considered the specifics of pitch to be secure enough

22. L. D. Reynolds and N. G. Wilson, *Scribes and Scholars: A Guide to the Transmission of
Greek and Latin Literature* (Oxford, 1974), 83. For the "Carolingian Revival," see 82–94.

23. Treitler, "Reading and Singing," 140. Also see Hucke, "Die Einführung des
Gregorianischen Gesangs im Frankenreich," in *Römische Quartalschrift* 49 (1954): 172–85;
"Gregorianischer Gesang in alt-römischer und fränkischer Uberlieferung," in *Archiv für
Musikwissenschaft* 12 (1955): 74 -87.

24. Treitler, "Reading and Singing," 207. Also see Susan Rankin, "From Memory to
Record: Musical Notation in Manuscripts from Exeter," in *Anglo-Saxon England,* no. 13,
97–III.

in professional memories to sustain this somewhat casual treatment by the early neumes." Essential to the system, he concluded, was "a dependence on memory for much of the information about pitch." Accordingly, by the time the repertory was cast in neumes "the singers' memories were stocked with the full complement of melodic information."[25] Levy calls to our attention, however, that though the rationale for most Gregorian chants "lies in distinctive melodic profiles, in formulations that are unique as to melodic detail," many chants may have drawn their basic materials from "a common fund of conventional modal-melodic gestures," yet each of them, according to Levy, "turned out as a distinct melodic entity, with singular twists given to the familiar gestures."[26]

The Rise of Notation as an Autonomous System

Considering these debates, it is evident that an autonomous *system* of purely *musical* notation is nowhere in sight. The picture delineated so far is anything but a description of a musical world coherent unto itself and rid of ambiguities. Although there is a bridge here between oral and written traditions, the scene has not yet been set for a claim that the history of Western notation may be read as a succession of stages—subsequent to the one we have just discussed—that add up, albeit retrospectively, to an evolutionary story about notation, that is, to a world that meets Nelson Goodman's requirements of systems of signs that eliminate ambiguity as far as their denotation is concerned.[27] We turn now, therefore, to such

25. Levy, "On Gregorian Orality," 216.

26. Ibid., 217–18.

27. For a symbolic system to qualify as a notational system, Goodman tells us, it must answer to five definitional requirements. Two of the requirements are syntactic, and three of them semantic. Briefly, the symbol scheme of every notational system is notational. It consists of characters ('inscriptions,' 'marks,' 'utterances'), the essential feature of which is an "abstraction class of character indifference among inscription," that is, each inscription of a character is recognized as a true copy of the character, and no mark may belong to more than one character. The syntactic requirements of a notational system are that the characters be *disjoint* and *finitely differentiated*. Disjointness is assured by a classification that counts every difference as a difference of character. Finite differentiation is assured by a scheme of clearly differentiated inscriptions, so that if two characters have an inscription in common, it must be theoretically possible to determine to which of the two characters the inscription belongs.

Symbol systems consist of symbol schemes "correlated with a field of reference." A symbol, however, may or may not denote that to which it refers. A mark is ambiguous if it has different compliants at different times, even if it is an inscription of a single character. If scores are to be correlated with performances, whatever is denoted by a

a description, cautioning again, however, against a deterministic reading in which intentionality is attributed to the sequence of stages. To repeat, each stage in this development was adapted primarily to immediately specific tasks and was not a move toward a more general explicit goal. Nevertheless, a review of some highlights of these stages will offer convincing evidence that ambiguities were increasingly eliminated in the course of the development of Western musical notation, so as to enable the notation to contain a visual record of the music it aimed to represent.

Reviewing the early development of musical notation, one is impressed that, from the start, musical notation incorporated certain cognitive aspects that clustered, at first, around attempts to find a proper way to record pitch, and only later around the ways in which durations were to be related. As far as pitch is concerned, it is interesting to note that the metaphors of "high" and "low" and the concomitant metaphor of "directionality"—so essential to the understanding of Western music—evolved autonomously. So, for that matter, did the understanding of melody as a "semblance of movement," to use Suzanne Langer's phrase. By comparison, controlling time so as to convey the *passage* of time in a Bergsonian sense—not time as measured by a fixed unit—presented major problems, for it involved what one might call the *quantification of qualities.*

It is important to remember that the selection of pitches, embedded as they were in formulae, preceded their notation. One can even argue that committing to notation what had already been formulated orally only heightened awareness of the constituent elements that were implicit in the oral system. If the notation was to contain what must have been most important to practitioners, namely, the ensuring of some kind of identity between the symbol of the pitch and the pitch as produced, the array of pitches had to be spelled out. In this respect, it is interesting to observe the transformation in the function of notation as it developed from the

---

symbol must comply with it. The three semantic requirements upon notational systems are thus: *unambiguity, disjointness,* and *finite differentiation.* Unambiguity pertains to invariance in compliance relationships; disjointness stipulates that "no two characters have any compliant in common"; and finite differentiation assures the theoretical possibility to determine that a given object does not comply with the first or the second of two characters, which have different compliance classes if that object does not comply with both.

These five requirements, Goodman tells us, are not optional, but a must, if a symbol system is to function as a notational system. Standard musical notation, Goodman suggests, is a prime example of a notational system, for identity of work and of score "are retained in any series of steps, each of them either from compliant performance to score-inscription to true copy." See Nelson Goodman, "The Theory of Notation," chapter 4 in his *Languages of Art* (New York, 1968).

early neumes, which indicated only direction, to the "diastematic" intervalic notation, which indicated *how far* up or down. This is a story about
music becoming increasingly aware of itself—defining its own building
blocks, as it were—in the process of moving from an oral tradition to the
creation of a system for proper recording. It is a story also about the transformation of a system of signs designed to indicate the inflections of language into a notation of discrete pitches that are isomorphic with musical,
that is, with sounded, configurations.

Pitch

In the course of this early development, and before the stage at which
a full diastematic intervalic notation was reached, there had been attempts to reduce ambiguity with regard to intervals through the *naming*
of pitches, through the designation of the *succession* of the intervals, and
through other alphanumerical devices. Though more accurate in a sense,
they did not take root, for they failed to convey the metaphors of directionality and movement that are so crucial to the understanding of music.
So it seems in retrospect, at any rate (see examples 1–3).

Although the long development of mensuration consists of many stages
at which the requirements of an unambiguous notation are only partially
and gradually fulfilled, the development of the notation of pitch was relatively brief. Indeed, at the moment when it was absolutely clear what it
was that one wished to signify, a notational solution presented itself rather
straightforwardly. Unlike duration, which has to be treated in several differentiated stages, paralleling changes that took place in musical thought,
it is legitimate to sum up the realization of the notation of pitch as if it all
took place at one and the same time. In line with Goodman's requirements
concerning notational *systems* (see note 27), one could summarize briefly
what took place in the following way: A neumatic notation that differentiates between only two signs cannot qualify as a notational system since the
differentiation is too general and is lacking in distinctions. The need to increase the amount of information in the system constituted a drive for the
creation of signs that were more varied, and as a result there emerged the
compound neumes. Although containing more information, these compound neumes did not differentiate clearly among their constituent elements and thus cannot meet Goodman's syntactic requirements, namely
that the characters be *disjoint* and *finitely differentiated* (see note 27). Nor
do they eliminate ambiguity as far as their "compliants," that is, what they
refer to, are concerned. Only with the transition to pitch notation, which
views a change in pitch as the movement between two stations, is the way

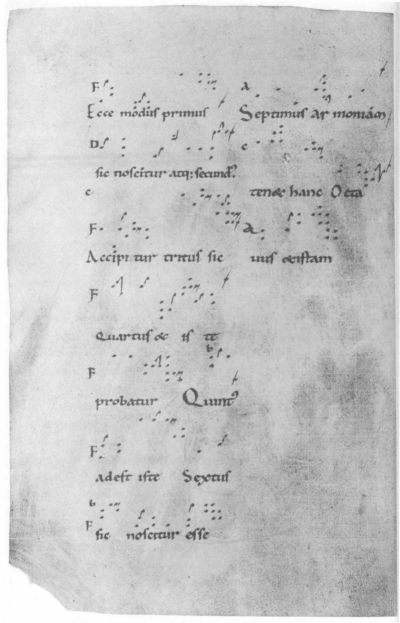

PLATE IV. Paris, Bibliothèque Nationale, Lat. 7211, fol. 127v. Late 11th Century

EXAMPLE 1. These pages are from a tonarium—a vocal exercise for learning the modes—and both contain the same musical material. Plate IV (on the left) is in Aquitanian neumatic notation and plate V (on the right) is in the so-called Guidonian letters, which employs only the letters A-G. In the latter, note the diastematic placing of the letters, which, though redundant, conveys 'directionality' visually. (From Carl Parrish, *The Notation of Medieval Music* [New York: Norton, 1957], plates IV and V.)

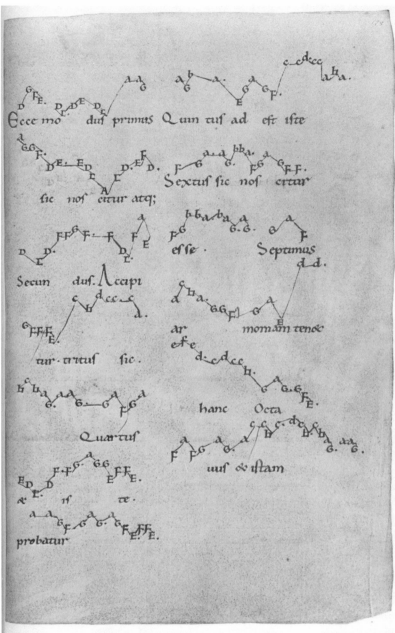

Ecce mo dus primus Quin tus ad est iste

sic nos citur atq; Sextus sic nos citur

Secun dus. Accipi esse. Septimus

tur · tritus sic. ar moniam tenet

Quartus hanc Octa

& E. is te. uus & istam

probatur

PLATE V. Paris, Bibliothèque Nationale, Lat. 7211, fol. 128. Late 11th Century

EXAMPLE 1. (*Continued*)

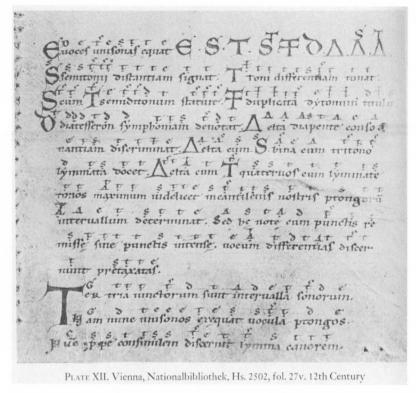

PLATE XII. Vienna, Nationalbibliothek, Hs. 2502, fol. 27v. 12th Century

EXAMPLE 2. This is an example of a succession of intervals designated by letters as devised by Hermannus Contractus (d. 1054). The letters, which are placed above the text, each represent a melodic interval. Thus "e" (*equaliter*) means repetition of the same note; "s" (*semitonium*) indicates a half step; "t" (*tonus*) a whole step; "ts" (*tonus cum semitonus*) a minor third, and so forth. (From Carl Parrish, *The Notation of Medieval Music* [New York: Norton, 1957], plate XII.)

paved for the fulfillment of Goodman's requirements. The alphanumerical notations addressed themselves only to the stations, as it were, while the diastematic system imposed an organization onto the neumes by introducing lines, at first imaginary and later real, that could graph the coordinates where each pitch, one by one, could find its particular location.[28]

28. The evolution of the diastematic neumes was increasingly stabilized through the adoption of staff lines, first one, then two, and finally four. The invention of the staff proper is ascribed to Guido d'Arezzo (ca. 990–1050). The horizontal lines of the staff (today always five in number) enabled the writing of musical notes on and between lines, thereby indicating their pitch. The four-line staff has been preserved to the present day for the notation of Gregorian chant.

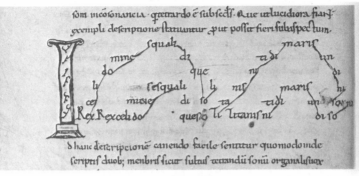

PLATE XXa. Paris, Bibliothèque Nationale, Lat. 7211, fol. 9v. 11th Century

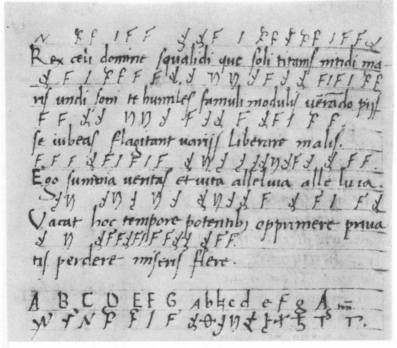

PLATE XI. Paris, Bibliothèque Nationale, Lat. 7369. 15th Century (?)

EXAMPLE 3. Plate XI (the lower part of the example) is in the so-called Daseian notation attributed to Odo of Cluny, which was first used in the *Musica enchiriadis*, a ninth-century treatise. The notation is based on the tetrachord principle of Greek musical theory, using different shapes and inversions of the letter *f* plus four additional signs that occur as the upper note of the half step in each tetrachord to indicate pitches. The example in plate XXa (the upper part) shows the Daseian symbols placed vertically at the beginning while the words of the text are placed sequentially at a height corresponding to their pitch, in each of the two voices. (From Carl Parrish, *The Notation of Medieval Music* [New York: Norton, 1957], plates XI and XXa.)

As baffling as all of this may sound, it will be readily understood by those familiar with the history of Western notation.

Duration

As far as mensuration is concerned, it is all the more important to repeat that it evolved through interaction between *musical* thought and stylistic and notational requirements. In this development, one can discern a gradual building up of a field of reference, increasingly differentiated from within. Unlike the choice of pitches, the concern here was not with a choice of durations but with decisions and assessments concerning durational relationships within a time span. To illustrate this, I shall briefly describe some aspects of early notational practices in the West, placing these in the context of the musical needs that they served and the currents of musical thought that constituted the driving force for notational changes. As we proceed, I shall try to locate these developments with reference to Goodman's requirements. This time, the idea is not to catch the moment at which Goodman's notational requirements are fully realized but rather to observe the emergence of a Goodmanian system from the process of responding, in script, to certain primary *musical* requirements.

It is largely the development of polyphonic music—in which the coordination between voices became necessary—that brought forth an awareness of problems calling for theoretical and notational solutions. The St. Martial repertoire from the end of the eleventh century is a good place to begin.[29] In addition to the two-voiced compositions that move in parallel motion, we find compositions in which voices move freely, as if independently of each other. Coordination between voices—which were unequal

29. European music history, explains Treitler, "has been understood since the Romantic era to begin in the Middle Ages with Gregorian chant" because Gregorian chant "is the oldest European music that we know, and by virtue of that priority it has been granted the presumptive right to be regarded as the progenitor of European music." According to Treitler, "scholars have long been engaged in the identification of quintessentially 'European' principles in that music, even to the extent of identifying them with principles that dominate the music of Beethoven." More interesting , however, is his observation that "this works both ways: the definition of what is 'European' is informed by the traits of the chant that has come down as 'Gregorian,' and the traits of European music that have been identified as such since the nineteenth century operate tacitly as teleological ideas for the recognition of those traits in chant. This double role continues to affect both large-scale accounts and detailed descriptions of the music, bringing into play a music conception that was not held by its contemporaries." See Leo Treitler, "The Historiography of Music," in *Rethinking Music,* ed. Nicholas Cook and Mark Everist (Oxford, 2001), 360.

in the number of notes—was apparently accomplished by ear, taking care that the voices met on the same note or on an admissible interval, that is, on intervals that were considered "consonant."[30] It must have taken a lot of practice, for the written notation does not differentiate between long and short notes, and thus the nature of the movement is not yet controlled (see example 4).

The elementary requirement for control of the movement of two voices unequal in length is that there should be a differentiation between a long and a short note. The introduction in theory of this distinction, toward the end of the twelfth century, led to the establishment of patterned sequences of longs and shorts and thus to the so-called rhythmic modes—that is, rhythmic patterns in ternary meter. Altogether, in contrast to its slow development in the eleventh century, the development of polyphonic music in the twelfth century is more rapid. It is characterized by greater rhythmic precision, by an increase of the number of parts that constitute polyphonic compositions, and, most important, by musical activity stepping out from the obscurity of anonymous and collective creation. The development is paralleled by a development of notational signs and methods of which the rhythmic modes are a part.

The sources of the Notre Dame school, when compared with the preceding period, reveal a difference in notational characters, that is, the neumes assume more definite shapes. Also, there existed a fundamental notational distinction resulting from the dichotomy of styles related to two different treatments of texts. Texts might be treated either syllabically, that is, with one note or occasionally a few notes to each syllable, or melismatically, that is, with extended groups of notes to each syllable. Syllabic treatment is represented primarily by single signs and melismatic treatment by tones that are written in group-character, in the so-called ligatures (see examples 5 and 6).

The rhythmic modes that take part in these styles are indicated, where possible, not through a visual differentiation between shorts and longs but via particular sequences of ligatures. To this there was added an understanding that the binary ligature—the two-note ligature—has a "natural" order, that of a short followed by a long. Thus, the first mode, which has the rhythmic sequence long-short-long-short-long, was presented in notation through a sequence of binary ligatures, preceded, however, by an initial ternary ligature to assure the desired sequence. The second mode, which, unlike the first, begins with a short, is presented through a sequence

30. I shall discuss intervals, tonality, and so forth later on.

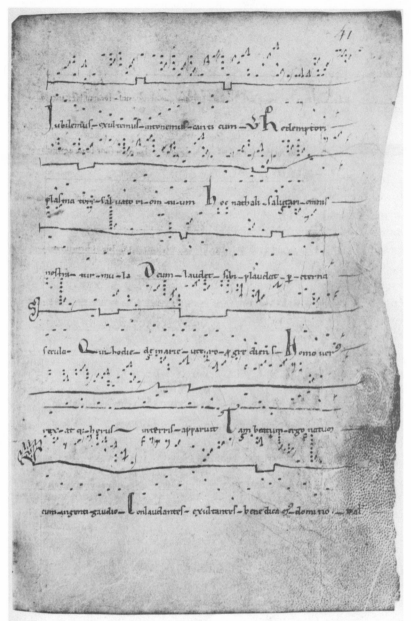

PLATE XXI. Paris, Bibliothèque Nationale, Lat. 1139, fol. 41. Early 12th Century

EXAMPLE 4. This is a two-voice composition from St. Martial sources that gives no basis for differentiating between long and short despite the obvious difference between the two voices in the number of notes. (From Carl Parrish, *The Notation of Medieval Music* [New York: Norton, 1957], plate XXI.)

FACSIMILE 53

MS Wolfenbüttel, Herzogliche Bibliothek *677*, formerly *Helmstedt 628*
(13th century)
Page 71

EXAMPLE 5. An example of syllabic notation. (From Willi Apel, *The Notation of Poly-phonic Music 900–1600* [Cambridge: Mediaeval Academy of America, 1953], facsimile 53, p. 259.)

FACSIMILE 46

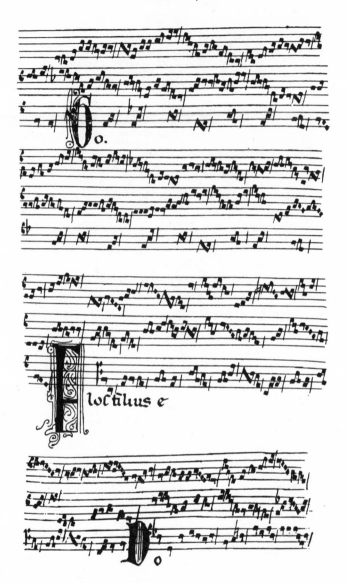

MS Florence, Biblioteca Medicea-Laurenziana *plut. 29.1*
(13th century)
From pages 11, 11′

EXAMPLE 6. An example of melismatic notation. (From Willi Apel, *The Notation of Polyphonic Music 900–1600* [Cambridge: Mediaeval Academy of America, 1953], facsimile 46, p. 229.)

Combination	Example	Transcription
1. *3 2 2 2 2*		
2. *2 2 2 2 3*		
3. *1 3 3 3*		
4. *3 3 3 1*		
5. *3 3 3*		
6. *4 3 3*		

The small vertical stroke which appears at the end of each *ordo* is the so-called *divisio modi*, which indicates a rest.

EXAMPLE 7. The different combinations of ligatures for the six rhythmic modes. (From Willi Apel, *The Notation of Polyphonic Music 900–1600* [Cambridge: Mediaeval Academy of America, 1953], p. 225.)

of binary ligatures, but with a ternary ligature at the *end* of the sequence. The third mode begins with a single note followed by ternaries to indicate the rhythmic sequence that consists of a so-called perfect long, that is, a long equaling three shorts, followed by a short and then a prolonged short equaling two. Had the notation introduced binaries, which consisted of a short equal to one and a long equal to two, the sequence of this mode could not have been maintained (see example 7).

But this is not the place to go into detail about these or the other rhythmic modes, nor into the way in which they were used in the Notre Dame school. The point to emphasize is that there is not yet at this time any *visual* differentiation between longs and shorts, a fortiori, between different kinds of longs and different kinds of shorts; it is only the modal context that establishes which is which. Even so, the rhythmic modes made it possible to organize and coordinate between several voices. However, since the notation itself does not differentiate between longs and shorts, since it lacks disjointness and finite differentiation, on the syntactic level this notation does not function as a notational system inasmuch as the identity of works, that is, their actual sound, is subject to a particular method related to style and is not inherent in the notation itself.

Although the organization of voices through the rhythmic modes allows for a certain degree of independence among the voices, the overall flow of the music is rather rigid. Two related types of attempts were made to broaden the limited frame of the rhythmic modes. One involved a unit of organization, called "ordo," which is larger than a modal pattern; the other concerns what might be called "musical densities." The ordo is an organizational unit consisting of a number of modal repetitions corresponding to a musical phrase, creating, as it were, a time-latitude (see example 6). Once the latitude of the unit is established, what is contained within it can be tampered with; thus, one can increase or reduce the number of notes. For example, if a given short is missing in a sequence of long-short-long-short-long-short-rest, in the first mode the long that preceded it is lengthened so as to encompass the duration of the missing short. Inversely, where additional notes exist in the same sequence, the duration of the preceding notes may be shortened to accommodate the additional ones in order to preserve the proper modal sequence. Moreover, additions and deletions may occur in the same phrase. What this means is that one obtains different densities, since the overall latitude of the ordo has not changed. While these innovations provide additional control over the flow of time by encompassing larger musical units and giving more flexibility within units, they neither encompass nor control the entire musical composition. Moreover, the varied densities of the ordo reduce the possibility of maintaining identities, since the solutions may vary within the context of a given ordo. I shall forgo enumerating further rules concerning changes within ordine and, for that matter, also the whole discussion concerning the different notational signs and methods as they paralleled different musical forms and styles during this period. Nevertheless, I would like to show that the strain to control the nature of the flow of time over an entire composition and to make certain that identities are maintained may be assumed to have been increasingly felt.

It must have become increasingly clear that the solution lies in disconnecting all of the elements from each other, for only disjointness can free the individual notes to enter musical combinations that are not dictated by form or style (though the style will be no less well served, as well). The overburdening of the basic modal framework brought about its breakdown and led to solutions that bring us a step closer to Goodman's requirements. Just as the ligatures and their arrangements plus the natural order of the binaria were essential to the earlier stage in which certain rhythmic combinations were desired, it now became essential to get rid of such con-

textual dependencies in order to make possible more and different combinations. It became increasingly evident that categories external to the
notation itself limit the potential of the system. But how, and in what way,
should one invest in the notation so that it should be flexible enough to
accommodate stylistic change, on the one hand, and strict enough to assure the identity of specific works, on the other? Such concerns, of course,
imply a change in attitude toward music, that is, toward the musical composition and the idea of *composing* music.

The process of eliminating an external system while creating a system
inherent in the notation was a long and tedious one. It oscillated between
corrections introduced in the vocabulary of visual signs and the introduction of new signs to designate note values of smaller duration. The corrections entailed the differentiation between longs and shorts and changes in
the ligature formations such that, standing each on its own, they should
lend themselves to unambiguous reading. Such changes not only gradually introduced disjointness and finite differentiation on the syntactic
level but increasingly eliminated ambiguities with respect to compliances
on the semantic level. Not only could the "natural order" (of the binary
ligature) now be dispensed with, but later the ligatures could be dispensed
with altogether.

Still, the differentiation between the different kinds of longs and the different kinds of breves remained contextual for a long time, and was related
to the concept of 'perfection,' whereby the note value of a long was considered "perfect" if it equaled three breves and "imperfect" if it equaled only
two breves. The same holds true for the relationship of breves to the next
shorter note value, and so forth. The designations "perfect" and "imperfect" depended on the context in which a shorter note value could imperfect, as it were, the longer one preceding it, and join with it to form a single
'perfection.' Readers unfamiliar—and, a fortiori, those who are familiar—
with medieval and early Renaissance notation will forgive me, I hope, if I
forgo any further attempt to oversimplify and jump to the generalization
that internal contextual considerations had to be taken into account in the
decoding of musical notation for a long time, even after disjointness and
some differentiation had been introduced and serious attempts had been
made to reduce ambiguity. Clearly, so long as a simple breve had the same
look as an 'altered breve' (equaling two shorts) or an 'imperfect longa' had
a different look from an 'altered breve,' finite differentiation did not yet
obtain at the syntactic level. At the semantic level, however, semantic differentiation was achieved within a given composition inasmuch as the use

of two different signs to mark the same duration was forbidden in order to avoid the overlapping of compliance classes. It might be noted in passing, however, that while the existence of two signs for the same object is superfluous, it does not create ambiguity, whereas the reverse—two objects marked by one sign—does, of course, create ambiguity.

From the middle of the thirteenth century until the beginning of the fifteenth, roughly speaking, the various notations created the possibilities for rhythmic variety while trying to control the order of events and the density of events within given latitudes, that is, the momentary and the overall flow of the music. By the thirteenth century, notation had already bridged the Augustinian rhythmical theory based on poetical-quantitative notions, that is, on a mathematical approach to the concept of time, and the Aristotelian qualitative approach, which defines time as an attribute of motion.[31] These new notations were further attempts to quantify qualities, namely, to present time as a measure of motion. The vertical axis of pitch and the horizontal axis of time were interrelated from the start through the ordering of pitch sequences. With the clarification of durational relationships—which needed to be clarified again and again with the introduction of smaller note values—it was only natural for the individual pitches, for the sound events, to carry, so to speak, the time element as well. The various 'rests,' interestingly, retained their proper duration even while forgoing the sounds, thus themselves becoming *musical* events. Although the Italian notation of the fourteenth century with its so-called divisions contributed to the institutionalization of mensuration by means of the differentiation among densities and their control within units that functioned like a bar, it is the French notation that allowed for the flow across bar lines, so to speak, not least because of the introduction of syncopation. While each of the various notations addressed specific requirements and aesthetic desiderata, together they contributed to the emergence of a notational system.

Concerning Notation: Concluding Remarks

The history of notation is, of course, more elaborate than the picture delineated here. It was accompanied by serious theoretical deliberations and interesting debates, as well as the wealth of music to which it gave rise. Via

31. See Dorit Tanay, *Noting Music, Marking Culture: The Intellectual Context of Rhythmic Notation, 1250–1400, Musicological Studies and Documents* (American Institute of Musicology) 46 (1999), 23–47.

a few concrete examples that lend themselves to relatively nontechnical rendition, I have tried to provide some *insight* into the ways in which this development proceeded. At any rate, the crystallization of notation in the West culminates in the fifteenth century, at a point where Goodman's five requirements are fulfilled. To repeat, this does not mean that there is a tight relationship between the development of notation and Goodman's system; it does not mean that every change was in the "right" direction, or that there was explicit striving toward a clear-cut goal. The claim, rather, is that one can speak of the history of Western musical notation up to this point as if it were a development aiming to preserve within the notation the *identities* of musical compositions independent of form and style.[32] The

32. The notion of 'identity,' however simple it may seem to the layman, is not so considered by philosophers. In fact, Goodman's five analytical requirements of a symbol system, if it is to function as a notational system (see note 27), have encountered serious philosophical debate. His claim that standard musical notation is a prime example of a notational system, because the "identity" of work and score are "retained from compliant performance to score-inscription," also has been seriously challenged by those familiar with the history of music and its performance practice. Indeed, as composers increasingly conceived of their music as *enduring works,* they also wished to control their performances by new notational precisions that introduced changes in the language of notation. Even without raising the issues involved in 'intention' and 'interpretation,' it is abundantly clear that Goodman's theoretical conditions fail to agree with their functioning in practice, and that his claim about the identity between the 'score' and the 'work' leaves many queries unsatisfactorily answered. Musical 'works' clearly entail complex structures of sound that interrelate composers, scores, and performances in ways that affect their essential features. Yet in the absence of such complex structures of sounds, questions pertaining to the definition of "works" and the maintenance of their "identity" become meaningless. Indeed, questions of this sort could hardly have preoccupied the theorists that accompanied the early development of music in the West. Rather, their attempts to "specify" what seemed essential to *them* paved the road that enabled music to become the "complex world in sound" that it had become. In fact, without the "common sense" notion of 'identity' that accompanied the early development of notation and its preoccupation with pitch and duration, the "sophisticated" deliberations on 'identity' might have never emerged in the way they did—as far as Western music is concerned. Whatever criticism one may launch against Goodman's theory of notation, it proved helpful in pinpointing the fundamental "stages" in the development of notation in the West and "conceptualizing" its achievement. I have used history, one might say, as a "compliance" to Goodman's "requirements" in order to benefit from their "rigor," which helped to isolate the essentials of the transition from an oral musical tradition to a written one, from descriptive signs to a prescriptive musical notation. Rose Subotnik, however, reminds us that, until the advent of the tape recorder and the computer, "music in Western culture has traditionally been defined as an intrinsically participatory art, in which the survival of the composer's original construction (by way of notation) did not discourage but actually required active physical participation by others beside the

development is not such that one can talk about an orderly "progress," for it oscillates between notational innovations and new musical thoughts. Major notational changes were preceded by theoretical clarifications concerning the contents and qualities that "wanted" to be notated. For example, the desire to contrast long and short, and the decision about a proper order, constituted a foundation for the rhythmic modes. It is worth noting that Goodman himself insists that theoretical decisions *must* precede notational considerations.

The dynamic of the entire process was dictated by the interaction between new musical thought and the limitations of the available notational forms; theoretical clarifications resulting from the impasse led to notational change. In fact, the subservience of notation to external factors time and again thwarted adaptation of notation to new musical requirements. The changes that came about may be thought of, therefore, as responses to a purely musical drive—rationalistic, autonomous, and even revolutionary in character—that strained to achieve *inner* notational clarifications. Looked at historically, however, it is not only the constant changes that loom large but also the continuities that underlie them. The reinterpreting and relabeling so familiar to us from the study of history is paralleled in the reinterpretations and relabeling of signs in the history of symbol systems. Old signs are reinterpreted and sometimes dropped and occasional new ones are added. In this process of continuity and change, music in the West also gave rise to and was governed by other important systems, including the modal, harmonic, contrapuntal, and so forth. The system discussed in the previous pages concerns only the *identity* of musi-

---

composer, that is, by performers. Still, in this medium, there remains a tension between the ideas of the composer and the interpretation of the performer; and the more actively performers are involved in re-creating a work, the more opportunity they have to make changes, whether accidental or deliberate, in the original." In music, argues Subotnik, "it is certainly possible for physical response to destroy the original identity of an artwork. In music, however, until now our culture has found it neither necessary nor desirable to restrict its mode of response so as to prevent such destruction, even in the case of art music. For just as the development of the concept of art music in the West has been virtually inseparable from the development of notation, so, too, Western art music has almost by definition been notated music. And within boundaries of cultural continuity, a notated musical composition is far sturdier than a painting is with respect to its original identity." See Rose Subotnik, *Developing Variations: Style and Ideology in Western Music* (Minnesota, 1991), 261. For a thought-through review of the debates and issues that Goodman's theory gave rise to, see Lydia Goehr's seminal essay in the philosophy of music—*The Imaginary Museum of Musical Works* (Oxford, 1992), part 1, chap. 1.

cal "compositions" (addressing the notion of 'identity' as understood in the early development of music), stressing the point of their *definitiveness*.[33]

Musical notations the world over differ not only in their visual aspect but also in the choices of parameters that they notate. These may even include extramusical elements that may constitute an inseparable part of the musical conception. In theory, there are but four purely musical parameters—pitch, duration, loudness, and timbre (disregarding the interdependence among them). In practice, however, subdivisions in any

33. Philip Bohlman opens his interesting article about the "ontologies of music" with the following declaration: "Music may be what we think it is; it may not be." Given his familiarity with many different musical traditions, his declaration functions both as a concluding remark and as a statement that invites substantiation. Indeed, his article makes amply clear that thinking about music does not only vary among cultures, but that some cultures created "complex categories" for thinking about music, whereas others saw no need whatsoever to contemplate music. Thinking of music as an "object" is, in and of itself, an ontological assumption that is not shared by all cultures, not even by a single culture at all times. Bohlman reminds us that "the assumption that music exists prior to being found by composers, performers, or even mathematicians is surprisingly widespread, both culturally and historically." On the one hand, the assumption often lays claim "to scientist explanations for music"; on the other, "it is often the clearest evidence that explanations for creation have simply been suspended for lack of any way to prove them." Bohlman outlines the "contrasting ways in which the act of creating or composing music takes place" in the West. The first component concerns itself primarily "with the materials of music, hence the acts performed upon these by a composer or agent of creation." The second "seeks to explain the existence of musical works—in other words, pieces that obtain and retain their own identity." In Western art music, we are told, "notation has become the primary means of retaining an identity—framing it, that is, in a score, which then becomes 'the work.'" However, since "what music is remains open to question at all times and in all places," scores cannot adequately represent the changes that take place over time in a musical tradition. Scores thus only leave "traces" that provide "the essence" of an identity and "make it possible for that identity, however sketchy, to persist through time and through the acts of many performers." See Philip Bohlman, "Ontologies of Music," in *Rethinking Music* (Oxford, 2001), 17–30. The last statement about the relationship between notation and performance still lends the musical "text" a privileged role in its diverse instantiations, for it still considers the instantiations as performances of some "time-resisting" features. The idea of "musical works" and their reification emerged rather late (as we shall see) in the development of music in the West, yet "it is only when you have started thinking of music as performance," argues Nicholas Cook, "that the peculiarly time-resisting properties of works in the Western 'art' tradition come fully into relief." The cultural study of music, suggests Cook, should find new ways to deal with music "*as* performance," rather than deal with the performance "*of* music." See Nicholas Cook, "Music *as* Performance," in *The Cultural Study of Music*, ed. Martin Clayton, Trevor Herbert, and Richard Middleton (Routledge, 2003).

one of these—for example, glissandi, various types of vibrati, and delicate shadings of intonation in the parameter of pitch—may be viewed as musical parameters unto themselves. If they are central to a particular style, one may wish to indicate them in the notation, and in such cases a detailed, mostly oral, tradition typically exists to guide the manner of their execution.

In a symbolic system such as ours, based on purely musical laws, the reduction of ambiguity in the notation of musical materials depends on their dismemberment into separate parameters, each of which, in turn, is broken up into the smallest particles that are still recognizable and available for comparison. The degree of clarity obtained from the division of a parameter into segments (e.g. different pitch intervals, ratios of duration) varies among parameters and largely depends on the possibility of arraying the segments on a single scale. The latter is facilitated by the possibility of establishing a basic unit, the multiples of which create the various segments. The parameter of pitch, according to these criteria, is the easiest to notate, followed by duration. Timbre, for example, cannot be arranged on a single scale, nor is there a clear-cut definition for a quantifiable unit of timbre. Consequently, comparisons between timbres are correspondingly vague. Loudness, on the other hand, can be ordered on a single scale provided that a clear-cut definition of a basic unit is established. In short, the more it is possible to separate a parameter from other parameters and the more it is possible to define its units, the more possible it is to notate the parameters unambiguously and to recognize their share in the organization of the entire composition. On the other hand, the more interconnected the parameters at an initial stage, lacking in discreteness of both parameters and units, the more they reduce the number of possible new combinations, by virtue of already existing combinations in the primary phase of the musical organization. In fact, different choices with regard to parameters and their type of interrelatedness may affect not only the degree of complexity of the musical style but also the pace of stylistic change, and, where notation of any sort exists, the degree of dependency of the written on the oral part of a musical tradition.[34]

In retrospect, it seems that Western notation, as it evolved over the course of a few centuries, rid itself of constituents that are not strictly musical, and a priori of inner relationships among them; it also excluded pa-

---

34. See Dalia Cohen and Ruth Katz, "The Interdependence of Notation Systems and Musical Information," in *Yearbook of the International Folk Music Council*, vol. 2 (1979).

rameters that did not lend themselves to the reduction of ambiguity. Pitch and duration, thus, became the prime parameters in the organization of musical compositions and the key to their identification. The notation of pitch and duration, moreover, increasingly gained in efficiency as the number of visual signs it employed was reduced.[35] Indeed, notational complications are inversely related to the complexities of the musical materials they can notate.[36] On the other hand, the more efficient the notation, the more complex, varied, and extended the music it can handle. In sum, with the aid of a fully articulate symbol system that leaves no room for ambiguity, an independent overall language of sounds was created in the West that could contain many varied, though congeneric, musical utterances. With minor additions, this symbol system seems to have answered basic musical demands until the twentieth century, during which it gradually broke down.

MUSICAL FRAMEWORKS AS REFERENTIAL SYSTEMS

Musical notation, as we have seen, invariably *refers* to the music that it represents, though it may choose to do so in several different ways. The various notations, in fact, run the entire gamut from descriptive to prescriptive representations—from signs that function as "reminders" of sorts, assisting the memory of those who are already familiar with the music, to signs that enable even those who are unfamiliar with the music to actually produce it. Naturally, one has to learn *to read* the signs, whether descriptive or prescriptive; notation invariably involves a kind of literacy. Western notation, I have tried to show, gradually moved from a descriptive to a prescriptive kind of notation in which the relationships between the signs and their signifiers allow us to move from score to performance, and the other way round, by virtue of having supplied the symbol system with a

35. The visual information for duration in the West eventually consisted largely of six different signs that can easily be differentiated from one another: an empty circle, a fully darkened circle, a horizontal bar, a vertical bar, a dot, and a connecting tie. With the aid of these signs and their combinations, it is possible to construct many different kinds of durations, which are well defined. The limited number of signs employed, for a single duration or for combinations, derives from the system that dictates that any additional sign, save the tie, designates either an increase or a reduction in a fixed proportion (not in a fixed quantity). Consequently, some of the signs are "abbreviations," as it were, that incorporate combinations of smaller units.

36. See Cohen and Katz, "The Interdependence of Notation Systems and Musical Information," vol. 2, 105.

symbol scheme correlated with an unambiguous field of reference. Before this development, music apparently rested on a formulaic tradition that guided its composition and the manner in which it was employed.

Like notation, the systematization of the *relationships* between pitches— whether as modes, scales, tonal relationships, and tonal functions—must have rested on an oral prehistory, involving "melody types" of sorts, that is, melodies that employed typified motives and the manner of their use. The practice of resorting to traditional melodies—to their melodic formulas, stereotyped figures, ornamentation, rhythmic patterns, tonal progressions, and so forth—as *reference* for the creation of new compositions seems to have constituted a fundamental stage for most subsequent theoretical developments, irrespective of culture or civilization. Theoretical developments, however, may take on a life of their own, sometimes involving fundamental issues pertinent not only to the context that excited them but also to other attendant conditions for which they carry significance or relevance. Indeed, theories are known to have wandered across civilizations, often bequeathing an already formulated "mental heritage" that may function as a starting point for what is yet to be developed. There is no denying that the civilization that developed in the West inherited much of what was already formulated in ancient Greece, including some aspects pertaining to music as an *organized* auditory phenomenon.

The Greek Heritage: Music as an Organized Auditory Phenomenon

Historically, the so-called *nomoi*—the stock melodies that were used as the basis for improvisations in ancient Greece—preceded the Greek theoretical abstractions, though, once launched, these abstractions seem to have taken on a life of their own. A fundamental tetrachord, accordingly, which was bounded by the fixed notes of a perfect fourth containing three subdivisions,[37] the so-called *genera*, gave rise to the Greater and Lesser Perfect Systems of the Greeks. The "Greater" consisted of two pairs of conjunct tetrachords, in descending order, with a disjunctive tone between them and an added bottom tone (a' g' f' [e' d'] c b—a g f [e d] c B—A), while the "Lesser" consisted of three conjunct tetrachords (achieved through the addition of a conjunct tetrachord above the first two). These systems, in turn,

---

37. The highest of the three intervals of the tetrachord (a g f e) was widened from a whole tone (a g) into an interval of three semitones (a f#), or four semitones (a f), in which case the remaining half tone (f e) was halved, producing two quarter tones.

gave rise to the *tonoi* (double-octave scales), which gave rise to the octave-species.[38] In the absence of a representative body of musical examples, however, neither the theoretical treatises that have come down to us from the Greeks nor the vast knowledge we possess of the culture of ancient Greece is sufficient to establish an unequivocal image of the music itself or of its influence on the subsequent development of music in the West.

The fact that in Greek music only the tuning of the perfect fourth (and only the notes connected with it) was fixed while the others were mobile leaves queries unanswered even concerning the concept of a 'scale.' The scale is one of the more obvious concepts that were supposed to have come from the Greeks into the music of the Middle Ages. The Greek *tonoi,* which are often described as transpositions of the *harmoniae* — "scales" derived from the Perfect Systems — were, in fact, keys whose development into an organized system was very intricate and not altogether clear.[39] To be sure, the Pythagorean tradition of harmonics, based on the principle of expressing intervals by ratio — indeed, the entire doctrine of expressing the universe in numbers — has commanded a respectable place in the Western theory of music. Tuning notwithstanding, however, such mathematical thinking did not strongly manifest itself in the practice of music as an art. It is still not clear to what extent this elaborate theory, which developed over a number of centuries, guided or affected the art of music and its "making" even in ancient Greece, not to speak of the immediate and direct influence it may have exerted on the early development of European music (despite Boethius, Cassiodorus, and other intermediaries).[40] Given the inconclusive evidence, some scholars have gone so far as to claim that when the ancient theorists measured musical intervals, whether by ratio or by units, they had no practical purpose in mind.[41] The tradition of harmonics, according to this claim, was a "self-propelled" science interested in the nature of the universe rather than in music as art,

38. For further detail, see chapter 2 in Gustave Reese, *Music in the Middle Ages* (New York, 1940), 11–53.

39. See ibid., 28–44.

40. Boethius in his *De institutione musica* (sixth century) transmitted the theories of Pythagoras, Nicomachus, Aristoxenus, and Ptolemy. Cassiodorus's *Institutiones* (sixth century), which dealt with the liberal arts including Greek speculative thought concerning music, became the principal source for the liberal arts in monastic circles during the seventh, eighth, and even ninth centuries.

41. See, for example, Isobel Henderson, "Ancient Greek Music," *New Oxford History of Music,* vol. 1 (London, 1957), 342.

aiming at a theoretically satisfying scale conceived as a structural element in the cosmos.[42]

Indeed, it seems undeniable that this harmonic science was part of a cosmological doctrine that embraced an idea of music not necessarily related to its actual aural qualities. As in many other ancient cultures, the Greeks attributed universal significance largely to the "unheard" part of music, rather than to the part that was heard.[43] Nonetheless, the notion of music as an organized system, which manifests itself in its various realizations, left an indelible impression on Western thought and was brought to great heights in the audible music that it created.

The Musical Heritage of the World That Gave Rise to Christianity

Though more plausible, the conjectures concerning the origin of the medieval church modes are not flawless either. The modes, as will be recalled, are assumed to owe their formation and formulation to the Byzantine melody types, to the so-called *oktoechos*.[44] Although it is very likely that through a process of "rationalization" the modes developed from that earlier system of melody types, it is not altogether clear how this process happened. What is clear, however, is that the category of "melody types" was, and still is, a widespread phenomenon covering many civilizations and cultures; it was certainly practiced in the world that gave rise to Christianity. It is likewise evident that the modes, which were formerly understood by many as referring to scales with a given ambitus and center tone, constitute a more elaborate musical framework, comprising typical motifs, kinds of progressions, and designated uses. This holds as true for the Hindu *ragas,* the Arab *maqāmāt,* the Javanese *patet,* and a number of other such traditions, as it does for the Greek *nomoi,* the Byzantine and Armenian *echoi,* the Syrian *risqole,* and for the framework that governed Gregorian chant.

42. Ibid., 341.

43. The "harmony of the spheres," for example, was based on the Pythagorean concept of the cosmos as consisting of separate spheres that move around the earth at different velocities, producing different sounds. In the Middle Ages this concept caused Boethius to state that the music of the world is in fact what is produced by the concordance of sounds caused by the motion of the heavenly bodies.

44. The *echoi*—the system in ancient Syrian and Byzantine chant that corresponds to the system of modes—existed in the same number (eight) as the Western church modes. They were collectively referred to as *oktoechos.*

Discussing notation, I mentioned earlier that for many years it was believed that Gregorian chant, which developed in different parts of Europe, had a common origin in the East—in the church of Jerusalem and its environs and possibly even in earlier Jewish practice. This belief, unfortunately, led to a search for early *documents,* that is, for written evidence, rather than to the musical *practice* of the inhabitants of the region that gave rise to Christianity. Indeed, as long as the whole category of melody types was viewed in terms of the modes in their limited sense, the search for the characteristics of older music largely focused on choices of pitches and the relationships among them, in distinction to the diatonicism of later music.[45] By now, however, it has become abundantly clear that the cantillation signs of the Bible, for example, which have survived to the present day, functioned as reminders of melodies already known, rather than referring to definite pitches or intervals. In his comparative study of the musical traditions of Eastern and Western Jews, Abraham Idelsohn was able to show that the oral tradition associated with these cantillation signs preserves some fundamental elements of the Hebrew chant to this very day.[46] The ancient chant, accordingly, was free rather than metrical and made use of short musical figures. A mode, he suggested, was in fact composed of a number of motives serving different functions—some of which were employed for the beginnings and endings of compositions, while others for conjunctive and disjunctive purposes—so that melodic formulas, not fixed melodies, characterized the different chants.

As for the original *oktoechos,* there is no actual evidence on which to base a claim that they derived from Greek or any other scale theory or, for that matter, from any purely musical considerations. Traditional melodies, suggests Reese, must have been assigned their places in the *oktoechos* "according to such symbolical meaning as were attached to them and as ostensibly rendered them suitable for particular liturgical occasions."[47] Though particular motives must have become accepted as entities unto themselves,

---

45. See, for example, Reese, *Music in the Middle Ages,* 9 n20.

46. See Abraham Zevi Idelsohn, *Hebräisch-orientalischer Melodienschatz,* vols. 1–10 (Leipzig, 1914 –32). The work, as indicated by its name, was originally conceived as a collection of melodies of Oriental Jewish communities. Idelsohn, however, decided in the early '30s to include the songs of European Jews, believing that the music of Ashkenazi Jews also contained genuine Oriental elements. For the methodology employed by Idelsohn, see Ruth Katz, "Exemplification and the Limits of 'Correctness': The Implicit Methodology of Idelsohn's *Thesaurus,*" in *Yuval* 5 (Jerusalem, 1986): 365–71.

47. Reese, *Music in the Middle Ages,* 75.

and may have acquired a specific musical status, they were not recognized as conforming to particular scales. While more can be said, I wish only to emphasize that neither the Syrian nor the Byzantine *echoi* fit a scale-doctrine. The extent to which these may have had some bearing on Gregorian chant must be sought in the musical practice and functions of the melody *types* that seem to have crystallized into idioms and, as such, passed on to the Christian world, continuing to inform its chant tradition and performance practice. Indeed, serious scholars, such as Peter Wagner,[48] Egon Wellesz,[49] Amédée Gastoué,[50] Otto Gombosi,[51] Otto Ursprung,[52] and Eric Werner,[53] have not only endorsed the theory about the role and function of melody types in the pre-Christian world, but also saw fit, like Idelsohn, to seek their influence on early Christian musical practice. The rarity of ancient melodies makes it, of course, difficult to compare their basic stylistic features and to establish unequivocally what they have in common. If it were not for the fact that the authenticity of the church melodies can be upheld,[54] the comparison could not take place altogether.

The Greater Perfect System was evidently retained by early medieval theorists, yet the octave-species, as understood by the Greeks, had apparently no practical meaning, either in the East or in the West. It is agreed among scholars that the Western system of eight modes followed rather than preceded the formation of the Roman repertory, and that it might have taken place together with its diffusion to the Frankish kingdom. Scholars have tried, and still do, to trace the development of the classification system that brought the chant repertory under control. The Frankish

48. See his "Der gregorianische Gesang," in Guido Adler's *Handbuch der Musikgeschichte* (1930), and his *Einführung in die gregorianischen Melodien* (1895). Part 1 of the three parts of the *Einführung* also appeared in English as *Introduction to the Gregorian Melodies: Part I, Origin and Development of the Forms of the Liturgical Chant up to the End of the Middle Ages* (1907).

49. See his "*Die byzantinische und orientalische Kirchenmusik,*" in Adler, ibid.; also see his "*Das Alter der Melodien der byzantinischen Kirche,*" in *Forschungen und Fortschritte* (1932), and *Der Stand der Forschung auf dem Gebiete der byzantinischen Kirchenmusik* (1936).

50. See his "*L'Origine lointaine des huit tons liturgiques,*" his "*Chant Juif et Chant Grégorien,*" as well as his "*Les Origines hébraïques de la liturgie et du chant Chrétien,*" in *La Revue du chant gregorien* 34 and 35 (1930–31).

51. See his "*Studien zur Tonartenlehre des frühen Mittlealters,*" in *Acta Musicologia* 10 and 11 (1938–39)

52. See his *Die katholische Kirchenmusik* (1931–33).

53. See his *The Sacred Bridge* (London, 1958).

54. The facsimiles contained in the *Paléographie Musicale* provide remarkable evidence for the persistence of the tradition.

cantors, suggests Richard Crocker, were probably the ones who organized "the standard collections derived from an archetype, or at least compared them with each other." Although little is known about how this happened, says Crocker, "we do have the end result, the system—systems—referred to as 'the four finals,' or 'the eight modes,' and the coordinate system of eight psalm tones."[55] A psalm tone refers to a pitch on which the psalm as a whole is intoned. These pitches function as reciting tones; they are surrounded by certain melodic configurations of whole and half steps that accommodate the usual structure of the verses of the psalm. The Franks seem to have classified the antiphons of the Office (the short texts set to music that embrace the psalm) in the system of eight modes. These modes were coordinated with the system of eight psalm tones. The classification by finals was thus made for practical reasons; it did not derive from the analysis of the melodies. It is the eight modes, as classified by finals, that were apparently placed upon the diatonic scale inherited from the Greeks—that is, the Greater Perfect System.

Finals, however, "are not good guides to the melodic structure of earlier chant," says Crocker, "and letter-locations on the diatonic scale make comparison between modes difficult." Solmization—which provides precise designation of interval structure, involving tones and semitones without reference to letter names—is the best way, says Crocker, "to compare internal structure directly." Solmization according to the hexachord—*ut, re, mi, fa, sol, la* (as in modern movable *do* practice, with *ut* instead of *do*)—was developed, according to Crocker, "soon after the year 1000, seemingly just for this purpose." This medieval solmization, he claims, "is the most appropriate for description of chant."[56] Crocker also convincingly demonstrates how the traditional psalm tones and antiphons move either within the pitch set represented by *ut-re-mi-fa* or within the diatonic system with pitches below *ut* descending through a tone, a semitone, and a tone, or descending through a semitone, a tone, and another tone. All of the psalm tones and antiphons, says Crocker, can be easily compared by using one of these combinations. Moreover, solmization not only calls attention to the "prominent position of the set *ut, re, mi, fa* throughout the repertory" but also "provides a means of differentiating melodies and groups of melodies

55. See Richard Crocker, "Chants of the Roman Office," in *The Early Middle Ages to 1300* (new ed.), vol. 2 of *The New Oxford History of Music* (Oxford, 1990), 165.

56. Ibid., 149.

on the basis of their interior substance rather than just their final (or final and range) as in the modal classification."[57]

While the tension between theoretical models and the practice of the chant seems to have continued for quite some time, it is the chant as practice that apparently provided the eventual base for the tone structure of Western theory. There exist numerous treatises that portray attempts to derive from the Greater Perfect System a scalar formation that would accommodate both the scalar patterns and the classes of chant. Although this is hardly the place to discuss each of them separately, it is important to mention that the development of neumatic notation with more definitive pitches led to a group of theoretical writings that also incorporated a concern for the exactitude of intervals (employing the monochord and the use of the alphabet A to G, with repetition in the upper octave). Yet the scale and notation found in the *Dialogus*—a seminal anonymous treatise that appeared shortly before 1000—"did not immediately supersede all others," says Crocker, "but eventually it provided the basis for the scale and nomenclature that found its way to modern times."[58] The thoughts expressed in the *Dialogus* were advanced by Guido d'Arezzo (ca. 990–1050), who tried to reconcile the scale of this anonymous treatise "with the advantages of the short scalar fragments surrounding the finals and represented by the tetrachord of the finals." This, we are told, resulted in the tonal structure of the hexachord, "which can be conceived as the tetrachord of the finals with a whole tone added on to each end."[59] Although the complete system and nomenclature did not appear until later, Guido provided, according to Crocker, "the solmization that came into general use for this formation: *ut / re mi fa sol / la*." The same formation, we learn, was also arrived at, almost at the same time, by Hermannus Contractus (1013–1054) in Switzerland. Furthermore, we learn that "with the development of the hexachord around 1050, the search of the early Frankish theorists for a simple, rational tonal construct reached its goal."[60]

As an aid for memorizing, Guido used the initial syllables—*ut, re, mi, fa, sol, la*—of the first six lines of a well-known hymn to St. John, whose melody begins one tone higher with each successive line. In medieval theory that dealt with practical musical matters, the compass of tones was thus

57. Ibid., 150.

58. For a discussion of several of the treatises that contributed to the crystallization of the scale, see 'Frankish Music Theory' in Crocker's "Medieval Chant," in *The Early Middle Ages to 1300*, 278–83.

59. Ibid., 282.

60. Ibid.

obtained not by joined octaves but by overlapping hexachords—groups of six tones following each other in the intervalic sequence of *t t s t t*. In the diatonic scale of C major, accordingly, there are but two hexachords, one starting on c, the other on g. A third hexachord, starting on f, could be included provided a b-flat was added. The first of these hexachords was called *hexachordum naturale,* the second *hexachordum durum* (because it contained the b natural), and the third *hexachordum molle* (because it contained the b-flat). Since medieval theory did not consider tones of higher or lower octaves "identical," there were seven hexachords in the scale from G to e"—two *naturale,* three *durum,* and two *molle.* In order to accommodate melodic progression exceeding the compass of one hexachord, two or more hexachords were interlocked by a process of transition, the so-called *mutation.* Though this method also produces the scale, it does so without at the same time establishing tonality. The hexachord system, it must be remembered, developed independent of the Greek system of the tetrachord, in which a group of four tones served as the generating segment for the construction of the entire scale. The system, moreover, began rather late and did not appear in full form before the beginning of the fourteenth century.[61] Still, the tonal material offered by the system was eventually grouped into a series of eight octave-scales having modal significance.

The turning point, however, in the history of medieval modal theory is related to the efforts to superimpose a scalar modal system upon an already existing independent body of music.[62] Though the Greek transposition scales were increasingly mentioned by theorists, they had no effect on the music as practiced. The study of Gregorian chant, moreover, has continually revealed the reluctance of the modes to conform to a single scale, reasserting that melodic idioms were more conclusive in fixing the character of a mode than was the scale structure by itself.[63] Whatever the history of the church modes, they eventually lead, at least in theory, to the authentic and the plagal modes, each consisting of four combina-

61. The system, including the three hexachords, the compound pitch names, the mutations, the Guidonian hand, and so forth, only appeared in full around 1300 in the writing of Hieronymus de Moravia (Coussemaker, *Scriptorium,* vol. 1).

62. See Reese, *Music in the Middle Ages,* 154–55. The *Alia musica* (tenth century), according to Reese, is the earliest treatise in which both the formulas as well as Greek theory (based on Boethius) is being discussed. Though the *tonoi* were mistaken for modes in this treatise, it merged the formulas and the scales for the first time, ascribing modal functions to degrees within octave-scales.

63. The identity of the intervalic structure, for example, of the Dorian and Hypomixolydian scales and the diversity of their finals, tenors, and so forth illustrate the importance of formulas in the modal concept.

tions of pentachords and tetrachords. Since the admissible pentachords in these series were *t s t t; s t t t; t t t s; t t s t;* and the admissible tetrachords were *t s t; s t t; t t s;* the modes reveal that the diminished fifth and the augmented fourth were clearly inadmissible species. Thus, the classified species of the Middle Ages were bound by the fourth, fifth, and octave, that is, by the medieval consonances. The hexachord, though used for practical purposes, could not be included in the modal species since its *t t s t t* structure never varied. The sixths, it must be remembered, constituted dissonances in the early Middle Ages. The frequent appearance of b-flat in the chant repertoire disturbed the symmetry established by medieval theorists in their modal system.[64]

There is much more to be said about the early stages of modal development, yet all I wish to stress is that melodic idioms or formulas were more conclusive than the scale structure in fixing the character of a mode. Although it is clear that distinctive melodic formulas are likely to have different underlying scales, the deducing of these scales apparently belongs to a later stage of modal development. Still, though the relation between modal character and scale structure was not determined at this earlier stage, the theoretical deliberations attest, nonetheless, to a growing awareness that one need not adhere solely to formulas for a sense of orientation, since the modal color can be retained provided that the scale structure is retained with its degrees in the capacity of final notes. In fact, the analyses of Gregorian melodies reveals that the degrees on which melodies began and ended, independent of the designated formulas that were employed, assumed an ever growing importance for practical reasons, that is, to guide the singers in performing their task. This must have sensitized the singers not only to the intervalic relationships between degrees but, in all likelihood, also to the differences in the underlying scale structures of the formulas, since some of these formulas were markedly different from each other. Scales, after all, represent the tonal material of the *actual* music, arranged in an order of rising pitches. If scales differ from each other it is because the tonal materials that they represent are different. Different cultures, hence, are often represented by different scales, by virtue of having chosen different tonal materials. Yet the tonal material that consti-

64. The tritone is, of course, avoided by the introduction of b-flat, but Reese also calls to our attention the fact that transposition of portions of the melody could cause the whole melody to seem as though it were principally in one mode. In other words, were real modulations to take place, too many phrases would end on tones other than the final of the intended mode. See Reese, *Music in the Middle Ages,* 157–58.

tutes the substratum for the music of a given tradition may undergo many changes before it becomes crystallized.

The opting for a "particularized scale" rather than a "generalized tune," or even opting for both at the same time, depends, in and of itself, on the particular culture. The choice, in fact, may reveal a preference for ideal categories that contribute to the overall theoretical grasp of the music, or for melodic aspects that provide guidelines and norms for more practical purposes of composition and improvisation.[65] The Islamic musical tradition, for example, opted for both, whereas the Western tradition seems to have been concerned with theoretical aspects in a steady and cumulative fashion. Theory, naturally, follows practice, but basic theoretical principles, once codified and formalized, tend to affect the subsequent development of music in practice.

Disregarding intonation, the diatonic scale, as we have seen, was already used by the Greek theorists. Moreover, the *mese*—the upper note of the third tetrachord, the nucleus of the Greater Perfect System—is referred to in pseudo-Aristotle's *Problems* as the "leader" and described in the following way: "In all good music *mese* occurs frequently, and all good composers have frequent recourse to *mese,* and, if they have it, they soon return to it, as they do to no other note. . . . [M]ese is as it were a conjunction among sounds, and more so than the other notes, because its sound occurs more often."[66] Such a predominant tone tends to yield a sense of tonality. We learn in addition from the theory of "Ethos" that the Greek writers attached ethical characteristics to their various scales.[67] This seems to suggest not merely that their octave-scales were segments of the Greater Perfect System, all using the tonal nucleus of the predominant tone of the Dorian (é-e), but also that each of the scales must have had its own predominant tone, so as to produce a variety of modes, each with a "character" of its own, similar to those found in plainsong. Indeed, there must have been a number of such tones, if the Greeks were able to distinguish between scales and attribute to each a distinct influential power.

65. See section 1, no. 2, in Harold Powers's outstanding article on "Mode" in *The New Grove Dictionary of Music and Musicians* (vol. 12, 376–450). "Particularized scale" and "generalized tune" are telling phrases coined by Powers.

66. Quoted in Reese, *Music in the Middle Ages,* 47.

67. For the basic characteristics of the theory of "Ethos," see Curt Sachs, *The Rise of Music in the Ancient World* (New York, 1943), 248–52. Also see sections from Plato's *The Republic* and Aristotle's *The Politics* in Oliver Strunk, *Source Readings in Music History* (New York, 1950), 3–24.

We must, however, remember that even if we adhere to the notion that modes are composed from a number of motives, the total group into which the several motives fit tends to give rise to a distinct tonality. To be sure, the method employed in Gregorian chant for the recitation of psalms rested on eight tones, one for each church mode, on the fifth degree of the mode. But, however suggestive it might be about the function of the dominant in the hierarchy of the degrees in our scale system, this procedure did not emerge from theoretical considerations; it was established, as we have seen, for practical reasons—to provide the singer with a "point of reference." In this particular case, it was meant to ensure the relationship between the psalm and its enclosing antiphon,[68] which determines the psalm tone. While it helped to orient the singers, it bestowed an added distinction on each of the modes, independent of their formulaic nature.

Scales, it turns out, are not only the tonal material of music arranged in an order of rising pitches; they contain, as it were, a "home tone," to which the other tones of the scale are subordinated. Although the Hexachord System, which was also based on the diatonic scale, gave no preference to any given tone, the church modes, by contrast, designated *each* tone of the diatonic scale as a center tone. Thus, within the modal framework, for example, the C-major scale would be termed the "C mode of major scale," the Dorian mode would be termed the "D mode of the diatonic scale," while the modes of any given scale may begin on various pitch levels, resulting in "transposed scales," that is, different keys. All of this gives all the more reason why the term 'scale' should be avoided in discussion of the modes, with their manifold centralized scales.

Western music, as we all know, eventually settled on two types of scale, the major and minor, but their definitive establishment as the tonal basis of music took place during the seventeenth century. Before this, music continued to be based on the church modes, all of which differ from major and minor in some of their degrees. The major and minor interval sequences, interestingly, first entailed the enlargement of the number of modes, before only two modes, one with the major third, the other with the minor third, became fully adopted. Glareanus is considered the first

68. The term refers to short texts, mostly from the scriptures, set to music in a simple syllabic style and sung before and after a psalm or canticle. On greater feasts the entire antiphon is sung both before and after the psalm, while at other times only the first word or so is sung before, and the whole after.

to have introduced (1547) two new diatonic scales, one built on C (the Ionian mode) and the other built on A (the Aeolian mode), thus enlarging
the number of modes from eight to twelve.[69] Still, the situation in musical
practice was quite different, even by then. Modal theory kept rational-
izing and reintegrating, as far as possible, not only the voluminous corpus
of the chant repertoire but also new musical compositions that no longer
owed their inspiration to chant melodies as such.

Nonetheless, with the growth of polyphony and the extension of counterpoint, more and more attention was given to the rhythmical, rather
than the melodic, aspects of music, since modality had little to offer that
would guide the simultaneity or the successions of voices. Unlike a key in
later periods, a mode was not an abstract general pattern of tonal relationships inherent in the grammar of a musical language that also establishes
a relationship between tonality and harmony. So long as chant melodies
constituted the baseline on top of which voices were added, guided by the
admissible intervals, to enrich the musical texture, there was, of course, no
real need to devise rules for the successions of simultaneities. Yet with the
development of counterpoint the need was increasingly felt for directives
that would integrate all of the elements of a musical composition into a
well-synchronized whole. Once established, such directives could also allow, inter alia, for the expansion of musical compositions into extended
works, since the integration of the whole is assured regardless of size.

The Formal Organization of the Chant Repertoire

Before proceeding further with the systems that gradually matured and
the rules that were devised that enabled music to develop a language of
its own, a word must be added about the formal organization of the chant
repertoire—the musical corpus that was so crucial to the development of

---

69. The date refers to Glareanus's *Dodecachordon.* It must be remembered that Glareanus was committed to the integrity of the octave-species, as were other theorists who
preceded him who were concerned, as he was, with the classificatory and scalar aspects
of the modes. The need to classify and categorize—so prominent in Western theoretical
deliberations—is exemplified by the development of modal theory, especially the phase
from Marchetto's *Lucidarium* (1318) to Zarlino's *Institutioni harmoniche* (1558). Though this
important phase cannot be covered here in detail, it should be noted that the Greek diatonic species of the octave, as transmitted via Boethius (who referred to the distribution
of tones and semitones filling in an octave consonance by step), obviously loomed large
in this intricate and fascinating development.

Western art music. The following discussion of some of the formal aspects of Gregorian chant aims to draw attention to the kind of dependence on language that music displayed at this early phase of its development. Naturally, the more music was able to develop intramusical understandings, the less dependent it became on extramusical factors or, for that matter, on rudimentary schemes of repetition applied to short, easily recognizable, musical snatches. Indeed, as formal organizations became able to completely rely on the syntax of the musical language, they could detach themselves from language, if so desired, without detriment to their communicative power.

Though the compositional activity of Gregorian chant centered less on new melodies than on adapting old phrases to new liturgical purposes, the music was, nonetheless, cast in a great variety of forms. The formal laws that actually governed the categories of plainsong were but few, but they were able in their various combinations to create apparent recognizable distinctions. To begin with, the styles of the melodies were determined by the kind of relationship they established between the number of notes and the number of syllables. The *syllabic* style, that is, one note to each syllable of the text, rendered simple melodies. The *neumatic* style, which gained its name from the fact that neumes of two or three notes were attached to certain syllables of the text, rendered slightly more elaborate melodies. The *melismatic* style, in which single syllables were sung to many groups of notes, rendered florid melodies. The hierarchy from simple to florid was exploited in the liturgy in a number of ways: to differentiate between the Office and the Mass, between the degrees of liturgical solemnity, and between ordinary and holy days. The different styles were also used intra the Office and intra the Mass in order to differentiate among the Office hours and among the various sections of the Mass, granting a richer style to the principal hours of the liturgical day—Lauds and Vespers—and a more florid style to the Gradual, Alleluia, and the Offertory of the Mass. The ability of the performers was also taken into consideration. The "simple" style, accordingly, was entrusted to the ministers and the people, while the more elaborate styles were entrusted to the trained choirs and their solo singers. All of these cross-related possibilities were entertained in the musical setting of particular texts, taking into account their respective places in the liturgy. The practice of music was thus guided by the ritual and its various texts, so that melodic formulas were chosen on the basis of their suitability to particular liturgical occasions, independent of their musical aspects.

Gregorian melodies, however, were affected not only by the liturgical texts and their placements but also by the grammatical accents of the text, bestowing on the melodies an oratorical quality. Regardless of the number of notes an accented syllable received (depending on the style to which it belonged), the tonic accents of words were meant to coincide with melodic peaks. This, naturally, affected the intervals, whether ascending or descending. Without discussing their actual sizes, it is clear that these intervals affected the curve of the melody. In fact, the so-called Gregorian periods mostly created convex curves, the tonal range of which could be as large as an octave. Yet each period was constructed from smaller melodic units, which were constructed from yet smaller ones. Since the melodic particles could be related to each other, they created a variety of forms. Though specific melodic formulas contributed to, and were a part of, the resultant structure, their choice was based, nonetheless, on their suitability to the liturgical texts that they were expected to serve, and was dependent on the particular functions that these texts were supposed to fulfill in the church ritual. This multidimensional matrix of requirements must have given rise to occasions in which not all of them could be accommodated. Indeed, the study of Gregorian chant reveals many such occasions, but the adjustments they evoked also became regulated.

A simple glance at the four main classes into which the chants are generally grouped reveals as well that their formal organizations derived from the texts that the chants were meant to serve. The *strophic* compositions, which are characterized by the immediate repetition of melodic sections of some length, resulted from groups of textual lines, each of which contained a prescribed number of feet, like the stanzas of most hymns, for example. The *psalmodic* compositions, which also employ immediate repetitions of a musical formula, arose from the desire to accommodate the verses of the psalm. Though the latter is composed of nonmetrical verses, and each verse is divided into two parts (like a question and answer, for example), these parts jointly create the sense of the verse. Unlike these, the *commatic* compositions do not use the same melody for different texts. Moreover, each of the units that make up a phrase may carry different melodic materials. The musical inflection of these chants, however, depends on the tonic accent of each word of the text. The fourth class of chants, the *monologues and dialogues*, obviously belongs to a category of performance practice, as the name implies. The monologues, accordingly, are sung by the officiating priest, and the dialogues take place between the priest and the choir or the congregation.

Of course, these brief discussions have barely touched upon the important topics that they addressed. Indeed, to those familiar with the materials discussed—given the scholarly attention to the theoretical treatises and the expertise with which detailed issues have been handled—it may appear as oversimplification. At the same time, to those unfamiliar with the issues raised (even though they are familiar with the music involved), my "shorthand" explanations of some theoretical aspects may appear to be overly complicated and hard to grasp. Although it is difficult to strike a middle course that would satisfy all concerned, this essay aims neither to teach music history nor to uncover new information. Rather, on the basis of what is already known, it tries to draw attention to the nature of the sifting processes that created the infrastructure that affected the various manifestations of Western art music as well as its delineation as a whole. It invites those immersed in these materials to entertain a "new look," as it were, at what they already know and at the knowledge of which they might have themselves contributed. As far as others are concerned, it tries to impart some insight into the processes whereby a culture structures its musical tradition. In order to persuade the erudite, some familiarity with the intricacies involved is essential. These intricacies, however, may introduce the less learned to processes that they have never considered before, even if they are not able to fully grasp the details of one thing or another.

At any rate, the discussion up to now has focused primarily on the ideational factors that guided the choice of the "musical building blocks" that went into the 'making' of the tradition that this essay tries to examine. Though the process unfolded over a number of centuries, each of which witnessed changes in the political, social, and cultural spheres, not to speak of the stylistic changes that were affected thereby, the stages it underwent nonetheless built on each other in a significant way. While adding clarifications and refinements of issues that were already raised, each newer stage seems to have augmented the referential power vested in abstract theoretical systems as they became increasingly solidified. As we have seen, such systems may encompass new musical possibilities by virtue of supplying an orienting frame that subsumes particulars, though the latter also stand to benefit from their "relocation," as it were. Yet the very aspects that enlarged the scope of the music they could potentially handle also circumscribed music's confines. It is confines of this sort, as we shall see, that became the main characteristic of Western art music.

Although it is undoubtedly true that music is not a language spontaneously appreciated by listeners of differing cultural backgrounds, it is fair to assume that it is easier to become acquainted with music that has divorced itself from extramusical references than with music that heavily depends on them. Abstract musical systems can more readily be acquired than entrenched interrelated cultural patterns. Although this hardly explains why the Japanese saw fit to adopt Western art music into their intellectual and artistic domain during the Meiji Restoration (1869–95), it goes a long way to explain its success.

TWO

Systematizing Musical Laws

THE SELF-CHOSEN CONFINES OF ART

Confines, as we have seen, add characterization to what they delimit. Thus, a sonnet is not a sonnet unless it is a fourteen-line poem. Although the length of the lines of different sonnets may vary, rhyming in accordance with one of various definite schemes, a sonnet must both retain its inner consistency as well as conform to the number of lines that are allotted to the delivery of what the poet set out to express. Art, as opposed to nature, invariably refers to a human skill, to an ability of execution that becomes manifest in the objects produced. Without wrestling with the definition of 'Art'—a concept that has been defined and redefined time and again—our condensed account, so far, has merely tried to disclose the kind of "making" (in an Aristotelian sense) that was involved and the "skills" that it entailed. The latter, clearly, become apparent only in reference to the sensuous world that they seem able to master. These sensuous worlds, however, derive their existence not only from the building blocks that they create but also from the manner in which they are employed and the functions they aim to serve.

Although nothing stands still in history, not everything changes at the same time, and certainly not at the same rate. Given that all of Culture is man-made, individual cultures display not only unique assemblages of interrelated cultural components but also different hierarchical relationships among them; their relative importance and presumed roles may be assigned as causes, as effects, or as mutually contingent. Clearly, the more interrelated and mutually contingent the cultural components of a given culture, the slower their pace of change and the less likely they are to give rise to subcultural domains that define their own boundaries and independence. Moreover, in cultures that experience little need to introduce differentiation, the direction that governs the relationship between antecedent and aftermath is indeterminate. Although differentiation makes the relative standing of different concerns more apparent, it also clarifies, albeit to varying degrees, the parameters that lend the different concerns their distinction.

It would be wrong, however, to conclude that divorcing music from extramusical factors excludes music from societal functions other than purely musical ones. In fact, though the church ritual affected the kind of music to which it gave rise, it was better served, as we have seen, the more music was able to devise intramusical references that assured these functions. Indeed, the more systematized a music becomes on the basis of purely musical laws of organization, the freer it is to adapt itself to different occasions, lending each a physiognomy of its own. This physiognomy, moreover, may be achieved in a number of ways, in tandem with both function and occasion. Naturally, such "speech acts" presuppose a "language" that the group holds in common, even if members of the group—though familiar with its vocabulary and the ways in which it is used—may have never bothered to become acquainted with the laws and rules of action that govern the language they have inadvertently imbibed. Such recognized laws and rules of action nevertheless exist; furthermore, they were devised and developed by the very group that understands and uses the language. A musical "language" is, correspondingly, a collective product whose fabricated schemes provide the "natural" base for its multiple musical expressions within its self-chosen confines.

HORIZONTAL AND VERTICAL ELEMENTS: A GENERATING AND CONTROLLING FORCE, RESPECTIVELY

So far we have discussed melodic lines and the musical frameworks by which they can be governed. The chants, as we have seen, contain residues of a former musical practice, characteristic of "melody types" of various sorts, despite the church modes that attempted to provide a more abstract umbrella for this corpus of melodies. Once established, these modes were able to provide an adequate orientation for newly composed melodies that abided by the dictates of its framework. Though we have not yet had occasion to discuss modal polyphony, which raised new problems that needed addressing, we have had reason to discuss the coordination between voices as far as duration is concerned. The rise of staff notation, as we have seen, was primarily prompted by a desire to enrich the melodic line vertically, that is, to variegate the sonority by introducing additional voices. Once these additional voices no longer consisted of the same number of notes as did the original melody, the coordination between the voices called forth specific "laws" that enabled their independence, while ensuring the desired coincidence among them.

The concurrence among voices invariably contributes to the musical texture of compositions. Given that music unfolds in time, the ability to control its flow makes it also possible to control musical textures, provided one has clear ideas about desired and undesired sonorities, which become most apparent when the voices converge or coincide. Music, in fact, consists of horizontal and vertical elements: the former are the successive sounds that form melodies; the latter are the simultaneous sounds that form harmonies. The effects produced by certain intervals, whether agreeable or disagreeable, are the foundation of harmonic music. In harmonic music the consonant intervals, that is, the agreeable ones, represent the element of normalcy and repose, while the dissonant intervals, that is, the disagreeable ones, represent the no less important element of disturbance and tension. Of course, what is considered "pleasant" or "unpleasant" can, and did, change during the course of history, but the ways in which these intervals functioned and related to one another were invariably circumscribed and regulated. How and by what means they were regulated we shall presently discuss, yet it is important to mention from the outset that the Pythagorean theory of consonance and dissonance guided Western music for a long time.

According to the Pythagorean theory, the smaller the numbers that express the ratio of the frequencies of intervals, or of the lengths of the corresponding strings, the more consonant the intervals. The order, from consonant to dissonant, is thus: unison (1:1), octave (1:2), fifth (2:3), fourth (3:4), major sixth (3:5), major third (4:5), minor third (5:6), minor sixth (5:8), second (8:9), major seventh (8:15), and minor seventh (9:16). Indeed, the order obtained conforms, more or less, to the order in which these intervals were entertained in the harmonic practice as it developed. Although the craft of composing music had to bear in mind both the consonant and the dissonant intervals, treating them in accordance with rules that controlled the ways in which they were used, the rules themselves kept changing, along with the shift of the dividing line between consonant and dissonant. In other words, what was considered consonant kept continuously moving in the direction of the ratios expressed in higher numbers, incorporating intervals that were previously considered dissonant. Moreover, dissonant intervals were differently conceived at different times. Whereas in the thirteenth century, for example, the progression 3–1, – 3–5, and 6–8 were the result of passing tones (4–3–1 and 5–6–8), in the fourteenth century these progressions were conceived as a movement from an imperfect to a perfect consonance through contrary motion by half and whole steps.[1]

Musical texture, as already mentioned, stands out particularly clearly in music written in a given number of parts. Though each part may represent a horizontal line of individual design, it is connected with the other lines by the vertical relationships that they create. It is not surprising that harmony came to be appreciated considerably later than polyphony, since the latter originated from the simple superimposition of voices—note against note—using only consonant intervals (i.e., intervals whose frequency ratios are expressed in the smallest numbers in the Pythagorean series). In fact, the term 'counterpoint' derived from the practice of *punctus contra punctum* (note against note), though it became identified with more complex music in later periods and eventually with the systematic study of voice combinations. Indeed, the freer the horizontal element of the texture became, that is, the more independent the individual voices became (admitting both contrary motion and several notes against one), the more need there was to mediate, somehow, between the horizontal and vertical elements. It must have become increasingly evident that the horizontal and vertical elements are inseparable, representing a generating and controlling force, respectively, despite the distinction between them. The mediation between voices engendered, naturally, many theoretical treatises that attest to the various practices as they proceeded.

Theory follows practice. It tries to unveil the principles that guide the practice. Once unveiled, these principles may turn into practical instructions that control the standard of compositional conduct for a while. However, by uncovering the "reasoning" that determines the constructions whereby every new practice in a given tradition relates, in one form or an-

1. According to Anonymous XIII (quoted by Dahlhaus), "The third composed of a whole tone and a semitone requires a unison after it, and that of two whole tones requires a fifth after it. The sixth composed of a semitone with a fifth requires a fifth after it, and that of a whole tone with a fifth requires an octave after it." See Carl Dahlhaus, *Studies on the Origin of Harmonic Tonality* (Princeton, 1990), 78.

other, to what preceded it, theory is also able to amend—refine, broaden, and unveil—the overriding frames that subsume individual practices as they emerge. Thus, while new practices may challenge theory, theory discloses the "rules," inferred from past practices, in a codified and systematized manner. As such, theory reflects the infrastructure of the musical "language," which the various practices helped build, and in relationship to which their particularities are assessed.

Interestingly, while the unison, octave, fifth, fourth, and the third (which was still considered an "imperfect consonance") were admitted in theoretical treatises by the fourteenth century, they did not govern the relationship between all of the voices, either in theory or in musical practice. Two-voice counterpoint, of course, created no problems in this respect, since it was relatively easy to govern the flow of the voices so as to ensure the desired consonance at points where they coincide. In three-voice counterpoint, however, the governing principle was that the third added voice must be in consonance with either the first or the second of the two other voices, though not necessarily with both.[2] Needless to say, the vertical combinations that resulted from such a principle could hardly avoid dissonant intervals, as far as the relationships between the other voices were concerned. The idea that the consonant principle should apply to the relationship between all of the voices obviously created problems, even after it was stated that all parts must be consonant.[3] Interestingly, the treatment of consonant intervals as "normative" called attention, willy-nilly, to what seemed unavoidable—the regulation of dissonant relationships. Given the initial practice of successive rather than simultaneous composing, the fundamental rhythmic relationships between the voices had to be solved, as we have seen, as soon as the upper parts became more flexible. Thus, how to write a melismatic upper part above the various intervalic progressions of the tenor long preceded the theoretical discussion of florid counterpoint. The latter, unlike the former, was increasingly forced to devise rules concerning *dissonance* (in addition to the rules that governed

---

2. Franco of Cologne, whose *Ars cantus mensurabilis* (ca. 1260) contributed greatly to the improvement and standardization of mensural writing, was also the first to discuss three-voice counterpoint. "He who shall wish to construct a triplum," writes Franco, "ought to have the tenor and discant in mind, so that if the triplum be discordant with the tenor, it will not be discordant with the discant, and vice versa." See Oliver Strunk, *Source Readings in Music History*, 155.

3. Jean de Muris, who defended de Vitry's *Ars nova* and was himself concerned with problems of mensuration, was probably the first to state that all three parts must be consonant; see his *Ars discantus* in Coussemaker's *Scriptorum de Musica Medii Aevi*, vol. 3, 68.

the consonance), for the more independent the voices became, the less possible it was to avoid the occurrence of those undesired intervals.

Freedom calls forth restriction, while restraint invites overcoming! Evidently, the desire to secure the "proper" relationships between the various voices, that is, the preferred relationships, gave rise to procedures controlling the melodic unfolding of the individual voices. Hence, what is commonly considered "voice leading" came into being out of a consideration for the composition as a whole, which imposed regulations on the components from which it was constructed. Indeed, the history of Western art music reveals not only a desire to relate individual segments, or parts, to the wholes they are able to construct but also an ever growing aspiration to vest the parts themselves with the "tendency" of the whole, creating a kind of internal referentiality, not unlike the relationship that pertains between a referential and an integral in calculus. However simple such a scheme might sound, it was neither premeditated nor quickly achieved.[4]

While the earliest document that contains examples showing how to write a melismatic upper part above the various intervalic progressions (c-d, c-e, etc.) of the tenor goes as far back as the middle of the twelfth century,[5] the first treatise that discussed florid counterpoint and gave definite rules concerning dissonance treatment only appeared in the second half of the fifteenth century.[6] And it is not until the beginning of the sixteenth century that it first dawned upon theorists that it might be easier to control the relationships among the melodic lines by composing simultaneously, rather than successively.[7] It took as long as it did to arrive at such a

4. Altogether, long-term plans do not befit the arts, since artists invariably relate to their own times, based on *past* experience. This, by the way, holds equally true for Wagner, despite his "Artwork of the Future."

5. The statement refers to the Vatican treatise from ca. 1150. See Frieder Zaminer, *Der Vatikanische Organum-Traktat (Ottob. Lat. 3025)*, (Tutzing, 1959)

6. The statement refers to Tinctoris's *Liber de arte contrapunti* of 1477. Tinctoris is considered one of the most important music theorists of his time; his writings constitute a major source of information on fifteenth-century musical practice. Although Tinctoris is best known for his *Terminorum musice diffinitorium*—the oldest printed music dictionary—his *Liber de arte contrapunti* is the most comprehensive treatise treating the principles of consonance and dissonance. Differentiating between note-against-note counterpoint and florid writing, Tinctoris provides compositional rules based on the supremacy of consonant intervals.

7. The first theorists to state that all the parts are best composed simultaneously were Johannes Cochlaeus (*Musica*, 1507) and Pietro Aron (*Libri tres de institutione harmonica*, 1516). The idea of composing simultaneously gained momentum from then on. Zarlino's well-known *Institutioni harmoniche* (vol. 3, 1558), however, is the first comprehensive study of counterpoint. Traditional counterpoint, as taught by Zarlino, became the basis of the

conclusion not for want of clever thinking, but rather for lack of genuine need. In fact, many of the problems that emerged in the interim, in actual musical practice, were quite ingeniously handled. It is the cumulative process, in practice and theory, that gradually and inadvertently led to what seemed like a pertinent shift in the "management" of musical construction. Though of momentous historical significance, it should be viewed as an act of expediency in its time, rather than a feat forecasting the future. Yet the reconceptualization of musical construction helped usher in a system that was able to govern both the harmonic as well as the melodic movements of musical compositions.

Cementing the Relationship among Successively Composed Voices

Attempts to govern the progression of voices—so as to achieve desired relationships among them—called attention to the modes and the extent to which they provide unifying frames for polyphonic compositions. It also heightened the awareness of the overlapping among voice lines, which essentially operated in the same voice range. The overall range of melodies could of course be enlarged by combining the authentic modes with their plagal correlates, as already exemplified by many of the chant melodies. Polyphonic compositions could, likewise, avail themselves of such mixed modes, if so desired, by assigning the whole composition to their finals. Yet Renaissance polyphony, like that of the Middle Ages, neither opted to subsume all of the voices by a single mode nor to forgo the overall distinction between authentic and plagal modes. In other words, though it had become clear that the simultaneous handling of diverse voices might ease the task of controlling the proper relationships among them, the voice lines retained their individual "fields of reference."[8] Thus, the order in which the different voices were to be *conceived* continued to preoccupy composers and theorists, regardless of the manner in which they were actually set down. In retrospect, it seems that only tonal chord combi-

---

systematic instruction of the subject (today better known, among music students, by the name "Palestrina counterpoint"). Aware of the fact that the thirds and sixths were not considered consonant in the ratios handed down by Pythagorean theory, though essential components of modern part-writing, Zarlino extended the limit of consonant intervals from those produced through four divisions of a string to those produced through six divisions. This, naturally, had consequences not only for counterpoint but for harmony as well.

8. See the discussion of the subject by Powers, "Mode," 400.

nations that have become stabilized as conventional formulas could constitute a guide for the successive composition of voice parts. In fact, the
conception of successively composed voices and tonal harmony are not
mutually exclusive, provided that the former presupposes the latter as a
foregone conclusion.

Since polyphony germinated from the vertical embellishment of plainchant, the part that carried the cantus firmus, that is, the preconceived
melody, became the basis, the *vox principalis,* for the addition of the other
parts. This voice came to be called "tenor" in connection with the development of melismatic writing, in which the notes of the cantus were drawn
out and sustained. The addition of a "discant"—an upper voice (originally
designated by this name)—called for special care and ingenuity, with utmost regard for the preexisting tenor. The addition of a *bassus*—a voice
below the tenor (a contratenor)—had to be executed with the "sweetness
of the harmony" (as Tinctoris put it) in mind. However, with the development of four-part writing, the "tenor" continued to provide the reference
for the composition of the soprano, while the bass gradually became the
reference for the alto, the second to the lowest part. With an alto subject to a bass and a soprano subject to a tenor, it became possible to think
of the voices as functioning in pairs. From there on, principal cadences
were mostly formed by the tenor and soprano, with the bass supplying
harmonic support and the alto harmonic filling. The tenor-soprano pair
seems to have established the mode referred to by the composition, by
virtue of having most cadences. The latter, as expected, related to the final
of the mode. This was not enough, however, to bring modality and counterpoint into a symbiosis that could resolve all of the problems as they
emerged.

"The Function of Closure"

Polyphonic compositions were naturally longer than the chant melodies
that they employed. The longer the composition, the more attention it
called to its formal design, and to the need to distinguish between the
conclusion of compositions and the momentary conclusions of sections
and phrases. The need to convey distinct *impressions*—that of momentary
conclusions and that of permanent ones—gave rise to set formulas. Set
formulas, once agreed upon, effectively convey what they stand for. While
the history of music is replete with "communicative coinages" of various
sorts, each period of music history had but a limited number of cadential
formulas, characteristic of their period and subject to the theoretical dic-

tates of their time. This also explains why cadential formulas serve so well as identifying marks for the different periods. Designations such as *perfect, authentic, plagal, mixed, imperfect,* and *deceptive* cadences—a nomenclature well known to music students—did not come into full array overnight. Like all else, such distinctions evolved only gradually, in line with the development of musical "language" and its adeptness. It must be remembered, however, that each step in this development resulted from the concurrent practice of musicians, who introduced modifications into inherited practices according to their own needs and aesthetic desiderata.

Indeed, the cadences of early music differ sharply from those of later periods; familiar progressions such as V-I and IV-I, for example, are hard to find in music prior to the sixteenth century. Yet all of the cadences, regardless of time, saw fit to employ the first step of the mode or scale for purposes of closure. It is, however, the *finalis*—a major "point of reference" in chant melodies—that eventually determined the modal frame to which a given chant belonged. Since music unfolds in time, clear notions about points of closure may, in fact, supply a better sense of orientation than do the points at which a composition or a section thereof begins. Closure, furthermore, affects the way in which it is to be approached. In fact, the more a closure functions as a definitive destination to be reached, the more influence it is likely to exert on the unfolding of the music leading to it. Cadences, as it turns out, have obvious implications for what precedes them, yet the extent to which they are able to exert influence on the unfolding of the music leading up to them depends on the "syntactic" structure of the musical language to which they belong. A musical language that possesses schemes that function hierarchically is clearly better furnished to govern the "direction" of the musical unfolding. Moreover, it is also better equipped merely to allude to points of destination, without actually getting there, thus prolonging the musical "journey." With a reliable "compass" in hand, one can afford to take detours!

From Imperfect to Perfect Consonance—Relating Voices and Sonorities by Interval Progressions

The musical language delineated above actually came to pass in the West, but it was slow in developing. Given the practice of adding voices successively, practically all of the cadences of polyphonic music prior to 1450 were based on the progression II-I in the tenor, since the most frequent cadential motion in Gregorian chant was that of the descending second. Ascending motion was much rarer in Gregorian chant and mostly limited

to the ascending second VII-I, but never as a leading tone. It should be
noted that as late as the thirteenth century the half step was still experienced as a problematic interval not easily understood, and no "tendency"
was perceived of the lower tone toward the upper, or of the upper toward
the lower. If polyphonic music admitted two half steps—one before the
octave and the other before the fifth, a practice common both before and
after 1400—it must be viewed in connection with interval progression,
rather than be mistaken for "leading tones." In the fifteenth century, we
encounter yet another modification in which the contratenor jumps up an
octave, from the fourth below the final to the fifth above it, foreshadowing
the V-I movement in the lowest part of the authentic cadence. However,
rather than being viewed as cadences intimating future developments,
they ought to be viewed for what they were—modifications of the basic
II-I progression. In contrast to the function of chords in tonal harmony,
the structural significance of interval progressions—those progressing
from imperfect to perfect consonance with a half-step connection in one
of the voices—is independent of the underlying scale. Though the principle for connecting sonorities independent of the underlying scale may
seem foreign to us, one should beware of projecting present-day perceptions onto past conceptions. The addition of the bass to the musical texture was apparently responsible for the increased use of the V-I progression (a seeming "authentic cadence"), in addition to the IV-I progression
(a seeming "plagal cadence"), which it introduced. Still, the third, the most
characteristic interval of the Western harmonic system, was mostly omitted in the final chords of these cadences.

It should be noted that the third fared quite well otherwise, despite
having been judged by French treatises of the thirteenth century as an
imperfect consonance. Thirds were in fact used on the Continent, in
one form or another, both before and after their categorical appraisal. In
England, moreover, they were considered as "excellent consonances" quite
early,[9] a statement well supported by the English repertoire. Interestingly,
the English medieval two-part compositions, which were based on thirds,
were called *gymel* (from the Latin *gemellus,* meaning twin), clearly allud-
ing to the perception of the third as a concordant bond. The early use of
the sixth-chord style in England (which reached its culmination in the
compositions of John Dunstable) presented, likewise, a challenge to the

---

9. So we learn from Anonymous IV, himself an Englishman and the best known of
all of the anonymi for having provided the key to our understanding of the historically
important Notre Dame school. See Coussemaker, *Scriptorum,* vol. 1, 358.

consonances considered perfect. At any rate, that which flourished early in England became, in due time, the preferred sonority. To support this statement, it will suffice—at least for those acquainted with the history of music—to mention the Burgundian and Flemish schools of the fifteenth century (whose composers were influenced by this English predilection); it is the preference for full sonorities, based on vertical combinations, that made for a lessening of independence between voices.

Tinctoris wasted no time on proper voice-leading or melodic considerations in his *Liber de arte contrapunti* (1477)[10]—having derived the word 'counterpoint' from something purely vertical—because the linear dimension was taken for granted at that period. This taking for granted of the linear is what enabled Tinctoris to endorse the "pleasant sounds" of composers such as Johannes Ockeghem, John Dunstable, Gilles Binchois, and Guillaume Dufay.[11] Tinctoris remarks, in this regard, that in the compositions of his predecessors dissonances happened more often than consonances, though they occurred—in improvised counterpoint—only in short note values and on unaccented beats, or as suspensions. With his contemporaries in mind, Tinctoris set forth some principal rules of counterpoint, yet he dealt almost exclusively with vertical problems, since, as already mentioned, the linear idea was basic. Interestingly, as long as dissonances were regarded only as bad sounding, the way they were in earlier periods, they were kept off the accented parts of the measure as much as possible, without being subjected, however, to any particular rules. In the course of the fifteenth century the laws for the conjunct treatment of dissonances became more established, not only in actual practice but also in theory (as formulated by Tinctoris). At any rate, the syncope dissonance, or suspension, came to be used frequently under circumstances that clearly signified a conscious attempt to exploit its effect.

If the harmony of the fifteenth century still strikes us as somewhat thin, the compositions of the period—during which vocal polyphony flourished—distinguish themselves, nonetheless, by a wealth and variety of tonal combinations. Empty fifths and octaves were much suppressed and were rarely chosen for the sake of their sound; they were motivated mostly by the movement of the melody, by voice leading, imitation, or the like.[12] The overall tendency toward fuller sonorities came to the fore

10. See Coussemaker, *Scriptorium*, vol. 4, 76–119.

11. Ibid., 77.

12. Imitation, however, only began to play a principal role in musical construction during the sixteenth century, when its pedantic stiffness underwent a great deal of refinement, not least due to a new attitude toward the text. This new attitude became

clearly in the two improvisational methods of singing that developed in this period—the so-called fauxbourdon and English discant—involving 6/3 harmonies using a cantus firmus. In the one, the lowest and the highest parts were notated and the middle part was improvised, whereas in the other only the lowest part was noted. In the fauxbourdon, accordingly, the chant melody appeared in the uppermost voice, with a contrapuntal part moving along at the lower sixth; the middle part was added by the singer at the lower fourth, doubling the chant melody. In the English discant the chant melody appeared in the lowest part, and the singers supplied the 6/3 harmony above it. These sixth chords, however, should not be viewed as "inversions," for the triad was not yet recognized as the basis of tonal harmony. Nor should the frequent use of the third be confused with its future role as the most characteristic interval of the Western harmonic system, which is based on triads.

Concerning the use of the modes as the tonal basis of polyphonic composition, there is no evidence, as we have seen, of an overall methodical treatment. The compositions of the fourteenth century were still remarkably free in their tonality, as is also evident from the liberal use of tones other than those in the diatonic scale (generally referred to as *musica ficta*). Nondiatonic tones, by the way, already appeared in the earliest examples of written music; they were even discussed at length by some theorists.[13] Such accidentals, however, whether present in the manuscripts or merely hinted at, should be viewed (at least until the late fifteenth century) as tones that resulted from melodic modifications or from transpositions of the church modes rather than from a conception of chromaticism that applies to all of the five whole tones of the diatonic scale equally, yielding twelve tones to the octave.[14] It is the tonal language to which accidentals belong that determines, in the final analysis, the functions they serve.

---

especially prominent in the music of the later sixteenth century. It was accompanied, to be sure, by a musical technique that displayed greater architectonic mastery of melodies, greater fullness of chords, and stricter use of dissonance. Palestrina's music, for example, may be characterized in these terms.

13. Reference to nondiatonic tones is already found in the "Scholia enchiriadis," a companion treatise to the earliest treatise dealing with polyphony, the "Musica enchiriadis" (ca. 900). Odo of Cluny, Magister Lambert, Walter Odington, and Jean de Muris are among the prominent theorists that dealt with the subject, from the tenth to the fourteenth centuries.

14. *Musica ficta* raises serious problems for the modern editor of early music, for there are many musical sources in which the chromatic alterations are not indicated, though implied. By means of copious editorial accidentals, some editors have revealed a tendency to transform the tonal language of the Middle Ages and the Renaissance into

Given the evidence of musical practice, one may conclude that polyphonic compositions reveal considerable freedom as far as their tonality is concerned until the latter part of the fifteenth century, when the Flemish school renewed interest in the Gregorian tradition and sacred music. The Gregorian tradition had been neglected for a while in favor of a broadening of compositional procedures—employing freely composed tenors and popular tunes, a variety of textures, imitation techniques, freely moving rhythms, four-voice settings, and so forth—producing many secular works on the way. With so enlarged a compositional scope, composers could entertain sacred music anew, more attentive to the Gregorian modal framework. To be sure, there were other historical factors that affected both sacred as well as secular music. The present essay, it must be repeated, only endeavors to unveil the nature of the musical *reasoning* that accompanied the development of Western music (as opposed to other kinds of music), and not the sociopolitical factors that instigated historical changes, which affected musical desiderata. At any rate, it is only in the sixteenth century that we first find polyphonic compositions assigned to a definite mode, like the polyphonic settings, for example, of the Magnificat in the various modes, using the tenor as the determining element.[15]

Yet despite the modal designations that were applied to various kinds of compositions, and despite the cadential formulas that the music employed, one can hardly speak of an overall embracing tonality, even without mentioning the problems raised by *musica ficta*. The treatment of the successive conception of the voices (with the tenor as the constitutive voice and the discant and countertenor as the first and second counterpoint) was apparently still operative. The fact that the tenor is a cantus firmus means not that interval progressions were related only to the tenor but that the tenor represented the mode of the entire composition, even if the individual voices differed in mode. However, representing the mode does not mean that the preexisting cantus also served as the reference voice of compositional technique. In the sixteenth century, in fact, the two different functions of the tenor were compressed into the distinction between the bass as a contrapuntal reference voice and the tenor as

---

that of major and minor; the later the source, the greater the temptation to do so. For a reliable and well-researched study of *musica ficta*, see Karol Berger, *Musica Ficta: Theories of Accidental Inflections in Vocal Polyphony from Marchetto Da Padova to Gioseffo Zarlino* (Cambridge, 1987).

15. In the Roman Catholic rites the Magnificat (the canticle of the Virgin) is sung at the Office of Vespers by alternating choruses to one of eight recitation chants (similar to the psalm tones), in connection with an antiphon.

a representative of the mode. The contratenor bassus, thus, replaced the soprano as the second voice in order of conception. While the reference of voices to the bass became the norm of compositional technique, the simultaneities were *not* understood as directly given unities. Indeed, the principle of tonality, though often presented as "intrinsic" to music in the West, was a stage gradually reached from the coalescing of certain musical developments. Propelled by a variety of objectives, these developments disclose not only different musical conceptions but variation in musical perception as well.

Since the rules of interval progression unsettled the modes, some scholars, interestingly, felt compelled to conclude that *musica ficta* already shows in practice, though "not yet" in theory, the major-minor system.[16] Yet the many chromatic alterations become abundantly clear if the correlation of half-step connection with the progression from an imperfect to a perfect consonance is assumed. Nonetheless, the effect produced by the interval progression from imperfect to perfect (with its chromatic correlate) was gradually destroyed with the increased tendency to enrich the sonority, so as to avoid, as it were, the empty sonority of the perfect consonance. Still, the tendency to enrich the sonority, including the granting of independence to the imperfect consonance, did not basically alter the concept of interval progression as a type of musical perception. In fact, the constructive linkage of sonorities depended on interval progressions for a long time, and the complete triad was not conceived as a chord, despite its "fullness," because root progression was still not the governing principle for combining sonorities. Though Pietro Aaron[17] rejected the successive conception of the voices in 1523, it is the flow of the voices that he had in mind, and not a perceived chordal context. And when Zarlino[18] in 1558 declared that the third and the fifth must be present in what he named "per-

16. See, for example, Hugo Riemann, *Verloren gegangene Selbstverständlichkeiten in der Musik des 15. Bis 16. Jahrhunderts* (Langensalza, 1907). Riemann is by no means the only one to have engaged in such speculations, but he was the first to have structured a "theory" around it.

17. The treatises of Pietro Aaron (1480–1550), especially his *De institutione harmonica* (1516) and his *Toscanello* (1523), are probably the best general treatises of his generation for they clearly and comprehensively discuss the musical practice of the time, in particular that of counterpoint.

18. Zarlino (1517–1590), who was already mentioned, was both composer and theorist. His aim was to unite speculative theory with the practice of composition; he believed that the perfection of music depended on the close relationship between the two. His *L'institutioni harmoniche* (1558) is considered as one of the most important works of Western music theory.

fect composition," he still required a half-step connection when passing from an imperfect to a perfect consonance. Indeed, "the criterion for the chordal character of sonorities is," as Dahlhaus points out, "the principle of connecting the sonorities by root progressions. What contradicts the concept of chord is not the independence of the voices, but the method of linking sonorities through interval progressions. The categories 'chord' and 'root progression' are in a reciprocally dependent relationship. The tones of a chord form a unity in relation to a chordal root. And it only makes sense to speak of a root when the succession of roots establishes a recognized musical context."[19]

BESTOWING A SEMBLANCE OF "ONENESS" ON PARTICLES

It should be argued, however, that focusing on what seems missing does an injustice to what is clearly there—magnificent music, which not only pleased its contemporary audiences but elicits our admiration as well. Indeed, the "lack" of an overall embracing tonality appears like an assessment that proceeds from a later point of view. However, once we center our attention on its *integrative* force, it becomes readily apparent that such an all-embracing framework resulted from the ever growing quest to integrate the musical elements of extended compositions, so as to be able to give each composition a physiognomy of its own. The reverse is equally correct: the more it became possible to integrate the various musical elements, the more it became possible to extend the compositions, secured by the cementing devices that controlled its particles. Devices that manipulate particles, so as to interrelate them, are usually subsumed by a system or some kind of "theory," which furnishes the needed directives. In either case, it is the rationale behind the strategy that constitutes the *reference* for the phenomenon observed. A well-established reference is endowed with "power," yet "whatever has powers, as reference does, also has roots"[20] (as we have seen in connection with notation, for example).

19. See Dahlhaus, *Studies on the Origin of Harmonic Tonality*, 93. In order to fully comprehend the structural significance of interval progressions (from imperfect to perfect consonance, with a half-step connection in one of the voices independent of the underlying scale), it pays to examine chapter 2 in its entirety. The chapter is replete with musical examples, references to theoretical sources, and persuasive arguments. Last but not least, it magnificently portrays a "Dahlhausian" intellectual ability, which invariably evokes admiration.

20. This phrase was used by Nelson Goodman, introducing the first of the Paul Carus

Indeed, it is impossible to divorce the theory from the practice that gave rise to it, as it is impossible to divorce the practice from a theory concerning its efficacy.

Be that as it may, the *pre*history of the system that was able to control musical compositions in their entireties is replete with attempts that aimed to bestow a semblance of "oneness" on musical compositions, by merging their constitutive elements in one way or another into "wholes." Familiar terms such as 'repetition,' 'sequentiality,' 'imitation,' 'transformation,' 'development,' and 'formal structure' denote procedures often assigned to music qua music, vested as it were in its manner of articulation. However, given that music is man-made, it incorporates ipso facto the ways employed for its realization; they are, in fact, part and parcel of the very "making" of music. By limiting the contexts to which they apply, theoretical systems are able, as we have seen, to provide *cognitive* frames of reference. Musical "operations," by contrast, function on a more immediate level, that of *perception*. Via numerous strategies that basically oscillate between "variance" and "resemblance," musical operations of certain kinds are able to create readily recognizable patterns of design. It is noteworthy that already in the fourth century BC, long before cognitive studies ascended the stage, Aristoxenus—the great Aristotelian music theorist—presupposed that music is an activity of collecting and building up "impressions" in one's mind: "Since music is a successive production, its comprehension," he suggested, "depends on two faculties, sense-perception and memory." "Musical cognition," he added, "implies the simultaneous discernment of a permanent and of a changeable element." The "discrimination of particulars," Aristoxenus observed, is part of "sense-perception," while their "functions" are "contemplated by the intellect."[21]

One need not be as astute as Aristoxenus apparently was in order to realize that a "successive production" like music—which relinquishes to the "past" every "present" moment, by continuously introducing new ones—calls for some kind of linkage between musical moments, all of which are transitional in a way. In fact, the full meaning of a "successive production" only comes to the fore, paradoxically, once the "production" has come to its end. Musical "productions," as it turns out, employ both internal and external devices to achieve structural relationships. Although

---

Lectures delivered by Willard V. Quine, one of the most celebrated analytical philosophers. Quine's three Paul Carus Lectures provided the content for his book *The Roots of Reference* (Illinois, 1973).

21. See Aristoxenus, from the *Harmonic Elements,* in Strunk, *Source Readings in Music History,* 27–30.

FIGURE I. Pythagoras (center) holds an open scroll with the word "number" on it.
Aristoxenus (lower left) plays a bass viol, insisting, as it were, that the ear, not the
intellect, should determine the consonance of intervals. The engraving appears as
the frontispiece in Iamblichus, *In Nicomachi Geraseni arithmeticum introductionem,* ed.
Samuel Tennulius (Arnhem, 1668).

art, generally speaking, consists of elements arranged in an orderly fashion according to both obvious and subtle relationships, music cannot be
conceived without them. Premeditated designs concerning the "layout"
of musical contents, accordingly, differ considerably from the schemes
that govern the unfolding of the content itself. Although both constitute
formal structures, the "layout" is essentially independent of the content,
whereas 'form' and 'content' are indelibly intertwined in the unfolding of
the content. The external design and the one brought about from within
may also interact with each other in significant ways, provided that their
different functions are clearly understood.

External Designs

External designs may be applied to music even in the absence of schemes
that govern the overall structural unfolding of a composition. In fact, they
are often employed as a means whereby short compositions may be extended. They are in a position to lend a sense of structure to music that
stands on its own, though they germinated from the connection between
music and language. The musical forms that were used in conjunction with
French medieval poetry, for example, consisted of a couple of short musical
lines that were manipulated in various repeat forms so as to correspond to
the structure of the poem—stanzas, lines, rhyming versicles, refrains, and
so forth. Yet the forms of the virelay, rondeau, and ballade, the so-called
formes fixes, were eventually adapted as musical forms, independent of the
poetry that they initially accommodated. Whether of French, Spanish, or
Arab origin,[22] the virelay form is evident in many musical repertoires under different names, in different countries, and different periods.[23] The
same holds true for the other forms. However varied the poetic structure
might have been, and however varied the content of its various stanzas,
the texts could be accommodated by a couple of short musical lines that
differed from each other, creating, thereby, simple musical structures. The
three stanzas of a ballade, for example, have an identical structure, each
consisting of seven or eight lines, the last one or two of which are identical
in all the stanzas, thus forming a refrain. While the form of the stanzas is
either a b a b c d E *or* a b a b c d E F, the form of the music is either AAB or

22. The issue has been debated in musicology. Although it was formerly assumed
that the virelay was a form of trouvère music, it is now considered of Spanish origin and
ultimately of Arab origin, tracing back the Spanish *zejel* to the Arabic *zajal.*

23. These include, among others, the Spanish *cantigas* and *villancico* and the Italian
laude and *ballata.*

AABB (A = a b; B = the remaining lines).[24] Though the musical form seems quite simple, we should not fail to note the instantly perceived operations that it contains, that of *repetition* and *contrast*. Although repetition and contrast may be achieved in numerous ways, they all build on the fundamental role played by "variance" and "resemblance" in our mental processes. Since music is an abstract art—a language without a semantics—it took some time to evolve the kind of syntax that is able, at one and the same time, to structure coherence as well as support the various operations that help to convey what music endeavors to express.

While the ability to distinguish between "difference" and "likeness" plays an important role in our mental processes, "difference" and "likeness" inhere not in the objects observed but rather in the way we conceive them—in the aspects that define them. The following anecdote may serve to illustrate this point: I was once asked by a Samaritan singer, who forgot to turn off the radio (after having listened to the news), what it was that some people appreciate in "that stuff which sounds all alike." He was referring to Beethoven's Fifth Symphony resounding in the background. To make himself clear, he sang a three-note melody—essentially a pivot note with a heavily vibrated upper and lower auxiliary—expecting me to appreciate its "richness." We obviously perceived different things, in line with our preconceived notions about what needs discerning. In fact, what guided *his* listening became the subject of my search. People apparently perceive only what they are looking for, and what they are looking *at* is defined by what they expect to see. Though it presents a challenge to the conceived distinction between perception and cognition, it certainly holds true for art and for music in particular.

In chapter 1, we had the occasion to discuss the difference between the Eastern and European conception of the "identity" of melodies. As we have seen, the Eastern conception does not conceive of the melody as a series of fixed "immovable" notes, but rather as a characteristic musical gesture that can be performed in a number of ways. The different renderings of a melody, therefore, may be considered identical, as long as the character of the specific gestures is maintained. Since the gestures consist of typified motives and the manner in which they are employed, the different versions of a melody do not change its *substance,* but are left to the discretion of the well-versed performer. European music, as already remarked, came to be fundamentally different from the music of the rest of

---

24. The schematically designated AAB is of course also relevant to the German bar form with its two *Stollen* (section a) and an *Abgesang* (section b).

the world because of the growth of harmony and the development of staff
notation, which contains prescriptive signs securing musicians from taking "wrong steps." Differences of this kind have far-reaching implications
for what things might be perceived as resembling each other. Although
almost anything may stand for almost anything else, the representation of
an object or idea invariably refers to and, more particularly, denotes it.[25]
Reception and interpretation are not separable; they are interdependent,
provided they are able to evade built-in contradictions. The musical tradition that opted for a notation whose symbols denote what they refer to,
that is, which leave no room for ambiguity, had no choice but to adhere to
the dictates of the system by means of which it effected musical variance
and resemblance. The musical operations (whichever and whenever) that
evolved in the West rested "naturally" (in the double sense of the word) on
this "perceptual readiness."[26] Evidently, there is no such thing as an "innocent ear"; our audile perception, like our visual perception, is influenced
by culture.[27]

   In Western music a formal design such as AAB implies that the second
A is a literal repetition of the first A, the same holds true for ABA, and so
forth. Literal repetitions of this kind mostly apply to the external overall
structural outline of musical compositions, though even there the repetition need not be carried out in its entirety, in which case it might or might
not be indicated by different designations, like AA'B, for example. External outlines, especially when applied to compositions whose alternating
sections are relatively short, are readily recognizable. No wonder they
emerged early in the development of music, for they served as an effective
means for extending musical composition while bestowing on the whole a
perceptible structure. Structural forms of this kind are already evident in
the chant repertoire in which the "through-composed" chants like those
of the Gloria and Sanctus stand side by side with strophic chants like those
of the hymns, where every verse is sung to the same melody, and in re-
petitive forms like those of the Kyries, Agnus Dei, and the Sequences. In
secular music, the *formes fixes* exemplify well the structural coherence that
overall outlines are able to achieve. Overall outlines of this sort eventually
turned into blueprints that composers had in mind when they set out to

   25. On "denotation," see Nelson Goodman, *Languages of Art*, 3–10.
   26. See Jerome S. Bruner's "On Perceptual Readiness," in *Psychological Review* 64
(1957), 123–52.
   27. See Ernest Gombrich, "The Analysis of Vision in Art," in his *Art and Illusion* (New
York, 1977), 291–329. Also see Melville J. Herskovits, *The Influence of Culture on Visual
Perception* (Indianapolis, 1966).

write their compositions. In fact, almost every period in Western art music has used certain traditionally established formal schemes as compositional "molds" into which varied musical contents could be poured, in line with stylistic musical preferences.

The Development of Inner Cohesion

The inner cohesion of the content, in contrast to external outlines, developed more gradually, in line with the development of music in theory and practice. Given their kinship to melody types, recurring melodic motives already characterized many chant melodies. Yet with the addition of contrapuntal voices, the chant melody as a whole or a part thereof became the basis of polyphonic compositions. Thus, the earliest polyphonic composition— the *organum*—was based on the entire chant, whereas the *clausula* was only based on a fragment, on the melismatic section of the original chant that became rhythmicized. More important than the connection of the *clausula* with the older organum is its connection with the later motet. Most of the early motets are, in fact, *clausulae* with an added text in the upper part, or parts. However different from each other these compositions turned out to be, the preexisting familiar musical material provided the cementing element for each of them.

The fact that even familiar melodies become unrecognizable when they are unduly stretched out did not seem to bother those who wished to embellish the chant, aware as they were of its place and function. Yet the use of an existing melody as a cantus firmus, that is, as the basis of a polyphonic composition, drew special attention to the "power" vested in it. Indeed, once detached from their natural mooring, the *canti fermi* were bound to undergo changes in order to fulfill their unifying function. That they were considered a binding force is supported by the fact that composers continued to employ existing melodies, including secular ones and even abstract subjects, for their polyphonic compositions for a long time. The cantus firmus, which appeared most frequently in the tenor, was at first characterized by long notes of unequal value that contrasted with the more florid added parts. The tenor, as we have seen, represented not only the mode but provided a reference for the establishment of consonant relationships as well. By the thirteenth century, the tenor was determined by the rhythmic modes, thereby introducing a further change in the original chant. And via the extension of modal patterns, a newly reiterated scheme of time values for the presentation of a liturgical cantus firmus was introduced, the so-called isorhythmic structural scheme, a scheme frequently used in the motets of the fourteenth century. The isorhythmic principle of the tenor was also applied, consequently, to the upper parts, though more freely. Interestingly, a motet whose voice parts became strictly isorhythmic created, as it were, "melodic variations" on a fixed *rhythmic* theme.

Since the cantus firmus provided the initial line to which *contrapuntal* voices were added, the freely composed voices could bolster their anchorage by "echoing" some of its melodic features. It is fair to assume that imitations of various sorts grew from the desire to add cohesion to individual compositions via variances that did not stray too far from their bases. Paradoxically, it is the Western musical understanding of "identity" that made it easy to engage in various schemes of musical operations by granting them the kind of saliency that is difficult to achieve otherwise. If the repeat of a motive or a short phrase at another pitch level is perceived as a "shift," it is largely due to the fact that the pitches themselves leave no room for ambiguity. Sequential writing, in fact, entails repeats of single parts of short musical phrases at other pitches, usually at the second above or below. It should be noted, however, that the sequence manages to create both similarity and difference via a relatively simple operation, not to speak of the musical extensions that can be achieved thereby. Sequential writing need not, of course, restrict itself to a single voice; it can take place among voices.

Change, apparently, is only perceived in reference to something that is taken for granted. The various extensions and reductions of the time values in the early ordo, as we have seen, rested on the constancy of the overall time latitude of the ordo. The various isorhythmic schemes built on the constancy of time values. The sequential shift takes pitch sameness for granted. Melodic shapes, likewise, differ from one another only where the self-sameness of intervals, regardless of the particular pitches that bound them, is retained. Hence, for melodic shapes to resemble each other the exact pitches become irrelevant; it is the intervals and the order in which they appear that needs attention. It is learned understandings of this kind that guide our perception, though they appear perfectly natural once fully internalized. Moreover, such understandings build on one another in significant ways, making it possible to introduce additional understandings without having to start all over again.

Imitation, as it turns out, may be achieved in numerous ways, depending on the determinants one wishes to emphasize. Indeed, imitation invariably functions as an integrating force, provided that the factors that serve to create the associations are from among those that have been clearly defined. Reviewing the early development of musical notation, I had occasion to mention that the selection of pitches preceded notation, for they had already been formulated orally without awareness of the constituent elements. To ensure the identity between the symbol of the pitch and the pitch as produced, one had to spell out the array of pitches. The neumes, which only indicated directions, succumbed, as we have seen, to a diastematic intervalic notation indicating *how far* up or down. Interestingly, there previously had been attempts to reduce ambiguity with regard to intervals through the naming of pitches. Though more accurate in a sense, they did not take root, since they failed to convey the metaphors of "high" and "low" and the concomitant metaphor of "directionality," as well as the understanding of a melody as a semblance of "movement." Whatever their linguistic or philosophical standing, "directionality" and "movement" are both crucial to the understanding of music. Once the representation of pitch was secured, melodic curvatures could be readily imitated, not only in a single voice line but in different parts of a contrapuntal texture.

In contrast to the problems related to pitch, which took a relatively short time to solve, the problems presented by the time element took a long time to resolve, despite the "semblance of movement" that was introduced almost from the start. Controlling the time element, so as to convey the *passage* of time, that is, its felt quality, called for a kind of "quantification of qualities" that did not disclose itself in full array at once. In fact, it is the solutions that were suggested that *created* the qualities that they enabled. Thus, every mensural system had a different impact on the flow of time. Though all of them allowed various rhythmic patterns of repetitions, within their confines such patterns were subject to the particular system to which they belonged, which limited the range of possibilities in line with the system's overall conception of the progression of time. However, with the clarification of durational relationships—which needed to be clarified again and again with the introduction of smaller note values— it was only natural for the individual pitches, that is, for the *sound event,* to "carry" the time element as well. It is by no means a coincidence that with the introduction of polyphony only the sections that were intended for soloists were recast for several voices, while the rest remained choral monophony.[28] Choral polyphony, in fact, only commenced once all of the ambiguities were eliminated.[29] Moreover, while early notations, as we

28. See Manfred F. Bukofzer, "The Beginnings of Choral Polyphony," in his *Studies in Medieval and Renaissance Music* (New York, 1950), 176–89.

29. Although the earliest choir books are apparently of Italian origin, the chorus-minded composers were mostly of Franco-Flemish descent. According to Bukofzer, choral music developed from its beginnings about 1430 to the "liturgical and chorus-

have seen, were closely wedded to the musical styles that they "noted," the emancipation of the sound event from its particular context allowed *varied* styles to avail themselves of the same notational system *because* it left no room for ambiguity (see chapter 1, pp. 34–36).

With the elements of pitch, time, and intervals clearly defined, no wonder that imitation took on an increased structural significance. Though each of these elements was exploited for purposes of integration as soon as it was clearly defined, together they were able to yield numerous and varied combinations that were held together, as it were, by an acquired "perceptual readiness" on the part of composers and listeners alike. The growth of imitative counterpoint in the fifteenth century is, ipso facto, related to the fact that the deliberations that dealt with the primary musical parameters seemed finally resolved. In fact, the relatively reserved use of imitation by composers such as Dufay and Ockeghem gave way to a more deliberate use by composers such as Jacob Obrecht and Josquin des Prez, so that by the end of the century imitation became an essential element of musical style. Yet a further stage was reached with Nicolas Gombert, who introduced what is known as the "through-imitative style," which is commonly associated with the sixteenth-century motet in which the *entire* composition was based on the principle of imitation. From there on, imitation remained a basic element of contrapuntal writing, employing old devices and developing new procedures through which it could be achieved. Once the structural significance of imitation was reformulated and enhanced, as it was toward the end of the fifteenth century and during the sixteenth century, devices such as augmentation, diminution, melodic inversion, and fugal procedures of various sorts continued to be developed in the seventeenth century, reaching an apotheosis in the eighteenth century in the musical works of Johann Sebastian Bach.

Imitation of entire melodies was, of course, already displayed in the earliest of Western polyphony, in parallel *organum*. The contrapuntal device of canonic writing, whereby a melody or long passages are strictly imitated by other parts in their entirety, was also used early and continued to be used. Those familiar with the history of music will no doubt

---

conscious music of Ockeghem, Obrecht, and Josquin, the poly-choral extension of the choral idiom with Willaert and the Venetian School, and the synthesis in Palestrina and Lasso." The other trend, that of soloist singing, became manifest particularly in the secular literature of the chanson and madrigal. Since polyphonic choral music developed out of the Gregorian unison chorus, it first occurred within the precinct of the church. This, according to Bukofzer, also explains why the secular compositions were slow in taking up the "new fashion." See ibid., 185–89.

recollect several thirteenth-century motets, the Italian *caccia* and the French *chace* of the fourteenth century, and a number of fourteenth- and fifteenth-century motets and Mass compositions that open with a section in canonic imitation, not to speak of those fifteenth-century Masses that contain various canonic treatments of the *L'Homme armé* melody. Yet the stylistic development of the Flemish motet between ca. 1450 to 1550 is of special importance, for it provided fertile soil for all kinds of stylistic developments and innovations largely because of its ever increasing use of imitation of the kind that could culminate in the through-imitative style. Though pervading imitation is often referred to as "motet style," the motets of the latter part of the fifteenth century used imitation only sporadically. It is precisely the sporadic use, coupled with the full understanding of the technique that it involves, that lends a special kind of saliency to imitation when juxtaposed, in the same composition, with other distinct stylistic features. The composition becomes, in fact, characterized by the unique variety that renders the semblance of the whole. Josquin, for example, often introduced full points of imitation alternating with sections that create different musical textures, thereby displaying a high degree of awareness of the power vested in the integration of various musical skills in the same composition.

Points of imitation, it should be noted, are distinct not only because they may alternate with other stylistic sections—homophonic, free contrapuntal, and so forth; they are of special significance because they occur within the polyphonic texture itself, adding to it both variety and distinctness by introducing imitation only on a single subject, related to but a small division of the text. And though they are diagonally marked off, causing the conclusion of one point to overlap with the beginning of the next, such points of imitation contribute to the structural coherence of the composition. There is evidently a vast difference between imitation that employs whole melodies and the kind that enlists small fragments thereof or a single subject of a polyphonic texture that it manipulates. The use of whole melodies, one might say, seems more "static," since the imitation imparts a sense of repetition, while the latter seem more "dynamic," since the working out of the musical material imparts a sense of continuity. The former, no doubt, is more likely to create what is often referred to as "closed forms," whereas the latter is more likely to create what is commonly understood under the rubric of "open forms." Yet with respect to the external design of extended musical works, they need not necessarily exclude each other's features.

Although canons, even the earliest of them, display a contrapuntal sophistication, involving the coincidence among voices that a single melody may engender through properly spaced repetitions, the duplication of a melody at the lower fifth or fourth, as in parallel *organum,* seems like the "safest" step one could take in order to thicken the texture of a melody. However, in free *organum* the *vox principalis* (later called tenor) was embellished by the added voices in a way that introduced a change in its own course and in its musical function. Thus, by the thirteenth century the tenor already served as a substratum for other voices with an identity of their own. It is the preexisting melody, which functioned as a *foundation* for the added voices, that came to be called cantus firmus. The borrowed material was clearly differently used, in line with its reconceived function. Compared to the Masses that based each of their movements on a different liturgical cantus firmus (the so-called plainsong Masses), a single melody could also function as the foundation for all of the movements of a Mass, creating a unified cycle (the so-called cyclic Mass). The fact that the tenor could also appear in the topmost voice, albeit with some rhythmic alterations and melodic embellishment (creating the so-called paraphrase Mass), attests to the fact that the *cantus firmi*—the preexisting materials that provide the foundation of these compositions—are employed as "wholes" and are expected *as such* to fulfill an integrative function.[30] In fact, the notion that melodic "rows," however used, may constitute a cementing device for an entire composition has accompanied the development of Western art music into the twentieth century.[31]

30. It has often been claimed that Guillaume de Machaut's Mass is unified musically by recurrent motives. Bukofzer, however, pointed to the fact that the motives are figures and formulae that are not characteristic enough and are not placed conspicuously enough to serve "a really unifying function." The unity displayed by Machaut's Mass, claims Bukofzer, "is primarily that of the liturgy, not of musical material." The Mass cycle, on the other hand, creates a *musical* unity. "It takes a very bold and independent mind," says Bukofzer, "to conceive the idea that the invariable parts of the Mass should be composed not as separate liturgical items, but as a set of five musically coherent compositions. In the latter case the means of unification are provided by the composer, not the liturgy." He actually proceeds to demonstrate how, to use his words, "the absolute work of art begins to encroach on liturgical function." The beginnings of the Mass cycle, according to Bukofzer, coincides with the beginnings of the musical Renaissance. Moreover, the cycle of the Ordinary of the Mass, asserts Bukofzer, "was the focal point on which all the artistic aspirations and technical achievements of the composer converged. It held as dominating and prominent a place in the hierarchy of musical values as the symphony did in the eighteenth and nineteenth centuries." See Bukofzer's "Caput: A Liturgico-Musical Study," in *Studies in Medieval and Renaissance Music,* 217–18.

31. The twentieth century witnessed a revival of contrapuntal writing in which the thematic figures produce and control the totality of sonorous textures. Thus, for example,

Bukofzer's brilliant study of the "Caput" masses of Dufay, Ockeghem, and Obrecht beautifully reveals the "scaffolding" function of the cantus firmus and the ways in which the composers were free to set up their compositions in accordance with their own imagination. Though the cantus firmus established the framework of the musical structure of these compositions, it nevertheless took its shape from the compositions it underlay—distinctive rhythms and the type of counterpoint and "harmony" envisaged by the composer. In tracing the origin of the shared cantus firmus of the three Masses, Bukofzer was able to establish that the Masses were founded on a section from the antiphon *Venit ad Petrum* of the Sarum use, more specifically on its final word, which is adorned by a huge melisma (an expressive vocal passage sung to one syllable), itself characterized by internal·repeats. *Cantus firmi* were in fact often chosen on the basis of their "fitness" to serve the function that was allotted to them.[32] Quoting Bukofzer, Taruskin agrees that the cycle of the Ordinary of the Mass became "the focal point on which all the artistic aspirations and technical achievements of the composer converged." He draws our attention, accordingly, to the *intricate ways* in which this new *musical unit* gradually came into being, taking note, of course, of the fact that its individual parts have different histories, different structures, and served different functions. The musically integrated Mass Ordinary, we learn from Taruskin, was not only "the most potent demonstration yet of the abstract shaping powers of music," but it conveyed, as such, "their potential import in mediating

---

the twelve-tone system consists of a series of intervals involving all twelve tones of the chromatic scale in any order chosen by the composer in advance. In order to retain the "tone row" chosen, no tone may be repeated until the other eleven have appeared. The order of the series, in other words, remains unchanged throughout the composition, except for some permissible modifications (such as transpositions, retrogrades, octave position, and inversions). Needless to say, such procedures discard traditional rules and conventions. We shall have occasion to discuss the implications of serial music in chapter 5.

32. See Bukofzer, "Caput." Bukofzer's outstanding liturgico-musical study should, however, be carefully read not only for the information it contains (some of which has been challenged in recent years), but for the picture delineated by its totality. He manages to combine, at one and the same time, an exciting "detective story" (the search after the origin of the "Caput" cantus firmus) with an interesting narrative concerning the rise of a historically important musical genre. Moreover, historical erudition informs the analysis of the works he set out to compare, and the analysis, in turn, portrays the continuity and change in stylistic features over a time span. The period covered bridges from Dunstable, through the Burgundian and the Franco-Flemish, to the Flemish composers. To top it all, he succeeds in delineating, thereby, the emergence of Renaissance style. It is this kind of exemplary study that elicits both awe and envy, even if some of its "facts" have undergone corrections due to further investigations and historical scrutiny.

between the human and the divine." The Ordinary of the Mass, argues Taruskin, in fact "acquired prestige as a symbol of ecclesiastical power."[33] Taruskin persuasively demonstrates how composers subsequently tried to emulate one another's achievements, while also attempting to lend their compositions individual characteristics. With great expertise, insight, and new findings, Taruskin takes us, step by step, through the musical developments that led to the cyclic Mass and its historical cultural significance. Scholars, to be sure, have invariably paid tribute to the contribution of the English to the development of the cyclic Mass, but no one has analyzed its crystallization and diffusion as persuasively as Taruskin, who has also been able to contribute astute observations based on his experience as a practicing musician.[34] Indeed, the *study* of music, not unlike music itself, is a cumulative process of "continuity and change," of additions and alterations that provide "new looks."

What became evident in thirteenth- and fourteenth-century motets and fifteenth- and sixteenth-century Masses was indeed upheld in later compositions such as the organ Magnificats, the chorale preludes, the chorale choruses of cantatas and Passions, and has even been reaffirmed in some atonal twentieth-century compositions. Whether plainsong melodies or secular melodies, Protestant chorales or abstract subjects, they are all meant to serve an integrative function. There is, nonetheless, a striking difference between the earlier use of preexisting materials and some of the later uses of the same. In the earlier periods the preexisting materials, including the familiar secular melodies, underwent a kind of "dismemberment" into particles, often to the point of losing their readily recognizable physiognomies. They provided the composition with a "footing," as it were, at the expense of their own "visibility." Since the later examples became increasingly less dependent on the structural anchorage that the preexisting materials formerly supplied, the materials themselves were allowed to surface as recognizable entities. It also became increasingly possible to wed the two treatments in the same composition, secured by new understandings that evolved in the meantime. In the twentieth century, however, the original function of preexisting materials was reinstituted with far-reaching structural implications. What did these new understandings consist of in the interim?

---

33. See Richard Taruskin, *The Oxford History of Western Music* (Oxford, 2005), vol. 1, 460.

34. To fully appreciate Taruskin's important contribution concerning the cyclic Mass, see the whole of chapter 12, ibid., 453–500.

THE RISE OF HARMONIC TONALITY

The fact that *cantus firmi* constituted the reference voice for compositional technique does not imply that interval progressions were necessarily related to the tenor. As we have seen, the characterization of a tenor as the basis of the whole relationship among voices only meant that the tenor represented the *mode* of the entire composition, if the individual voices differed in mode. In fact, the two functions of the tenor, that is, as cantus firmus and as reference voice, were divided between different voices. By the sixteenth century, the differentiation of functions was consolidated into the distinction between the bass as a contrapuntal reference voice and the tenor as a representative of the mode. Nonetheless, the sequence in which the voices should be composed continued to engage theorists for some time. In other words, the *simultaneous* conception of the voices did not imply a reference to a "bass," nor did the reference to a bass imply chordal composition; and chordal composition, of course, did not imply tonal harmony.

'Tonality' has often been broadly defined as "loyalty to a tonic." It is quite remarkable that throughout the evolution of music, including the music of non-Western cultures, practically every single musical formulation gave preference to one tone, which became a center, or reference, to which all other tones are related. Our discussion of Gregorian chant, for example, made clear the need for a point of reference. However, once the church modes were construed as constituent scales, tonality emerged in different varieties, limiting the definition of the term. Indeed, although almost all of music is tonal in the sense of giving preference to one tone, the means of achieving tonality have varied throughout history, giving rise to a variety of tonal systems.[35] Moreover, whereas the relationships among tones in monophonic music are purely melodic, harmonized music creates, as we have seen, a more complex situation.

---

35. The pentatonic scale, for example, which has only a five-tone octave, occurs in the music of nearly all ancient cultures, including that of American Indians, Celts, and Scots. A considerable number of Gregorian melodies are also purely pentatonic. However, there are different kinds of five-tone scales—with or without semitones—and by using different tones of the scale as a tonic five different "modes" can be derived from each of them. More recently, it has been argued that the Western selection of a seven-tone scale, based on twelve distinguished notes, maintains a kind of equilibrium between proliferation and scarcity, which is an optimal choice of a well-defined maximum. See G. J. Balzano, "The Group Theoretic Description of 12-fold and Microtonal Pitch Systems," in *Computer Music Journal*, no. 4 (1980): 66–84.

Though harmony came to be appreciated considerably later than counterpoint, certain intervals were considered as sounding better simultaneously than others, even in the earliest days of counterpoint. The progress of counterpoint necessarily entailed an increased consideration of harmony, since the horizontal and vertical elements of a musical texture invariably represent a generating and controlling force, respectively. As a *primary* building material of music, however, harmony was not entertained by composers until relatively late, though they revealed preferences with regard to certain sonorities. Considering the development of art music in the West, the vertical element could, in fact, only crystallize in tandem with the development of counterpoint, whose beginnings were closely associated with an entrenched monophonic chant tradition. Yet even when musicians began to think of harmonies as a primary building material, it took more than a century for harmonies to be formally recognized as structural and compositional elements.

The Move from Desired Coincidences among Voices to a "System of Chords"

Dahlhaus, in his outstanding studies on the origin of harmonic tonality, takes us step by step through a historical development that makes clear that harmonic tonality was not conceived as a displacement of a horizontal musical conception by a vertical one. The evolution, rather, is characterized by gradual transformations that built on one another in significant ways. Nothing was ever completely discarded in the process, while everything underwent change, adapting itself to novel nuances that reflected aesthetic preferences. Polyphonic music thus moved from the desired coincidences among voices created by interval progression to the spacing of voices that differentiates among essential and "filling in" voices, to the intrarelationship among voices that serve different functions for each other, to preferred sonorities still linked by interval progressions. Although the latter eventually included complete triads, they were not conceived as 'chords'; their purpose was merely "coloristic," since root progression was still not the governing principle for combining sonorities. In the psychology of perception, Dahlhaus reminds us, there is no primary category known as "sonorous unity"; perceived unity is an "object of conceptualization." Accordingly, individual tones and intervals of a chord do not "fuse" but rather relate to the preceding and succeeding chords *as a whole*. The independence of voices, in other words, is not what contradicts the concept of 'chord,' but the method whereby sonorities are linked. The tones of a chord form a unity in relation to a chordal root, and it only makes sense to speak of a root "when the succession of roots establishes a recognized musical context."[36]

Indeed, while the reference of voices to the bass becomes the norm of compositional technique in the sixteenth century, the simultaneities were not understood as given unities. And though many of the *frottolas,* for example, clearly display a discant-bass framework, this merely points to the fact, says Dahlhaus, "that the interval combinations have stabilized as formulas conceived or grasped directly in four voices." "The origin in successively composed voices," admits Dahlhaus, "is canceled out by the result—the sequential schema." Yet, he continues, "the fact that one counts only the intervals between the outer voices suggests that the 8–6–3 chords could have been replaced by 8–5–3 chords—thus that these simultaneities are not chords and representatives of chordal scale degrees, but mere fillings in of the octave with consonances." In other words, the distinction between chordal root and bass is still meaningless.[37] Even the characteristic schemata of tonal harmony—complete cadences, circle-of-fifths progressions, and the major-minor parallelism—typified in the compositional formulas of the sixteenth and early seventeenth centuries do not justify a tonal interpretation, according to Dahlhaus. The outward correspondence, in other words, can be misleading. Although earlier practices have been interpreted, at times, with the aid of later theoretical conceptions, Dahlhaus tries to avoid such pitfalls. He takes us step by step so as to disclose the process whereby the system of chords arose from a "coalescing of formulas," which have crystallized over time. Interestingly, the principle of tonality, which in a theoretical presentation appears as "the first step," is historically, nevertheless, the "last to be reached."[38] Obviously, the "last step" applies only to a specific historical process, that is, to the cumulative attempts to lend music a semblance of a *logically organized body,* as it were, with connected interdependent parts. Individual musical utterances were expected to gain in coherence thereby and, consequently, be more readily understood by those familiar with the syntax of the musical language.

The thoroughbass—the "stenographic" system developed toward the turn of the sixteenth century and used everywhere during the baroque period—generally pertains to a method for indicating an accompanying

---

36. See Dahlhaus, *Origin of Harmonic Tonality,* 92–93.

37. Ibid., 98–99.

38. Ibid., 102. See the entire section: "Compositional Types and Formulas in the 15th and 16th Centuries," 94–111.

part by the bass notes with figures designating the chief intervals and chords to be played above the bass notes. Yet from F. Thomas Arnold's comprehensive study of thoroughbass practice we learn that in the initial stages of its development one of its major functions was to enable organists, or other instrumentalists, to fill the vocal gaps left by absent singers whose parts were nevertheless necessary for the performance of a polyphonic composition.[39] On the other hand, Lodovico da Viadana wanted his famous *Cento Concerti* (1602) to accommodate singers "wishing to sing to the organ, either with three voices or two, or a single one by itself."[40] Indeed, rather than finding ways to fill in the missing parts of a given polyphonic composition, he composed concerti for single voices, and others in a variety of combinations, always trying, so he claimed, "to give satisfaction thereby to singers of every description, combining the parts in every variety of ways, so that whoever wants a soprano with a tenor, a tenor with an alto, an alto with a cantus, a cantus with a bass, a bass with an alto, two sopranos, two altos, two tenors, two basses, will find them all, perfectly adapted to his requirements." "I have, to the best of my ability," he added, "endeavored to achieve an agreeable and graceful tunefulness in all the parts by giving them a good and well-sustained melodic progress."[41]

Like all else, the figured bass had an antecedent that guided its function. The practice of improvising an accompaniment over a given bass was known for some time before the figured basses were used. The accompaniment over a given bass consisted of chords *and* counterpoint suitable to the vocal melody in question. Thus the figured basses of Jacopo Peri, Giulio Caccini, and Emilio de' Cavalieri, which represent the earliest extant use of figures as a method of indicating harmony, provided an unbroken accompaniment to the voice part. More than functioning as a 'figured bass,' they functioned as a 'basso continuo.' Yet it was Viadana's *Concerti,* which enjoyed wide circulation, that brought the basso continuo into general notice, though he did not use figures. Arnold draws our attention to the fact that were the vocal bass (of a composition for several voices) to be

---

39. F. T. Arnold, *The Art of Accompaniment from a Thorough-Bass as Practiced in the 17th and 18th Centuries,* Dover ed., 1965 (first published by Oxford in 1931). References will be made to the Dover edition.

40. The invention of the 'figured bass' was for a long time attributed to Lodovico da Viadana. Viadana's basses, however, do not exhibit figures, save for occasional signs generally denoting a sharpened or flattened third, while Jacopo Peri, Giulio Caccini, and Emilio de' Cavalieri, somewhat earlier, did use figured basses.

41. See Viadana's preface to his *Concerti* in Arnold, *Art of Accompaniment,* 4.

figured so as to provide the basis of an accompaniment, it could not function as a basso continuo, for it would stop whenever the vocal bass was not in operation. But if the organ, for example, were to be supplied during the pauses of the vocal bass, with "whichever voice part in the composition that happened at the moment to be the lowest, and therefore the real basis of the harmony, the result would be a continuous part, pervading and supplying a foundation to the entire structure."[42]

Playing from an un-figured bass, Arnold tells us, organists were chiefly dependent on their ear as a guide to the correct harmony, and many went to the trouble to prepare their own full scores. Relying on the ear, we are told, did not always lead to satisfactory results; contemporary references are marshaled to prove this to have been the case. Opponents of the "new invention," accordingly, advised their pupils to study as many Masses, motets, *ricercari,* canzone, and madrigals as possible, in order to attain the highest perfection in playing the organ, since each type "has its special advantage for musical education." The advocates, on the other hand, maintained that one must practice diligently so as to "listen very attentively."[43] The basso continuo, in other words, was treated as a mixed blessing, not on account of any inherent demerits, but because it absolved some of its practitioners from the necessity of cultivating other important musical skills, such as the art of improvisation and a solid knowledge of counterpoint. Moreover, passion for the "new invention" often resulted in adding a basso continuo to works that hardly stood to benefit from such additions, such as some of the works of Giovanni Pierluigi da Palestrina, for example.

From the picture delineated by Arnold, it becomes clear that the thoroughbass did not provide a foundation for compositional technique; rather, it functioned primarily as a tool of performance practice. The figures, it turns out, supplied a fragmentary notation of counterpoint at times, and at other times a rudimentary notation of chords that assured desired sonorities. The accompaniment, to be sure, gradually acquired the character of an harmonic background to the polyphony of the principal parts "without any attempt at arranging the intervals of the chords in the same order as that in which they appeared in the latter," as Arnold puts it. The accompaniment, moreover, became increasingly freer, partaking in the shaping of the overall musical texture.[44] The reciprocal relationship

42. Ibid., 6.
43. Ibid., 80–81.
44. See Arnold's summary of the beginnings of the basso continuo and figured bass, ibid., 236–39. Also see Dahlhaus, *Origin of Harmonic Tonality,* 135–41.

between the whole and its parts, however, was still foreign to the basses of the early seventeenth century, for "an individual scale degree of the bass formula," as Dahlhaus insisted, "is inserted into the whole by custom, not by the mind's proclivity for seeking relationships." A bass formula, he concluded, represented nothing but itself, for "it is not legitimized by a system and has a direct effect only as a concrete Gestalt."[45]

Indeed, in the harmonic language of the late sixteenth and early seventeenth centuries, chords seem to progress in an immediate relationship to each other, not according to an extended overall plan. In contrast to later periods, they do not give rise to the impression of a goal-directed development that is so characteristic of tonal harmony. The dynamic impression imparted by tonal harmony is, in fact, due to the *reciprocal* relationship between the part and the whole, and to the resultant distinction between what is given and what it implies. The harmonic language that preceded that of tonal harmony was clearly governed by a different principle. In contrast to the principle of "subordination" that governs tonal harmony, Dahlhaus set forth the principle of "coordinate structure" as the regulating force of the earlier harmonic language.[46] The coordination between particles, of course, does not require, ipso facto, that they be defined by the tendency of the whole.

Harmonic tonality does precisely that—the whole defines the tendency of the particles and the coordination among them. Chords, to begin with, are regarded as a *primary* element in harmonic tonality, regardless of the difference between homophonic and polyphonic styles. The simultaneous sounding of three or four notes, in other words, constitutes indivisible units, rather than end products of combinations of three- or four-part counterpoint. Whether a chord presents an entity or a combination of intervals depends on the function it fulfills in the musical context. The recognition of harmonies as building elements depends on 'tonality,' the musical framework that superseded polyphonic modality. In the modal use of intervals, the cadence point represented one of the means of defining a modal center, yet the intervallic progressions that occurred elsewhere in the context mostly remained modally neutral. Tonality, by contrast, made the overall conception of a piece possible from a harmonic point of view. Unlike modality, which refers to the use of the church modes, tonality re-

45. Dahlhaus, ibid., 141.

46. For a comparison between "coordinate" and "subordinate" structure, see ibid., 141–61.

fers to the use of "keys" (major or minor).[47] The key of a composition refers to the main note to which all its other notes are related, including the
meaning of the entire tonal material.

A key differs from a scale in that it allows the use of notes extraneous
to the scale, such as chromatic variants, without forgoing the tonality. The
idea that a chord presents a primary unit, rather than a combination of
intervals, was of course bound to affect the conception of the nature and
function of dissonances. Notes foreign to the chord or to the harmony do
not create fundamentally dissonant chords in harmonic tonality, for they
appear as *adjuncts* to chords and their resolution is not dependent on a
change of harmony. Since the seventeenth century, keys have been constituted by constructional means as well as note relationships. It is not sufficient, therefore, to define a key by a major or minor scale, for a key also
refers to the harmony. Harmony, in turn, refers to the structural principles
underlying intervals and their combinations, or chords and their relationships. While the two-note consonance constituted the foundation of the
old tonal system, the three-note consonance constituted the foundation
of the new. Given the fact that in tonal harmony chords present *primary*
units, the new tonal system came to be based on 'triads,' with each note of
the scale serving as the "root" of a chord of three notes, consisting of the
root and a third and fifth above it.

The triads based on the first, fourth, and fifth degrees of the scale were
steadily gaining in prominence during the seventeenth century. They were
more frequently used than those based on the second, third, and sixth degrees (the "modal" degrees), while the one based on the seventh degree
was only rarely used. This development led to the eventual acceptance of
three principal chords—the tonic, dominant, and subdominant—as *the*
characteristic chords of the harmonic system, the carriers of the harmonic
as well as the melodic movement. A key, at any rate, can be unmistakably
defined only by correlating a given scale with a "fundamental bass," that
is, with the roots of the triads. The roots of chords are of course no longer their bass notes when the chords are inverted, yet in tonal harmony it
is the roots of chords, linked together, that form the *fundamental* bass, unlike the basso continuo, which is the sequence of actual bass notes.

---

47. Discussing the church modes, I noted that Glareanus (1547) enlarged the number
of modes from eight to twelve, so as to include the two scales on -a- and the two scales on
-c'-. The Aeolian mode (the diatonic scale on a) is essentially our minor mode, while the
Ionian mode (the diatonic scale on c) is essentially our major mode.

The Systematization of Harmonic Tonality

Harmonic tonality operates under the proposition that chordal inversions are but different manifestations of an identical harmony, that is, the bass note of the root position is invariably conceived as the *reference* for the other notes, regardless of their changed position. Although the concept of inversion had been anticipated long before Jean-Philippe Rameau, he was the one who incorporated it into a comprehensive theory of musical coherence.[48] By revealing the *interdependence* of the chord (as a primary and indivisible unit), the root note, the proposition of the fundamental bass, and the hierarchy between the fundamental degrees, he created an integrated theory that persuasively accounted for the musical practice of his time. As a theorist, Rameau (1683–1764) addressed the music of his time, and as composer he wished to put his theory to the service of practicing musicians.[49] Yet in his famous *Traité de l'harmonie* (1722) and other theoretical essays, he attempted to reduce music to a science based on universal harmonic principles derived from natural causes.[50] Rameau thus maintained that *all* music is founded on harmony, which arises from natural principles derived from the mathematical and physical basis of a vibrating

48. For the precursors of Rameau, see Dahlhaus, *Origin of Harmonic Tonality*, 114–21.

49. In his impressive study of Rameau, Thomas Christensen reminds us that it is important "not to confuse music theory as we understand it today with *musica theorica* of the seventeenth century. The latter discipline was much more narrowly defined and, at least until Rameau's day, concerned itself with speculative matters. The disciplines of counterpoint, harmony, and thoroughbass that we today consider a part of music theory were in most cases considered as components of *musica practica*." Rameau's most significant accomplishment, Christensen tells us, "lay in the *rapprochement* he was able to effect between these two traditions" and in his ability "to integrate practice and theory into a coherent whole." See Thomas Christensen, *Rameau and Musical Thought in the Enlightenment* (Cambridge, 2004), 29–31.

50. The idea that music is based on "universal harmonic principles derived from natural causes" was hardly new; it had accompanied the development of music until the middle of the sixteenth century. Music, which until then was viewed as reflecting the order of God's harmonic creation, was from then on guided by a new legendary vision, that of the ethical power of music, that is, music as a medium capable of imitating passions. I shall say more about it later. Yet those familiar with the history of the art will have surely recognized, at this point, the cause for Jean-Jacques Rousseau's attack on Rameau's fundamental claim. Though music and language had a common origin, argued Rousseau, language eventually provided the tool for rational thought, while music constituted the medium for the expression of the "passions of the soul." The commensurability of music and the emotions is a subject that continued to preoccupy both aestheticians and scientists even after the conceptions of the role and function of the art had drastically changed.

body. Using the acoustical studies of Marin Mersenne,[51] and aware of the growing body of acoustical knowledge, Rameau argued that the essential unity of harmony is already represented in the fundamental sound. The latter generates the parts from which the primary consonances in music are derived in an order of relative perfection: octave, fifth, and major third. Their combination, therefore, forms the "perfect" chord, the major triad. It is from the *physical* nature of the fundamental sound that Rameau developed the basic concepts of his harmonic theory—harmonic generation, harmonic inversion, and the fundamental bass—believing that he had provided music with a sound scientific basis.

Despite Rameau's scientific claims, it was clearly musical practice that ultimately determined his rules and laws of harmony.[52] The principle that the lowest sound is the source or generator of the perfect chord (the major triad) was also expected to yield, in addition to the major third and perfect fifth, all of the harmonies that were in use at the time—the minor mode, the subdominant, and the various dissonant chords. Since these could not be directly extracted from the fundamental bass, Rameau postulated that the principle that determines the structure of chords also determines their succession, that is, that the intervals of the fifth and the third also serve as the most perfect intervals for the progression of the fundamental bass. Although acoustics provided Rameau with some guiding principles, he clearly based much of the rest on the inherent logic of tonal harmony. In his chordal syntax, accordingly, each chord within a key has a unique function. The tonic, dominant, and subdominant are the essential chords of a key and do not have overlapping functions as long as the key is maintained. The functions of the remaining chords are derived from these essential chords. The tonic chord (major or minor) is the most important chord in defining a key, for it is the only chord without a dissonance. All the other chords in a key must have a dissonance, implied or expressed; dissonance is normally created by the addition of a seventh to a perfect chord. Since each of the essential chords can give the impression of being the key, it is the dissonance attached to the harmony of a fundamental chord that is not the tonic that clarifies which key is intended. However, given (in addi-

---

51. Mersenne (1588–1648) was the first to formulate rules governing vibrating strings, based on an understanding of the variable factors on which pitch depends—length, diameter, tension, and the mass of the vibrating body. He was also the first to discern the nature of partials related to a fundamental note.

52. For the following summary of Rameau's theory, I am indebted to Cynthia Verba's profound analysis of Rameau's theoretical writings and development. See chapter 4 in her *Music and the French Enlightenment* (Oxford, 1993).

tion) that the tonic is the only chord that can follow the dominant seventh chord, the progression down a fifth from dominant to tonic constitutes a "perfect cadence."

For the establishment of the tonic, Rameau also included an "irregular cadence," the one created by the progression *up* a fifth, from the subdominant to the tonic. This cadence, unlike the others, rests on the addition of a major sixth to the perfect chord on the subdominant, which is the only chord that may carry this dissonance and progress in this way. The remaining dissonant seventh chords are patterned after the perfect cadence — each considered the dominant of the chord a fifth below. Regular seventh chords, or simple dominants, cannot proceed directly to a perfect chord or tonic; they must proceed to other simple dominants until they reach a dominant seventh, which then proceeds to the tonic. The perfect and irregular cadences, then, together with the progression of the seventh chords by a fifth, constitute the basic premises of Rameau's chordal syntax. Rameau actually succeeded in reducing the many chords and chord progressions that characterized the music of his time to three essential chords, governed by a few underlying principles. More than delineate music as a physical phenomenon, Rameau unveiled and systematized the "logic" inherent in harmonic tonality. The musical practice that he described had indeed reached a high level of interconnectedness — coherence arrived at through the "submission" of musical particles to the tendency of the musical whole. Regardless of Rameau's own assessment of the scientific significance of his work, harmony, as an expressive artistic means, is as man-made a phenomenon, as is the rest of music.[53]

The fact that the I-IV-V-I cadence relies, in addition to the wholeness of the scale, on the effect of the fifth progressions in the fundamental bass and on the effect of the characteristic dissonances that are enlisted so as to establish continuity led Hugo Riemann[54] to claim that the three chords of the fundamental cadence *gave rise* to the keys. The scale, he suggested, is actually deduced from these chords (C-E-G, F-A-C, G-B-D=C-D-E-F-

---

53. Rameau's rationalist position concerning music as a science did, in fact, evoke a heated debate among leading figures of the French Enlightenment. Rousseau went all out to defend music as an "expressive art." Jean D'Alembert, a scientist himself, was more open to the notion of music as science, but he did not accept the ways in which Rameau conceived of the subject. In reaction to the arguments advanced by Rousseau and d'Alembert, Denis Diderot advocated a synthesis between art and science. For a thorough discussion of this debate, see Verba, ibid., chapters 3–5.

54. In addition to his famous *Musik-Lexikon,* Riemann (1849–1919) is considered a foremost theorist and outstanding music researcher of his time.

G-A-B-C). Since the chords and their relationships are taken as given, the scale may undergo alterations without the key becoming unrecognizable. His theory of harmony, thus, replaced the theory of fundamental notes with a theory of functions, in which function refers to the dependent relationship of a particular harmony to one or several other harmonies. The tonic triad, accordingly, is dependent on its dominant and subdominant. Every chordal structure, Riemann suggested, can be traced back to these functional triads, and each triad can be represented by one of its constituent pitches or intervals. The fact that the chords, in a major or minor key, are defined by their relationships to the tonic does not exclude the set of chords from being limited to the system of diatonic scale degrees. But whereas the theory of fundamental progressions emphasizes the limitation by the diatonic system, the theory of functions stresses the relation to a center. It is the functional system of tonality that makes every kind of modulation and other alterations of the harmonic function of a chord possible, according to Riemann. Since harmony comprises not only the structure of chords but also their movement, the term tonality came to designate (historically) the *intrinsic* governing principle of key, as distinct from its outward aspect, which is associated with the idea of a given diatonic scale. Moreover, if the intrinsic principle transcends the boundaries of the key, tonality can even be taken to mean a complex of several related keys, covering a broad key area.[55]

To be sure, the baroque era was tonal, but it evolved a different conception of the flow of music. The basso continuo, as we have seen, could not always be reduced to a fundamental bass, for the melodic bass itself often appeared as a primary factor and the harmonic elaboration as secondary. Many of the harmonic procedures were determined by genuine melodic movement in the bass, rather than by an imaginary fundamental progression. Yet after the decline of the figured bass with its series of notated chords, it was the tonal *functions* that established harmonic continuity, serving in the background of the music as an abstract regulative force. In its attempt to articulate the unfolding of musical structure in all of its components, the new conception of the flow of music attacked both the horizontal independence of the voices and the vertical independence of the harmony. It is amazing how fundamentally different this conception of music is from that which considered harmony as a by-product of simultaneously melodic lines.

---

55. See Hugo Riemann, *Vereinfachte Harmonielehre oder die Lehre von den tonalen Funktionen der Akkorde* (London, 1893).

Shifting Concerns — From Musical "Rules" to Music's Communicative "Powers"

It will be recalled that Zarlino, the foremost theorist of the sixteenth century, was still of the opinion that harmony arose out of melodies sounding simultaneously, though he addressed technical musical aspects more than any theorist before him. Since Zarlino dealt principally with the practice developed by composers in the Netherlands during the first half of the sixteenth century, his "rules" could no longer fully apply to the style that prevailed thereafter. The earlier composers, in fact, revealed a freer treatment of the melody than did Palestrina and his contemporaries, whose restraint with regard to voice leading became their major stylistic hallmark. If Palestrina nonetheless became the greatest representative of the sixteenth century, it is because he represented a musical ideal that aimed at order, that is, one conforming to rules easily comprehensible and evading all that seems "superfluous." It must be remembered that the sixteenth century, unlike many later periods, had little understanding of ideas such as "originality" or "uniqueness." Composers were expected to go about their art in a way that could be readily understood and enjoyed by those they served. In fact, according to the recommendations of the Council of Trent (1545–1563),[56] sacred music, in particular, was to be so ordered that it "may reach tranquility into the ears and hearts of those who hear them, when everything is executed clearly and at the right speed." The whole, moreover, was to be constituted "not to give empty pleasure to the ear, but in such a way that the words may be clearly understood by all, and thus the hearts of the listeners be drawn to the desire of heavenly harmonies, in the contemplation of the joys of the blessed."[57] Although neither Palestrina nor the other great masters of his epoch wrote theoretical works, it is not at all surprising that the restraint so characteristic of Palestrina's music—his refraining from experimental artistic expansion, coupled with a sureness and propriety as far as the texts are concerned—should have become ideal models for pedagogical purposes. Future generations, as it turned out, viewed Palestrina as a composer seeking a primary "natural"

56. A council of cardinals of the Roman Church (held at Trent) that dealt, among many other things, with issues pertaining to the dignity of the service, including important decisions regarding church music.

57. From an extended quotation, see Gustav Reese, *Music in the Renaissance* (New York, 1954), 449.

expression—a kind of universality that rejoices in the fulfillment of "laws" in which the "old represents the eternally new."[58]

The musical situation at the end of the sixteenth century, however, clearly tended toward a more expressive style, which resulted in the new musical forms of the seventeenth century—the opera, the cantata, the concerto, and so forth. Yet the attempt to make music serve the ends of poetic expression was already manifest in the sixteenth century, not least through its rejection of the "superfluous" that "gives empty pleasure to the ear." The insistence on the "drawing of hearts" to words that are "understood by all" initiated, as we shall yet see, a new understanding with regard to the communicative "powers" vested in music, an understanding that went hand in hand with a process that created, rather than unveiled, them. At any rate, by the time full-fledged harmonic tonality came into being, that is, once the new conception of the flow of music attacked both the horizontal independence of the voices and the vertical independence of the harmony, Palestrina's counterpoint could no longer serve as a sole model for composers who wished to master those techniques that would be particularly useful to them in practice. Even the special pedagogical exercises that Johann Fux devised (based on Palestrina's style) in his *Gradus ad Parnassum* (1725)—involving special difficulties, proceeding from simple to complex, from easier to more difficult, the so-called five species—could not withstand the competition presented by Bach's technical accomplishment (harmonically and contrapuntally) in the first half of the eighteenth century. If Johann Philipp Kirnberger, a student of Bach, finds the rules presented by Fux too strict, complaining that his textbook takes up the fugue too quickly, it is because Kirnberger is utterly committed to the style that he himself had thoroughly imbibed. To this one must, of course, add Kirnberger's admiration for the one who had "completely at his command—as is attested by his works—rhythm, melody, harmony, in short, all that makes a composition really beautiful."[59] Nonetheless, by the end

58. Knud Jeppersen, *Counterpoint, the Polyphonic Vocal Style of the Sixteenth Century* (New York, 1939), 23. For a full delineation of the style of Palestrina and the place it occupied in pedagogical developments, see 13–53. In more recent years an interesting theoretical reformulation of the rules of Palestrina counterpoint allowed a comparison of various forms of vocal expression (speech and music), proposing an explanation of the sources of tension in vocal expression and, in particular, the deeper sources from which Palestrina's rules of counterpoint emerged. See Dalia Cohen, "Palestrina Counterpoint: A Musical Expression of Unexcited Speech," in *Journal of Music Theory* 15 (1971): 84–110.

59. Quoted by Jeppersen, *Counterpoint,* 43. Since Bach never wrote anything theoreti-

of the eighteenth century and the beginning of the nineteenth century, the *Gradus ad Parnassum* was still being used by composers to instruct the young—their potential successors. Yet the study of composition had to reckon, as well, with the theory of harmony, certainly after Rameau's *Traité de l'harmonie.*

Although the theory of harmony was bound to receive a more fundamental and more refined working out by later generations, there is no denying that harmonic tonality effected a major change in the conception, perception, and construction of music. This was in no small measure achieved by isolating the musical phrase, thereby imposing a higher level of periodicity on the inner progression of individual elements. The musical phrase and combinations thereof contributed to the continuity of the composition as a whole in a way that could be readily perceived by the listener. Rather than emphasize a definite formal pattern, musical form now aimed to impart a feeling of proportion, texture, and, above all, direction. If the sonata was chosen to contain all of that, it is largely due to the fact that 'sonata' did not indicate a single defined pattern in its antecedent history; it referred mainly to *played* rather than sung compositions, comprising varied musical structures.

Although there is more to be said about harmonic tonality, and more has been said,[60] it should be remembered that this discussion of the subject has aimed only to display the determination of Western art music to integrate musical laws and practice, so as to lend music a coherence of its own based on references intrinsic to the musical language. Looked at in retrospect, Western art music tenaciously aspired to lend music a physiognomy of its own. Even in conjunction with texts, composers have continuously tried, as we have seen, to devise features identifiable in musical terms alone. Harmonic tonality, however, is the culminating point of a cumulative process that increasingly fortified what is called in musicological parlance "absolute music," that is, music that is free from extramusical reference.

With so high a degree of self-sufficiency, no wonder that instrumental music, at this juncture, began to flourish as it never had before. Relying on music's self-referential system, instrumental compositions could be extended and manipulated in interesting and novel ways. Although harmonic

---

cal about music, Kirnberger set out to reduce Bach's teaching and method to its basic principles in his *Die Kunst des reinen Satzes in der Musik aus sicheren Grundsätzen hergeleitet unt mit deutlichen Beispielen versehen* (2 vols., 1774, 1779). For a brief comparison between Fux and Kirnberger see Jeppersen, *Counterpoint,* 43–48.

60. For an illuminating discussion of the historical development of the tonal system, see Dahlhaus, *Origin of Harmonic Tonality,* 162–92.

tonality is no doubt the musical language that made the classical style possible, much must be attributed to the pliability of the language, which lent itself to changes and elaboration without losing its fundamental syntactical structure. Still, if the tonal outline of larger scale compositions was to be accessible not only to music connoisseurs but also to ordinary music lovers, who steadily grew in number, the pace of harmonic change had to be of a kind that can be readily perceived.[61] In fact, an ostentatious change of harmony was not only considered less comprehensible, but became regarded as "baroque"—overembellished from an aesthetic point of view. Compared to the fast harmonic change in the baroque period, the "harmonic rhythm" in the classical era slowed up considerably. In fact, the motor force of the new style was not the harmonic sequence but the periodic phrase. While the articulation of the phrase demanded a corresponding movement from the harmony, the harmony could be manipulated in various ways as far as the illusion of motion was concerned, striking a balance between expression and proportion. Supported by a rhythmic texture of great variety, with the different rhythms passing smoothly into one another, periodic phrasing, in fact, heightened the sensitivity to symmetry.[62] Naturally, where the unity of music had to be conveyed without text, it was necessary to provide each of the individual movements of an extended

61. Compared to the music in the classical era whose aim was also to appeal to the growing public of musical amateurs belonging to the middle class, the music of the baroque era was primarily bound socially to the aristocracy. Aristocratic music naturally addressed a restricted audience. The church was the only place where music was regularly accessible to the citizens. Yet both church and state used the arts as means of representing supremacy, the authority of the nobility and the clergy. Although the display of splendor was one of the main social functions of the arts in baroque courts, the grandeur in the arts, including that of music, became an end in itself. Music involving the middle class was first organized in consorts of trained *amateurs* and in music clubs. It is these provisional institutions, however, that constituted the forerunners of the modern concert hall and the concert audience. Though comic opera is associated with the middle class, opera remained an exclusive institution even when it was commercialized by professional companies. Opera, which was initially an exclusively courtly institution, continued to serve those who backed the commercialized companies, that is, the smaller noblemen and wealthy patricians who could not afford so costly an institution on their own. For a good summary of the sociology of baroque music, see Bukofzer's *Music in the Baroque Era* (New York, 1947), chap. 12. While meticulously addressing the changes in musical style and practice, Bukofzer is invariably aware of the fact that the conception of music must be seen as an integral part of a general history of ideas. Sensitivity to the interdependence of form and style, and of musical thought and practice (see chaps. 10 and 11) enables Bukofzer to locate music in the milieu in which it functioned and to which it contributed its share.

62. See Charles Rosen's discussion on the subject in *The Classical Style* (London, 1971), 57–65.

work with its own tonal layout, so as to avoid a jumble of musical ideas. But as soon as the comprehensible layout of keys could sustain the unity of whole movements and of large musical forms, attention was directed toward the articulative elements of the musical unfolding, such as the structure of phrases, the combination of phrases that effect larger musical unities, metrical relationships, certain kinds of motivic development, and the like. Attempts were made to relate these rhythmic, harmonic, and melodic aspects to each other so as to reinforce the *abstract* regulative force by employing procedures that convey audibly that which can be *immediately* perceived. Exposed to a musical language so integrated, the music lover was expected to follow the "sense" of a composition while listening to its actual unfolding. He was invited, in fact, to be privy to a process, engendered by the composer, whereby musical form is being formed.

This does not mean that music so endowed ceased to serve extramusical purposes. As such, it could be enlisted to bolster, intensify, or underpin the implied messages that the various texts intended to impart. To be sure, the history of music, prior to this stage, is replete with interesting attempts to wed music to texts, also involving expressive interpretations by various musical means. From *musica reservata*[63] to opera, including the different stages in its development, varied approaches were enlisted to tighten the interplay between music and texts.[64] Yet the ability to make all structural and stylistic elements of music audible independent of texts—whereby tensions are lowered and raised, expectations fulfilled and frustrated, dispositions sustained and changed—reinforced the power of music to "spell out" that which the text, paradoxically, could only intimate.

This, of course, was made possible because the reverse is equally true: absolute music could admit "conflict," "reconciliation," and other designations such as "tense," "relaxed," "tender," "passionate," "graceful," and so forth, without foregoing its autonomy. The sonata form,[65] for example, the form that gradually constituted the dominant "mold" of instrumen-

63. A term first used by Adrian Coclico (1552) to describe the music of Josquin and his followers, pointing to the expression of the text by musical motifs and chromaticism, or as indicating the "reserved" character of music of high cultural standing. Later on, however, the term occurs as a designation for expressive interpretation of the text.

64. Although Fux, no doubt, dealt with Palestrina's counterpoint as the ultimate standard of musical strictness and purity, it must be remembered that this excellence was originally wedded to the texts it served in a manner that greatly contributed to the heightening of Palestrina's ideal—to constitute an adequate expression for divine worship.

65. The term does not apply to the overall form of the sonata, but to the form frequently used for single movements of sonatas (symphonic, chamber, or solo instruments).

tal music, encapsulates a dramatic scheme in which each of its sections—
exposition, development, and recapitulation—performs a unique function in the unfolding of an organic construction; the "drama," in fact,
resides in its structure. The exposition introduces two main themes,
mostly different in character, the second of which normally is in the key
of the dominant (if the tonic is major), or in the relative key (if the tonic
is minor). These themes are connected to each other via a modulating
passage (a "bridge," which connects the two tonal areas). The development section uses one or both of these themes as its point of departure,
engaging various melodic, harmonic, and contrapuntal techniques—
melodic fragmentation, rapid harmonic modulation, imitation of melodic
motifs, and so on. By virtue of the many procedures used to produce its
special dynamic character, this central section carries the major aesthetic
impact—intellectual and sensual—of the sonata form. If the placing of a
phrase in another context bestows a new significance upon it, the development section may be characterized as a continuous process of "reinterpretation" or transformation. While the recapitulation contains the material
of the exposition, the second theme now appears in the tonic, so that the
whole movement returns to the tonic, whence it commenced. Even this
oversimplified description of sonata form is loaded enough to suggest all
kinds of narrative readings.[66] Indeed, the dramatic qualities of the form
lend themselves to all kinds of extramusical meanings.

There is, of course, more to be said about sonata form, a fortiori about

66. Musical genres with narrative texts, like opera for example, are not as open to
alternate readings as is "absolute" music. In such genres, the correspondences between
musical and extramusical meanings provide more explicit guidelines. In the absence of
such guidelines, however, establishing a correspondence between internal and external
meanings must rely, willy-nilly, on one or more of the following: (1) authorial intent;
(2) subconscious intent as discerned by others, based on a shared criteria of judgment;
(3) audience reading; and (4) individual reading, whether or not intended, and whether
or not abiding by a shared criteria of judgment. To make this clearer, consider two different readings of the same musical form—Susan McClary's "gendered" reading of the
sonata form and David Schroeder's report on Haydn's "tolerant" reading of essentially
the same form. Schroeder worked from manifest authorial intent, while McClary attributed subconscious intent. Schroeder endeavored to unveil the extramusical thoughts
that Haydn wished to "translate" into a musical unfolding that "would lead his audience
through a process of discovery, the importance and function of duality, and the arrival at
an understanding of tolerance." See David P. Schroeder, *Haydn and the Enlightenment: The
Late Symphonies and Their Audiences* (Oxford, 1990), 20. McClary, for her part, proposed
that a "powerful narrative paradigm of adventure and conquest had underwritten the
symphony since its beginning." See Susan McClary, *Feminine Endings: Music, Gender, and
Sexuality* (Minnesota, 1992), 76.

the interesting development of the sonata in general.[67] In the extended history of the sonata there is virtually no known instrumental form that has not been included, at one point or another, under its title. Nonetheless, however different they were from one another, they were all *instrumental* pieces, which usually comprised a cycle of several contrasting movements. They embodied, moreover, the broadest structural principles available at the time, thereby providing *absolute* music with the most extended designs. And last but not least, these "designs" aimed to serve an *aesthetic* rather than a utilitarian purpose.[68] Given the coherence and intelligibility that music was able to effect, music could both elucidate the ambiguity of language and provide a fertile ground for metaphorical "possession."[69] Although the emergence of sonata form was a gradual development, it is no coincidence that it reached its most developed stage once music was fully able to "make sense" without being "predicated," that is, without being told what it is about.[70]

67. For the historical development of the sonata, see William S. Newman, *A History of the Sonata Idea* (North Carolina, 1959, 1966, 1972). Newman's monumental study is divided into three parts—the first treats the sonata of the baroque era, the second of the classical era, and the third of the period since Beethoven. Together they form a history of an *idea* rather than a history of a specified form whose antecedents are examined only from the perspective of so-called sonata form. As already mentioned, the latter term (also known as *sonata-allegro form*) applies only to single movements, mostly used (but not only) in the first movements of the later instrumental works.

68. This applies equally to the *sonata da camera* and the *sonata da chiesa*. These baroque terms indicate places of performance and not specific types or forms uniquely adapted to the location at which they were performed. The two terms, however, gradually became associated with larger forms rather than with single pieces. It was Arcangelo Corelli who standardized the *sonata da chiesa* as a composition consisting of four movements (slow-fast-slow-fast) and the *sonata da camera* as a suite consisting of an introduction and three or four dances.

69. Expression is invariably related to exemplification. Exemplification, insists Goodman, is a mode of symbolization based on labeling. A certain piece of music, for example, may be labeled sad. That which expresses sadness is metaphorically sad—actually sad, but not literally so—by virtue of "transferred application of some label coextensive with sad." What is expressed is thus "possessed"; the symbol takes on an acquired property. "Establishment of the referential relationship," says Goodman, "is a matter of singling out certain properties for attention, of selecting association with certain other objects. Verbal discourse is not least among the many factors that aid in founding and nurturing such association." See Goodman, *Languages of Art,* 85–88.

70. For an insightful and scholarly investigation of the historical argument according to which reason and sense impressions are reciprocally related to each other, and an analysis of the theories that claimed the simultaneous emergence of perception and conception that positioned metaphor in a philosophical context, see Michael Spitzer, *Metaphor and Musical Thought* (Chicago, 2004), chap. 5.

Indeed, music is the most articulate of media, though it cannot say what it is articulate about. The following chapter will try to elucidate the nature of this seeming paradox. Music, apparently, is better measured by what it makes possible than by what it is. Interestingly, once music reached the apex of its coherence, it was able to contribute significantly to the path-breaking juncture in the history of ideas that heralded the cognitive turn in Western thought.

PART II

The Crafting of
a "Shared Understanding"

THREE

Separating 'Sense' from 'Meaning'

NATURAL LANGUAGES: SOME RELEVANT POINTS

The cumulative process whereby Western music attained a language of its own explicates to a large extent the aforementioned paradox, namely that music is the most articulate of the media but cannot say what it is articulate about. The journey toward optimizing music's "independence," as we have seen, consists of ideas and innovations that, explicitly or implicitly, sought to interrelate internal musical references in order to achieve a well-integrated, self-reliant musical syntax.

The syntax of a language generally refers to the grammatical arrangement of words that show their connection and relations to one another within a given sentence and among sentences related to each other. Although the display may be, and frequently is, incorrect, it invariably presupposes the existence of certain customary uses of words in combination. In fact, the grammar of a language denotes the mode in which words are connected in order to express a complete thought, or a "proposition" (as it is termed by logicians). Thus the grammatical correctness or incorrectness of an expression depends upon its intelligibility, that is, upon the ordinary use and custom of a particular language. Whatever is so unfamiliar as not to be generally understood is also ungrammatical, for it is contrary to the habit of a language as determined by common usage and consent.

Since grammatical propriety is but the established usage of a particular body of speakers at a particular time in history, it follows that the grammar of a people undergoes changes concerning all those contrivances whereby the relations of words and sentences are pointed out in the language they hold in common. To establish the "historical grammar," or primary infrastructure, of a single language involves tracing language patterns as far back as documentary evidence allows so as to disclose—through their development and transformations—the morphological uniqueness of the language, that is, the sorts of distinctions and degree of distinctness its users found necessary to introduce. There is apparently no language that has completely forsaken the relations of elements with which it started. It is thought that this is due to the fact that the essential unit, that of the sentence, resides in the very relations of its several parts. Like the thoughts that they express, sentences are conceived as wholes; their parts are related to each other like the ideas they intend to convey. Such relations do not readily change once they succeed in facilitating the utterances and the understanding of the bearers of a given language. Solidifying what has been achieved, they are transformed only gradually, making room for novel ideas that seek expression. Thus, indices of grammatical relations may be placed differently in different languages, and some languages may allow for greater subtleties than others, yet fundamental structural relations, once established, do not drastically change their functions, though they may gain in refinement and coherence. It is obvious, therefore, why grammar constitutes the surest and most important basis for the classification of languages.

This brief discussion seeks only to stress that the object of language is to convey thought. So long as this object is attained, the machinery for attaining it is of comparatively slight importance. Yet it is the contrivances whereby the relations of words and sentences are pointed out that allow us to follow the thoughts *thus* expressed. Obviously, elaborate machinery is not necessary for simple designations, whereas abstract thought that rests on interrelated ideas, subordinated to one another in a variety of ways, requires machinery crafted to handle complicated mental processes. Although what refers to what and in what way may vary, complicated thought patterns invariably necessitate a multilayered referential system that is able to effect hierarchical structures in which the ideas that make up intricate and composite thoughts may find their proper places. The set of rules governing the grammatical arrangements of sentence structures and the relationships within and among them are cardinal factors for the act of conveying thoughts via language.

Although semantic factors are not essential to the identification of grammatical formulations or parts of speech, we would have difficulty in formulating the rules that make one correct expression acceptable and another not if the morphology of languages did not also include concepts of a higher order to mediate these phenomena of grammar, so as to correspond to the regularities that prevail concerning the behavior involved. Since "natural languages" relate *to* and function *in* culture, they are used not only for purposes of communication but also to code or categorize the environment, thereby constituting an important intellectual feature in the control of behavior. It has thus been suggested that linguistic systems follow an orderly sequence of increasing differentiation of significant features relating language development to perceptual development.[1] It has likewise been suggested that in addition to phrase structure, languages must also contain a set of transformational rules that, when used, serve to modify a statement from one type to another. Transformations, accordingly, rest on simple sentence models—basic forms of adult utterances—that are transformed, as needed, by the use of transformational rules such as the interrogative, the passive, the negative, and so on.[2]

Even the rudimentary considerations raised here are enough to convey the idea that natural languages obviously stand apart from other communication systems used by humans. This is largely due to the magnitude of their resources, but no less to the indisputable fact that every normal child is capable of using the language of his or her community, producing an infinite number of meaningful utterances at a relatively early age. While we are still far from understanding all of the characteristics of language, and

1. See Roman Jakobson, *Kindersprache, Aphasie, und allgemeine Lautgesetze* (Uppsala, 1941); H. V. Velten, "The Growth of Phonemic and Lexical Patterns in Infant Languages," in *Language* 19 (1943): 281–92; Roger W. Brown, *Words and Things* (Glencoe, 1958); and Lev S. Vygotskii, *Thought and Language* (Cambridge, Mass., 1962), first published in 1934.

2. Noam Chomsky has argued for a long time that a simple stimulus-response formation and habit utilization theory cannot cope with this conception of grammar. The psychologist George Miller, though he considers associations in language to carry significance, is also of the opinion that the mechanisms underlying the transformational grammar can hardly be of the associative kind. See Noam Chomsky, *Syntactic Structures* (The Hague, 1957), and George A. Miller, "Some Psychological Studies of Grammar," *American Psychologist* 17 (1962): 748–62. Both, and many others, have deliberated on these issues ever since, relating transformational rules to basic cognitive factors.

even farther from understanding the human nervous system that makes it possible, two things are clear, namely, that humans are capable of inventing both *symbols* and a *duality of patterning* in linguistic structure. Unlike signs, from which the existence of something else is inferred, a symbol is a special kind of sign, one with arbitrary, conventionally assigned meaning. It is apparently uniquely human to be able to assign arbitrary meanings to signs, that is, to invent symbols. Yet the symbols of language, unlike other symbolic systems, are divisible, that is, words divide into morphemes, which, in turn, divide into phonemes—the sound units of spoken language. These diverse sound units,[3] which are meaningless in themselves, are used for the construction of a huge number of meaningful units. It is this duality of patterning—the two-level structuring—that bestows on language a quantitative and qualitative superiority over other symbolic systems.

The fact that individual languages are transmitted culturally does not rule out, as we have seen, the possibility that mankind has certain unique inborn capacities for linguistic behavior, which culture "naturally" exploits. To be sure, the preoccupation with the innate capacities of the mind did not commence with linguistic studies; it has a time-honored, distinguished history. Nonetheless, because language is a *communal* achievement, an inseparable part of culture, which enables the development, elaboration, transmission, and accumulation of a culture as a whole, it is no wonder that the study of language should have focused on matters concerning structure and meaning, as related to manifest experiences and behavior. Yet when a particular word, in common usage, designates the object it refers to, the meaning of the word resides in the individual minds of the users of the language; it is not, however, a "thing" they have in mind but, rather, a *relationship* that associates words and objects. In other words, even the minimum units that participate in the arbitrary relationships of meaning, that is, the lexical part of language, already rest on a mind capable of entertaining relationships of this sort. However, since the links between such structural units and meaning are arbitrary, it is their *regularity* that reflects the integration between language and the rest of culture. Again, it is not surprising that regularities of this kind should have attracted the attention of linguists and anthropologists. It is the regularities displayed in the use of language that disclose, after all, not only its syntactic structure but also its semantic meanings and the culture that contributed to their formation.

By analogy to language, music lacks a semantic layer. Yet music, I re-

---

3. Every language uses a small number of these meaningless units, usually less than fifty, to build up meaningful units.

peat, is the most articulate of media though it itself cannot say what it is articulate about. In order to "make sense," Western art music, as we have seen, strove to achieve coherence *without* having to resort to extramusical factors. Wedded to many texts in different manners and varying degrees of dependency, the expressive power of music became increasingly apparent with the elaboration of *internally* related referential schemes that could be manipulated in a variety of ways. However, unlike the grammatical arrangements of words in sentence constructions, which also code or categorize the environment as perceived and conceived, music is able to create its own sensuous environment via sheer construction, which enables both idiomatic procedures and the individuation of familiar musical coinages. Western art music, in other words, became increasingly endowed with the power *to occasion* an "atmosphere," a desired ambiance, without recourse to language. In fact, music was increasingly able, as we shall see, to "disambiguate" the "inconclusiveness" inherent in language.

THE POWER TO OCCASION AN ATMOSPHERE

No musical institution contributed more than opera to unleashing the powers of music. The institution of opera may be conceived as a "laboratory" for continuous exploration of the hidden powers that lurk in the interaction between words and music.[4] Altogether, the *Gesamtkunstwerk,* as Richard Wagner would later refer to his music drama, constituted a fertile ground for the assessment of the limits and the uniqueness of each of the participating arts. Curiously, their distinct contribution to the workings of the music drama came to light not least owing to the "adjustment" they had to make in order to achieve a satisfactory union among them. Although the history of opera, and of opera theory and criticism, can almost be written as a scientific exploration aimed at charting the domain of each of the arts, it more particularly and most vividly has delineated the domain and powers of music. Opera, in fact, partook in the process that undermined the Aristotelian understanding of Nature, an understanding that was primarily based on the perceptible, visible world. As is well known, the scientific revolution of the late sixteenth and early seventeenth centuries reversed this understanding, hoping to extrapolate from the factual world the *invisible* laws of nature—its *hypothetical* fundamental laws. Indeed, the

4. See Ruth Katz, *The Powers of Music, Aesthetic Theory, and the Invention of Opera* (New Brunswick, New Jersey, 1994), chap. 2: "Opera as a Laboratory for Defining the Powers of Music."

scientific revolution ushered in a new kind of search, a search that aimed to *unveil* the "secrets" of nature via theories that gained credence through novel processes of verification.[5] Opera thus should not be viewed as a "setback" on the way toward musical autonomy, but rather as a musical institution that contributed to the "unveiling" of the *communicative* powers of music and to the ways in which they may be used to assist language to pinpoint its intent. There is no denying, however, that opera also partook in a new vision of "what music was for." If prior to the scientific revolution music represented the judicious embodiment of the harmony that God conferred on the universe, from the early seventeenth century onward music became increasingly viewed as a medium capable of expressing the emotional qualities of objects that texts represent, but do not express.[6] The early seventeenth century, says Karol Berger, ushered in a "new paradigm," a paradigm that highlighted the "mimetic aims of music." The idea of music as a mimetic art "able to imitate passions," says Berger, "stirred the imagination" only of some "visionaries" inspired by humanism in the middle of the sixteenth century, yet by the last quarter of the century it had become the dominant opinion "in more advanced circles." It did so, Berger tells us, "without eliminating the idea of harmony." Moreover, "the two ideas had to coexist," he tells us, through the third quarter of the eighteenth century.[7] Indeed, the new paradigm embodied and exemplified the intellectual trends that underlie early modern culture, which provided among other things the foundation of a new musical aesthetic.[8]

Drama Aspiring toward the "Condition of Music"

The union between words and music drew special attention—engaging both devotees and critics of the opera—since relations between these two were especially problematic. Though the dramatic, the musical, the deco-

5. For old and new perspectives on the scientific revolution, see David Lindberg and Robert Westman, eds., *Reappraisals of the Scientific Revolution* (Cambridge, 1990).

6. Representation—according to Goodman's theory of symbols—relates a symbol to things it applies to, while expression relates the symbol to a label that metaphorically denotes it. We shall have the opportunity, somewhat later, to discuss the difference between 'representation' and 'expression' at length.

7. See Karol Berger, *A Theory of Art* (Oxford, 2000), chap. 3: "The Genealogy of Modern European Art Music," 127–28.

8. For musical aesthetic elements that were impacted by the new science, see Paulo Gozzi, ed., *Number to Sound: The Musical Way to the Scientific Revolution* (Boston, 2000). Also see Timothy Reiss, *Knowledge, Discovery, and Imagination in Early Modern Europe: The Rise of Aesthetic Rationalism* (Cambridge, 1997).

rative, and so forth are temporally changing characteristics, marking the manifestation that is opera and the changes in its form, there is no denying that singing is the "fixed axis" that distinguishes opera from all other art forms; the music drama rests, in fact, on the convention that it is sung. All art, to be sure, rests on conventions, a convention being a tacit agreement to take something for granted, however bizarre, and accord it legitimacy at a given time and place. Yet, while painting has not been attacked for lacking relief, or sculpture for lacking color, or pantomime for being mute, opera has been challenged for using song as its natural speech. Its "fixed axis," as it turned out, could not easily be taken for granted; it could not easily be reconciled with the plain, but inevitable, narration of the plot. Indeed, to meet this challenge successfully required a thorough understanding of the characteristics and functions of the major participants in the opera— singing and telling, music and drama—and the unique relationship that they were bound to forge in constituting the melodrama. To handle the complexities with skill, that is, to avoid reminding the spectators that they are partners to an agreement, was, and still is, the challenge of opera.

The problem of the interaction between words and music is not that they appeal to the same sense, as has been suggested,[9] but more exactly that they employ the same sense differently. Although both unfold in time, they make different use of its duration; music takes more time—real time, not to be confused with musical time—than words. Music acts synthetically; it requires expansion to communicate a given "disposition"; whereas verbal communication, in its continuous movement, presents a succession of images and ideas. Music, in fact, may gather up the predominant elements described and analyzed by verbal and scenic images to express them in their totality. What, then, does happen when words and music wed in the opera? What is revealed about the power of music? Rather than simply echoing those critics who would restrict music to those places where it serves as the best vehicle of expression, opera opted to marry music to the kind of drama that "aspires toward the condition of music," that is, where drama strives beyond the representational toward the symbolic.[10] Or, as Susanne Langer puts it, "Anything that can enter into the vital symbolism of music belongs to music, and whatever cannot do this has no traffic with music at all."[11]

9. See, for example, Harold Child, "Some Thoughts on Opera Libretto," *Music and Letters,* vol. 2, 1921.

10. See Philip Heseltine, "The Scope of Opera," *Music and Letters,* vol. 1 (1920), 230.

11. Susanne K. Langer, *Feeling and Form* (New York, 1953), 152.

Aristoxenus, as we have seen, already realized that listening to music presupposes an intellectual activity whereby impressions are collected and built up in one's memory. Musical cognition, he suggested, implies the simultaneous cognition of a permanent and of a changeable element. If Aristoxenus was able to make so astute an observation in *his* time, it became substantially easier to follow his line of thinking centuries later. As a matter of fact, by the time Eduard Hanslick asserted (1854) that sound and motion (*"tönend bewegte Formen"*) constitute the essence of music[12] — of that "illusion begotten by sound" — it was naturally and almost fully endorsed by those who had a commanding knowledge of the métier. The existence of "absolute music," with the kind of self-sufficiency and coherence it embodied, only reinforced the long-evolving view of music as "the hidden arithmetical exercise of a mind, unconscious that it is calculating."[13]

While more will be said about music and the mind and the role the arts played in the pre-figuration of the cognitive turn in epistemology that took place in the eighteenth century, we may not relinquish the long unshaken belief in the *affective* powers of music. Musical traditions, the world over and from time immemorial, have attributed persuasive powers to music, enlisting them for different purposes and to varying degrees. There is also no want of theories trying to explain why music has such powers. Although some theories, old and new, have a cosmological ring and others a more down-to-earth "sound," once music was *believed* to have influential powers — however unproven — it could be, and has been, enlisted to produce desired effects.[14] In the musical tradition of the West, the centrality of the image of Orpheus and his lyre, and the preoccupation with this theologian-magician-musician, were in fact basic to the early history of opera and, more generally, to the history of music. Orpheus not only personified the concept of man's ability to *divine* (in the double sense of the word) the powers of music but became the symbol of unleashing them.[15]

12. Eduard Hanslick, *The Beautiful in Music* (1854), trans. Gustav Cohen (New York, 1957), 27.

13. Leibniz's famous statement (in a letter to Christoph Goldbach) concerning music. See Ruth Katz and Carl Dahlhaus, *Contemplating Music*, vol. 3, 427, 429–30.

14. Anthropological literature is replete with examples of the efficacy of music in this respect, highlighting the success of "autosuggestion."

15. See Katz, *The Powers of Music*, chap. 5. Much has been written about the Orpheus myth and the place it occupies in the Western musical tradition. I shall refer to some of the seminal works on the subject later on. I wish to call attention, however, to an interesting book that deals with "the attraction of cinema to opera" that employs the *distinction* that the Orpheus myth established, that is, between "a song that revives but

The Legacy of the Humanists

Magic is a form of *doing*, we learn from the experts, not just of contemplating; hence its kinship to science. It is, however, also a form of *manipulating* a supernatural world; hence its proximity to religion.[16] But whereas the Greeks were satisfied with speculation, and medieval Christians humbled themselves under the strict surveillance of God, the humanists[17] of the Renaissance, says Charles Trinkaus, "offered through their writings a new affirmation of the possibility and value of human action. They presented a vision of man controlling and shaping his own life . . . and they stressed a new conception of human nature modeled on their own image of the Deity."[18] The determination "to operate" was their innovation, says Frances Yates.[19] Thus, every account of the humanists reveals not only the influence that the ancient world exerted on them but also the way in which they enlisted that world to reinforce their own ideas, and in the process were influenced by what they found.[20] The humanists, as it turned out, were influential to the *camerata*—the group to whom the beginnings of opera is attributed—in somewhat the same way as the ancient world was influential to the humanists. The humanists, as is well known, revealed a profound preoccupation with the powers not only inherent in nature but also in the arts. In their attempts to gain access to the "harmonies" of the world, to influence and reshape them, the proper "tuning" of individual souls was high on their agenda. Oriented not only to observe God's Creation but also to act upon it, the "magic" of the humanists entailed the

---

is transient, and a gaze that kills and is permanent"(6). See Michal Grover-Friedlander, *Vocal Apparitions: The Attraction of Cinema to Opera* (Princeton, 2005), 1–16.

16. In his classic essay, "Magic, Science and Religion," Bronislaw Malinowski says it all and better. (See 1948 reprint of essay.) Many of the studies that took special interest in the hermetic tradition, especially those produced by scholars at the Warburg Institute in London, arrived at similar conclusions.

17. 'Humanism' generally refers to a doctrine emphasizing the importance of common human needs, resting on an image of man as a responsible and progressive intellectual being. Although the term 'humanists' refers to adherents of humanism, it also refers to students (especially in the fourteenth through sixteenth centuries) of Roman and Greek literature and antiquities.

18. See Charles Trinkaus, *In Our Image and Likeness* (Chicago, 1970), 767.

19. See Frances A. Yates, *Giordano Bruno and the Hermetic Tradition* (New York, 1969), 155.

20. For classical sources and their influence, see Frederick W. Sternfeld, *The Birth of Opera* (Oxford, 1988).

media of words and music, enlisting them for their projects of persuasion
and manipulation.[21]

In line with Plato, the humanists postulated that beyond the spirit that
flows in man there is an all-embracing *spiritus mundi*. The latter, they believed, serves to bind the "soul" and "body" of the cosmos, and transmits
the particular influences of each of the several planets. In order to enlist
the *desired* characteristics of the planets, music was especially recommended. The recipe recommended by Marsilio Ficino, one of the most
eminent humanists,[22] was based on the following argument: (1) given that
music has movement, it can be made to correspond to the movements of
the celestial bodies; through music, in other words, the human spirit can
refresh itself via contact with the cosmic spirits;[23] (2) because of the ability
of music to arouse singer and listener to particular emotions and moral

21. See D. P. Walker, *Spiritual and Demonic Magic from Ficino to Campanella* (London,
1958), and Gary Tomlinson, *Music in Renaissance Magic: Toward a Historiography of Others*
(Chicago, 1993). Discussing Marsilio Ficino's magical songs, Tomlinson takes issue with
Walker. Their interpretations of Ficino's writings with regard to the function of words and
music differ considerably. Walker differentiated between words and music, claiming that
Ficino attributed to the text alone the ability to carry intellectual content and thus to influence the mind. Through a reexamination of Ficino's writings, including the treatises that
provided the background for Ficino's thinking, Tomlinson endeavored to show that there
is no evidence in Ficino's writings to support Walker's distinction of "meaningful" words
and "non-meaningful" music, but that Ficino conceived the effectiveness of music through
other means, which Tomlinson dwells on and clarifies. Tomlinson, however, deserves
careful reading not only because of his judicious reinterpretation of Ficino's writings—according to which the effect of music, words, and magic inhabit a liminal place in Ficino's
theories, that between body and soul—but also because of its relevance to present-day
studies that try to "bridge" body and soul via a better understanding of the relationship
between mind and brain, cognition and perception, thought and sentiment, in an attempt
to unveil the "embodiment" of the soul, as it were, in the course of human development.

22. Marsilio Ficino (1433–1499) was the founder and head of the Platonic academy in
Florence. In addition to translating Plato's dialogues into Latin, he also translated works
by Plotinus, Iamblichus, Porphyry, and one of the most important hermetic treatises of
the Asclepius. Their influence is apparent in his writings. Ficino's major contribution to
humanism was his attempt to restore the link between philosophy, the product of man's
thought, and faith, which is given to him in revelation. Ficino sought to place philosophy
(which included the sciences) and faith on the same cognitive basis, for the truths of
both, he maintained, are similarly attained. For sections of his writings (in an original
translation into English) relevant to the above discussion, see Katz and Dahlhaus, *Contemplating Music*, vol. 1, 78–93.

23. Ficino's spirit is an airy substance that occupies a middle ground between body
and soul; "it conveys," Tomlinson tells us, "the animating force of the soul to the body
and the stimuli received by the corporeal senses back to the soul." See Tomlinson, *Music
in Renaissance Magic*, 106.

attitudes, it is also capable of arousing those emotions and attitudes that correspond to the moral character of the gods whose names the planets bear.[24] Ficino cautioned, however, that his formula for reaching the stars is not the equivalent of worshipping them. Rather, it is imitating them in such a way as to benefit from their spirit. Accordingly, he provided rules for stargazing and for attuning words and music to particular stars: include the power of the star in the text of the song; discover the people and places under the influence of a star and include their modes and meanings in your songs; imitate the variations in speech, songs, and actions that are induced under various aspects of the star, and include these in your song.[25]

Notice the operations: Ficino calls for systematic observations of the movement of stars in the heavens. He calls for inferential analysis of the influence of different stars from the changes in human behavior that accompany the changes in stellar behavior. He prescribes imitative behavior. He calls, in short, for a kind of applied science, as the camerata would later call for systematic and empirical analysis of "situations," the better to match them to appropriate music.[26] There is reason to believe that Ficino actually practiced his astrological music.[27] His texts were Orphic hymns

---

24. To fully understand Ficino's logic, it pays to cite his own summary of the relations of body, spirit, and soul:

> The soul and the body are very different in nature; they are joined by means of spirit, which is a certain vapor, very thin and clear, produced by the heat of the heart from the thinnest part of the blood. Spread from there through all parts of the body, the spirit receives the powers of the soul and communicates them to the body. It also takes up through the organs of the senses the images of bodies outside, images that cannot be imprinted directly on the soul because incorporeal substance, which is more perfect than bodies, cannot be formed by them through the reception of images. But the soul, being present in all parts of the spirit, easily sees the images of bodies as if in a mirror shining in it, and through these judges the bodies; such cognition is called 'sense' by the Platonists. While it looks at these images, by its own power the soul conceives in itself images similar to them, but much purer; and such conception is called imagination or phantasy. (Quoted by Tomlinson, *Music in Renaissance Magic,* 106)

25. See Walker, *Spiritual and Demonic Magic,* 17. The reader will have noticed that 'analogy,' 'correspondence,' and 'imitation' occupy central positions in Ficino's theories, as do 'image' and 'imagination.' Although this is hardly the place to treat each of these separately, I would like to call attention to the fact that all of these continued to play central roles in aesthetic and cognitive theories.

26. See Ruth Katz, *Divining the Powers of Music* (New York, 1986), 107–10.

27. For a more detailed analysis, see Gary Tomlinson, *Metaphysical Song* (Princeton, 1999), 9–33.

sung to the accompaniment of some sort of lyre. The Orphic hymns were considered suitable because Orpheus among the ancient theologians is the most ancient of the Greeks, the master of Pythagoras and, through him, of Plato. "In natural magic," says Pico della Mirandola, another illustrious humanist, "nothing is more efficacious than the Hymns of Orpheus, if there be applied to them the suitable music, and disposition of soul and other circumstances known to the wise."[28]

However interesting, Pico's conditional clause does not explain wherein the powers of music reside. And though Ficino's "music-spirit" theory tells us something about the way in which it is transmitted, he seems to have taken the powers of music for granted, *believing* that such exist. He also *believed* that the ancients could attune themselves to the cosmic spirits through music, and tried to do so himself. In his theorizing, he provided an explanation of the process by which the spirits inherent in man and in the universe could be contacted by musical rituals. The method for doing so he defined by observation and experimentation.[29] Interestingly, the members of the camerata were no less practical than Ficino, and no less theoretical. However, although they too believed that the ancients held the secrets to the powers of music,[30] they left off trying to understand them exactly, convinced only that a major clue to the nature of that music resided in some form of monody, that is, some way in which music could enhance the spoken word. Their theorizing insisted that music must cease to distort the words or merely to embroider them, but rather must cope with the problem of conveying their latent meaning. This meaning, they believed, could be transmitted from composer to listener.

Those familiar with the early history of opera will no doubt agree with these last statements. They might equally agree that from the camerata through the doctrine of affections,[31] the powers of music were not sim-

28. Walker, *Spiritual and Demonic Magic*, 22–23. Also see Yates, *Giordano Bruno*, 177.

29. The changes that took place in the relation between theology and science (from the Middle Ages until and including the scientific revolution) reveal, according to Amos Funkenstein, that "hypothetical reasoning" increasingly encouraged and complemented experimentation. See Amos Funkenstein's seminal study, *Theology and the Scientific Imagination from the Middle Ages to the Seventeenth Century* (Princeton, 1986).

30. Indeed, the idea that nature (including music) harbors "secrets" was hardly new, nor was the interaction between magic and science. The various interactions between the two, we learn from William Eaman's interesting study, actually bequeathed major attitudes and values that proved instrumental in shaping the scientific outlook of early modern culture. See William Eaman, *Science and the Secrets of Nature: Books of Secrets in Medieval and Early Modern Culture* (Princeton, 1994).

31. An aesthetic theory of the late baroque period, formulated by a number of eight-

ply described in empty words but became part of the technical aspect of the theory of composition. Thus, the camerata's campaign against music that "delights the ear" argued, for example, that the use of many notes was "artificial" and that the limitation of means held the secret for success.[32] Vincenzo Galilei, a key member of the group, also tried to supplant Zarlino's contrapuntal theory with a theoretical formulation of the harmonic practice of his contemporaries, thereby satisfying the need for a theory of chromatic and enharmonic music.[33] The latter, as is well known, loomed large in the attempt to endow music with greater expressive powers. Musical elements of all kinds were employed to qualify emotions, to match affects to musical procedures.[34] Indeed, like Ficino, the camerata tried to show how latent meanings could be transmitted from composer to listener—through observation, experimentation, composition, and performance. But while Ficino aimed primarily at healing the body and refreshing the spirit of man by connecting him to the cosmos, the primary aim of the camerata, cognizant of the hermetic tradition, was to connect men with men. Ethical persuasion preoccupied them all, but the camerata took a further step toward the humanizing and secularizing of music.

Empirical Observations and Aesthetic Theory

Joined with a theory based on empirical observation, magical operations became increasingly scientific. And so it was with music: aesthetic theory addressed to the nature of music found itself in the corridors of the same laboratory from which empirical science was emerging. It is fashionable nowadays to speak of the origins of modern science in the hermetic tradition of magic, operating on the will and the world. Somewhat similarly, via theorizing about the powers of music—"divining" them (figuratively and literally)—then joining composition and performance with theory and empirical observation, the theorists and musicians of the late Renaissance

---

eenth century theorists. It was treated in greatest detail by Johann Mattheson in his *Der Vollkommene Capellmeister* (Kassel, 1739), where he enumerates more than twenty affections and describes how they should be expressed in music.

32. See Claude Palisca, "Vincenzo Galilei and Some Links between 'Pseudo-Monody' and Monody," *Musical Quarterly* 46 (1960a): 347.

33. See Claude Palisca, "Vincenzo Galilei's Counterpoint Treatise: A Code for the Seconda Pratica," *Journal of the American Musicological Society* 9 (1956): 81–96.

34. Giulio Caccini, as is well known, gave detailed instructions about "how" to produce affective singing in the introduction to his collection of songs, which caries the noteworthy title *Le nuove musiche.*

and early baroque connected music with both magic and science. Indeed, science, no less than magic, rests on a mind properly tuned. Ficino was not so far off in this respect: he saw music as a mediator between men and the celestial bodies, operating through the common denominator of movement. The *spiritus mundi,* accordingly, constitutes the "channel of transmission" through which the soul of man can affect—via his spirit—the *spirit* of the gods (whose name the stars bear), and the other way round. In short: musical movement, received through the ear, stirs movement in the soul, which functions like a "remote control" thanks to a compatible channel of transmission. Though hardly sound physics, it has a quasi-scientific sound. We would do well to remember that Johannes Kepler's three laws of planetary motion derived from the same tradition, which supplied the overarching theories that he subjected to empirical testing. More succinctly, in line with the quadrivium tradition, Kepler linked astronomy and music in order to discover the harmony of the universe. His five-book work, *Harmonia mundi,* is devoted to that connection.[35]

The year Kepler died (1630), a work of almost the same name appeared—*Harmonie universelle.* The author was none other than Marin Mersenne, who was mentioned earlier in connection with Rameau's theory of harmony. It is noteworthy that Ficino—who is identified with the humanist strain that sought to integrate artistic, scientific, and social activity with Christian religious values—was not only the initiator and head of the Platonic academy in Florence but also a canon at the city's cathedral. More than a hundred years later, it was a French Minim friar—Mersenne—who became a central figure among the scientists of his day. In his various undertakings Mersenne brought together most of the thoughts and the scientific advances made in his time. His alertness to the cultural life that surrounded him also found expression in a wide-ranging correspondence with leading thinkers and scientists—René Descartes, Thomas Hobbes, Christian Huygens, Blaise Pascal, and other distinguished figures, including Vincenzo Galilei (the theoretical mentor of the camerata) and Giovanni Battista Doni (a profound student of ancient music), who took an interest in the early activities of the camerata.[36]

35. See Katz and Dahlhaus, *Contemplating Music,* vol. 1, 107–44 (includes an introduction and original translation of sections concerning music).

36. G. B. Doni (1594–1647) is the nobleman to whom the much-quoted letter by Pietro Bardi (son of Giovanni Bardi, Count of Vernio) was sent. In his letter Pietro describes the nature and composition of the camerata, the group that used to assemble in his father's house.

Mersenne was also of the opinion that arriving at the essence of things is beyond the reach of human reason, yet he did not negate the legitimacy of scientific knowledge of natural phenomena.[37] On the contrary, Mersenne regarded the possibility of improving and developing that knowledge as the religious answer to the contentions of skepticism. He believed that the relativity of the senses could be overcome by precise instruments and reliable observations, that the phenomena could be interrelated by a coherent system of laws, and that, thereby, a body of systematic knowledge of the world we experience could be created that would also help us to direct our activity. Scientific research, thus, has pragmatic implications and, consequently, far-reaching moral significance.

Under the influence of Descartes and others, Mersenne rejected the view that there was an essential connection between the world and language. However, whereas for Descartes the negation of the relationship between words and the things denoted by them did not have any special significance (since as far as he was concerned the relationship that pertains between mathematics and the physical world is sufficient to relate man to real phenomena[38]), for Mersenne the arbitrariness of language meant the loss of the possibility to penetrate and influence man's soul. In music, he hoped to find the principal heir to the effectiveness of language. This goes a long way toward explaining why he supported those who sought to strengthen musical expression over musical pleasantness, and why he extolled the polar texture of the basso continuo over the balanced polyphonic art. Mersenne, in fact, adopted the Italian theories about the effectiveness of music and endorsed the changes that they effected in the musical aesthetics of his time. Yet *how* and in *what way* music turns into a universal language, expressing the "thoughts of the spirit and the desire of the will," is a question that kept occupying him. Having accepted Des-

37. Six of Mersenne's twenty-four encyclopedic works, which are mostly devoted to the fields of mathematics, astronomy, and physics, are devoted to music. The following delineation of Mersenne's position with regard to music is based (almost verbatim) on sections from the introduction I provided to Mersenne's writings in *Contemplating Music*, vol. 2, 77–112.

38. Building on the great change that mathematics had undergone—from a collection of solutions to a limited number of problems to a formal science extending across realms—Descartes assumed the reduction of all of science to mathematical thought. He envisaged the organization of all knowledge as a tree whose roots are in mathematics, whose trunk is physics, and whose branches are all the other sciences. See my introduction to Descartes in *Contemplating Music*, 501–5.

cartes' arguments about the relativity of taste and aesthetic judgment,[39]
he rejected Descartes' contention about the *dis*connection between the
senses and reason, that is, between the senses and that which is able to
comprehend them. According to Mersenne, it is musical *praxis,* not inductive science, that dictates musical theory and musical *experience;* "like
the phenomena of nature themselves," it constitutes an object for study, a
power of influence that can be examined, in order to provide a basis for a
systematic musical aesthetics.

All of this finds expression in his *Harmonie universelle,* in which Mersenne sets up a system of experiments, treating even what is *not* subject
to observation and quantification as though it were an experiment. At the
base of his system he places his own empirical findings—the discoveries
in the field of acoustics that paved the way for the laws of Joseph Sauveur
(1701) and Rameau's theory of harmony (1722). To this he adds the findings
of Giovanni Battista Benedetti and Galilei,[40] shifting the basis of consonant relations from string lengths to pitch frequencies, thus preserving the
hierarchical system of intervals while removing the "substantive" nature
of the tones and presenting music as the pure movement of air. Increasing
or decreasing movement may, accordingly, explain empirical findings, such
as the listener's aesthetic preference, for example. Mersenne reinforces,
thereby, the Neoplatonic theory of 'spirit' as found in Ficino. By drawing
a tighter physical relationship between sound and its influence on man,
he is able to ground the assumption about the "natural" relationship between music and the soul. More concretely, in light of his own discovery
of several of the overtones above the fundamental (the full theory had to
wait for a later date), Mersenne concluded that the purity of the intervals
is not only relative but also context-dependent. Mersenne thus shifted his
entire search for musical effectiveness from the isolated components (e.g.,

39. Interested in aesthetic preference, Mersenne expected Descartes to answer his
query as to why one sound strikes us as more pleasant than another. Descartes' answer
contained the following statement: "'Beautiful' and 'pleasant' signify simply a relation
between our judgment and an object; and because the judgments of men differ so much
from each other neither beauty nor pleasantness," concludes Descartes, "can be said to
have any definite measure." See Descartes' letter to Mersenne, ibid., 525

40. Giovanni Battista Benedetti (ca. 1585) contested the claim that the celestial orbs
emit sounds, since sound requires that air enter a confined place. Failing to find the
harmonic proportions in the sky, he enumerated the ratios of the consonances as defined
by modern musicians (see Claude V. Palisca [1985], 186–87). Galilei's most significant
discovery was that the ratio of an interval was proportional to a string's length but varied
as the square of tension applied to the strings and as the cubes of volumes of air. He was
the first to show that the same ratio did not apply under all conditions.

intervals and modes) to the musical work, that is, from the movement of a single tone to the "movement" of the musical composition as a whole. The musical phenomenon was thus presented as analogous to man's emotional and moral activity, and, consequently, as a highly effective agent in influencing him. Much of the aesthetic emphasis is transferred in that way to the metaphorical factors of musical movement. While Mersenne refers his readers to the ancients, as well as to more recent predecessors who addressed this subject, he stresses the need for independent judgment on the part of the musician.

The musician, following Mersenne's line of thought, becomes a kind of psychologist-physiologist who bases his work and understanding on his own living musical experience. The camerata, as we have seen, tried to show (like Ficino) how latent meanings could be transmitted from composer to listener. Musical elements of all kinds were devised and employed to qualify emotions, to match affects to musical procedures. If Mersenne calls upon the musician to exercise judgment based on his *own* experience, it is due to the fact that the composer, himself, acts on what he understands as a well-trained listener. As circular as this argument might sound, it is less void than it might seem. Indeed, before the arts could be defined as symbolic languages through their own "sensuous form-giving character,"[41] one had to realize that "images," of whatever kind, are insufficient for the understanding; they have to be turned into symbols by the very intellect they address, using the content of perception and experience. Symbols, thus, are not just made but disclose themselves through their own making; they are, in fact, the cultural forms of human activities.[42] Looked at in this way, one might even say that awareness of the "interpretative capacity" of the arts preceded other cultural forms, including that of science, since the sensible worlds of the arts were first recognized as man-made. By rendering perceptible images into conceptual ideas, art lent the interaction between the two a kind of saliency lacking in other domains.

41. A phrase often employed by Ernst Cassirer, who maintained that the artist is as much a discoverer of the forms of nature as is the scientist a discoverer of facts or natural laws. Accordingly, art is expressive, but it cannot be expressive without being formative. And this formative process is carried out in certain sensuous media. See "Art" in his *An Essay on Man: An Introduction to a Philosophy of Human Culture* (New York, 1954), 176–217. For an exciting and illuminating acquaintance with his philosophy of symbolic forms, consult Cassirer's three volumes bearing this name (New Haven, 1955).

42. On the relation between opera and archetypal symbols, see Robert Donington, *Opera and Its Symbols: The Unity of Words, Music, and Staging* (New Haven, 1990).

DEMYSTIFYING AN ELUSIVE AGENDA

It has been suggested that the crystallization of problems and their solutions in art is analogous to the development of a "paradigm" in science.[43] And as E. H. Gombrich and others have suggested, style represents a kind of collective problem-solving by a group of artists.[44] In turn, such agreed-on solutions, or styles, are inherent, as Diana Crane suggests (see note 43), in "invisible colleges," that is, in social circles of colleagues whose informal networks of communication nurture the paradigm and fructify it. The sociology of art, Crane tells us, "requires an analysis of the developments of belief systems of such groups as well as sociometric analysis of the relations between their members, of the relations between such groups, and of the relationships of such groups to the larger social structure."[45] In the parlance of the sociology of science, the camerata fits rather closely the model of an "invisible college."

Of course, the idea of salons, the coffeehouse, or the café as a breeding place of artistic creativity is nothing new in the history of art or intellectual history generally. Indeed, the centrality of such meeting places for the exchange of views has often been noted.[46] Moreover, the weaving of bonds of mutual support among artists, of liaisons between artists and dealers, and the forging of common understandings between artists and critics has often been both the cause and consequence of sitting together. However, the idea that social circles of this kind—brought together through mutual interest—should share a common puzzle, which all are trying to solve,

---

43. The term 'paradigm' is used here with the full awareness of the ambiguities that have accompanied its widespread use. Indeed, Thomas Kuhn himself has discerned several different meanings attributable to the concept, electing to emphasize shared puzzle-solving techniques as the most useful definition. Others have used the concept to refer to a new way of seeing things, a "cognitive event," or to "a series of related assumptions—theoretical, methodological and empirical—which are generally accepted by those working in a particular area." See M. K. Mulkay, *The Social Process in Innovation* (London, 1972), 31–32. Whatever the uses, they all fit the subject treated here, especially the suggestion to view creativity in art as analogous to creativity in science. See Thomas S. Kuhn, *The Structure of Scientific Revolution* (Chicago, 1970), 161, and Diana Crane, *Invisible College: Diffusion of Knowledge in Scientific Communities* (Chicago, 1972), 29.

44. See E. H. Gombrich, "The Renaissance Conception of Artistic Progress and Its Consequences," in his *Norm and Form* (London, 1985), 1–10.

45. Crane, *Invisible College,* 131.

46. To mention but a few, see L. Coser, *Men of Ideas* (New York, 1965); Arnold Hauser, *The Social History of Art* (London, 1951); Bernard Rosenberg and Norris Fliegel, *The Vanguard Artist* (Chicago, 1965); Harrison White and Cynthia White, *Canvases and Careers* (New York, 1965); Arthur Loesser, *Men, Women, and Pianos* (New York, 1954).

came to the sociology of science only much later, and, as a result, to the sociology of art. Here one has only to think of a group such as the impressionists to realize that they were coping—as an "invisible college"—with a puzzle that each, separately and together, was trying to solve.

The Camerata: Custodian of a Paradigm

Gombrich notes how in the Renaissance new pieces of art came to be viewed as "contributions" and as "solutions" to problems, thus implying another analogy between work in the arts and the new arena of experimental science.[47] Indeed, as Crane notes in this connection, "similarity between this [Gombrich's] concept and Kuhn's idea of paradigm is startling."[48] In this sense, as already noted, the camerata's puzzle was to discover the ideal combination of words and music such that the two, each in its own way and in juxtaposition to each other, could be maximally effective in communicating not just sensory pleasure but also the specific meaning and emotions appropriate to the text. Reading the theoretical writings of members of the camerata, their letters and the introductions to their compositions,[49] one cannot but be struck over and over again by the attempt to solve this problem. No matter that they did not know exactly how the Greeks had done it (if they had); that was all the more reason to return again and again to the inadequacy of contemporary music, and to try yet another time to achieve the formula that would "move" the understanding.

It by no means detracts from the camerata's attempt to "solve a problem" to relate that the group was split in several ways: Jacopo Corsi and Giovanni de' Bardi, in whose homes the members convened, had their dif-

---

47. Gombrich, "The Renaissance Conception of Artistic Progress," 8–9.

48. Crane, *Invisible College,* 134.

49. Most of this material came to light due to the diligent and insightful work of Claude V. Palisca. See, for example, his "Musical Asides in the Diplomatic Correspondence of Emilio de' Cavalieri," in *Musical Quarterly* 44, no. 3 (1972); "The Camerata Fiorentina: A Reappraisal," in *Studi musicali* 1 (1972); "Scientific Empiricism in Musical Thought," in *Seventeenth Century Science* (Princeton, 1961); *Mei's Letters on Ancient and Modern Music to Vincenzo and Giovanni Bardi* (Rome, 1960); "Vincenzo Galilei and Some Links between 'Pseudo-Monody' and Monody," in *Musical Quarterly* 46 (1960); "Vincenzo Galilei's Counterpoint Treatise: A Code for the Seconda Pratica," *Journal of the American Musicological Society* 9 (1956). Also see Nino Pirrotta, "Temperaments and Tendencies in the Florentine Camerata," in *Musical Quarterly* 40 (1954). Oliver Strunk's *Source Reading* contains relevant materials (dedications and forewords) in section 8, "'Seconda Pratica' and 'Stile Rappresentativo.'"

ferences over the kudos of sponsorship and the character of group activities, with Corsi tending to be more interested in actual experiments with
the role of music in drama and Bardi, perhaps, more interested in theorizing. Peri and Caccini—both singers—accepted that their main goal was to
enhance communication through singing, yet Peri sought to bring singing nearer to speech, allowing the text and the action to dictate to the
music (Pirrotta calls this *recitar cantando*), while Caccini, more concerned
with the perfection of singers and the art of singing, was committed to
"affective reactions to dramatic situations," to words finding expression
in the music (Pirrotta calls this *cantar recitando*).[50] Their differences, thus,
provide a nice illustration of the "working out" of a paradigm. Outsiders,
says Pirrotta, would be impressed by the similarities rather than the differences. This, he adds, could only have been the product of their joint mem-
bership in the salon, where shared concepts arose from theorizing and so-
cializing.[51] Claude Palisca also remarks on the criticism of colleagues from
which members of the salon could benefit[52]—much like the "refereeing"
or "discussant" functions in scientific institutions.

Even the competition over "priorities" is reminiscent of the behavior
of scientists. The race to be first has to be reconciled in science with the
need and the norm of sharing. The scientists' role is above all to advance
knowledge, and knowledge advances through originality. "Recognition
and esteem," explains Robert Merton, "accrue to those who have best fulfilled their roles, to those who have made genuinely original contributions
to the common stock of knowledge. Then are found those happy circumstances in which self-interest and moral obligation coincide and fuse."[53]
Merton goes on to explain that the frequency of struggles over priority
does not result from the traits of the individuals involved but rather from
the institution of science,

> which defines originality as a supreme value and thereby makes recog-
> nition of one's originality a major concern. When this recognition of
> priority is either not granted or fades from view, the scientist loses his
> scientific property. Although this kind of property shares with other
> types general recognition of 'owner's' right, it contrasts sharply in all

50. See Nino Pirrotta, "Early Opera and Aria," in *New Looks at Italian Opera,* ed. William W. Austin (Ithaca, 1968), 52.

51. Ibid., 45.

52. See Palisca, "The Alterati of Florence, in the Theory of Dramatic Music," in *New
Looks at Italian Opera* (Ithaca, 1968), 22.

53. Robert K. Merton, *The Sociology of Science* (Chicago, 1973), 293.

other respects. Once he has made his contribution, the scientist no longer has exclusive rights of access to it. It becomes part of the public domain of science. . . . In short, property rights in science become whittled down to just this one: the recognition by others of the scientist's distinctive part in having brought the result into being. [54]

The behavior and rhetoric of Caccini, Peri, and Cavalieri is relevant in this respect, for they expressly fought over "priority rights." Pirrotta, interestingly, proposes three reasons why these men fought over "priorities," though the reasons are not mutually exclusive. One possibility is that they really believed they were in a race; a second possibility, which does not contradict the first, is that they failed to appreciate the differences in the kinds of experiments they were conducting; and, finally, they may each have experienced the fear of being overshadowed.[55] Attention should be drawn, however, to the fact that the conflict centered over priority rights with regard to a new *style*. Unlike individual compositions, style is a contribution to which the composer may cease to have "recognition of the 'owner's' right." As in science, property rights with regard to style are limited to the mere recognition by others of the composer's "distinctive part in having brought the result into being." The increased awareness with regard to musical styles in the early baroque may be explained, in part, by the tangible spirit of the scientific revolution.

In fact, the single-minded preoccupation with overthrowing the existing polyphonic paradigm and replacing it with expressive music—of a kind that would both carry the words and express the implicit intent of the text—ushered in the so-called *seconda pratica*.[56] The *seconda pratica* not only endorsed the novel style of monody but licensed as well the novel harmonic practice (exercised by the most distinguished composers of the day, including Monteverdi), as opposed to the established polyphonic tra-

54. Ibid., 294.
55. See Pirrotta, "Early Opera," 45.
56. Claudio Monteverdi, in the preface to book V of his Madrigals (1605), said that he adopted "*seconda pratica*" (referring to the "modern" style of music), claiming that it makes the words the "mistress" of music, rather than the other way round. 'Who' serves 'whom,' and in what fashion, is an issue that will continue to occupy, as is well known, subsequent generations. Monteverdi's assertion appeared in his extended retort to Giovanni Maria Artusi (a conservative theorist of the time), who criticized the innovations that had been introduced into polyphonic music by the greatest composers of the time. For the most recent analysis of the dialogue between Artusi and Monteverdi, see Massimo Ossi's *Divining the Oracle: Monteverdi's Seconda Pratica* (Chicago, 2003), 27–57.

FIGURE 2. A portrait of Monteverdi by Bernardo Strozzi (1581–1649).

dition of the *prima pratica* of the sixteenth century. "The second practice," says Berger, "differed primarily in its treatment of dissonance, introducing and resolving them in ways that Zarlino's rules of strict usage prohibited. The core of *seconda pratica* consisted in a relaxation of these rules, a relaxation understood not as an abortion whereby the rules were simply pushed aside as irrelevant, but as the introduction of licenses the expressive effect of which could be felt only against the remembered background of the strict usage." The *seconda pratica*, concludes Berger, "conceived of dissonance not as a threat to 'harmony,' a threat which had to be strictly controlled and subordinated to consonances, but rather as an independent expressive means, and expressive at least in part precisely because licentious."[57] In this novel style, words clearly assumed a new ranking—a less definitive one—and, as a result, the search for the "proper" wedding of words and music ensued. Although the text was accorded a significant role in the rhetoric of the time, it is the query about *how* music should be "grafted" to the text that led to a renewed interest in the "power of music." The purpose of music was now to "move" human affections. On these very grounds, Leo Schrade tells us, "modern time, which starts with the baroque, and old music, which ends with Palestrina, part company forever."[58] Of no less interest is his following assertion:

> For the sake of *ariosi spectacoli,* a term which ambiguously moves
> between 'airy' spectacles and spectacles of 'arias,' the composers,
> beginning with Monteverdi himself, strained all their efforts to build
> up a musical rhetoric expressive of passion, and carried the *stile concer-*
> *tante,* the style of competitive implements, to its widest range and to
> perfection. Now, the arias of passionate emotions—of jealousy,
> wrath . . . love . . . lament . . . misery and pain . . .—were all subject
> to the standards of style, with the structure and figurative materials
> establishing the scope of expression. And when the arias followed each
> other, driven by Amor, the mover of action, they came in succession as
> image followed image, truly ariosi spectacoli, and the whole was noth-
> ing less than a war of antagonistic forces, with the stile concertante
> being the most faithful interpreter of conflicting passion.[59]

Indeed, the idea that art resides in its making gained momentum in the course of the seventeenth century;[60] expressiveness and affect pervaded

57. See Berger, *Theory of Art,* 126.

58. See Leo Schrade, *Tragedy in the Art of Music* (Cambridge, 1964), 99.

59. Ibid., 67–68.

60. No composer illustrates this point better than Monteverdi, who in the course of a few decades "divined" the powers of music to such an extent that future generations saw fit to credit him as the true initiator of opera. Under the title "Opera from Monteverdi to Monteverdi," Taruskin traces step by step Monteverdi's contributions for the stage, which commenced in a courtly environment and culminated in a commercial "public space." He reminds us, however, that by the time Monteverdi composed his *Orfeo* (1607) for the Mantuan nobles, he had already made his mark as a distinguished composer for a quarter of a century, and that in the capacity of chief cathedral musician in Venice (a position he held for more than thirty years) he had attained the kind of prestige he could hardly have gained at court, although he did not publish the service music he wrote until

not only music but art in general, redefining the relations between Nature and the Arts. In the wake of the "new science," ushered in by the scientific revolution, the relation between the innate and the habitual was, likewise, assiduously reexamined; in fact, with the rise of 'perception' as an important subject for investigation, all of these reassessments, jointly, led (toward the end of the eighteenth century) to the inclusion of aesthetics (as a special branch of critical philosophy) in the Greek division of philosophy into physics, ethics, and logic. By then, however, a philosophy of culture, allied with a better understanding of the functions rendered by signs and symbols, was well on its way. Though entrenched beliefs still awaited clarifications, and newly emerging aspirations continued to elicit new frames of thought, the "conceit of the soul" was replaced, nonetheless, by the delineation of cognitive processes that gave substance to the elusive agenda of the camerata, namely, "to move the passion of *the mind*" (my italics), to quote Caccini.[61]

Much had to happen, however, before it became possible to conceive of

---

after he retired. He continued nonetheless to publish madrigals and set epic poems to music, increasingly employing a more lavish instrumentation while developing new musical strategies and techniques. Taruskin persuasively reveals how Monteverdi's musical innovations turned the textual narratives into "dramatic representations." Monteverdi, he tells us, created thereby a set of conventions "representing emotion in the musical theater," which acquired their meaning by "mere agreement among composers and listeners" that would remain standard "for the rest of the century and a good deal beyond." Taruskin, however, also enlightens us about the "routes" via which agreements of this kind are arrived at. Indeed, though mostly influenced by music, composers are also influenced by "larger societal forces." Taruskin, accordingly, delineates the nature of the music and its relationship to its audience—teaching us about the "politics" that affected its development, and the "politics" that influenced its retrospective portrayals—via his own insightful "representation of reality." See Taruskin, *Oxford History of Western Music,* vol. 2, chap. 20, 1–34. Also see Richard Carlton, "Florentine Humanism and the Birth of Opera: The Roots of Operatic 'Conventions,'" International Review of the Aesthetics and Sociology of Music 31 (2000): 67–78.

61. See the foreword to his *Le nuove musiche* (1602), in Strunk, *Source Readings in Music History,* 379. Giulio Caccini (ca. 1546–1618) was one of the most important members of the camerata. Whereas Galilei was of the opinion that solo melody should merely enhance the natural speech inflections of a good orator, Caccini (who was a singer) developed a style of song that admitted certain embellishments of the melodic line at appropriate places. The earliest surviving compositions in this style are the songs he wrote a dozen years before they were actually published (1602) under the above title, stressing their novelty. In 1600 Caccini and Peri (another singer and member of the group) jointly set to music Rinuccini's *Euridice,* based on the well-known myth of Orpheus and Euridice. Each composer published subsequently a version of his own. These two works constitute the earliest surviving complete operas.

the mind as operating symbolically, transforming sensations into a world of meanings in search of coherence and "truthfulness." And it took even more time before it became possible to realize that it is not the human mind that changes but the cultural artifacts, which are the *creation* of human consciousness. Those familiar with Giambattista Vico's *Scienza nuova* (1733) will have recognized, no doubt, the source of the last two sentences. Although more will be said later about the perspective gained through Vico's anthropological historicism, it should be pointed out that not until the twentieth century, with its own preoccupation with the mind, was its significance fully recognized. Vico's boldest contribution, Isaiah Berlin teaches, resided in the notion that there can be "a science of mind which is the history of its development, the realization that ideas evolve, that knowledge is not a static network of eternal, universal, clear truth, either Platonic or Cartesian, but social process, that this process is traceable through (indeed, is in a sense identical with) the evolution of symbols—words, gestures, and their altering patterns, functions, structures, and uses."[62]

Leading Conceptual Turning Points

It all began in the late Renaissance with the attempt to render art more expressive.[63] In music, as we have seen, this involved the quest for the lost formulae of the Greeks who allegedly knew how to use music to heighten the power of words. Whether they were real or feigned cultural archaeologists, those engaged in the quest identified new declamatory forms for effective song speech, from which dramatic music and related forms have emerged. This, of course, was not rediscovery, but invention, from which a semantic of musical expression gradually sprouted. The systematic marriage of words and music branded music with meaning, while music endowed words with affective specificity. This had consequences as well for "pure" instrumental music. The acquisition of meaning in music might have never taken place, however, if it were not for a change in the overall conception of art, brought about in the course of the Renaissance, that gave rise to a newly perceived common denominator of the different arts, that of "creativity."

62. See Isaiah Berlin, *Against the Current: Essays in the History of Ideas* (Oxford, 1981), 113.

63. The following discussion is based on my study (together with Ruth HaCohen) regarding the pre-figuration of the cognitive turn by the arts, in which music played a dominant role. For the historical unfolding and a detailed analysis of the processes that led to the re-conceptualization of the arts, see Ruth Katz and Ruth HaCohen, *Tuning the Mind: Connecting Aesthetics to Cognitive Science* (New Brunswick, New Jersey, 2002).

A Fundamental Change in the Conception of Art

The history of Western art reveals that painting was central to the move from the conception of art as 'techne' to a conception of art that emphasized *creativity* as a common denominator of the different arts. From the history of the visual arts we learn that in the course of the Renaissance artists were more and more expected to render reality as *if* it were taking place before their eyes, eternalizing, as it were, the fleeting moment.[64] From this point on, the role of true art, we are told, was no longer to imitate nature as such, that is, to produce appearances in the Platonic sense, but to present nature as *perceived* by the artist. Naturally, shifts of this kind do not take place in a "vacuum"; they are determined by circumstances, resulting from historical processes—social, political, and cultural—that lead up to them. Given the self-imposed limits of this essay to the conceptual development of music in the West, I shall resist the temptation of probing the social-historical circumstances that provided the impetus for this unique course. I shall note only that the epistemological implications of so decisive a shift in the conception of art were not fully grasped until the eighteenth century. By then, however, Nature was no longer perceived as explaining, or dictating, our understanding and construction of art. The latter entailed a thorough grasp of signs—cultural rather than natural ones—as cognitive tools.

Signs as Cognitive Tools

The development of modes of signification in Western music involved semiotic procedures familiar to us from other communicative systems. Powerful tropes such as metaphor, for example, were configured musically, and syntactic structures and narrative frames became tonally encoded. The cohesion of these schemes and procedures happened at an illusory level, revealing their efficacy in the fictive world that they fabricated. To accomplish a verisimilitude of this kind required, to begin with, a thorough investigation of signs, so as to unveil the mental processes that they instigate in the making of culture.

Unlike most ancient cultures, which saw signs as belonging to a supernatural order, the Greeks were of the opinion that signs could be defined. 'Idea,' they maintained, is located in the mind, whereas 'object' is in the world of *realia*. Idea and object, they postulated, are connected via 'form,' which is reflected in the mind. The "theory of forms," whether Platonic or Aristotelian, permeated Western philosophical thought. Yet occult tradi-

---

64. See Gombrich, *Art and Illusion*, 107–13.

tions kept insisting on the "magical" power of signs, employing symbolic devices of all kinds, understandable mainly to the initiated. This "circular" understanding, however, led in due course to a recognition of the artificiality involved. Nonetheless, attempts to explicate the power of symbols in the creation of worlds of knowledge continued to flourish, though increasingly in a demystified fashion.[65] The tendency to demystify symbols spilled over into philosophical deliberations that tried to cope with their epistemological implications, inviting a "new look" at the dichotomous notion of 'idea' and 'object.'

For Descartes, as we have seen, essences were no longer forms perceived but proportions conceived, establishing mathematics as the core of epistemology. Reality was thus split into two kinds of qualities, a primary and a secondary one; whereas the first was conceived as the product of rational deliberations, hence clear and distinct, the secondary was conceived as the sensual effects of the primary, hence clear and confused. The mind was thus viewed as a bundle of faculties, implying that sensual ideas could be formed even in the absence of external objects. Though primary and secondary qualities became an underlying premise for most of the believers in the new science who did not expect God to guarantee their epistemology (as we have witnessed in the case of Mersenne), mathematics provided only a methodological tool, formulating partial and subjective findings.[66]

Claiming that epistemological considerations start from secondary qualities, John Locke suggested that the mind itself works in that order, arriving at primary qualities through inferences. Locke thus conceived 'idea' as the representation and the perceptual act intertwined. Perceptions, he thought, are impressed on the mind's tabula rasa, becoming "the object of the understanding of a man thinking."[67] In the cognitive process, he assumed, developmental stages played a major role, thus turning the mind itself into an object of introspection. Language, according to Locke, is a mirror of a natural, primitive, yet reasonable mind, itself reflecting a reality rationally constituted. Free associations and imaginative deviations seemed erroneous to Locke, since impressions become ideas only through their conscious isolation. What is learned is thus explicitly known, acquired through processes of which the mind is aware. Reflection, hence, consists of the mind's ability to trace its own activities and operations.

65. For an interesting discussion of the "naturalization" of wonders, see Lorraine Daston and Katharine Park, *Wonders and the Order of Nature* (New York, 1998).

66. See Cassirer, *The Philosophy of the Enlightenment* (Princeton, 1951), 96–7.

67. Locke: *An Essay Concerning Human Understanding* [1690] (London, 1961), introduction, 8; as quoted by John W. Yolton, *Locke—An Introduction* (Oxford, 1985).

Ironically, it was Gottfried Wilhelm Leibniz, the rationalist, who entertained the thought that perceptions are neither logical nor distinct. He attributed the blur and confusion that he observed in perception to a "lower" cognitive faculty; and relegated those unconscious calculations that Locke rejected to a transitional phase that leads from unlogicized to logicized constructions of thought. Yet it was the "higher cognitive faculty" to which Leibniz paid his main attention. Believing in a preestablished harmony between mind and reality, he endowed the mind with the power to sift all kinds of components of thought in order to further their skillful manipulation. No wonder that Leibniz came to realize that the nature of such mental components is symbolic. The cognitive efficacy of signs, concluded Leibniz, is due to their ability to lead us into "the interior of things." Assisted by signs, he tells us, ideas may be resolved into those components of which they are composed. In other words, signs function as reasoning focal points; they set up, as it were, syntactical structures that are open to re-development. Through signs, guaranteed by logical and scientific reasoning, Leibniz maintained that the mind is free to create its own possible worlds, independent of ontological constraints.

As far reaching as this idea was for future developments, it only dealt with signs of a purely conceptual nature. Envisaging a language that would not only function in accordance with such a conceptual scheme but would also encourage thought and creativity, Leibniz, like Mersenne, enlisted music for that purpose. And like Mersenne, confusing the conceptual with the perceptual and the emotional, he expected a properly conceived music to evolve into "moving" songs, believing, in a true Platonic spirit, that the Beautiful, the True, and the Good are but different aspects of one perfect order.

Moral Philosophy and Its "Affair" with 'Beauty'

The acknowledgment of the sensual traces in the most abstract intellectual activities contributed to an awareness of the concrete aspects that symbols entail. Whereas Locke's theory of mind centered primarily on propositional thought, Leibniz's philosophy led back to symbolic systems, the nature of which are less clear and concrete. It is no coincidence therefore that Leibniz should have found interest in an English contemporary—the Earl of Shaftesbury.[68] The point of departure for both Shaftes-

68. The third Earl of Shaftsbury (1671–1713) was an enthusiast in the cause of virtue. The topics that most interested him were philosophy, politics, morals, and religion. During his extended travels he came in close contact with artistic and philosophical associations that exercised a marked influence on his thought. His profound classical education, however, he owed to Locke, who was entrusted with overseeing his early education.

bury and Leibniz was the harmony of the plenum, which found new expression through science. Thus, Leibniz tried to find a mathematical equivalent in this *"Reimung der Dichtung"* by means of his infinite calculus, while Shaftesbury was after the secrets of its 'beauty.' Drawing as they both did on Platonic sources, Leibniz's orientation was, in the main, Pythagorean, whereas Shaftesbury's was, in the main, Plotinian. The old identity of truth, beauty, and the good occupied Shaftesbury in his attempt to find a solution to the problem of the truth-value of sensation.

All beauty, Shaftesbury believed, springs from truth, but the full, concrete meaning of truth can be revealed only in beauty. Shaftesbury's concern was with intuitive, rather than theoretical, knowledge, which reveals itself primarily in the creative act by applying the knowledge that God entertained in the act of creation. One may thus discover all-inclusive truth through artistic acts, and the artist, moreover, may explore "possible worlds" hitherto unknown. The organic units created by art parallel nature itself, which art conveys through its designs, independent of verbal descriptions. Note that it is the work of art as a *whole* that carries so exalted a symbolic function. Unlike ordinary symbols, which carry distinct meanings that can be traced and stated, the work of art as a whole implies, rather than states; it signifies rather than indicates; in short, it creates an 'import,' to borrow a term used by Susanne Langer to express a similar idea.[69]

Shaftesbury, it must be remembered, was an enthusiast in the cause of virtue. He tried to assail the irreconcilable antagonism between social duty and self-love (so central to Hobbes's social theory) by exhibiting the *naturalness* of man's social affections, demonstrating the normal harmony between these and his self-regarding impulses.[70] Since man, by definition,

69. See Langer, "The Art Symbol and the Symbol in Art," in *Problems of Art* (New York, 1957).

70. In his impressive inquiry into the sources of modern selfhood, Charles Taylor naturally also deals with the development of moral sentiments. As an outstanding expert in moral philosophy, he grants Shaftesbury a significant role in having inspired moral sense theories. Shaftesbury, Taylor tells us, argued that "the highest good for humans is to love and take joy in the whole course of the world. Someone who achieves this love reaches a perfect tranquility and equanimity; he is proof against all the buffetings of adverse fortune; and above all, he can love those around him constantly and steadily, un-diverted by his own pain and disappointments, or his own partial interest. . . . Moreover, this love carries itself the greatest intrinsic satisfaction. Since by nature we love the ordered and beautiful, the highest and most complete order and beauty is an object of greatest joy." Taylor also calls to our attention that Shaftesbury refers again and again to music, architecture, and painting to establish that "the rule of harmony" is not a matter of "caprice or will," but rather conveys the artist's inward character—"the harmony and numbers of

must be considered part of a larger system, his impulses and dispositions are so balanced as to tend toward the good of the whole. Thus moral goodness in "sensible creatures" consists in a certain harmony of self-regarding and social affections. The pleasure one takes in goodness is due to what he calls the moral sense. As it turned out, Shaftesbury's theories provided a major turning point in ethical thought, whereby the introspective study of the human mind—observations of its impulses and sentiments—replaced the considerations of abstract rational principles.

It is, of course, the close parallel he drew between the moral and the aesthetic that interests us. Although Shaftesbury enlisted the faculty that apprehends beauty in the sphere of art in order to exemplify the workings of the faculty that determines the value of human actions, it is through his explication of the moral sense that we gain insight into his aesthetic theory. Both faculties are primarily emotional and nonreflective, though in the process of development they become rationalized by education and use. Yet the harmonious in art stands apart from external dictates, as morality does from theology. Mental dictates are the incentive of beauty just as the voice of conscience is the incentive of morality. Both reside in the mind, which aims at perfect harmony for its own sake. Guided by internal notions of harmony, the artist may be viewed as a "maker" of coherent wholes, in which the constituent parts are subjugated to that which is "proportioned in itself"—the work of art.

The influence of Shaftesbury's theories in the fields of ethics and aesthetics was considerable; it embraced also many of those who wished to better understand the relationship between 'man' and 'culture' (with or without a capital C).[71] For those who tried to bridge the sensual, psychological substratum of man and the sense-making, conceptual layer of culture, there was much in Shaftesbury's writings that could lend assistance and offer support.[72]

---

the heart and beauty of the affections." Shaftesbury's "subjectivization of a teleological ethic of nature" and his "transformation of an ethic of order, harmony, and equilibrium into an ethic of benevolence," Taylor tells us, are what inspired moral sense theories. See Charles Taylor, *Sources of the Self: The Making of the Modern Identity* (Cambridge, Mass., 1989), 251–55. To fully appreciate the role that the preoccupation with "moral sentiments" played in the development of modern identity, one should read chapters 15–17 in their entirety, since they deal not only with moral philosophy but also with the role of "sentiments" in the culture of modernity.

71. The list includes—to mention but a few—Francis Hutcheson, Hume, and Joseph Butler in England; Voltaire, Diderot, and Montesquieu in France; Gotthold Ephraim Lessing, Moses Mendelssohn, and Johann Gottfried von Herder in Germany.

72. For the influence he exerted on a particular group of his fellow countrymen—an

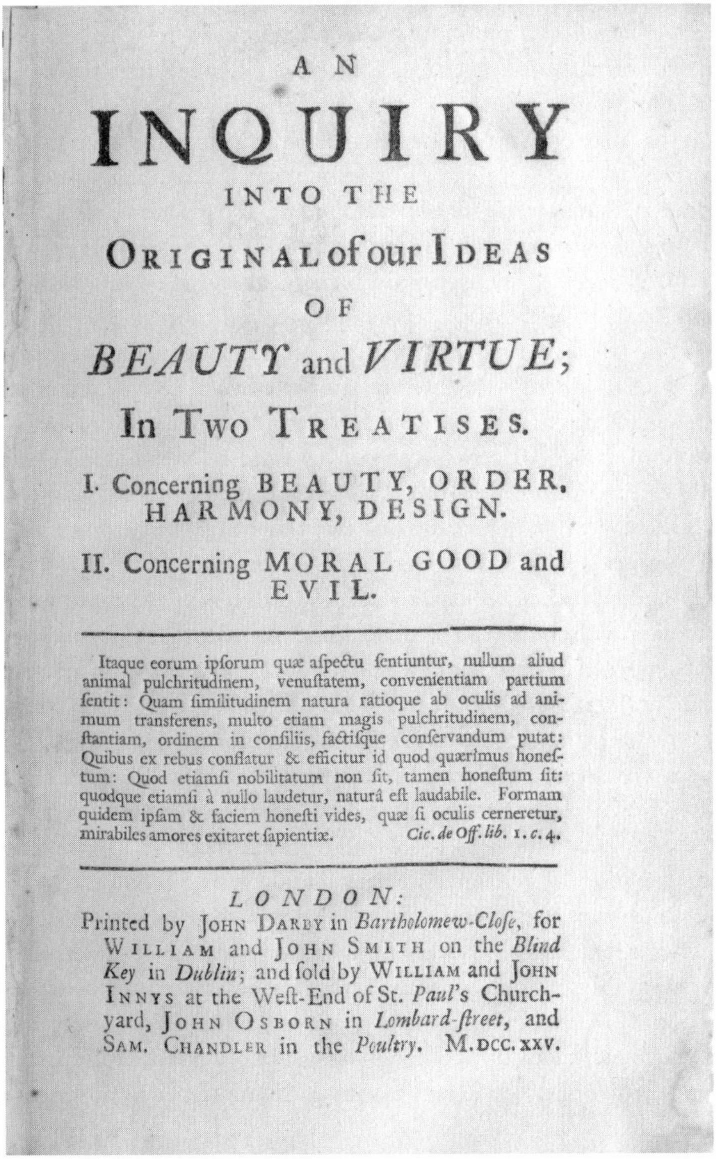

A N
INQUIRY

INTO THE

ORIGINAL of our IDEAS

OF

BEAUTY and *VIRTUE*;

In TWO TREATISES.

I. Concerning BEAUTY, ORDER, HARMONY, DESIGN.

II. Concerning MORAL GOOD and EVIL.

Itaque eorum ipforum quæ afpectu fentiuntur, nullum aliud animal pulchritudinem, venuftatem, convenientiam partium fentit: Quam fimilitudinem natura ratioque ab oculis ad animum transferens, multo etiam magis pulchritudinem, conftantiam, ordinem in confiliis, factifque confervandum putat: Quibus ex rebus conflatur & efficitur id quod quærimus honeftum: Quod etiamfi nobilitatum non fit, tamen honeftum fit: quodque etiamfi à nullo laudetur, naturâ eft laudabile. Formam quidem ipfam & faciem honefti vides, quæ fi oculis cerneretur, mirabiles amores exitaret fapientiæ.   *Cic. de Off. lib.* 1. *c.* 4.

LONDON:

Printed by JOHN DARBY in *Bartholomew-Clofe*, for WILLIAM and JOHN SMITH on the *Blind Key* in *Dublin*; and fold by WILLIAM and JOHN INNYS at the Weft-End of St. *Paul's* Church-yard, JOHN OSBORN in *Lombard-ftreet*, and SAM. CHANDLER in the *Poultry*. M.DCC.XXV.

FIGURE 3. Francis Hutcheson (1694–1747), like the Earl of Shaftesbury, may be regarded as one of the earliest modern writers on aesthetics. His importance, however, is due to his contribution to the field of ethics. For Hutcheson, as for Shaftesbury, the test of virtuous action lies in its tendency to promote the general welfare of society. Their moral philosophy rested on the analogy between beauty and virtue, implying that man is endowed with a special sense by which he perceives beauty.

Modes of Communication and Cognitive Expansions

In his treatment of language, Shaftesbury implied that the development of mankind can be traced through the various modes of communication that man employed. The ostensible dichotomy between the "non-reflective" and the "rationalized" can be placed, accordingly, on a single continuum, that of man's social development. What was merely intimated by Shaftesbury became fully explicated by others, albeit in diverse ways.

In his attempt to demystify both the Old and the New Testament, Bishop William Warburton, for example, related the stages in the development of writing to types of discourse:[73] pictures, he maintained, employ a "language of action"—gesture and movement—to convey directly that which one intends to express; hieroglyphs employ a "language of similes"—a variety of analogous means—to convey what is intended; an alphabet employs a "metaphorical language"—conventional abstract signs—to convey abstract ideas. Whereas the first two stages relate signs to things, the third commences with signs referring to whole words and ends with signs indicating single sounds. Given these basic differences, Warburton argued that modes of discourse can be understood only within the cognitive constraints imposed by the stage to which they belong. While each of these developmental stages replaced its predecessor, the various types of language, insisted Warburton, were preserved in the later forms of speech.[74]

Suggestive as it was, Warburton's theory failed to account for the process involved in passing from one stage to another; namely, the transition from the sensual to the perceptual, and from the perceptual to the linguistic and the rational, remained unclear. Thinkers who followed Descartes and Leibniz were not interested in the relationship between images and hieroglyphs, but in the way they function in processes of understanding. David Hume, for example, postulated that images constitute the representative aspect of symbols that make possible the mind's reasoning, as well as its imaginative activation. Though images in our minds are of particular objects, their application in our reasoning, Hume argued, is no longer that

---

"invisible college" that pioneered in relegating aesthetic criteria to the mind, while maintaining their sensual foundation and unique manifestations in the different arts—see Katz and HaCohen, *Tuning the Mind,* vol. 2, *The Arts in Mind.*

73. See William Warburton, *The Divine Legation of Moses Demonstrated from the Principles of a Deist,* in 2 vols. (London, 1738, 1741). Warburton's treatise was translated into French as early as 1744 and later also into German.

74. For the influence Warburton exerted on poetics and poetic practice, see Kevin Barry, *Language, Music and the Sign: A Study in Aesthetics, Poetics and Poetic Practice* (Cambridge, 1987).

of particulars. A particular idea becomes general due to a customary conjunction related to many other particular ideas, and readily recalls them in our imagination. Thus, though they are less lively than immediate impressions, ideas are of a more lasting nature and may be redirected toward associations, which are the mind's imaginative production.[75]

By claiming that all complex ideas relate to the mind's basic modes of association (similarity, causality, space, and time), rather than to a reality out there, Hume "de-rationalized" Locke's "copy theory" of ideas and deepened the gulf between reality and the mind. Hume relegated the combinatorial power of the mind to that which Alexander Baumgarten called the "lower cognitive faculty," though he himself did not believe in a faculty that stood above these modes of thought. Based as scientific thought is on causal relations, it, too, apparently rests on customary links that prove efficacious. Science and art thus share a common epistemological ground, though a different one from that held by seventeenth-century thinkers. Yet, while Hume's conception of the mind is markedly different from that of Leibniz, they share a profound recognition of the autonomy of the mind and its constructive powers.

Perhaps the most important contribution to the understanding of the cognitive nature of signs was that of Etienne Bonnot de Condillac,[76] whose main thrust was to show that it is only through utilizing signs that the mind learns to control thinking, even in its most primordial stages. His theory entails stages of development in which each stage is determined by a preceding one, but its realization is not ensured thereby. The mind's initial 'perception' of sense data, according to Condillac, first leads to consciousness — a mere awareness. The mind then learns to concentrate on certain such perceptions through 'attention.' Directed by wants and desires, this development leads to 'reminiscence' — the recognition that certain perceptions did occur. Four different cognitive stages are thus needed — commencing with 'perception' and terminating with 'reminiscence' — for the mind to become fully aware of what it perceived. By rendering consciousness as part and parcel of cognitive growth, Condillac, in fact, provided a bridge between Locke's conscious mental activities and Leibniz's unconscious processes: the mind, according to Condillac, activates 'imagination,' reviving images through recollection only when needed or when

75. For his detailed explication of the subject, see David Hume, *A Treatise of Human Nature* (London, 1739).

76. Etienne Bonnot de Condillac wrote his *Essai sur l'origine des connaissances humaines* (Paris, 1756) as "A Supplement to Locke's Essay on Human Understanding."

demands arise for doing so. In 'contemplation' awareness is enlarged so as to include what has vanished out of sight, that is, the whole context in which it appeared. This complex image connects with similar images through a *"laison des idées."* While the first four stages consist in the ability to individuate perceptual units by keeping them in mind, it is only in this fifth stage that the separate units connect with other such units to create a new reality. The power of signs manifests itself through their *use,* for it is through their use that mere consciousness turns into meaningful reflection, a state in which the mind is in command of itself.

Social Interaction as a Regulating Force

The formation of a systematic language requires, however, more than signs that evolve naturally from associations with specific objects. Modes of communication, Condillac postulated, must have derived from human interaction that entailed compassion no less than desire. Although the initial phase of interaction, he presumed, employed a "language of action" composed of gestural signs (motions, ejaculations, or combinations thereof, depicting behavior), these must have increasingly incorporated "modes of information" (assertions, interrogations, and the like), so that over a span of time "specific gestures" or "cries" came to be associated as well with particular causes of concern or contentment. Note that it is passion *and* sympathy that transform the natural into a social phenomenon, in which passion may turn from cause to referent with its own characteristic signs. It is this kind of differentiated sign, interacting with other such signs, that enabled the development of a linguistic system, according to Condillac. In discussing Condillac, we should not lose sight of the fact that by identifying gestures with mimicry, sound, and intonation, Condillac emphasized their *iconic* character. He insisted that gestures, though unanalyzable in terms of their constituent parts, constitute complete utterances—a basic condition of language—despite the fact that they do not derive from outer perceptions. However, since language also includes contextual surroundings that render perception persuasive, "languages of action" had to be "decomposed" and the relations among the resulting components conceptualized through syntaxes of various sorts in order to achieve linguistic systems. Signs once institutionalized into systems, Condillac tells us, permit not only economy, variety, and subtlety but also allow for the formation of new combinations of ideas, furthering our knowledge of the world. In sum, civilization begins once the natural is socialized, once the accidental and expressive are institutionalized.

Institutionalizing signs eventuates, nonetheless, in some cognitive loss.

Compared to "languages of action," linguistic systems seem to perform less well, certainly less succinctly, in communicating emotional states. Believing that the arts continued, as a rule, to employ "languages of action," Condillac turned to music, hoping to trace the early stages of language through the emotional powers ascribed to music. Since there exist at all times messages in which neither the sign nor the signified is clearly defined, music, maintained Condillac, joined expression and communication together from the start; music, in other words, functioned metaphorically from its very inception, for rhetoric was embedded in it as an integral part. No wonder, then, that the ancients refused to separate music from words; prosody, after all, set a perfect example in which expression and communication coincided. It is hence from early prosody, in all likelihood, that the different arts must have emerged, concluded Condillac.

That music is able to possess certain emotional meanings on its own, Condillac tells us, is due to the common origin of music and language—a state in which the sign and the signified, expression and communication, were not yet separated from each other. Music, hence, as an autonomous system, invariably needs a "lived context" whence it emerges and to which it relates; signs, activating the imagination, cannot, unto themselves, guarantee communication. Notwithstanding this limitation, music remains distinct from language in the cognitive processes that it involves and in the kind of signification that it conveys. To sum up: in his attempt to understand the cognitive nature of signs and their uses in the social development of humanity, Condillac sought exactitude in linguistic systems as they apply to the world outside, and exactitude in artistic means as they relate to the world as experienced. It is his implied division of the mind's faculties, despite his emphasis on the continuity of its operations, that brings him close to Baumgarten's aesthetic propositions.

The Sagacity of Sensate Discourse

Images, argued Baumgarten,[77] though internally fused, are perceived with clarity by the "lower faculty" of the mind—a faculty specially assigned to the reconstruction of sensate experiences and the activation of

77. Alexander Gottlieb Baumgarten (1714–62), renowned as the founder of aesthetics as a systematic field of inquiry, started his career with the publication of some notes on Horace's *Ars poetica* (see his *Reflections on Poetry,* 1735) and ended it with a perceptual theory in which art played a major part (see his *Aesthetica,* 1750). For a more detailed exposition of Baumgarten's aesthetic theory, see the introduction and annotations to Baumgarten's *Reflections on Poetry* in Katz and Dahlhaus, *Contemplating Music,* vol. 2, 571–613.

the imagination; hence, it is the true realm of the arts. Although it aspires to 'perfection' no less than does the "upper faculty," it does so by aiming at *construction* rather than analysis. The "lower faculty" befits the arts because all that pertains to science and logic is reversed in art: whereas science tries, with the aid of logic and concepts, to reduce complexity to "simplicity," art tries, via components *soundly* combined, to make the simple "flower." To convey what he means by components sensibly combined, and to establish the regularity of the sensate, Baumgarten enlisted the Leibnizian principle of "sufficient reason," insisting, however, that in sensate discourse it applies to associations based on 'resemblance' and fulfillment of 'expectation.' Given that it is imagination, rather than nature, that creates works of art, neither 'resemblance' nor 'expectation' can be reduced to strict grammatical, logical, or perceptual laws; such rules would, in fact, curtail the very essence of artistic creativity.

By opening before the arts the full array of the imagination, Baumgarten created, as it were, a parallelism between his world of fiction and the "possible worlds" of Leibniz. According to Baumgarten's aesthetic theory, all works of art turn into organic units located in one of the "worlds," that is, in one of the artistic media that defines its nature. And, like Condillac, he ascribed immense importance to sensate discourse, believing that it conveys certain intended meanings in a way that language, given its nature, tends to distort. Like Shaftesbury, Baumgarten maintained that the investigation of the ways in which man conceptualizes the world, attempting to comprehend the preestablished harmony between man and his surroundings, must not overlook the unique cognitive role played by the arts in the strengthening of man's sensibility.

Human Consciousness as a Creator of "Truths"

With the influence exerted by Baumgarten, Condillac, and their followers it became gradually clear that the understanding of artistic realms depends on a theory of perception, alongside a theory of culture. In fact, it became increasingly clear that only the intersection between the two may yield fruitful insights into the "workings of the arts"—the modes in which they are apprehended and comprehended. The man who most clearly understood this unique condition was Giambattista Vico (1668–1744), whose vision of the "wholeness" of man's activities has already been mentioned, but not explicated. Impressed with the new historiography and ethnography of his time, and utilizing data gleaned from philological discoveries and philosophical explications concerning 'knowledge,' he tried to form a "new science" based on the contention that "truths are made," rather than revealed.

Vico thought that history might uncover the principles governing man's behavior as he molds and shapes his worlds, since history deals with man-made worlds. Mathematics, accordingly, is nearer to history than to physics, for in both mathematics and history man is the maker of that which he eventually recognizes as 'true.' Philosophy must therefore be wedded to history, he thought, and more particularly to philology, since it is in language that cultures are formed. To bolster his theory, Vico set out to examine ancient primitive cultures—fables and myths, customs and rituals, language and song, labor and economy—in short, all aspects of social life. Such a historicizing of man lent epistemology a new kind of perspective, separating the distinctly universal from accumulated knowledge, whether systematized or practical. Moreover, it liberated man from the wiles of fate and from divine will and posited him as free creator of his own destiny, of his own humanity.

Creation starts from perception, Vico maintained. He argued that in order not to become immersed in a 'flux of sensation,' whereby each new sensation conceals a previous one, the mind fixes itself on a 'locus'—a point that is perceived as an image combining within itself the entire flux. The complete process, however, is inconceivable without 'memory.' In memory Vico discerned three stages that together form an inseparable totality: *memoria* brings to mind that which has vanished, *fantasia* reshapes it in a manner significant to the individual, *ingegno* formulates past acts so as to influence present ones. While fictive cognitive entities are guided by the individual's preconceived notions, the notions he entertains are guided by social consciousness, as in the case of language, which, by definition, is a socially shared phenomenon. Elaborating upon the rhetorical tradition, Vico insightfully observed that thinking, as we know it, is primarily metaphorical, for metaphors are 'particulars' concretizing wholes. Altogether, the mind operates symbolically, transforming all sensations into a world of meaning, permanently seeking coherence and "truthfulness."

It should be reiterated that it is not the human mind that changes, according to Vico, but the cultural artifacts, which are the creation of human consciousness. The Enlightenment, accordingly, was misguided in its attempt to construct a science of human nature on the model of physical nature, for the only basis for a science of culture and a metaphysics of mind is an investigation of the different encounters of human consciousness and nature, as they occurred at different times and in different situations and parts of the world. Although Vico's developmental theory had already exerted a strong influence in nineteenth-century historical and social thought, it was only in the twentieth century that it became possible, as already mentioned, to fully appreciate the boldness of his vision.

THE SIGN AND THE SIGNIFIED IN WESTERN MUSIC

Music, like all other man-made "worlds," is a cultural artifact that does not take shape in a vacuum. It takes place in a social environment that it both affects and reflects. The introduction to the present essay tried to convey this fundamental premise, and the first two chapters tried to show how "truths were made" in the musical realm of the West. The high point reached in the eighteenth century, as far as musical coherence is concerned, was mainly attributed to a tightly organized self-referential system that functioned like an "organism," in which the parts derived their meanings from the ways they related to each other and, jointly, to the whole—the individual composition. To "compose," "arrange," "compound," "shape," "form," and "settle" are designations found in the dictionary for the word *comporre*. All of these specifications were, in fact, incorporated in the construction of musical works, with a lucidity that listeners, and not only the musically competent, could follow. Indeed, having evolved over centuries a variety of modes that created internal references—a diversity of ways in which musical components referred to each other intelligibly—Western art music was increasingly able to shed external references that contributed to its comprehension.

In the "truth making" of music, musical signs acquired symbolic meaning. Yet the notion that the mind operates symbolically, transforming sensations into worlds of meaning seeking coherence, emerged only gradually in deliberations on the arts. In retrospect, it seems that attempts to better understand the relationships *among* the arts and the *uniqueness* of each succeeded in precipitating modern scientific notions of the arts more than did the inquiries into the relations between art and bona fide science. Though the establishment of the "modern system of the arts" in the eighteenth century meant recognition of the epistemological uniqueness of the arts—having brought to the fore the recognition of science and art as two distinct bodies of knowledge[78]—the conceptualization of that uniqueness

78. The distinction between the two was based on the recognition that certain fields seem to rest on an accumulation of knowledge resulting in a sense of progress, whereas in other fields the notion of 'progress' cannot be clearly established. See Paul O. Kristeller,

drew, and continues to draw, from a process of development *in* and *among* the arts. Although the camerata's effort to unveil the communicative powers of music around the beginning of the seventeenth century eventually won philosophical anchorage, the disclosure of the *ways* by which this was to be achieved *had* to precede such deliberations. In other words, the powers of music had to be constructed in ways that could be *so* understood.

The idea that the power of art does not reside in the objects it represents or imitates, but rather in the creative modalities that influence its messages, was far from being self-evident. If the theory of 'mimesis' lasted as long as it did, it was due not only to the philosophical heritage that the Greeks bequeathed to the West but also in no small measure to the effort of art itself to create "appearances" reflecting reality, focusing on the objects and the techniques involved in their re-presentations. From this point of view, music was always problematic, for what it supposedly imitates or reflects could not be apprehended from its appearances alone. Plato was, of course, aware of the power that the arts exert on man and, surely no less, of their *fictive* status; this was all the more reason to warn against "appearances" thus removed from the "truth." Interestingly, as long as music's numerology was considered capable of disclosing the secrets of world harmony, its lack of graspable referents was supplied by meanings imported from outside its own precincts, concealing a seemingly obvious question: How does a symbolic system like music, which unto itself defies translation of any kind, act cognitively?

While musical language was increasingly coming into its own, ways of thinking were gradually developing, as I have tried to show, that could deal with this question. The deliberations, however, that proved most efficacious did not necessarily deal with music directly; most of them, in fact, concerned primary issues, all of which required a fundamental array of theoretical conceptualizations. It eventually became clear that it is the very ways in which man conceptualizes the world, including his immediate surroundings, that requires close scrutiny. Thus it happened that music, the most symbolic of the arts, became, in the course of time, the testing ground for plausible hypotheses concerning the working of the mind.[79] The study of Western art music should not lose sight of this momentous event—a moment whereby music was able to contribute substantially to

"The Modern System of the Arts," in *Renaissance Thought and the Arts* (Princeton, 1965), 163–227.

79. For a detailed analysis of seminal treatises that dealt with the subject, see Ruth Katz and Ruth HaCohen, *The Arts in Mind* (New Brunswick, New Jersey, 2002). Also see "Sense, Sensibility, and Commonsense—The British Paradigm," in their *Tuning the Mind*.

the general conceptualization of knowledge.[80] The story, of course, is far more elaborate than the one delineated here.[81] In the present essay—dealing with the "making of a world in sound" that reached its utmost coherence in the "absolute music" of the eighteenth century—I wish, above all, to drive home the idea that the way we think about music, and the ways we go about making and understanding it, are invariably intertwined activities and reside in a broader world of ideas that encompasses, among a host of things, the realm of music as well. *How* and in what *way* music relates to the world of ideas of which it is an integral part in all cultures is, of course, what lends music, any music, its uniqueness.

Even when it was still barely developed theoretically, the concept of 'perception,' in relation to the arts in Western thought, was closely linked to another cognitive concept, the 'imagination.' The ability to perceive a "solution"—a sense of some whole—was deemed necessary in order for perception to complete its own organizational task. Interestingly, the more this ability was assigned a part in perception, not only with regard to the arts, the more it caused the "real world" to recede from man's grasp. From Leibniz and Shaftesbury onward, attempts were made to fathom the power of imagination as a constructive faculty, able to create its own referential systems. The world was not ignored thereby; it only seemed more and more out of reach as an entity independent of its human formulations. In due course, the world as perceived came itself to be viewed as a kind of "representation," circumscribed by the boundaries of cognition, as Immanuel Kant was soon to maintain. Paradoxically, while the tangible world received a fictive status, the fictive status of the arts acquired an ontological standing.

Having assigned the arts to the realm of perception, the eighteenth century produced an abundance of treatises dealing with the "correspondences and differences" among the arts. Just as the failure to deal with the lawfulness of human perception and irrationality had led to the separation of art from science in the seventeenth century, so did the later pursuit of perception lead to the separation of the arts from each other. Although terms such as 'nature,' 'imitation,' 'expression,' and 'perfection' continued to be employed, their meanings underwent significant changes, resulting from, as well as effecting, new qualifications within the twin domains of

80. See Katz and HaCohen, "Sense and Meaning Interlocked," in *Tuning the Mind*.
81. The short delineation that I provide here, is largely based, as already mentioned, on my and Ruth HaCohen's detailed study that resulted in *Tuning the Mind* and *The Arts in Mind*.

the "given" and the "made." The rising interest in perception, and the re-formulation of the epistemological standing of causal explanation, led to the employment of two distinct procedures, the one related to the reex-amination of the "given" and the "made" as *wholes,* the other referring to their internal investigation. While the former strove to unveil common denominators for each of the domains, the latter tried to reveal differ-ences that helped define uniqueness within them. Interestingly, the more one focused on the made, the more differentiated it became, even if many of its aspects still awaited definition. In the course of such clarifications, much of the "natural" underwent redefinition, relocating much that was previously considered as given. Thus, many of the queries that found their solution in the multiplicity of the seemingly "naturally given" faculties were now reexamined in light of the *unity* of the mind, which required better understanding. Such an understanding was in fact expected to en-hance the grasp of the made, which depends on perception *and* cognition, at one and the same time.

To be sure, comparisons among the arts had been made before, yet it was only now that they could be handled with increased rigor, given the tools that gradually became available for doing so. Thus the idea that the several arts were but different treatments of essentially the same sub-jects—an idea that predominated in widespread circles, primarily among consumers of the arts—yielded to the idea that different artistic media dictate the choice of compatible subject matter.[82] It is no coincidence that music, given its newly acquired status, should loom large in the trea-tises that dealt with the comparisons among the arts. This essay makes no room, of course, for a close analysis of these eye-opening treatises, or for a discussion of the interesting transformations that took place in the other arts, not to speak of the historical conditions that precipitated the changes in both art and thought. Yet, in the present context, it is rele-vant to state that the *fictive,* the "as if" world of the arts, became solidly grounded in the course of these transformations. It was embedded in an understanding of the "illusion" that it entails and the kinds of metaphors that it employs, so as to enable the arts to convey elusive meanings con-cretely and perceptibly.

Having drawn on the Platonic tradition, it is only fair to say a word about the other grand tradition—the Aristotelian. As important as the Platonic tradition was in the arts, especially the Plotinian and Neoplatonic off-

---

82. The eighteenth century is replete with illuminating treatises that deal with this issue, of which Lessing's well-known *Laocoön* is but one.

shoots, the entire gamut—from likeness to symbolic representation, from impression to expression, from conception to perception, from common traits to the uniqueness of the arts—could be entertained under the umbrella of 'imitation' as conceived by Aristotle. Art, for Aristotle, was a kind of "potency," a productive form of knowledge, while imitation partook in the cognitive process of *analogy*, a process that he considered a part of all learning. By emphasizing the productive aspect of art and by circumscribing imitation, as he did, by "purpose or design," Aristotle provided the arts with a concept open enough to accommodate many subsequent queries he himself could hardly have envisaged. It is no surprise, hence, that the eighteenth-century treatises that reexamined the "imitative arts" should have enlisted Aristotelian thought in their discussions of 'illusion' and the *realities* that it conveys. In fact, the greater the Aristotelian influence, the more the emphasis shifted from the artistic object to the "contriving and considering of how it may come into being"[83] and to the "import" it harbors.

Needless to say, the field of aesthetics gained in stature the more the theory of art freed itself from the constraints of the concept of 'imitation.' The disclosure that symbolic languages could more adequately be defined through their own organization and systems of symbolization rested on the acknowledgment that "images," of whatever kind, are turned into symbols by the very intellect that they address, using the content of perception *and* experience. The realization that symbols are not only made but disclose themselves through their own making, that they are the cultural forms of human activities, lent the arts—the first to have been recognized as man-made—a special place. Moreover, by highlighting the interaction between perceptible images and intricate conceptual ideas, art lent the issue a kind of saliency wanting in other domains. The arts, to be sure, were appreciated long before their cognitive standing merited explications; their "wonders"—their beauty and achievements—commanded awe and respect long before their unique communicative function was understood. However, once these aspects underwent faithful and scrupulous investigation, the arts were placed on a "pedestal" higher than ever before. If music became the envy of the other arts in the nineteenth century, it was due to the fact that it resourcefully displayed the "power of symbols" even *without* stating what they were about!

Music revealed that it is able to "make sense," though it lacks a bona fide semantics. It also made clear that it could be enlisted to communicate *directly* what words must circumvent. The extended affair between music and

83. Aristotle, *Nicomachean Ethics,* book VII.

language helped unveil music's unchallenged domain—the power to create an ambiance, to occasion a mood and a disposition of mind, without recourse to language. All of this was fully and most impressively exemplified in both vocal and instrumental music. This may, in fact, explain why philosophers and aestheticians continued to mull over what it is that music represents, trying to locate *decisive* attributes that would explain its success.

Accordingly, some aestheticians have come to view musical duration as the passage of life experienced as "expectations becoming now." Such passage, it is claimed, is measurable only in terms of sensibilities, tensions, and emotions, and differs from scientific time in measure as well as in structure.[84] Although the direct experience of passage is only in part perceived in actual life, it constitutes, nonetheless, the model for the "virtual time created in music." Langer tells us that "the primary illusion of music is the sonorous image of passage, abstracted from actuality to become free and plastic and entirely perceptible."[85] Music, in other words, gives quality to the passage of time.

Though Langer admitted that her "subjective time" is akin to *la durée réelle* that Henri Bergson tried to capture and understand,[86] she overlooked, as did many others, the important insight that can be gained from the development of Western notation. In our earlier discussion of the development of mensural notation, it was pointed out that "controlling time, so as to convey the *passage* of time, in a Bergsonian sense, presented a major problem, for it involved what one might call the 'quantification of qualities'" (see chap. 1, 36). Indeed, mensural notation involved the strain to control the nature of the flow of time; the various notations, in fact, increasingly coped—through rhythmic variety and control of the order of events—with the possibility of "quantifying qualities," that is, to present time as a measure of motion. 'Movement,' as we have seen, was the prime and earliest musical metaphor, the first to have been addressed by musical notation. Moreover, serious attempts were made later to relate the perceptual and the physical in music via 'movement.' Yet it is only in the eighteenth century that the relations between sound and sentiment could be explicated effectively, for it rested on a system that comprised built-in expectations that could be enlarged to include "the probable," that is, possible worlds that rest on the consistency within the fictive. This, how-

84. See Langer, "Feeling and Form," 109–16, 150. Also see Leonard B. Meyer, *Emotion and Meaning in Music* (Chicago, 1956), 23–32.

85. Langer, "Feeling and Form," 113.

86. See Bergson's *Matiére et mémoire* (1896), translated as *Matter and Memory* by N. M. Paul and W. S. Palmer (New York, 1911).

ever, required a series of prior understandings of the elements essential in
the perception of music, the mechanisms characteristic of affect, and the
compatibility between the labeling of affects and their experience. Thus,
the idea that expectations can be "temporalized," that music creates a succession of impressions, rather than of ideas, led to recognition not only
that music and poetry represent two different kinds of cognitive processes
but also that 'affect' is the bridge between the two.

Early attempts to relate sound and sentiments did not distinguish, as
we have seen, between the perceptual and the physical in musical movement; the relationship between that which moves and that which is moved
was construed as a simple causal relationship, shrouding the whole issue of
affects—their content as well as their identification—in Platonic mystery.
Though Mersenne, unlike Ficino, *did* separate the physical from the mental, he granted, nonetheless, naturalness to the relationship between the
two. And while he admired Galilei for having tried to make music more
communicative, he understood that the association between words and
music must reckon with affect as experienced, that is, with music perceived as "wholes." By delving into the nature of experiencing affect and
the associations it evokes, Descartes revealed that although the ability to
create associations is naturally given, the contents poured into them are
arbitrary, albeit historically explainable. Having understood Descartes'
emphasis on the cognitive aspect of affect, it is surprising that an astute
theorist such as Johann Mattheson should have reunited the physical and
the mental in a simple causal process in his *Affektenlehre* (instructions concerning affects), overlooking both Mersenne and Descartes.

Emotions felt do not guarantee preestablished identifications. It was
important, therefore, to distinguish first between the mechanism that
transmits the behavioral codes of emotions and the behavior itself, that
is, to realize that the former is neurological while the latter is psychological. Musical "movement" is, of course, psychological; it is also indeterminate, hence the commensurability between the unfolding of music and the
emotions. The categorization of emotions, moreover, is as dependent on a
palette of "semantic differentiation" as music is dependent on sentiments
borrowed from poetry.[87] However, to be able to accommodate a whole ar-

---

87. "Music borrows sentiments from poetry, and lends her movement," Daniel Webb
tells us in his insightful essay—*Observations on the Correspondence between Poetry and
Music.* See Katz and HaCohen, *The Arts in Mind,* 316. Among the enlightening treatises
written in the eighteenth century, Webb's three treatises—*An Inquiry into the Beauties of
Painting* (1760); *Remarks on the Beauties of Poetry* (1762); and *Observations on the Correspondences between Poetry and Music* (1769)—loom large. By insisting that music is not just a

ray of emotions and nuances of sentiment requires the prior identification of primary passions in order to provide the basic dimensions of the
mental space wherein specified leanings and particular dispositions can
be located. It is noteworthy that by the second half of the eighteenth century it became clear that the artistic world superimposes a semantic space
on the emotional one and that affect bridges the two.[88] Yet the attempt
to establish dimensions of emotions has lingered on, having gained special currency among present-day psychologists in search of the *principal*
dimensions of emotions, that is, the *key* factors that both determine and
enable a variety of emotions that have become, in one way or another,
semantically differentiated. Although the basic dimensions of emotions
are still far from being conclusive in theory, empirical research does prove
their tenability, as far as emotional semantic spaces are concerned. How
many dimensions there are and what they refer to is still an open question,
especially for those in search of universals.[89]

Although expressive musical idioms are related to specific meanings
of accompanying texts, they are more general and flexible in themselves.
They tend to be associated with other expressive patterns, creating complicated symbolic configurations. The same theoretical presuppositions
may, in fact, serve to unveil both the expressive potential of what seems
fixed though arbitrary (such as lexical or musical units) and the built-in
semantics of what seems free yet constrained (such as poetical or musical
movement). Affect, as it turns out, emerges as a guiding precept in both
stages, bridging the moving and the fixed. Though it was already suggested
in the eighteenth century that affect directs the search for a primordial

---

"succession of impressions" but that these impressions are meaningless *out* of context,
Webb contributed to our understanding of the relations between sound and sentiment
more than the other writers who tried to delineate the uniqueness of the individual arts.
Webb, one might say, anticipated Bergson's grasp of movement as an immediate and
unmediated construction of consciousness. 'Movement,' of course, was not the only issue
he addressed in his attempt to understand the relation between sound and sentiment; he
also delved into the procedure whereby affects are identified and the ways whereby compatibility between their "labeling" and experiences are established. For a close analysis of
Webb, see *Tuning the Mind,* chap. 5, and *The Arts in Mind:* "Daniel Webb."

88. Webb, to whom we owe much of this understanding, took into account not only
the inherent qualities of each field—music and the emotions—but the way by which
they come to be cognitively associated as well.

89. See, for example, Carrol E. Izard, *The Face of Emotion* (New York, 1971), and Rob-
ert Plutchik, "A General Psycho-Evolutionary Theory of Emotion," in *Emotion: Theory,
Research, and Experience,* vol. 1 (*Theories of Emotions*), ed. R. Plutchik and H. Kellerman
(Orlando, 1980).

communicative substratum, gradually leading to that which enables unique expressions,[90] current theories of 'affect' also entertain interesting connections between affect, metaphor, and creativity. Affect, it is argued, functions in certain cognitive processes as a semantically free, though identifiable, agent, connecting disparate domains by throwing them into relationships that convey new meanings. This process is considered central to the act of creativity, illuminating both the roots and routes of metaphor.[91] Thus, the *in*commensurability of emotion and music, of music and poetry—the basic problem that precipitated eighteenth-century theoretical attempts—turns out to be its solution: the relation between sound and sentiment involves an affective linkage that makes it possible for the aesthetic and the psychological to intertwine creatively!

All of these observations go beyond the work of art, related as they are to the workings of the mind. Indeed, the preoccupation with "problem-solving" in the domain of art involved assumptions and conceptions about the workings of the mind, in both theory and practice. The different modes of overcoming the discrepancies between the original object and the imitating medium—for example, creating in two dimensions the illusion of three, forging a semblance of movement in a static object, prefiguring in the audible what is not heard—amounted to the creation of perceptually tenable means for the achievement of desired ends. The means, in the process, became ends in themselves, involving the idea of contemplation. It is noteworthy that the association of means with contemplation was ingeniously exploited in moral philosophy. Shaftesbury, as we have seen, aimed to reveal the good in man via 'beauty.' Eighty years later, having entertained 'sympathy' as a regulating factor in human interaction, Adam Smith[92] considered contemplating means (abstracted from ends) instrumental to the unveiling of the secrets of the development of civilization, and as a method whereby the origin of the sentiment of beauty is revealed. In his essay on the imitative arts he explicitly states that man is pleased and happy to find that he can comprehend how the wonderful effects of the arts are produced, pointing to the double experi-

90. This was, in fact, one of Webb's key propositions in his investigation of the correspondences between poetry and music.

91. See David S. Miall, "Metaphor and Affect," in *Metaphor and Symbolic Activity* 2 (1987).

92. He is no other than the man who coined the well-known phrase "invisible hand," referring to an intangible factor that regulates economic affairs. The potency of the "invisible hand" rested, of course, on his understanding of the role played by 'sympathy' in human relations.

ence involved in the comprehension of art—the cognition embedded in its making and the *cognizance* of that cognition. This double-faced aspect of works of art, Smith argued, should reside in their very appearances, inviting the beholder to experience both. As far as art is concerned, reality is a contradiction in terms, for real art never conceals the "distance" it keeps from the imitated object.

Of course, Smith did not consider the origin of music as related to the heightening of the inflections of the voice or to other primitive communicative devices. Smith proceeded from the concrete to the abstract, from meanings that came to be associated with music to music's pure constructive elements. The nature of music as an independent artistic medium, Smith believed, is better revealed in what is purely instrumental, for it highlights the fabrication itself more than any other art form. Smith's view of instrumental music can be seen as a forerunner of Hanslick's, for the kind of independent beauty that can be ascribed to music implies for Smith (if not for Kant) "a high intellectual pleasure, like the pleasure derived from the contemplation of a great system in any other science."[93] Baumgarten's two cognitive levels are thus united into one—combining structure with expression by conceiving the former as meaningless unless related to a cognitive response. Smith linked the freeing of expression from specific content to the psychological resonance of meaningful structure. He did not deny the "semantics" of music, but insisted that music acquired it from verbal semantic attachments. Nonetheless, the referential and syntactical rules of music, Smith argued, are in themselves as complicated as the linguistic system, enabling coherence though it "signifies nothing."

Indeed, music is the most articulate of media, though it itself cannot say what it is articulate about. In this chapter I have tried to articulate this seeming paradox, by introducing some of the major ideas and issues that it implicated, and the kind of thinking that it engendered. Musical perception, clearly, became permeated with the aesthetic awareness and the postulates that this thinking engendered. Most of all, the chapter aimed to introduce the general reader—if not the expert—to the intricacies that this paradox involves and to its central role in the development of music in the West.

---

93. Katz and HaCohen, *The Arts in Mind,* 418. For an extended analysis of Smith, see Katz and HaCohen, *Tuning the Mind,* chap. 5, and "Smith" in *The Arts in Mind.*

FOUR

Probing the Limits of Musical Coherence

THE REFERENTIAL FUNCTION
OF LEARNED SCHEMATA:
EXTERNAL VERSUS INTERNAL REFERENCES

Musical coherence, as we have seen, owed much to an organized referential system that functioned like an "organism" in which parts derived their meanings from the ways they related to each other and, jointly, to the "whole"—the individual composition. The transparent devices that accompanied the musical structuring enhanced the ability of habituated listeners, not only of the musically competent, to follow a sophisticated musical unfolding. The ability of the individual to follow "naturally," as it were, what is synthetically constructed rests, paradoxically, on the individual's belonging to a *collective* that both guides and limits his understanding. Music is culture bound; it is a cultural artifact that takes place in a social environment that it both affects and reflects. A musical "language," no less than a verbal language, is internalized by those exposed to it from early childhood.

As we all know, children learn at an early age to communicate in the language into which they are born. However remarkable the achievement, it does not come as a surprise—not to them, nor to those from whom they acquired so significant a tool. Yet despite the self-evidence and "naturalness" of the appearance and experience, it is a *learned* phenomenon. Children apparently imbibe, albeit gradually, correct language usage, linguistic idioms, a richer vocabulary, concepts, metaphors, and so forth, that is, a manipulative agility within the confines of the particular language that they use. All of this may be achieved without conscious knowledge of grammar, sentence structure, and the like, and, a fortiori, without knowledge of the morphology of the particular language that they speak and understand. What seems "natural" is obviously learned through sheer belonging, exposure, and participation.

Although music the world over is culture bound, not all cultures felt the same need to abstract and formalize the guidelines of their musical traditions. And, if they did, the pace and the way they went about it was not the same. In the West, at any rate, a great deal of thought and theoretical speculation was vested in the construction of a "world of sound" that reached a point at which it could stand on its own without detriment to its coherence. It did not happen overnight, as we have seen; it was progressively constructed, steadily promoting ways that substantially built on each other. While musical styles were replacing each other, the ways whereby music was pointing to itself became more elaborate and the relationships among them grew tighter. In fact, the more music allowed for a variety of internal references, the more patent and overt became the "logic" whereby internal musical references were being created. Theory, as expected, followed practice, but practice was informed by prior theory that had become entrenched, providing the yardstick for deviations. Deviations, as we have seen, could be subsumed by broadening the theory itself, so as to accommodate the novelties under its umbrella. Providing that the essential premises of a theory are kept intact, it can tolerate a great deal of change. This is certainly true for theories that must reckon with historical changes that affect transformations in the very subject matter they address. At any rate, Western musical theory was fabricated in an additive, yet organic, fashion, responding to social-historical changes that became manifest in altered aesthetic desiderata.

So it is with listening to music. Once internalized, a musical norm serves as a reference for the unexpected. When a deviation from the expected occurs, our minds mobilize what has become second nature, enabling us to detect the change. Typically, a deviation is only perceived as such when what seems normal serves as a backdrop. When the deviations themselves become systematized and are situated in particular relations to what was considered normal, the enlarged scope of reference turns into the very yardstick by which further changes are gauged. Accommodating deviations through their systematization is tantamount to an increase in perceptible internal references, that is, to an enlarged network that allows for the prolongation or circuiting of "routes" without causing the listener to lose his "compass."

The reverse, however, may hold equally true. A tightly organized musical system may not quickly fall apart in the absence of a given internal link. A system that has time and again proven its reliability can afford, so to speak, to gloss over some missing ties, trusting that the listener will mentally supply them. Art even stands to gain by not spelling out the obvious, by leaving something for the imagination to complete. The high degree of coherence that absolute music managed to achieve provides us with a kind of artistic challenge. We may now ask, to what extent can so entrenched a musical mental blueprint continue to function as an auditory guide?

Tracing the development of internal musical references, that is, the primary means that allowed music to refer to itself, was relatively easy since all of these devices progressively built on one another. The process, moreover, was accompanied by an array of evolving ideas that sought to circumscribe the domain of the arts in general, and to determine the uniqueness of each of the arts within that domain. These processes, as we have seen, were interdependent, in the way that Vico suggested.

By comparison, the task ahead is considerably more difficult, for the changes that built on "absolute music" as a musical *prototype,* that is, the changes that rested on the coherence that music had achieved, resist sequential treatment. The new aesthetic desiderata, in fact, sought to exploit this hard-earned musical understanding in a manner that would not only sustain the introjections of extramusical contents but would also incorporate their "literal" meanings into the musical fabric. Although no less metaphorical, the point I wish to emphasize is that such tailor-made musical adaptations did not build on one another systematically. Their cumulative impact, however, effected a major change in the overall "portrayal" of music and in the manner in which musical import was to be enlisted and "depicted."[1]

It must be stressed that the introduction of extramusical contents into the very musical fabric should not be confused with the initial alliance between music and language, nor with the subsequent division of labor

---

1. I used the words 'portrayal' and 'depicted' advisedly, since much musical effort was exerted on *re*-presenting *images,* narrative and pictorial, alongside the awe they inspire and the moods they impart.

between them. However, once music became the envy of poetry, because music was perceived capable of conveying *directly* what words could only intimate, serious attempts were made to display *musically* specified ideas that music, by definition, is unable to spell out. Even while following purely musical laws, the results of such attempts were bound to replace seemingly objective musical idioms by subjective ones and absolute music by a kind of music that attempts to lend saliency even to "imaginary texts," as it were. Such attempts also inspired an opposite inclination, that is, to listen to vocal music "instrumentally," paying little or no attention to the existing text. What is most significant is the fact that these attempts rested heavily on music's most perceptible elements in novel and unique ways, introducing a great deal of refinement in music's rudimentary, self-evident guise. The way we listen to music and what enlists our attention is apparently, like all else, subject to historical change.

It has been shown that diverse musical traditions also display differences in their attitude to the time axis; some tend to focus primarily on the moment—emphasizing elements that are perceptible on the immediate level—while others employ the momentary to impart a sense of the "whole," via subtle interactions among musical "levels" that lend music a "forward push."[2] Music in the West, as we have seen, increasingly devised methods and means that enabled the various levels of its construction to interact in ways that made long-range directionality possible. This linear conception of music's temporal order became fully recognized only in the second half of the eighteenth century, however. It was subsequently, as we shall see, taken for granted. Indeed, a unidirectional "order of events" can be exploited in new ways, engaging imagination and memory in novel ways. Interestingly, among contemporary attempts to define "music and the aesthetics of modernity,"[3] Karol Berger suggests that the turn in the temporal order that took place in the late eighteenth century marks the

---

2. For elaborate discussions of different attitudes toward the time axis, as manifested in types of directionality (momentary vs. overall, clear vs. unclear, simple vs. complex), see, for example, Dalia Cohen and Ruth Katz, *Palestinian Arab Music: A Maqām Tradition in Practice* (Chicago, 2006). Also see Dalia Cohen and Ruth Katz, "Attitudes to the Time Axis and Cognitive Constraints: The Case of Arabic Vocal Folk Music," in *Perception and Cognition of Music* (East Sussex: Psychology Press, 1997), 31–45.

3. The phrase alludes to the title of a recent book—*Music and the Aesthetics of Modernity* (Cambridge, Mass., 2005)—that contains a number of essays that try to locate and define music's modernity in line with the place "the notion of modernity" occupies in the general history of the West.

beginning of modernity. This turn, he endeavors to show, was fundamental not only to music; it permeated all aspects of Western culture. It was more decisive and new, we are told, than any that had taken place in earlier periods, prior to the French and American revolutions. The late eighteenth century, argues Berger, changed the "relative indifference" to the temporal order, by shifting the attention that primarily focused on musical "invention" toward a disposition that also took "the flow of time from the past to the future seriously." Indeed, although musical events can never be presented at once, they nonetheless may highlight different aspects of the musical unfolding.[4]

It is by no means an exaggeration to claim that some of the novel ways in which this temporal order was exploited in the nineteenth century constituted a kind of rebellion against the "sense-making" capacity of music that seemed to have "superseded" the mysterious magical powers that man had attributed to music from time immemorial. Yet the mysterious and magical, the ineffable and enchanting, have attractions of their own; they are seductive by nature, overpowering and gratifying at one and the same time. Although calling for submission, they are awe inspiring once their transcendent qualities become discernible, that is, once they are concretized, particularized, and rendered palpable. With this in mind, it's little wonder that the new attitude preferred to highlight music's *in*definiteness over its habitual impartial regime. By creating new forms of expression, by challenging the old established ones, the Romantic composers wished to transport the listener into new enchanted realms.

These developments, as expected, called forth individual palettes of expression, all of which aimed, each in its own way, to bestow their unique "coloration" on the mythical powers of music, attempting to evoke reverence for their particularized interpretations of music's enigmatic potency. Of course, earlier composers also left their own stamp on the works they composed. Though not lacking in individuality, they seem to have endorsed the styles of which they were part (and to which they contributed), trying to excel rather than display originality. The several ways in which they employed the musical language they shared often led, to be sure, to novel ideas of musical construction, ideas that had not been entertained before in the particular style to which the composers and their works belonged. Yet once such novelties accumulated and became part of

---

4. See Karol Berger, "Time's Arrow and the Advent of Musical Modernity," in *Music and the Aesthetics of Modernity*, ed. Karol Berger and Anthony Newcomb (2005), 3–22.

the common core of music-making, a new all-embracing style was ushered in. Style is what they shared, not an amorphous attitude toward music; a concrete musical language occupied their universe, not a covenant with a transcendent "otherworldly" realm.

Indeed, while the Romantic composers made ample use of the coherence that music had achieved, it is their shared *attitude*—which nurtured and extolled 'originality'—that prevents us from describing their endeavors chronologically. Yet the new trends in music-making, taken as a whole, had far-reaching consequences for the development of music in the West. Naturally, by tampering with musical coherence as they did, composers were bound to probe the "limits" of the very system they employed. Though their daring eventually resulted in the overthrow of the system that they challenged, the music they created in the interim encompassed audiences that were larger than ever before—listeners who lent attentive ears to the sounds that swayed their souls. No music lover, however sophisticated, can honestly lament the course music took in the nineteenth century, for it produced magnificent music—rich in color, variety, and interest. Even if some of its doings precipitated the eventual overthrow of the system that functioned as a reliable audile compass, no music aficionado can genuinely afford to forgo the profound sensual experiences that the music of the nineteenth century managed to elicit.

It may be recalled that in my discussion of Shaftesbury I pointed out that he drew a close parallel between the moral and the aesthetic, between values and beauty. Mental dictates, he argued, are the incentive for beauty just as the voice of conscience is the incentive for morality; both reside in the mind, which aims at perfect harmony for its own sake. Although primarily emotional and nonreflective, both faculties, he believed, become rationalized in the process of their development by education and use. Though Shaftesbury exerted great influence on subsequent moral-sense theories, the Enlightenment had little use for either providence or for the providential order that guided Shaftesbury's moral philosophy. Instead, it anchored the pursuit of happiness in a new vision of the nature of man, a nature neither good nor bad. Man's nature, it was argued, is formed by circumstances, themselves subject to change and amelioration by mankind. Liberated from superstitions and customs, reason and education might allow man to grasp the broader picture of the human scene and lead to a kind of selfless benevolence, in which man himself becomes the source of moral motives.

The turn from "providential order" toward an order controllable by man naturally looms large in Charles Taylor's profound study of "the sources of the self." Taylor tells us that the idea that "we explore from within the human life form," coupled with the recognition that "certain matters are the invariable objects of moral sentiments, which are by their nature marked off from others by their unique significance," brings us closer to "modern culture" and the significance it bestows on "ordinary life." This transformation, he reminds us, was accompanied by a new conception of order, a vast *physical order* that also incorporated "thinking human beings." It is this enlarged perspective that

> can awaken a kind of awe, wonder, even natural piety. The reflection which moves us is that thought, feeling, moral aspiration, all of the intellectual and spiritual heights of human achievement emerge out of the depth of a vast physical universe which is itself, over most of its measureless extent, lifeless, utterly insensitive to our purposes, pursuing its path by inexorable necessity. The awe is awakened partly by the tremendous power of this world which overshadows us—we sense our utter fragility as thinking reeds, in Pascal's phrase; but we also feel it before the extraordinary fact that out of this vast blind silence, thought, vision, speech can evolve. We who think and see have a glimpse of how deep the roots are of our fragile consciousness, and how mysterious and strange its emergence is.[5]

To be sure, the eighteenth century was still largely rooted in religious and metaphysical beliefs, adhering to the long-held dualism between the incorporeal soul and the corporeal body. Yet the new perspective of the "emergence" of man, Taylor tells us, not only ceased to be an "outlandish, outside view" but also "helped to foster a new sense of cosmic time," which in turn generated "its own forms of personal and historical narration."[6] That this kind of naturalism should have been fostered by Romantic thought comes as no surprise. Although the limits of this essay make no room for a discussion of some of the major figures who left their indelible mark on Romantic thought (Rousseau and Herder, for example), it is important nonetheless to trace briefly the major steps through which Nature became a source of inspiration for Romantic expressionism.

5. Taylor, *Sources of the Self,* 347.
6. Ibid., 349–51. To fully understand the significance of this turn in the history of ideas—a turn that had an enormous impact on modern society and culture—one should read the entire chapter (chap. 19).

Toward the late eighteenth century, Taylor tells us, the new conception
of *human* nature—which placed the responsibility on man to chart his
course of life—also effected a change in the notion of "individual differences" by placing an "obligation on each of us to live up to our originality." Given that the access to Nature is but "through an inner voice or
impulse," says Taylor, "we can only fully know this nature through articu-
lating what we find within us." The new philosophy thus also brought to
the fore the idea that this realization in each of us "is also a form of expression." Consequently, the "individuation of expression"—a notion in-
comprehensible in earlier times—turned into "one of the cornerstones of
modern life."[7]

That the expressive view of human life should have changed our understanding of art is hardly surprising. Yet by calling our attention
to the "double sense" of expression, that is, to both its "formulating"
(working-out) and "shaping" (determining) aspects, Taylor revealed why
"most important human activity will partake of this nature." In the civilization wrought by the conceptions that expressivity entails, no wonder that
art "has come to take a central place in our spiritual life, in some respects
replacing religion," says Taylor. The awe we feel before "artistic originality
and creativity," he claims, "places art on the border of the numinous, and
reflects the crucial place that creation/expression has in our understanding
of human life." However, "in thus being made central," it is no wonder that
"art was also reinterpreted." Indeed, if to define oneself is "to bring what is
as yet imperfectly determined to full definition," and if "the paradigm vehicle for doing this is artistic creation," then art, says Taylor, can no longer
be defined in "traditional terms." The traditional understanding of art, he
reminds us, was "as mimesis"—art imitating reality. This tradition, however, "left a number of crucial questions open: in particular, the question
of what kind and level of reality was to be imitated. Was it the empirical
reality surrounding us, or the higher reality of the Forms? And what was
the relation between them?" The new understanding of art, Taylor claims,
replaced imitation by expression in the sense discussed above.[8] Thus the
new understanding, he concludes, "makes something manifest while at the
same time realizing it, completing it."[9] The important insights we have

7. Ibid., 374–76.
8. The shift from 'mimesis' to 'expression' has been treated extensively by other
scholars as well, most notably by M. H. Abrams. See his *The Mirror and the Lamp: Theory
and the Critical Condition* (Oxford, 1953).
9. Taylor, *Sources of the Self,* 376–77. To do justice to Taylor's erudition and profound
insights, one ought to read the entire chapter (chap. 21), which deals with the issues

gained from Taylor's impressive investigation of the "sources of the self" will help us better understand the "transformations" discussed in the following pages.

PERCEPTION REPLACING CONCEPTION

It can readily be shown that identical ideas have emerged in a variety of different historical contexts. Historians, moreover, frequently reveal that what passes for novel already existed in earlier times. Although factors of this kind must be taken into consideration in the general delineation of a period, they must be carefully scrutinized in the attempt to establish the uniqueness of its cultural expressions. Since time and place dictate the *prism* through which ideas and concepts are *perceived,* old ideas may be subsumed by new "looks." Perception, we are told, is "the action by which the mind refers its sensations to the external objects as cause."[10]

---

discussed above. "The musical art of expression," says Dahlhaus, "falls into a paradox. Yet this paradox cannot be disposed of as a flat contradiction, but must be grasped as a living tension, driving historical development onward." He reminds us that ever since the late eighteenth century the principle of expression constituted the driving force of music history. "If music is striving to become like language, eloquent and expressive," argues Dahlhaus, "it must do two things: on the one hand, in order to make itself understood, music must develop formulae (in opera a whole vocabulary took shape, which overflowed into instrumental music); on the other hand, as 'outpouring of the heart' and expression of someone's own inner being, expressivity demands avoidance of whatever is usual and taken for granted. Under the dominance of the principle of originality, traditionalists could be despised as mere imitators and epigones, though they were irreplaceable for musical culture. Expression, then, is paradoxically yoked to convention, the particular to the general." His explanation runs as follows:

> If expression, being subjective, is unrepeatable, yet at the same time, in order to make itself clear, it yields to a compulsion of becoming established. In the moment when it is realized in any tangible existence, it sacrifices its essence. But, precisely in its dialectic, the principle of expression has become definitive for a historical consciousness and activity in which progressive and conservative traits mutually condition each other. The paradox of the art of expression forces both the production of novelties in steadily accelerating change and the preservation of works from the past phases of the development; the paradox forbids what happened in earlier centuries—allowing older works to be discarded and forgotten as obsolete. The fact that musical expression, once achieved, is unrepeatable motivates the tendency to change; the fact that expression, in order to be understood at all, must be repeated, supports the maintenance of the past. Progress and historical memory belong together, as two sides of the same thing. (Carl Dahlhaus, *Esthetics of Music* [Cambridge, 1995], 23–24.)

10. See the Oxford Dictionary of Current English.

Thus, a shift of "vision"—a new perspective—does not apply solely to our understanding of past events, but may equally affect contemporary cultural activities. In fact, while absolute music no doubt triumphed by the turn of the eighteenth century, those who inherited its attainments—making ample use of its achievements—gazed at 'Music' through a prism reminiscent of former days.

The Return of an Enigma

It took great effort, as we have seen, to *de*mystify the "powers of music." The historical developments that accompanied this process disclosed the ways in which the seemingly mysterious is structured and valued, that is, the ways in which music is "divined" (in the double sense of the word). Although the division between Art and Science kept fluctuating, the carving out of a special domain for the arts was accompanied by an understanding of the uniqueness of each of the separate arts. Music emerged from these various deliberations as the most articulate of the arts—eloquent and expressive—and thus was invited to lend *specificity* to language. A poem or story, as we all know, need not express what it says or say what it expresses; linguistic utterances, unlike musical scores, are not the "end product," despite their semantic layer.[11] It may be said that music was enlisted to render *unambiguously* much that remains elusive in language.

It is this marvel—which rested on a "well-made world"—that the early Romantics addressed anew through their then current look. It is precisely the freedom of music to manipulate its own forms and symbols, without reference to reality outside itself, that invited speculations *beyond* the knowledge of the métier: if reality, as we know it, can only be grafted *onto* music, then music, unto itself, must represent a realm the presence of which we experience and relish, but fail to locate. No wonder then that the rhetoric of those captured by music's potency should be so highly charged by religious "overtones." Although all of the literary forerunners of musical Romanticism emphasized the close relationship between religious feelings and artistic creation, they mainly endeavored to penetrate the *mystery* of the spiritually "uplifting" power of music.

Jean Paul (1763–1825), for example, who was considered by many of his contemporaries the literary counterpart of Beethoven, attributed the character of Romantic poetry to Christianity, the religion "that gave shelter to

---

11. These are precisely the sorts of issues that Nelson Goodman tried to clarify in his *Languages of Art*.

romantic love." Venus could only be beautiful, he argued, but Mary sym-
bolizes this higher form of love—love that detaches itself from the earthly
by "transforming the beautiful body into the beautiful soul that one might
love the other—beauty, then, in the infinite."[12] Jean Paul, in fact, defined
Romanticism as "beauty without bounds—the beautiful infinite"[13] —an
expanse that "sets the imagination free." The "sharp, closed outlines" of the
Greeks, he thus claimed, exclude everything romantic by definition.[14] Yet
Romanticism, he tells us, is more than "the wavelike ringing of a string or
bell, in which the tone-wave fades into ever further distances, finally losing
itself in us so that, while already silent without, it still resounds within."
Romanticism, rather, is an *awareness* of something "larger than there is
room for here below"—an awareness of "a boundless spirit-world in which
the narrow sensual world dissolves and sinks from sight."[15] As time goes
on, Jean Paul prophesied, the writing of poetry "will become more and
more romantic, freer from rules or richer in them. . . . it will experience
greater and greater difficulty in maintaining a steady course."[16]

Although he did not write about music in a formal way, his conception
of the art may be inferred from the place he allotted to music in his literary

12. This statement, like the subsequent ones, is taken from Jean Paul's *Vorschule der
Ästhetik,* which appeared as early as 1804. A part of the section that deals with the nature
of Romantic poetry is included in Strunk's *Source Readings,* 744–49. For the above, see
Strunk, 748. Jean Paul considered "Platonic love" (748) as but "a pure unsullied friendship
between youths."

13. Ibid., p. 746.

14. Friedrich Schiller, in his *Über naïve und sentimental Dichtung* (1795–96), also attempted, though somewhat earlier, to differentiate between styles—between Grecian,
that is, antique, and "Modern," that is, subsequent styles. Jean Paul did not take kindly
to Schiller's differentiation, yet regardless of the nomenclature they used, these were
clearly attempts to delineate the critical features that distinguish what we might term
the "classical" and the "Romantic" style. It is interesting to note, in this connection, that
Heinrich Wölfflin—long after Jean Paul, and without religious "overtones"—in his attempt to define the difference between styles had the following to tell us:

As soon as the depreciation of line as boundary takes place, painterly possibilities
set in. Then it is as if at all points everything was enlivened by a mysterious movement.
While the strongly stressed outline fixes the presentment, it lies in the essence of a
painterly representation to give it an indeterminate character: form begins to play; lights
and shadows become an independent element, they seek and hold each other from
height to height, from depth to depth; the whole takes on the semblance of a movement
ceaselessly emanating, never ending. Whether the movement be leaping and vehement,
or only a gentle quiver and flicker, it remains for the spectator inexhaustible. (Heinrich
Wölfflin, *Principles of Art History* [1915], trans. M. D. Hottinger [Oxford, 1929], 19.)

15. Strunk, *Source Readings,* 748.

16. Ibid., 749.

works. For example, the "Garden- Party" in his *Hesperus*[17] creates an exquisite setting not only for sentiments but also for "romantic love" as well. The resounding music, we learn, assuages the "longing" and "desire" of Victor—the designate lover of the scene. Jean Paul, to be sure, does not leave us pondering, for he tells us explicitly that music "stills the longing of the soul—a desire to which nothing can give a name." "Songs and harmonies name it to the human spirit"; they convey what the soul yearns for, where "there is no place for words."[18] Music, thus, may also accompany "one's own inner melody, turning instrumental music into vocal—inarticulate sounds, as it were, into articulate ones, not permitting the lovely succession of tones, to which no definite object lends alphabet or language, to glide from our hearts."[19] This should not be mistaken, however, for the kind of sympathetic correspondence between music and the emotions that was discussed earlier. Rather, it should be attributed, according to Jean Paul, to the "echoes" that music gathers "from the joyous sounds of a second world." These are the echoes that music conveys to our "mute hearts," bringing "past and future together," for they "truly come from a shout that, ringing from heaven to heaven, dies out at last in that remotest, stillest heaven of them all, consisting only of a deep, broad, eternally silent rapture." Man, concludes Jean Paul, "is unhappy only on the earth."[20]

17. For a section of the "Garden Concert" from the *Hesperus,* see Strunk, *Source Readings,* 764 –74. Strunk clearly included this section for its many relevant statements about music.

18. Ibid., 767–78. It is worth noting that Arthur Schopenhauer, somewhat later, viewed music as an art that men are "content to understand directly" but renounce all claim "to an abstract conception of this direct understanding." Schopenhauer, of course, emphasized the *will* at the expense of the intellect. He recognized the fact that his explanation of the "inner nature of music" and its "imitative relation to the world" assumes and establishes a relation between "music as idea" and that which "from its nature can never be idea." Music, therefore, has to be regarded "as the copy of an original which can never itself be directly presented as idea." According to Schopenhauer, music, like the other arts, is a "way of *viewing* things independent of the principle of sufficient reason," but it is "by no means like the other arts the copy of the ideas, but the copy of the *will* itself whose objectivity the ideas are." The effect of music is more powerful and penetrating than that of the other arts because "they speak only of shadows, but it speaks of the thing itself." See *The World as Will and Idea,* trans. R. B. Haldane and J. B. Kemp (London, 1950), 282–83.

19. Strunk, *Source Readings,* 771.

20. Ibid., 773. The "death wish," as is well known, became an important topos in the nineteenth century, yet it is Wagner's '*Liebestod,*' in his *Tristan and Isolde,* that represented self-destruction as the highest rapture, the transmutation of sensuousness into an optimal level of spirituality.

Music's Spiritual Peculiarity as Distinct
from Its Mundane Technical Aspects

It is amazing how close Jean Paul came to the description of the *poetic* side of musical composition. Without delving into technical matters, he expressed what many leading composers of the nineteenth century experienced and envisaged. They were not, after all, in quest of musical guidance, for they had plenty of that; they were in search of appraisals that would lend support to their individual "toil" *and* "troubles."

No one expressed the distinction between the practical side of music-making and its aspiration more succinctly than Wilhelm Heinrich Wackenroder (1773–98).[21] Although he, too, emphasized the close relationship between religious feeling and the mystery of music, he elaborated on the "purifying" function of music for the "properly tuned" listener. Music thus "uplifts" Wackenroder's fictional hero—a devout music lover—from a "prosaic life" to a "beautiful poetic ecstasy."[22] Since music can evoke so powerful a spiritual existence, the hero resolves that one's "whole life must be a piece of music." Music, in short, has the power to *aestheticize* one's existence on *this* earth![23]

It follows that Wackenroder's poetically inclined music lover should also long to participate in the *construction* of that dominion that he has so wholeheartedly endorsed. He experiences a *calling* to become a "distinguished artist,"[24] and turns, of course, to music's patron saint to assist him in the fulfillment of his destiny. The following prayer addressed to Saint Cecilia tells it all, but in the hero's *own* verses:[25]

---

21. The section describing "The Remarkable Musical Life of the Musician Joseph Berlinger," from Wackenroder's *Herzenergiessungen eines kunstliebenden Klosterbruders* (1797), is included in Strunk, *Source Readings,* 750–63. The section is divided into two parts, the one dealing with an inspired *reaction* upon listening to music, the other with the feelings that accompany the "down to earth" musical practice.

22. See ibid., 753.

23. Wagner, it may be remembered, aspired to render his services to an aesthetic ideal of redeeming German civilization by elevating its reality to the level of his fiction. He saw his work as reaching a climax in which fiction and reality fuse to create a level of heroic existence on the ruins of the "basely materialistic" bourgeois order. Wagner, of course, was not the only one who tried to "aestheticize life." In fact, the attempt to elevate reality to the level of fiction is often discussed as one of the characteristic features of fascist regimes.

24. See Strunk, *Source Readings,* 756.

25. We shall have occasion to discuss the whole notion of the poet-musician somewhat later.

FIGURE 4. A depiction of Santa Cecilia by Denys Calvaert (1540–1619).

See me comfortless and weeping,
Solitary vigil keeping,
    Saint Cecilia, blessed maid;
See me all the world forsaking,
On my knees entreaty making;
    Oh, I pray thee, grant me aid.

    . . .

Let the hearts of men be captured,
By my music's tones enraptured,
    Till my power has no bound;
And the world be penetrated,
Fantasy-intoxicated,
    By the sympathetic sound.[26]

Inspiration from above is what the artist most needs, not the hard-earned knowledge of the métier, for the "wondrous gift of music"—the "power to affect us"—is the greater "the more dark and mysterious its language."[27] It comes as no surprise, then, that our hero should experience a tremendous letdown once his wish has been fulfilled. The mundane task of music-making makes him long for those innocent days, when he was untroubled by the "details" of how music achieves its *overall* impact.[28] It is Art that one should worship, he concludes, not the artist; the latter is but a "feeble instrument" in the hands of the Creator, who grants the power to make use of "nature's eternal harmony." Our desolate musician realizes, moreover, that the striving to make of oneself an "artist for the world" is a delusion of the "greatest of visionaries"; an artist should be "artist for himself alone, to his own heart's exaltation, and for the one or two who understand him." Yet the *spirit* of art "is and remains for man eternally a mystery . . . at the same time, it is eternally an object for his highest admiration."[29]

The Changed Status of the Artist

The "self-portrait" of Wackenroder's hero—as ardent admirer of music, yet desolate musician—contains many of the themes that surfaced in the

26. Ibid.
27. Ibid., 754.
28. See ibid., 759.
29. Ibid., 760, 761, 763.

nineteenth century regarding art and artists in general. It also granted music a uniquely elevated status. Jean Paul and Wackenroder were of course not alone in their regard for music, but they were unusually expressive about the changed climate that so conceived of the art. It is largely due to their eloquence—their ability to verbalize what so many tried but failed to express—that they turned into "influentials": their words fell on receptive ears. There were, of course, others whose rhetoric is not so markedly different, considering that all of them were spokesmen for a social-political world whose sensitivity toward 'Culture' had drastically changed. The question of how it happened that the concern with culture became so widespread, and why its expressions took shape as they did, is, of course, beyond the scope of this essay. Apart from arguing that cultural expressions must be properly contextualized, I have refrained from dealing with general historical—social and political—changes, except for those ideational changes that affected music conceptually as well as perceptually.

Thus I shall not attempt to answer the question of why the century that followed the so-called Age of Reason should have seen fit to conjure up inexplicable worlds, preferring to traverse remote and "distant lands." Yet, the question of why music—which not so long ago had reached the pinnacle of coherence—was chosen to "echo" the remotest of illusions can be readily explained. The answer, clearly, resides not in inherited Platonic-Pythagorean thought—in the belief that music makes the order of God's Creation audible—but in the pursuit of music's hypothetical "engulfing sphere." This "chase" produced an unavoidable rift between Music's "enigmatic location" and the actual standing of those who dealt with the practical side of the art. Composers could no longer be satisfied merely to partake in the various functions that diverse institutions—whether church, theater, or concert hall—took it upon themselves to fulfill. They now felt called upon to live up to an *ideal* that, to say the least, transcends ordinary proficiency or even marked ability. Yet to be a "messenger" conveying an "exalted vision" is not easy, a fortiori to merit a position among its chosen apostles!

Expert musicianship and superior skills were not discarded, of course. These remained the sine qua non of music-making, but they were no longer viewed as the main source of inspiration, which was supposed to derive from an ostensibly undefined sphere. Thus, to have been born into a family of musicians—which was often the case in the past—provided no more of a head start than to have been born into an enlightened middle class family with cultural aspirations. Until the end of the eighteenth century, composers had a clear idea of where they belonged and whom they were serving. Consequently, to have been born into a music-making environment provided an obvious advantage, the more so since compositions were primarily produced for immediate use (however "personal" they may strike us in retrospect).[30] Now that composers became emancipated artists," free to follow the dictates of their hearts, they faced a new, unanticipated constraint—they had to create their own publics.[31]

Emancipation, evidently, is not wholly a blessing because the emancipated need to rely on their own resourcefulness and to surmount unforeseeable difficulties on their own. In fact, once the composer was totally cut off from his preexisting institutional position, he had to engage in the difficult task of securing his own *preferred* audience—anonymous listeners appreciative of his individual endeavors. Given the double task of achieving their objectives in an unpredictable social setting, it is no wonder that composers experienced a sense of isolation, often leading to outright alienation. Those failing to obtain immediate acceptance, or some modicum of success, could console themselves, however, by blaming the audience for its insufficient understanding of what they were trying to achieve. An imagined audience came thus into being—a "future audience" that might be better equipped to appreciate what the preceding generations had failed to comprehend. Like music—which was presumed to echo a remote realm—recognition, too, was placed at a distance, entrusting final judgment to posterity.

30. The drift toward a self-conscious art had already been noted by contemporaries toward the end of the eighteenth century. In an interesting essay concerning the "beautiful in Mozart," Scott Burnham argues that Mozart brought "sentimental self-consciousness to naïve grace" with his beautiful dissonance, intimating thereby "the ungraspable with perfectly grasped musical language." See Scott Burnham, "On the Beautiful in Mozart," in *Music and the Aesthetics of Modernity* (Cambridge, Mass., 2005), 39–52. Discussing the alleged modernity of Georges-Louis Leclerc de Buffon's "Discourse on Style," Henri Zener claims that Buffon (a well-known figure of the Enlightenment) "differentiated between the substance and the tone of style." Buffon's statements (quoted by Zener) that "style is nothing but the order and movement that one gives to one's thought" and that "to write well is to have, all at once, wit, soul, and taste," and that "it is only ideas that constitute the substance of the style," clearly convey, argues Zener, a "new move" in the conception of the role of the individual in bringing about a successful work of art. See Henri Zener, "A propos of Buffon's *Discours du style*," in *Music and the Aesthetics of Modernity*, ed. Berger and Newcomb, 53–62.

31. George Frideric Handel, apparently, was the only eighteenth-century composer to have built his own public. Franz Joseph Haydn (toward the end of his life), Mozart, and, certainly, Ludwig van Beethoven already experienced the social transition that led from the musical amateur to the citizen of the concert hall.

The Merger of the Arts

In Music's all-engulfing sphere, the arts clearly merged again. Though 'Music' was regarded as a "primal cause" from whence all the arts sprang, it also constituted the "womb" to which they were to return. The specific nature of Music could best be recognized in music whose "sole content is the infinite," that is, instrumental music. It is 'absolute music,' says E. T. A. Hoffmann (the poet-musician), that discloses to man a realm "that has nothing in common with the external sensual world that surrounds him, a world in which he leaves behind him all definite feelings to surrender himself to an inexpressible longing."[32] Thus, to read definite emotions into that which by nature remains "*in*expressible" reveals a basic lack of understanding of what Music is about. However "otherworldly" Hoffmann might sound, it must be remembered that this kind of aesthetic contemplation was largely assisted by the fact that instrumental compositions of sizable lengths had already come into being by then, compositions that magnificently displayed the coherence that music had achieved—a musical unfolding that could readily be "possessed" by meaning and succumb to interpretations of various sorts. But we must also take note of Hoffmann's *nonmimetic* approach to music, for it counteracts the mimetic paradigm that governed the arts until then. Though nonmimetic, Music exemplifies nonetheless a *fundamental* metaphysical realm, a realm inaccessible to language but accessible to audible sounds. Music, accordingly, expresses a kind of awareness of the spiritual power embedded in Nature—in the totality of existence. No wonder that music came to be addressed as a form of religious worship, or as a substitute thereof.[33]

32. See E. T. A. Hoffmann, "Beethoven's Instrumental Music," in Strunk, *Source Readings,* 775–76.

33. However novel this metaphysical approach may have appeared at the time, it is somewhat reminiscent of music's outstanding position in the Platonic tradition, which attacked in its way the imitative tendencies in art. Considering music's mathematical and physical components, music was related to world harmony as a static system. Ignoring the fact that music is experienced as unfolding in time, music was conceived as the art that makes the harmony of the world audible. Concerning the "autonomy" of instrumental music, Dahlhaus reminds us that our taking for granted the right of music "to exist even if it expresses neither a text nor a program" was not so viewed around 1800; it was, in fact, "considered something of a paradox." It is particularly revealing, says Dahlhaus, that the "proponents" of "musical-hermeneutics" were fond of "fabricating tacit programs in order to explain away the puzzling aspects of what E.T.A. Hoffmann called 'pure instrumental music.'" See Carl Dahlhaus, *Foundations of Music History,* trans. J. B. Robinson (Cambridge, 1999), 146.

Hoffmann's "longing" clearly has no address; it is a state of being—an unconscious region of uncontrollable feelings and agitation. Beethoven, accordingly, disclosed this state of being more than any of his predecessors, for his music "sets in motion the lever of fear, of awe, of horror, of suffering, and wakens just that infinite longing which is the essence of romanticism."[34] This last statement is especially noteworthy since it unites three independent issues into one: it identifies inexpressible yearning with *boundlessness;* it recognizes *generalized* emotions, that is, seats of passions "without cause"; and, most important, it sanctions 'absolute music' as the undistorted conveyer of a *contemporary disposition.* Amazing though it may be, different points of view apparently create a divergence in the understanding of the selfsame manifestation. Given the new perspective, no wonder that the function of music allied to language was reformulated as well. Music, accordingly, was no longer perceived as lending *specificity* to emotions suggested by means of words, but as a garb that clothes them in "the purple luster of romanticism," so as to be guided "out of life into the realm of the infinite."[35]

Poetry, however, was not dislodged by music, for the "voices" emitted from this faraway land made them partners in a state of "bliss"; as "members of a faith, related in the most intimate way."[36] In spite of his statement that "only that opera in which the music arises directly from the poem as its inevitable offspring is a genuine opera," Hoffman reminds us that in "the language of romance," words turn into "sounding music" and that music is at home "only in the land of romance."[37] Thus, in the joint affair between music and poetry, it is "the magic force of poetic truth which the poet representing the marvelous must have at his command" to deliver us into "a romantic existence in which language, too, is raised to a higher power, or rather, is borrowed from that faraway country . . . where action and situation themselves . . . take hold of us and transport us the more forcefully."[38] Since "no good line can form itself . . . except it comes forth as music," poetry need not envy music, but join forces so as to create a higher means of expression.[39]

Painting, too, sought to capture the sublime, which music so eloquently

34. Strunk, *Source Readings,* 777.
35. Ibid., 776.
36. See Hoffman, "The Poet and the Composer," in Strunk, *Source Readings,* 787.
37. Ibid., 788.
38. Ibid., 788–89.
39. Ibid., 790–91. For an insightful explication of the merger between music and poetry in the nineteenth century and the way in which it differs from the eighteenth-

represented. In their attempts to transcend the objects depicted, painters chose Nature—its undisturbed calm and long forgotten eruptions—
in order to *arrest,* as it were, a domain that was, is, and will last forever.
Landscapes of all kinds were exploited to allude to the realm that music
managed to echo. Painters, thus, concentrated on majestic, awe-inspiring
sights: aged volcanic rocks, exalted mountains, awesome cliffs, raging
seas shrouded in mist, little villages in the dusk of spectacular twilights,
and "tiny people" in vast panoramas—in an all-embracing, overpowering
universe. Poets tried "drawing" in words what their fellow artists tried to
picture. At any rate, Nature described as 'romantic' is seen through a veil
of associations and feelings extracted from poetry and literature. Indeed,
undefined states of mind can be projected onto Nature, which evokes an
abundance of unlabeled moods.[40] Composers, in turn, were affected by
poets and painters who aimed to achieve what music was most qualified
to express.

Inspiration, however, was deemed necessary to achieve these goals; it
was, after all, not easy to bring about tasks so highly placed. Artists, accordingly, needed to be *illuminated* by an undefined, unknown stimulus that
provided an incentive for their creativity. Thus inspiration—the primary
impetus—occurs in a "dreamy condition," in a condition in which the artist is not fully conscious, though it leaves its imprints on the artwork once
completed. The "rest" was of course not neglected, but it was considered
"a mechanical technique," albeit "essential to success in any art and attainable only by constant application and steady practice."[41] Knowledge
of musical theory, therefore, no longer assured a proper understanding of
Music; nay, it could even lessen the joys of that higher realm.[42] Music, evidently, can be enjoyed by listeners whose understanding of what they hear
does not depend on music's "mechanical technique." No wonder that so
many composers of the century celebrated authors whose thoughts could

---

century conception of the relationship between them, see Lawrence Kramer, *Music and
Poetry: The Nineteenth Century and After* (California, 1984), 1–24.

40. In my discussion of "Moral Philosophy and Its Affair with Beauty" in chapter 3, I
highlighted the importance of intrinsic sentiments and their "harmony-seeking" nature,
but did not emphasize the changed view of Nature itself. The new view of nature, we
learn from Taylor, endorsed nature "as the source of right impulse or sentiment," no
longer as "a vision of order, but in experiencing the right impulse." "Nature as norm," we
learn, became "an inner tendency," ready to become "the voice within . . . and to be transposed by the Romantics into a richer inwardness." See Taylor, *Sources of the Self,* 284.

41. Strunk, *Source Readings,* 785.

42. This was also one of the points that Wackenroder stressed. See Struck, *Source
Readings,* 787.

hardly be better expressed by "inspired musicians." Composers, of course, had to *actualize* these thoughts in the compositions they produced, in order to convey them in a manner discernible to their audience.

TANTALIZING THE EAR AND LURING THE MIND

Regardless of their new perspective, composers were still bound to exploit the coherence of the musical system they had inherited. In fact, taking its systemic linkages for granted enabled them to achieve much of what they set out to accomplish. Intelligibility, after all, depends on what is implied, yet what is implied must be made manifest in the music itself.

The Reformulation of Musical Structure

Irrespective of the way in which he was perceived, Beethoven never broke the unity of the whole. Though his passion sometimes led to a seeming freedom in the manipulation of form—in its dynamics, in the sharp alternation of contrast, in the *crescendi* and *decrescendi* and the like—its shaping was nonetheless controlled by an inner musical necessity. The Romantics naturally emphasized Beethoven's "emancipation" in preference to the inner necessity of the musical work. The latter was eventually relegated to "exegetical" interpretations—like a text that needed deciphering—to which Beethoven's unique musical approach no doubt contributed. Classicism—the stylistic preference for well-proportioned "balanced" forms—became altogether suspect as being antiquated, pedantic, and dry. Romanticism, by contrast, unleashed fantasy; it freed the imagination in directions never entertained before. Now that the role of the creative artist was to transmit, as it were, other-worldly transcendence, or to voice man's inexpressible longing, form was bound to give way to imaginatively conceived content.

Though a tendency to recognize the importance of imagination in works of art may be discerned in the eighteenth century, it should not be confused with the Romantic attitude toward the subject. The age that gave rise to the study of perception could hardly overlook the role of imagination in the establishment and formulation of 'meaning.' The Romantics, by contrast, were less concerned with the exact grasp of meaning and more with the particular emotion aroused in the person who contemplates it. In other words, the Romantic focused not on the properties of the objects described but on the reactions they aroused in him. He assumed a subjective character, hoping to convey *his* experience to an impressionable, sympathetic audience. The subjective element, paradoxically, was deemed compatible with that magical and evocative art that aspires to remote and unknown regions that affect Man as such. Why is it, asked Jean Paul, that everything that exists only in aspiration and is remote possesses a magical transfiguring charm? Because "everything, when inwardly represented," answers Mario Praz, "loses its precise outline, since the imagination possesses the magic virtue of making things infinite."[43]

This new way of "seeing" things clearly altered the relationship between sound and structure. Timbre, register, the spacing of voices, tone color, orchestral color, resonance, sound effects, and the like became far more prominent then they had ever been, including the use of dynamics, which had already been intensified by some classical composers. In short, all that engaged the ear on an immediate level gained momentum and was treated with utmost care because it could elicit instant attention. Compared to sound, structure is more neutral in character; it is more conceptual than perceptual, less sensual and more ideational. However, since the familiar structures rested on relationships among musical factors guided by a system capable of arousing expectations, the new attitude toward sound impelled composers to take account of immediate impressions and deferred satisfactions in ways that diminished the importance of musical expansion—of that prolonged structural development that aimed to engage the listener's mind.

Unlike extended compositions that integrate several parts into larger wholes, the idea of something small, as if torn away from an extended whole yet self-contained and complete unto itself, came into being. Replacing the placid perfection of classical beauty, little works of art could now abound in dynamic interest despite their limited extent. The century thus gave rise to an abundance of condensed little works that delighted music teachers as well as their romantically inclined students. The notion of a self-contained "fragment" clearly entails a contradiction, yet therein resides its assertion, that of a deliberate act of detachment from the surrounding universe. Though separate and complete unto itself, the fragment, nonetheless, hurled into the universe this very act of defiance. Subjective ruminations of this kind were expected to reverberate in the souls

---

43. See Mario Praz, *The Romantic Agony* (translated from the Italian by Angus Davidson), 2nd ed. (Oxford, 1951), 14. Jean Paul attempted to define the essence of the Romantic sensibility in an essay entitled "Magic of the Imagination." It is in this essay, according to Praz, that Jean Paul posed his question. Praz also quotes Novalis's dictum according to which "*Alles wird in der Entfernung Poesie . . . Alles wird romantisch.*"

of sympathetically tuned ears, equally inclined to listen to their own inner voices, divorced from all else.

Expression, regardless of kind, must, however, crystallize into recognizable communicative patterns, so much more so if 'ideal nature' is to be sought not only in Nature but in works of art as well. Nature without living creatures, argued Schiller somewhat earlier,[44] can become the symbol of the human either as a representation of feelings or as a representation of ideas. Landscape paintings, accordingly, become anthropomorphized via ideas, which are symbolized in the painting itself, whereas music evokes feelings not by portraying their contents but by rendering their "forms." The specified contents of feelings, claimed Schiller, are supplied by the imagination of the listener. Thus the re-formulation of the world, by highlighting its *expressivity*, calls for discernible *artistic* essences that lend themselves to the carrying out of the task. Seeking universal essences in the "atmosphere" that envelops specific subject matters, and in the feelings they evoke, was bound to yield new "insights," which in turn became "translated" into new modes of communication. Although giving rise to novel musical procedures, this process of "concretization" rested nonetheless on *acquired* cognitive formations, in much the same ways as did the earlier procedures that attempted to convey "affects." Yet the idea that shared cognitive dispositions, more than identifiable forms, are responsible for communication came to full fruition only now, based less on theoretical constructs than on artistic intuition.

The emphasis on inexplicable and ephemeral essences was likely to depreciate the accepted defining lines between units. By imposing on self-contained units an altered "external appearance," by loosening their structural "tightness" via an array of sound factors that directly meet the ear (timbre, densities, spacing of voices, dynamic changes, and so forth), composers were in fact able to convey readily recognizable dispositions as well as their "experiences," that is, their individual "responses" to that which they allegedly represented. Thus, textural transparencies no less than textural densities, hidden melodic contours no less than rustling sounds, sustained sonorities and crossing of voices no less than the oscillations between melody and accompaniment were all used to dissolve form. Once musical figures appeared as units whose primary function is to re-merge with their designated environment, musical representation seems to have acquired a set of stylistic procedures that markedly differed from those

---

44. Schiller was not only a well-known poet and playwright but also a theorist who dealt with aesthetic queries with equal force and comparable impact.

that were used for rendering a coherent outline with a clear beginning, middle, and end. The reflection of the infinite—as opposed to the world of appearances—called, after all, for a new palette of representation.

Though the beliefs concerning a well-tempered world—in which body is tuned to soul and to the universe—had been closely related for some time to the idea that a unique atmosphere, a certain *Stimmung* (mood) surrounds Man,[45] it now became an obsession to capture its representational characteristics, highlighting *interpretation* as a central feature of perception. What seemed like an immediate reflection of the world or a particular state of mind involved, however, not only active participation on the part of composers but of the listeners as well. Thus, a dynamic mode of listening replaced the more static way of perceiving that primarily rested on the implementation of "logical" procedures, on those learned cognitive schemata shared by composer and listener. By "fabricating" new modes of observation and perception, composers and their audiences may be said to have opted out of the "canon of authorized responses," facing 'ideal nature' in a "fluid state" that required a "corresponding creativity" on their part.[46] Though the dual purpose of presenting the represented—that is, presenting the emotions aroused in the composer contemplating what he is representing—enlisted interpretation, it also gave rise to compositional procedures that sought to guide the imagination of listeners.

Unlike the former delineation of "affections," the characterizations of the *cosmic* spirit turned music itself into a cosmos, granting composers the power to inhabit it in their own particular ways. The silent music of the spheres was thereby transformed into processes whereby the unheard was given form by musicians who felt at one with its spirit and with the

45. See Leo Spitzer, *Classical and Christian Ideas of World Harmony* (Baltimore, 1963).

46. The last phrases are borrowed from Umberto Eco's discussion of baroque form, suggesting that it was dynamic through the indeterminacy of its effect. Baroque art, he observed, "conveys the idea of space being progressively dilated. Its search for kinetic excitement and illusory effect leads to a situation where the plastic mass in the Baroque work of art never allows a privileged, definitive, frontal view; rather, it induces the spectator to shift his position continuously in order to see the work in constantly new aspects, as if it were in a state of perpetual transformation." For the first time, he argues, "man opts out of the canon of authorized responses and finding that he is faced (both in art and in science) by a world in a fluid state which requires corresponding creativity on his part." See Umberto Eco, *The Role of the Reader* (Bloomington, 1981), 52. Although Eco's observations are well taken, they primarily relate to the eventual consideration of 'discovery' as the creation of systems, and 'creation' as the discovery of how systems may be used—an understanding endorsed by writers in the second half of the eighteenth century.

predicament of Man. While inspiration was thought to guide the recondite content, the composer shaped its external appearance into a work of art. Though inherited musical forms and musical elements continued to underlie the compositions of the nineteenth century, their formation underwent changes through the modifications that individual composers introduced, leaving a distinct mark on their compositions. Never before did a musical period abound in so many individual styles and in so many different types of composition as did the Romantic era.

From General "Language" to Particularized "Speech"

Apart from the place of music in the initial development of language, or music's lasting contribution to the prosodic layer of languages, it is fair to claim that music also developed a language of its own, comprising, as we have seen, unique musical characteristics. However, once music came to be looked upon as a disembodied spirit, as the primordial source of the varied utterances that facilitated activity and communication among humans, languages came to be viewed as part of a process of *de*composition, emphasizing their commonality rather than their distinctiveness. As both source of all languages and the "whole" that represents them, 'Music' was assumed to interact smoothly with its parts, so as to render the particular in the general. The particular, explained Johann Wilhelm Ritter,[47] could be raised thereby to the intelligibility of the general, which is understood by all, regardless of the tongues they use, since it constitutes an integral part of man's *consciousness*. Given that this "general language" is part of man's consciousness, it does not come from man himself; man only serves as its "translator" from the particular into the general. "Only in expressing himself is man conscious."[48]

The idea that awareness implies a representation to oneself was already central to the philosophy of Johann Georg Hamann (1730–88), whose thinking exerted considerable influence on the Sturm und Drang movement in German literature of the late eighteenth century. The tendencies

47. Ritter was a contemporary advocate of *Naturphilosophie*—a mystical, Romantic philosophy of science.

48. It should be noted that the explanation that identifies music not only with speech but with consciousness itself was advanced by a scientist. Ritter was a renowned German physicist who also enjoyed the friendship and admiration of the Schlegel brothers and many other men of letters whose interests reached beyond the confines of their professional activities. For the citation that identifies music with consciousness, see Charles Rosen, *The Romantic Generation* (Cambridge, Mass., 1995), 59.

of the movement were reflected in music as well, through a "labored" kind of musical expressiveness. As one of the most important critics of the German Enlightenment, Hamann attacked the undue authority given to reason over faith. Faith, he believed, consists in an immediate personal experience, inaccessible to reason. The reification of ideas, the artificial abstraction of reason from its social and historical context, he considered a fallacy, stressing instead the role of language in the development of reason. The instrument and criterion of reason, he argued, was language sanctioned by tradition and use. Hamann also attacked the critical philosophy of Kant for its purification of reason from experience. The task of philosophy, he claimed, was not to introduce "dualisms" of all kinds but to unify all the various functions of the mind, viewing 'reason,' 'will' and 'feeling' as an indivisible whole. His sharp break with eighteenth-century rationalism also came to the fore in his aesthetics, which defended the metaphysical supremacy of art. In Hamann's aesthetics, Kant's 'space' and 'time' turned into preconditions of *expression*—the one for painting, the other for music—and perception emerged as an active rather than as a passive phenomenon. Awareness, consequently, implies a representation to oneself by definition.

As far as Hamann was concerned, perception of the world *in time* is already language, and music is its most general form, since temporal ordering is the incipient musical structure. The idea of Music as a "general language," of which the separate languages are "fragments," is an idea that Ritter appended to the philosophy of Hamann. According to Rosen, it is the idea of music as a "general language" that influenced Robert Schumann and which Hoffmann also picked up and developed in the portrayal of his whimsical "Kapellmeister Kreisler." The cycle of eight piano pieces (strongly contrasting in mood) that Schumann named "Kreisleriana" reflects the idea of "general language," says Rosen. It affected as well Schumann's technique of songwriting, in which "the general musical line is individualized only intermittently into words: the full line is either in the piano or passed from piano to voice." Rosen attributes to Schumann the originality of the technique whereby the complete phrase is only "incompletely realized by either voice or accompaniment," and claims that this approach "radically transformed the traditional relationship of song to accompaniment."[49]

Indeed, the departure from the traditional relationships between song

49. See ibid., 60–61.

and accompaniment affected the function each served and the division of labor between them. Up to this point, accompaniment mainly served the function that is implied by its name, that is, it provided either the harmonic underpinning of the melody or the doubling of the melody plus added harmonies. The accompaniment, at times, also opened and closed with salient sections borrowed from the melody, so as to anticipate or round out the vocal line instrumentally, or to intercede between its repeated stanzas, as in the aria, for example. In these procedures the independence of the melodic line was hardly ever challenged. The invasion of the vocal melody by the accompaniment, or the actual taking over of the melodic line while introducing musical materials that compete with its supremacy or slant its interpretation, clearly altered the functions they served for each other, resulting in an inability to disentangle the two.

The erosion of the traditional relationship of song to accompaniment would be inconceivable without the changed attitude toward music as a general language, which presumably gave birth both to verse and to the languages that specify its meaning. The dividing lines between the parts and the whole became diffuse, for the parts no longer carried the separate functions they were believed to serve for each other. The oneness of the whole was also expected to override the significance of its inner derivatives, since masking the various divisions seemed more congenial to the enigmatic ambience and illusive import the composer wished to convey. Obscuring the division of labor among parts does not mean, however, that the character of the "wholes" necessarily resembled each other; they could in fact differ from each other markedly depending on the "ingredients" used and the manner in which they were employed. Particular "mixes" were evidently determined by *reactions* to certain life experiences that resulted in states of mind that bear general "labels"—such as 'delight,' 'longing,' 'reminiscing,' 'distress,' 'solitude,' 'anguish,' and the like—which in turn suggested artistic procedures suitable for their representation. Yet such representations must ipso facto rest on decodable signs.

The old debate as to whether music serves the words or the other way around became irrelevant in this new aesthetic outlook. Once music was conceived as the *precondition* of speech, which becomes individualized into words, the emphasis was bound to shift from music that particularizes or embellishes words to that of music "becoming language." "The fusion of music and poetry," says Rosen, "was supposed to result from the coincidence of meaning of two independent forms of expression. In practice, of course, this ideal fusion is attainable only intermittently, and either poetry or music must step down and be made to serve the other."[50] Although this goes some distance toward explaining the changed relationship between song and accompaniment, it also contributes to an understanding of the changes that were introduced into seemingly independent pieces—vocal or instrumental—that were understood and performed as *parts* of a larger whole.

Stringing together the independent parts of an extended composition invariably calls for a scheme that justifies their belonging together. Tradition and fiat, however, often suffice to explain an entrenched norm. While the number of movements a classical symphony contains and the order of their occurrence, or the ordering of the dances in a baroque suite, belong to the first category, the number of parts and their ordering in a Mass composition belong to the second category. This by no means implies that traditionally sanctioned norms are void of aesthetic considerations. The character of the individual parts may in fact contrast with each other in a number of ways—for example, fast versus slow, homophonic versus polyphonic, simple versus intricate rhythms—so as to create a balanced variegated composition. The scheme may apply to internal as well as external factors, including repeats of sections already heard.

There is a vast difference, however, between musical forms that are based on repeats of sections already heard—such as a rondo, a *da capo* aria, or a sonata reprise—and compositions that employ "returns" of various sorts in an unanticipated manner. The latter, unlike the former, are not dictated by a preexisting formal structure, but may be determined by some extramusical content that affects the nature of the musical unfolding. Indeed, recurrent musical events prescribed by a preconceived structural design differ considerably from a series of seemingly independent compositions that jointly form a "cycle" that converges on a theme or idea taken from life. A cyclical musical form that circles around an idea progresses linearly, yet its parts contain constituent elements that intrude on each other, forming, as it were, a seamless "ring." Intruding on each other's individual domains highlights the *external* theme that the series holds in common. All those familiar with the famous song cycles of the nineteenth century will no doubt agree that it is impossible to ignore their extramusical impulse and thrust. This, of course, holds equally true for the symphonic poems, which tried to represent by direct sensuous means what ostensibly was the essence of the poem. This enabled Franz Liszt to consider the symphonic poem a more intimate union of poetry and music

50. Ibid., 66.

than song, opera, and other genres that include literary language. Liszt, in fact, viewed the total "absorption" of literature into music as the most adequate representation of the modern way of feeling.[51] A new mixture of literary and musical elements came to the fore in opera as well, whereby the "limits" of the participating arts were similarly dissolved, as it were.[52] Yet here, too, regardless of the rhetoric that opera engendered, music remained its expressive center. Even Wagner, keen as he was to highlight the dramatic aspects of his operas, only shifted the brunt of expression from the singer to that of an enlivened symphonic orchestra.

For the Romantic composer, music provided a receptive framework in which recollections, associations, and a free flow of consciousness could be expressed via audible means. Music was made to echo sentiments and states of mind by relocating musical materials, including the associations they evoked, in new surroundings. Without exhuming past events, present moments were made to include residues from the past by diffusing them in a way that aptly represented the consciousness of composers, or their protagonists. Reflections of this kind—which both "mirror" and "remind"—created links among seemingly independent parts and bestowed a sort of unity on the whole. While individuating the whole, these reflections also conveyed the composer's attitude to the represented material. Free from preconceived structural dictates, the composer could also give vent to his changing states of mind, or that of his actors, without having to resort to "labels." Though semantic differentiation may offer subtleties that music, given its synthetic nature, is unable to supply, words that aspire

51. See Liszt's *Gesammelte Schriften* (Leipzig, 1882), vol. 4, 58.

52. Among the various attempts to delineate "music's modernity," Hermann Danuser argues that the history of music was not sufficiently attentive to the "social dimensions" imparted by music's "self-reflexivity." While self-reflexivity had been observed and discussed in the twentieth century (as in Richard Strauss's *Capriccio,* for example), the phenomenon itself, argues Danuser, was overlooked, though the self-reflective qualities that comic strategies created were already rife in eighteenth-century opera. Comic strategies, by virtue of being able to create situations of contrast to given norms, establish contradictions between "form and content," a kind of "mediation between our sensual experience and the signs, which reflects a tendency towards modernity." By "inverting given structures," comic strategies imparted to modernist aesthetics "tools" that, according to Danuser, "set the powers of creative fantasy free because by liberating societal norms, they contribute to a loosening of artistic norms." Indeed, the relationship between "societal norms" and "artistic norms" is, like all else, subject to change. As we shall see, this very issue will increasingly gain saliency and will be openly debated by composers. See Hermann Danuser, "The Textualization of Context: Comic Strategies in Meta-Operas of the Eighteenth and Twentieth Centuries," in *Music and the Aesthetics of Modernity,* 65–97.

to represent Music—in its enlarged sense—may stand to benefit from the subtleties that the eloquence of music is able to offer. Indeed, 'Music' may have been redefined, yet that which differentiates music from the other arts remained unchanged; its hard-earned "powers" were just differently employed, dictated by a new vision.

Let us not forget that musical compositions were not only intended to convey the experiences and emotional reactions of the artist; they were also meant to evoke comparable emotional reactions in the listener, based on his own experiences. To assure rapport between composer and listener, the composer incorporated in his structural design elements that aimed to guarantee shared associations, always related to the context in which they appeared. Readily perceived musical gestures—musical metaphors that imitate familiar sounds from nature; emphatic musical accentuation that convey assertions and affirmations of all kinds; lingering musical motions that disclose hesitation, indecision, and the like; and many other metaphorical devices—were used in ways that evoked the prelinguistic function of music as a vehicle of communication. While music as a "general language" was reinforced thereby, it was employed as a kind of "particularized speech" of 'Music'—the inexplicable primeval cause whence all the arts sprang and the "womb" to which they return.

It is fascinating to observe how music's self-referential power, its pure unfolding, and its potential for expressive coinage became viewed as its a priori "condition," in which "the end is not distinct from the means, the form from the matter, the subject from the expression," as Walter Pater defined it.[53] Yet it is only as a symbolic system that could "make sense" *without* predication that music remained "open" to extramusical interpretation, that is, to metaphorical "possession" of various sorts, including the metaphorical interaction with the other arts. Heir to the sonata form and the powerful expression it had achieved in the symphony, the Romantics chose, nonetheless, to emphasize Beethoven's impulsive attitude over the immanent logic that his compositions observed, taking the latter, as it were, for granted. Altogether, attitudes to symphonic form became more relaxed, with extramusical contents being toyed with in one way or another. Although this relaxation appeared most clearly in the works of Hector Berlioz, who was strongly animated by extramusical ideas, it also affected other composers whose mastery of the form leaves no room for doubt.

53. See Walter Pater, *The Renaissance* ([1893] Los Angeles, 1980), 109.

A General Theory concerning the Function
of Symbol Systems in the Arts

Though Georg Wilhelm Friedrich Hegel declared that music was the archetypal Romantic art and poets and painters marveled at music's freedom to manipulate its own forms and symbols without reference to reality outside itself, it was not Music that tantalized their ears, but a particular kind of music. Its overall guidelines were well entrenched in their minds, regardless of the discourse that accompanied it. This holds no less true for nineteenth-century philosophers who actually exerted influence on subsequent musical theory and thought, Arthur Schopenhauer for example. They all related to a "world of sound" that rested on a unique historical development that increasingly tightened the internal references of that sphere, relating musical events to each other *inwardly*. Pure instrumental music—*the* source of their admiration and wonder—employed all of those elements that enhanced the coherence of musical compositions. Although the 'absolute music' of the eighteenth century created a heightened consciousness of listening, music *with* words, it should be noted, still remained in the forefront of that century's musical activity.[54] The nineteenth century, by comparison, exploited the readiness to forgo the lexical function of words in order to take advantage, ironically, of their referential ambiguity. Since language invariably refers to something outside itself without circumscribing its field of reference, music could be enlisted to eliminate or to further the search for referents, by emphasizing either music's *un*ambiguous nature or its ephemeral "content-free" existence.

Discussing the development of music in the West, I emphasized the significance of the symbolic language in which it is written. Although the evolution of Western music is inconceivable without writing, the notational system it eventually chose also circumscribed its overall "idiom." Tracing the development of notation in the West revealed that it persistently eliminated ambiguities and reduced its dependence on any particular style. Once Goodman's five requirements for a notational system were fulfilled (see chapter 1, note 27), *work* preservation, not score preservation, was ensured; the latter is clearly "incidental," compared to the paramount significance of the former. Though all symbol systems consist of a symbol scheme correlated with a field of reference, discursive languages—unlike

54. For an interesting discussion on the subject, see R. J. Sondheimer, *Die Theorie der Symphonie* (Leipzig, 1925).

notational systems—meet only the two syntactic requirements, that is, the disjointness and finite differentiation of characters, but are exempt from the three semantic requirements, that is, from unambiguity, disjointness, and finite differentiation regarding their field of reference. In discursive languages, accordingly, a definition or set of coextensive definitions is seldom uniquely determined by a member of the class defined, whereas the basic purpose of a notational system may be served only if the compliance relationship is invariant.

A concise summary of Goodman's more comprehensive theory of symbol systems and the ways they function in the arts will contribute a great deal to our understanding of the manner in which they were employed by the Romantics.[55] Given that symbols invariably refer to something, Goodman found it necessary, in his *Languages of Art,* to establish from the outset that 'resemblance' is not necessary for reference and that almost anything may stand for almost anything else. A picture that represents—like a passage that describes—an object refers to and more particularly denotes it. 'Denotation' (what is implied or signified), argues Goodman, is the core of representation and is independent of resemblance. Given that 'representation' is not a matter of imitation, 'reception' and 'interpretation' are interdependent, for in representing an object one does not copy the interpretation, but *achieves* it. Although anything may be denoted, only 'labels' may be exemplified, argues Goodman. Exemplification of an unnamed property usually amounts to exemplification of a nonverbal symbol for which we have no corresponding word or description. The gestures of a conductor, for example, are "labels" applied in analyzing, organizing, and registering what we hear. Though actual labels are often ostensibly applied to fictive things, fictive labels, Goodman reminds us, cannot be applied, for a label that is used exists.

'Exemplification,' explains Goodman, is a mode of symbolization related to 'expression.' Though not all exemplification is expression, all expression is exemplification, and what is expressed is *metaphorically* exemplified. Metaphors, however, require attraction as well as resistance, an attraction that overcomes resistance. In metaphor, Goodman tells us, a term with an extension established by habit is applied elsewhere under

55. Since the following summary is entirely based on Goodman's *Languages of Art,* mindful of his definitions of the major concepts he uses, I shall at times keep some of his own wording intact without quotation marks and without reference to isolated page numbers. My summary primarily aims to trace and present faithfully the *logic* of his arguments and their interrelatedness, focusing on those aspects that are relevant to our own discussion.

the influence of that habit; there is both departure from and deference to precedent. When one use of a term precedes and informs another, the second is the metaphorical one. The understanding of metaphor requires recognition that a label functions not in isolation but as belonging to a "family," for we categorize by *sets* of alternatives. The aggregate of the ranges of extension of the labels in a schema Goodman calls "a realm." A realm thus consists of the objects sorted by the schema, that is, the objects denoted by at least one of the alternative labels. The shifts in range that occur in metaphor, Goodman explains, amount to a "migration of concepts, an alienation of categories." It is not, however, the whole "class" that moves from realm to realm, nor are attributes somehow extracted from some objects and injected into others. It is, rather, a set of alternative labels that is transported, and the organization they effect in the alien realm is guided by their habitual use in the home realm. Although a schema may be transported almost anywhere, and the choice of territory for invasion is arbitrary, the operation within that territory, Goodman insists, is almost never completely arbitrary. We are free, for example, to apply temperature predicates, say 'warm,' to sounds, hues, personalities, and so forth, but which elements in the chosen realm are warm, or warmer than others, is then largely determined. In sum, metaphorical force requires a combination of novelty with fitness, of the odd with the obvious. Metaphor *creates* similarity, and with repetition a transferred application of a schema becomes routine, no longer requiring or making allusion to its base application. Thus "what was novel becomes commonplace, its past is forgotten, and metaphor fades to mere truth."

Given that "what is expressed is metaphorically exemplified," it follows that what expresses sadness, for example, is metaphorically sad, and what is metaphorically sad is *actually* but not literally sad, for it comes under a transferred application of some label coextensive with "sad." Thus what is expressed is "possessed," argues Goodman, and what a face or picture expresses need not (but may) be emotions or ideas that the artist wants to convey, or the thoughts or feelings of the viewer or of a person depicted, or the properties of anything else related in some other way to the symbol. The properties a symbol expresses are, however, its own property, but they are acquired property. They are not the features by which the objects that serve as symbols are classified literally, but are metaphorical imports. Furthermore, properties expressed, we learn from Goodman, are not only metaphorically "possessed" but also "referred to, exhibited, typified, and shown forth." In short, "whereas almost anything can denote or even represent almost anything else, a thing can express only what belongs but did not originally belong to it. The difference between expression and literal exemplification is a matter of habit, a matter of fact rather than fiat."[56]

Establishment of the referential relationship, as we have seen, is a matter of *singling out* certain properties for attention, of selecting associations with certain objects. Verbal discourse is not least among the many factors that aid in founding and nurturing such associations. Yet musical expressions are no less relative and variable; music may exemplify rhythmic patterns and express peace, pomp, or passion. With respect to verbal symbols, however, Goodman reminds us that ordinary usage is so "undiscriminating" that a word or passage may be said to express not only what the writer thought, felt, intended, or the properties possessed by or ascribed to a subject, but even what is described or stated. Though a verbal symbol may express only the properties it metaphorically exemplifies, *naming* a property and *expressing* it are apparently different matters. Clearly, a tale of fast action may be slow and a description of colorful music drab. To exemplify or express is to *display* rather than describe. From all of these various related modes of symbolization, that is, kinds of reference, the arts may select and organize their "universe" and be themselves in turn informed or transformed.

It is at this point that Goodman introduces his notational theory, but not before having clarified some questions concerning authenticity. His discussion of the subject reveals that in the different arts a work is differently localized; Rembrandt's own brushstrokes must obviously be considered differently than Bach's handwriting, however telling. Goodman distinguishes, accordingly, between "autographic" and "allographic" arts, between works that represent individual objects, as in painting, and those that represent a class of performances compliant with the work, as in music. He now proceeds to present his notational theory in order to show that a musical score is in a notation that *defines* a work, and that a picture is not in a notation but is *itself* a work, and that literary script is in a notation and is itself a work. Evidently, in the different arts a work is differently localized.

Though both music and literature are in a notation, taking into account Goodman's five requirements of a notational *system,* music is both syntactically and semantically articulate, whereas literature is only syntactically articulate but semantically "dense," that is, its field of reference is not finitely and unambiguously differentiated. In other words, though a literary work is articulate and exemplifies or expresses what is articulated, various

56. Goodman, *Languages of Art,* 89. For much that was said above, see 52–95.

readings of the text are always required in order to determine precisely what is exemplified or expressed. Although further and projective decisions have to be made with discursive languages, no such questions arise using a notational system as music does. Nothing is, however, intrinsically a representation; status as representation, we learn from Goodman, is relative to symbol system, and a scheme is representational only insofar as it is dense. Hence, despite the definition of works by scores, exemplification of anything beyond the score is reference in a semantically dense system, and a matter of infinitely fine adjustment.

Representation and description are clearly markedly different from exemplification and expression. While representation and description relate a symbol to things it applies to, exemplification relates the symbol to a label that denotes it (and hence indirectly to the things in the range of that label), and expression relates the symbol to a label that metaphorically denotes it (and hence indirectly not only to the given metaphorical but also to the literal range of that label). Thus, to exemplify or express is to display rather than to depict or describe. Since expression is what concerns us most, let us have a look at Goodman's own summary of expression. If 'a' expresses 'b,' then (1) 'a' possesses or is denoted by 'b'; 2) this possession or denotation is metaphorical; and (3) 'a' refers to 'b.' Were we to substitute music for 'a' and emotion for 'b,' Goodman's summary would state the following: if 'music' expresses 'emotion,' then (1) music possesses or is denoted by emotion; (2) this possession or denotation is metaphorical; and (3) it refers to emotion. Let us not forget, however, that expression must be *displayed* and that the utterances of music are *end products* because music is both syntactically and semantically articulate.

Although there is no want of aesthetic theories that deal with music's expressivity, I know of no theory that covers the interrelated functions of symbols pertinent to the arts as rigorously and as succinctly as Goodman's does. Yet there is no denying the importance of Ernest Cassirer's contribution to the philosophy of symbolic logic, with which Goodman was apparently well acquainted. As an arresting representative of Continental philosophy, Cassirer employed his vast learning to unveil the symbolizing activities through which man has expressed himself and given form to his experience.[57] As an analytical philosopher, Goodman's main objective in

57. See Ernest Cassirer, *The Philosophy of Symbolic Forms* (New Haven, 1955, vols. 1–3), translated from the original three volumes (1908–29) by Ralph Manheim. Also see *Symbol, Myth, and Culture: Essays and Lectures of Ernst Cassirer, 1935–1945,* ed. Donald Phillip Verene (New Haven, 1979).

his *Languages of Art* was to unveil the *logic* whereby the denotation of symbols is acquired and circumscribed. Although the symbolizing activities through which man expresses himself are subject to change, affecting the forms to which they give rise, the forms themselves, we learn from Goodman, invariably abide by limiting factors that are necessary for their understanding. Thus how and in what way representation functions in the various arts is independent of the particular choices that are made; works of art must ipso facto take into account the various modes of symbolization, that is, kinds of reference, in order to disclose their preferred objectives.

THE FLAUNTING OF IDENTITIES:
INDIVIDUAL AND COLLECTIVE

The idea that the arts differ from each other in decided ways that affect their choice of subject matter emerged only gradually. Yet once it took hold, the division of labor among the arts was tacitly employed in the interaction among the arts, whether in song, dance, or theater. Though the Romantic conception of 'Music' seems to have blurred this division of labor, it increased the sensitivity to the symbolizing functions that each of the arts is able to render. Cognizant of metaphorical exchanges of various sorts, the invasion of each other's territory was carried out with utmost discretion, guided by the distinctions that different modes of reference seem to supply. Indeed, the changes that occurred in music, its manifold relationships with discursive language, including that of landscape descriptions, reveal a heightened sensitivity to the ways in which music may enhance the communication of specified meanings. The ability of music to refer to something outside itself rested, however, on a metaphorical possession that took for granted the sophisticated "syntax" that music had developed. In short, music expressed what it denoted, and what it denoted was an acquired property exemplified by "labels." The adequacy of music to display that by which it was only metaphorically possessed created the illusion that music, more than the other arts, is able to capture the representational characteristics of 'Music.' Many composers tried, each in his way, to lend credence to this illusion.

Intimacy Made Public

The Romantic era, I suggested somewhat earlier, may be characterized by a kind of "opting out of the canon of authorized responses," a facing of 'ideal nature' in a "fluid state" that required a "corresponding creativity"—

free yet compelling. If the period gave rise to an abundance of individual styles, this is largely due to the fact that composers were now called upon to be *persuasive*. Beyond displaying a supreme mastery of their craft, they were expected to employ their artistry in ways whose "faithfulness" to the *human* spirit, if not to the cosmic one, could pass unchallenged. Inasmuch as 'Music' embodies a kind of cosmic spirit that affects the spiritual condition of Man, displaying human states of mind via *music* was supposed to yield insights into the workings of Music. Yet insights of *this* kind are rare; they are, as we have seen, reserved for the few who are properly "inspired." They occur, moreover, only among those who are both capable of making and ready to undertake a scrupulous and candid examination of self. Indeed, introspection became a sine qua non for those insights that the uninspired were expected to recognize—identify and acclaim—once they were made public.

Though valuable insights are to be gained from introspection, the scientific observations of the human soul or mind were clearly not derived in this way. While the field of psychology, as is well known, gained considerable momentum in the nineteenth century, this is hardly the place to delve into the historical circumstances that affected its course. Rather, the point I wish to draw attention to has an immediate bearing on the artistic creativity that concerns us here. To disclose one's own emotions, it may be recalled, was considered in poor taste—"uncivilized"—in the eighteenth century, unless it was properly framed by legitimizing circumstances. Although intimate moments were expected to provide "clues" that could mitigate embarrassment, shared styles of behavior solicited attention to their implementation rather than to the personal feelings that accompanied them. The nineteenth century seems to have reversed these tacit understandings. Revealing one's innermost reflections and feelings, accordingly, could provide clues that concern the general public, and a highly individualized artistic mode of expression could harbor "revelations" that transcend their unique appearance.

Without entering into a discussion about private versus public spheres, there is no denying that the nineteenth century altered the attitude toward both. Much that was considered private turned into concerns that engaged the public, and public concerns that were previously attended to by a select few engaged the interest of far greater numbers. Though the dichotomy between private and public was retained, their spheres became differentiated along different lines. The reshuffling of the boundaries between private and public is generally precipitated by social and political factors that redistribute reticence, commitment, and responsibility.

These, in turn, become manifest in cultural activities of all kinds, including the functions served by the arts and the ways they carry them out. Yet inasmuch as specific cultures relate to particular types of intellectual development, every stage in such a development is informed by a mental frame of thought, one that precedes it and is of consequence for that which follows it. Accordingly, while music now "licensed" the flaunting of intimacy in public, it was still informed by a previous "frame of mind," that of music's systemic internal relationships, which linked the "spirited" composer and his public.

The Particularization of Publics

"Soul searching" was also applied at the group level. Thus, the political creed that underlies the cohesion of modern societies, that is, nationalism, is of comparatively recent historical development. But this familiar form of political organization—viewed as a framework for all social and cultural activities—was unknown before the eighteenth century. The idea that each form of nationalism is conditioned by the social structure, the intellectual tradition, the cultural history, and the geographic location in which nationalism asserts itself is a notion of modern European history closely linked with the theory of government by the active consent of the governed. As a politically revolutionary movement, nationalism, of course, tried to overthrow past claims to authority based upon divine ordination or hereditary rights. But it also tried to establish new political entities coextensive with geographic, ethnic, linguistic, and cultural frontiers. Thus, political self-determination of a people—the goal of nationalism—entailed separateness, distinctness, and independence from other nations, yet equal to them. Though the Enlightenment had already expressed some of these aspirations in its persistent strivings to further "individualism" and "democratic equality," it is the nineteenth century that transferred these demands from the individual to the collective. From the early nineteenth century on, nationalism carried with it the demand for "national" foundations for all cultural and intellectual life. The nationalists placed great emphasis on *cultural* self-determination because they believed that only thus could the people become autonomous subjects, an end in itself, instead of being a means for the policy to achieve the goals of others. The quest for cultural self-determination was in fact perceived as the ground for political self-determination.

These developments seem to mark the beginning of a long process whereby supranational and theoretically universal claims are in decline, being steadily replaced by emphases on local cultural traditions, including folk traditions that facilitate the accessibility of the nonlearned to culture. In retrospect it appears that the decline in theoretically universal cultural assets harbored from its inception implications for ideas that were to reach fruition only toward the turn of the millennium, as manifested in postmodern thought and multicultural trends. It must be remembered, however, that this extended process was accompanied by an ever growing conviction that explication in the cultural sphere must be holistic, that is, that characteristic human activities—such as art, religion, law, and language—must be included within the scientific worldview. This implied, moreover, that human actions, regardless of their kind, had to be understood in their historical and cultural contexts and not simply viewed as instances of a causal regularity between events. The human spirit is essentially free; it may express itself in a variety of ways not circumscribed by a predetermined order. It expresses itself, however, within organically integrated wholes, embodying the practical and profound wisdom of convention and tradition, subject to time and place. Abstract analytical segments cannot be separated from these cumulative organic products, for to do so is tantamount to slighting the complex interdependence of the web of social life. The philosophy of Romanticism clearly influenced this view of society; for that matter, the overall tendency to subordinate form to content has its roots in Romanticism.

Romanticism, to be sure, underwent many phases, and each locale placed its own stamp upon it. Yet of all these, early German Romanticism is of special importance in the history of Western thought. The primary aim of Romantics such as Friedrich Schlegel, Friedrich Schleiermacher, Friedrich Schelling, and others was essentially social and political. They wanted to overcome the alienation created by modernity through a renewed unity with oneself, with others, and with Nature. As already mentioned, they advocated an ethics of love and self-realization in opposition to the Kantian ethic of duty. Among their many novel ideas, they developed an organic concept of Nature against the mechanistic worldview of Cartesian physics. Ethics, politics, and aesthetics, they claimed, should all be seen in the light of a cultural goal—to cure humanity of "homesickness" and make the individual feel "at home" again. As a central figure in the German intellectual renaissance of the late eighteenth century, Johann Gottfried Herder (1744–1803) exerted immense influence upon Romanticism and German idealism. Indeed, he exerted no less influence on the development of historicism and nationalism.[58] Although his achievements spanned every domain of philosophy, he was among the first to defend the value of ethnic poetry and the need for a historical, culture-bound understanding of a text. He believed, moreover, that creative work can be done only in one's own folk language and that great art has always been the expression of, and determined by, the *Volksgeist* (the "national" spirit). As part and parcel of a *Volk,* the individual imbibes its characteristic spirit "naturally." Processes of this kind are assumed to lend confidence to artists and credence to their works. Great art, accordingly, must be "genuine," and nothing can be genuine without self-evident conviction. It is important to specify the context that gave rise to Herder's conception of "genuineness," for taken out of context the loftiest of ideas may be misconstrued. Herder's main aim was to develop naturalistic, nonreductive explanations for the realm of culture; he did not seek criteria for cultural "incompetence" or exclusion. Later Germans, of course, would find it all too easy to do precisely that (not that others are exempt).[59]

58. In his interesting study of the German phase of the Enlightenment, Peter Reill has persuasively argued that the German Aufklärers ("enlighteners") sought to reconcile extreme rationalism and self-conscious Pietism and that their conception of history, and their preoccupation with aesthetics, psychology, and religion stemmed from a desire to mediate between normative and subjective modes of understanding. The German Aufklärers, says Reill, confronted the tension between change and communal being, between will and reason; they recognized that societies were regulated by shared communal feelings—habits of heart and mind that are embodied in custom and law—that form the "character or spirit of the times." This "spirit" constitutes, in turn, the only true basis upon which effective change could be achieved. "The true revolutionary (one who effects basic changes in society) was, in their eyes," says Reill, "the man or group of men who saved tradition from stagnation and breakdown by a creative reinterpretation of that tradition. In their evolving analysis, the Aufklärers differentiated among three types of spiritual influences: the vaguely defined *Geist der Zeit;* the more specific, though equally hazy, national character; and the active spirit, soul, or moral apprehension of the original genius, who acted within and against the other two. With these root concepts, the Aufklärers sought to describe the *Ideenwirkung* (the rational and emotional effect of ideas) on history." The German phase of the Enlightenment, unlike its French and English counterparts, affirmed the "irrational substratum of life. And, finally, they formulated a theory of historical understanding that established a duality between nature and spirit and recognized that all historical understanding is relative to the milieu in which it is generated." See Peter Hanns Reill, *The German Enlightenment and the Rise of Historicism* (California, 1975), 161–62, 218–19.

59. The German culture acquired by the Jews, Wagner claimed decades later, remained "very thin"; even their language was recent, he wrote. They "stuttered" in the new language of music, he said, pointing to Meyerbeer. Art grows in the soil of culture, Wagner asserted, and the Jews are altogether out of touch with its roots. Wagner's aims

It is fascinating to observe how the selfsame ideas served to sanction the uniqueness both of the individual and of the society to which he belongs, allowing for a free interaction between the two without encountering contradictions. Individual "spirits," accordingly, could betray elements of collective significance, and the collective "spirit" guaranteed the freedom of the individual to do so. Whether on the individual or societal level, a kind of "soul-searching"—a turn of mind inward upon itself through an examination of one's own thoughts, feelings, and mental processes—was deemed to harbor a promise of liberation. If the Enlightenment hoped to deliver Man from prejudice or superstition by emphasizing reason and individualism against tradition, Romanticism overlooked the potential danger embedded in a theory that overemphasizes the interdependence of the *Geist* of the individual with the *Volk*. The realization that mental processes—thoughts and feelings—are, in one way or another, "conditioned" and cannot be detached from their "pastures," does not prevent prejudice and the like, of course; it may, in fact, encourage such phenomena under certain circumstances. One might argue that awareness of the fact that the human "spirit" is at all times inadvertently informed by external factors is all the more reason for reinstating *universal* criteria that limit both human rights and duties, entitlements *and* liabilities. This, however, is hardly the subject of this essay.

Introspection of all kinds, as argued earlier, was evinced in many compositions of the nineteenth century and in the individualized styles that characterize their composers. Nonetheless, the art of musical representation managed to develop a psychological system of signs, so that even the experience of landscapes turned into perceptual musical emblems. Moreover, along with the emancipation of the creative artist and his apparent isolation from his immediate surroundings, the political and social developments of the nineteenth century unveiled a subtle, fortuitous bond between them—a kind of "transaction" of which artists were previously unaware. To be sure, the historical development of music took place all along in national currents, and significant phases in this development crystallized in different geographic locations. Though composers became increasingly conscious of stylistic choices and national propensities, these seemingly individual phases—including the famous feuds around Italian

---

included, in fact, a desire to infuse music with the German folk spirit and to highlight the pre-Christian and Teutonic foundations of the culture. Wagner is not responsible, of course, for the ways in which he was used in the Third Reich, but he certainly made it easy.

versus French opera—contributed to the diachronic development of music. Yet before 1800, insists Alfred Einstein, "a strongly national coloring was shown only by those composers whose stature did not reach the lofty heights of greatness."[60] "Greatness," according to Einstein, entailed an awareness of the gamut of musical means (however acquired), which were skillfully employed by composers who paid no attention to the "national tag" that might be attached to their work. In other words, national coloring was characteristic of those who did not know any better, that is, to the less sophisticated among composers. To the extent that great composers availed themselves deliberately of national coloring, it mostly functioned as a kind of "parenthesis"—subordinate to the overall musical expression, not guided thereby. This situation was of course bound to change once 'culture' was redefined in the way the nineteenth century redefined it.

The unveiling of "souls"—that of the nation and that of the individual—and the processes whereby they are connected shifted attention to local traditions, highlighting historicity no less than authenticity. As a critique of the normative, ostensibly antihistorical epistemologies of the Enlightenment, the nineteenth century, as we have seen, emphasized the historicity of all knowledge and cognition, insisting on the radical segregation of human from natural history. By recasting human nature in the light of science, the Enlightenment believed in an idea of progress anchored in reason and individual self-reliance. The "historicism" of the nineteenth century, by contrast, launched doubts concerning the notion of a general all-encompassing "historical progress." For example, Herder's claim that human history is composed of fundamentally incomparable national cultures led to an argument against the construction of history as a kind of "linear progress."[61] Yet some years later, Hegel conceived of the historically situated individual consciousness as but particular moments within an all-encompassing process that has as its goal the recognition of Reason *through* reason, that is, the recognition that our perception of objectivity is determined by Reality, which plays a significant role in constituting the subject of both cognition and knowledge. Reason, as Hegel understood it, is not a quality attributed to human subjects, but the sum of all reality. Knowledge of reality, he claimed, is only possible if it is reasonable, for otherwise it could not be accessible to cognition. Since we can know only what is real, this calls for a unified theory of reality that will systematically

---

60. Alfred Einstein, *Music in the Romantic Era* (New York, 1947), 18.

61. For a discussion of Herder's "Outlines of a Philosophy of the History of Man" (1784), see R. C. Clark, *Herder: His Life and Thought* (California, 1955).

explain all of its forms: physical, organic, and psychic phenomena, social and political forms of organization, as well as artistic creations and other cultural achievements.[62] Historicism, as it turned out, followed both Herder and Hegel. It attempted to do justice to an objective kind of history, while trying to determine general patterns of historical change. This elusive approach to history eventually encountered much criticism on the part of theorists and historians alike, yet in the meantime it succeeded not only in creating an awareness of cultural differences and national uniqueness but also in encouraging their emergence.

National self-consciousness clearly tried to assert itself in music as well. It did so first in the countries that were nearest to the nations whose music had earned universal standing, that is, whose music-making exerted influence on the countries nearby. Prior to that moment, composers tried hard to emulate the achievements of those who had prevented them—largely for political reasons—from developing their own national life. Having been relegated to an inferior position, composers naturally aspired to the "trademarks" of those whose cultural activities resulted in widespread acclaim. Indeed, the whole notion of "cultural centers" underwent a revision with the growth of national self-consciousness. In earlier periods, dominance in musical activity moved from country to country, and the aesthetic predilection of each of these countries left its mark on the development of Western art music as a whole. Composers seeking employment also moved from place to place, guided by the availability of attractive positions. Nineteenth-century national self-consciousness could not eradicate what had been achieved over centuries by composers who contributed to the overall development of music despite their different national origins. Given the new climate, however, composers tried to lend distinct "dialects" to the musical "language" that they inherited. These dialects allotted composers a new avenue of pride, since nationalism not only revived and sanctioned the interest in local traditions but also insisted that each tradition harbors the "spirit" of a particular "folk." The national emphasis in music is thus strongly connected with a kind of "folk coloring." It was of course most genuinely represented by the incorporation of actual folk songs.

To trace the development of national music in each individual country is obviously beyond the scope of this essay. It must be stated, however, that the development in each country was largely affected by the musical activities that preceded it, that is, by the sort of relationships the country

62. For an introduction to Hegel's "Philosophy of History" (1826), see Charles Taylor, *Hegel* (Cambridge, 1975).

had previously maintained with "universal" music, and by the degree of patriotic sentiments in search of outlets. Even widely acclaimed composers faced the possibility of being accused of not being patriotic enough, though their music bore clear signs of their homeland. Pyotr Ilich Tchaikovsky, for example, was accused by an important group of Russian national composers of being too "Western."[63] Although it is unquestionably interesting to trace in what way and by whom the "spirit" of the "folk" was expressed, I have had to limit myself only to sketching the process that led to the emphasis in music on national characteristics. Ushered in by Romanticism, nationalism became a distinguishing feature of the Romantic era in music.

One must distinguish, however, between the historical development of a national character in music and the deliberate emphasis on national characteristics. By the eighteenth century, the Italians, the French, and the Germans had clearly developed what might be termed a "national character in music." Proud of their tradition, the French were even ready to debate the relative merits of French versus Italian opera—a quintessentially Italian genre. Yet outside the field of opera, which involved not only music but dramatic considerations as well, the French enthusiastically endorsed the German symphonists and tried to emulate their achievements. Given his outstanding mastery of the musical art, Bach was largely venerated by musicians everywhere. And one need only think of Mozart to realize how ubiquitous Italian music had become. Since the time of Peter the Great, Russia, for example, had been musically an Italian province, for most of its musicians were obtained from Italy. There are endless examples that attest to the fact that there was no contest for authority among the three national characters in music, despite their professed predilections; none of them distinctively emphasized its own national traits, for they all aimed at a universal standing. Even in those cases where folk tunes were employed, these mainly served as thematic material, as building stones, like any other. Stereotyped musical idioms of "remote lands" were at times employed in order to add a tinge of exoticism or a comic touch to the music; they were hardly prompted by *ethnographic* concerns. Although the attitude to "national coloring" had already shown signs of change toward the end of the eighteenth century, it is clearly the Romantic era that developed national *dialects* out of a universal musical language. The demarcation lines between "universal" and "national" varied from country to country, depending on

63. The group consisted of Mily Balakirev, Modest Mussorgsky, César Cui, Nikolai Rimsky-Korsakov, and Alexander Borodin. The group was later referred to as the Mighty Five, not least because of its patriotic fervor.

past experience and future aspirations. Though this holds equally true for individual composers, their "greatness" was still judged by what they had accomplished rather than by whom they represented.

MUSIC AS A CULTURAL SUBSYSTEM

While cultural change requires social actors as agents, and social change is likely to have cultural counterparts, changes in certain cultural subsystems may also be viewed in terms of an autonomous evolution. Science, for example, is a cultural tradition, preserved and transmitted from generation to generation because it is valued in its own right, irrespective of the changes it undergoes and the factors that influence the course of its development. A language may likewise be viewed in terms of autonomous evolution, regardless of the social and cultural factors that affected its development. As a cultural subsystem, the development of music in the West seems to have shared some aspects characteristic of the development of science and others characteristic of the development of language. For example, the primary purpose of scientists, like that of composers since the tenth century onward, has been change through discovery. Yet, unlike discoveries in science, innovation in art, as in language, lacks explicit criteria to determine whether an innovation, however unto itself appreciated, is an improvement over an existing tradition.[64] Some of the norms implicit in the public conduct of scientists, on the other hand, such as universality, neutrality, rationality, and communality, also characterized in the main the conduct of composers prior to the Romantic turn. The evolution of the musical language of the West revealed, moreover, a high degree of consensus with regard to its *theoretical* underpinnings, not unlike scientific movements in the seventeenth and eighteenth century, which viewed science as a model for attaining progress objectively and by common consent.[65] But whereas the professed aim of the natural sciences was, and still is, to unveil

---

64. Paul Kristeller claimed that the debates over the "modern" vs. the "ancient" in the arts brought to the fore the recognition of virtually two distinct bodies of knowledge — science and art. The progress of the moderns over the ancients, argued Kristeller, can clearly be demonstrated only in fields "where everything depends on mathematical calculation and the accumulation of knowledge." See "The Modern System of the Arts," in his *Renaissance Thought and the Arts* (Princeton, 1965), 163–227.

65. The "scientific revolution" of the seventeenth century placed great emphasis on the theoretical part of science. Theory, in fact, became the substratum of all the sciences, irrespective of their experimental approaches, until the "information revolution" of the twentieth century, which the advent of the computer brought about.

laws, music, like language, virtually *created* the laws whereby an independent coherent world of sound was constructed. Though the developmental process that steadily improved the communicative self-sufficiency of
music reached full fruition only in the eighteenth century, this point of
"self-sufficiency" was not only admired in the nineteenth century, but addressed as a "condition" intrinsic to music as such.[66] Once music was entertained as a "natural" phenomenon, albeit a singular language, composers could call special attention to the ways in which it was employed—to
the uniqueness and persuasiveness of musical utterances.

The Blend between Past and Future in Romantic Thought

The redefinition of 'Music,' as we have seen, went hand in hand with the
view of Man in the context of great cosmic and historical movements that
envelop him in an "infinity" that is beyond his grasp. Nevertheless, compared with the Enlightenment, the Romantic movement seems to have
enhanced man's *capabilities,* since the wider vision that man yearned for required faith *and* ingenuity, intuition *and* creativity, feeling *and* understanding. Compared to the supposed "rational man" of the Enlightenment, the
man driven by insight and will became actually more many-sided, though
by far more complicated. Nobody reflected this new state of affairs better
than the artist—the *creative* composer. Indeed, though "lost" in a boundless universe, composers could now, more than ever before, become visible as creative individuals. Adjusting to *human* nature—of which reason
was by no means considered the greatest part—they exploited the musical
language they so fervently appreciated, creatively. Thus, despite the quasi-
organic theory that emphasized man's spiritual ties to historically growing
communities and their institutions, the theory did not negate Romantic

66. In her interesting discussion of tonality (what it represented and what it could
accomplish), Susan McClary reminds us that "the eighteenth century was a period of
almost unparalleled confidence in the viability of a public sphere in which ideas could
be successfully communicated, differences negotiated, consensus achieved: thus the
concern with compiling encyclopedias and with codifying language, the arts, and even
thought itself, as well as the widespread standardization and adoption of convention."
Though the cultural practices came from the "top down," people who "identified with
liberal causes," we are told, "also put a premium on intelligibility and the efficacy of
shared discourses." Tonality, according to McClary, "constructed musical analogs to such
emergent ideals as rationality, individualism, progress, and centered subjectivity." The
musical procedures that evolved did not merely reflect their times, but "participated
actively in shaping habits of thought on which the modern era depended." See Susan Mc-
Clary, *Conventional Wisdom: The Content of Musical Form* (California, 2000), 64–65.

individuality, as might have been supposed; to the contrary, the latter was even deemed necessary, as we have seen, for the free development of the individual's personality.

Yet a mixed feeling about past and future became blended in Romantic thought, which affected music no less than other cultural spheres. Although the "resurrection" of the fatherland emphasized its unbroken historical succession, commanding respect for a past out of which one had grown, visions of the future entailed actual "missions," prophesying societal change and improved social conditions. This blend of Romantic thought became manifest not only in nineteenth-century nationalism but also in its historicism, which tried to bridge temporal individuality and historical continuity. The empathy with past epochs gave rise, for example, to an interest in early periods such as the Middle Ages, valorizing the latter's *spiritual* force as opposed to its material forces. The interest in the future, however, tended to reflect sentiments of revolt and a vision of social improvement, shifting the emphasis from spiritual to material forces in historical explanations.[67] This unique blend of past and future became manifest in music as well. Alongside the determination to affect the future of the art, an interest in early music came into being, emphasizing its "spirituality." The tendency was reinforced by the attraction to things remote, by a fascination with their obscurity. Thus, those in search of the primordial powers of Music were more inclined to endorse the "vagueness" of medieval music than the "obviousness" of an ordinary recent symphony. In whatever guise, the preoccupation with the past harbored implications for the historical and systematic study of music, while the preoccupation with the future contained the seeds of the oncoming overthrow of the referential system that music had developed over centuries.

Trying to restore unity among Man, God, and Nature in an alienating, unfriendly world that had turned prosaic, the Romantic movement clearly constituted a revolt against the "modernity" represented by the scientific Enlightenment. Yet aware of the fact that they were living in a world of an endless "becoming," the Romantics tried their utmost to affect its advance. The philosophical concerns with the *nature* of historical understanding originated primarily as part of a general protest against the Enlightenment's tendency to regard the natural sciences as representing

---

67. While Marx and Marxist theory serve as prime examples, Marx is not the only philosopher-historian whose interests shifted from the spiritual to the material domain. Indeed, many partook in this shift, trying, among other things, to avert the implications of *social* Darwinism.

the paradigm of all true knowledge. Yet despite early objections, such as Vico's, to the validity of extending modes of interpretation employed by the physical sciences to human studies, the methods established in areas of inductive inquiry continued to guide historical inquiry throughout the eighteenth century and were constantly reaffirmed by positivistic-minded theorists in the nineteenth century. Thus, while cultivating a sentimental relationship to the past—viewing the Mass compositions and the motets of the sixteenth century, for example, as the purest embodiment of an "unearthly" music—the nineteenth century also gave rise to a new discipline based on "objective" musical research. The study of music was in fact expected to render an unbiased picture of the historical development of the art—of its theoretical and aesthetic unfolding, as evinced in its manifold, diverse styles—not yet aware of the fact that music manifests itself in the interplay among the written score, its interpretation, and modes of reception. Yet by the time the discipline received its official formulation, toward the end of the century, some of its theoretical premises no longer suited the "imprudent" behavior of certain composers, who became noticed despite their "careless" conduct. Although their compositions revealed decided deviations from accepted norms, they could not be accused of not having mastered the knowledge of the métier.

The study of music, as is well known, was not regarded as an independent discipline until the second half of the nineteenth century. Prior to being treated as a science in its own right, music was handled as part of a general theory of knowledge. As a physical phenomenon, music benefited early on from the scientific methods developed in the natural sciences, yet, as a cultural phenomenon, it had to wait for the development of the cultural sciences and their modes of investigation. Modern humanistic scholarship, however, only commenced with the Enlightenment, with that current in European intellectual history that was as interested in the worlds created by Man as it was in God's Creation. To be sure, treatises concerning music—referring to both theory and practice—were also written before then, and a host of musical manuals guided students who wished to become familiar with the art. Of course, philosophy throughout the centuries abounded with deliberations regarding music, and serious debates about musical issues occupied musical practitioners, involving their publics as well from time to time. Yet despite its venerable place in the medieval *quadrivium*,[68] music, prior to the eighteenth century, was not treated as an autonomous subsystem. Padre Martini's three volumes

---

68. The medieval university courses were divided into two groups, the *quadrivium*

(1757–81), which dealt with the music of antiquity, already displayed original research and a critical historical evaluation, as expected of a "scientific" study. The same holds true of Martin Gerbert's two volumes (1774) on the history of church music. The general histories of music that followed, that of Charles Burney (4 vols., 1776–89), John Hawkins (5 vols., 1776), and Johann N. Forkel (2 vols., 1788, 1801), revealed a similar concern with music as an autonomous subsystem whose development, they believed, deserved critical evaluation. The fact that all of these works suffered from an insufficient knowledge of primary source material—mainly insofar as the early ("distant") periods were concerned—was all the more reason for scholars in the nineteenth century to "unearth" materials that would shed light on the historical development of music.

Most historians of music will no doubt agree that in the course of the eighteenth century the center of gravity of musical activity gradually moved from the southern to the northern part of Europe. Yet by the nineteenth century music-making in the German-speaking countries was accompanied by a contemplative component that was largely influenced by German idealism, which, as we have seen, also affected the historicism of the century, and, of course, the liberal arts. Since inductive inquiry persisted in guiding historical inquiry in general, musical studies, particularly the historical ones, were likewise expected to abide by the standards that had long been adopted for the natural sciences—trustworthiness and objectivity. But scientific deliberations concerning a field of knowledge require a proper stage for the exchange of ideas. Beyond societies of various sorts, they require adequate source materials and publications of all kinds, if the deliberations are to be of any consequence. Yet publishing houses, no less than institutions of learning, have first to recognize the value of such deliberations in order to lend them support. Although the problem of the chicken or the egg is often difficult to sort out, it seems likely that the principle of supply and demand affected the printing press more readily than it did the institutions of higher learning. Paradoxically, the more entrenched these institutions became, the less readiness they exhibited to explore new venues. As is often the case, those who stand to lose are less willing to dare; longstanding traditions, good or bad, resist change as long as they can.[69] At any rate, Germany, in the course of the nineteenth

---

and the *trivium*. The first consisted of arithmetic, geometry, astronomy, and music; the second contained grammar, rhetoric, and logic.

69. This widespread phenomenon should not be viewed, however, as a kind of "obstinacy," that is, as a refusal to confront novel ideas, but rather as set mental frames that delimit their "vision."

century, not only supplied the greatest number of historically outstanding composers but also contributed largely to the establishment of the necessary frameworks that promoted scientific deliberations on music.[70] Eventually, however, it is the German university system of the nineteenth century that strongly supported the scientific study of the liberal arts that created the proper framework for the new discipline, not least because of the proximity of other fields of knowledge that had a direct bearing on the study of music. To be sure, once musicology was officially established, not all of the German universities saw fit to include the subject among the disciplines they offered, not even by the 1930s. Nonetheless, compared to France, England, and Italy, it is the German university system that created an environment hospitable to the scientific study of music.[71]

The preoccupation with the past, as it turned out, had a decided influence on the historical study of music, yet the realization that social sentiments have only a precarious existence without symbols challenged

70. Leafing through the entry "Editions, Historical" in the *Harvard Dictionary of Music* will suffice to corroborate this point. German printing presses seems to have supported the publication of critical editions, bibliographies, catalogs, dictionaries—in short, all that was deemed necessary for the furtherance of musicological research—more readily than their counterparts in other countries.

71. Given this development, many a student interested in musical research traveled to Germany to acquire an education not obtainable in their countries of origin. What was well recognized in most of the European countries was doubly appreciated in the United States, which eventually contributed a major share to the development and strengthening of the field. Thus Oscar Sonneck, the first important American musicologist, chief of the Music Division of the Library of Congress (1902–17), received his training in Germany. Otto Kinkeldey, another figure associated with the beginnings of musicology in America, was likewise trained in Germany; he became the head of the Music Division of the New York Public Library upon his return from Germany in 1914. The first chair of musicology was established sixteen years later (1930) by Cornell University, and was offered to Kinkeldey. Oliver Strunk, one of the founders of the American Musicological Society (1934), a student of Kinkeldey's, spent his early twenties in Germany studying under Johannes Wolf, Friedrich Blume, Curt Sachs, and Arnold Schering. In fact, the first generation of American musicologists was inspired by or came into direct contact with the leading figures of German musicology in those days. Though musicology was steadily growing in America, it was still in its infancy, however, when so many uprooted musicologists landed on its shores, in the late 1930s and '40s. Only a few universities included musicology in their curricula, and there were but few institutions that could absorb these unfortunate newcomers, most of whom were German Jews. However, by giving salience to the field, these newcomers helped create the very jobs that were not available when they arrived. As is well known, it is these struggling scholars who became leading figures in the second generation of American musicology. By transferring their experience with German musicology to the United States, they contributed immeasurably to its development.

music's theoretical foundation.[72] Although the structuring power of symbolic patterns was bound to give rise, in due course, to a science of signs in its own right,[73] a goodly number of nineteenth-century composers consciously manipulated symbols so as to leave indelible marks on their compositions for future generations to decipher. Altogether, the idea of treating a musical score as a "text" that invites "decoding"—rather than as a guide for performance—in order to grasp the unique ways in which the composition was structured had become increasingly prevalent ever since Beethoven's symphonic "texts," which engendered, as we have seen, interpretive "readings" of many kinds. Such "readings" inevitably gave rise to theories concerning the "author's" *intention* as well as theories concerning the "modes" of public *reception*. Although the tendency to treat musical scores as "texts" goes a long way toward explaining the central position that theory and analysis gained toward the end of the century (from which earlier composers could naturally benefit as well), it is also closely related to the conscious desire of nineteenth-century composers to "originate"—to introduce compositional novelties into their works. Once the composer felt the need to "innovate," he hoped, in addition to securing his own public, to find favor in the eyes of future historians who would applaud the way in which he contributed to the advance of music. All of the aspects discussed above—the new attitude toward sound, musical structure, the relationship between melody and accompaniment, the relationship between music and language, and above all toward Music's ineffable, transcendent nature—were exploited not only to engage the attention of contemporary listeners but also to impress the concertgoer of the future by unique compositions that would be, as it were, "copy-proof."

72. Symbols, to be sure, were employed in the arts even in the absence of a theory concerning symbolic phenomena. Emile Durkheim, for example, one of the founders of sociology, only came to recognize the importance of symbolic processes once he became interested in religion. Durkheim, of course, had an enormous influence on later sociologists, who preferred, however, to see him in the light of his works that emphasized social constraints and social facts, rather than the important functions that symbols perform in various social settings. However, since interest in cultural studies highlights the analysis of symbolic phenomena, sociology, too, increasingly emphasizes what it had previously overlooked. See Jeffrey C. Alexander, ed., *Durkheimian Sociology: Cultural Studies* (New York, 1988).

73. Ferdinand Saussure, who is widely acknowledged as the first to have conceived of modern structural linguistics, conceptualized "semiotics" as the science of signs. Claude Lévi-Strauss's structural anthropology, for example, insists that societies must be studied in terms of symbolic classifications.

Internal References Challenged

I have repeatedly stressed that nineteenth-century composers were in possession of a musical language that could "make sense without predication," that is, cohere without having to resort to extramusical references. The introduction of external references into the musical fabric in the nineteenth century rested, in fact, on the ability of composers to manipulate an entrenched musical syntax, and on music's aptness to *display* what it metaphorically denotes (see chap. 4, pp. 159–60). Moreover, a tightly organized musical system, certainly the organic system developed in the West, does not necessarily fall apart in the absence of a given link. A system that has time and again proven its reliability can afford not only to gloss over some missing links but may also alter some accepted procedures, trusting that the listeners will be guided mentally by the musical system, that is, by harmonic tonality, the very system that constitutes the starting point for the composer as well.

By revealing the interdependence of the chord (as a primary and indivisible unit), the root note, the proposition of the fundamental bass, and the hierarchy between fundamental degrees, Rameau, as we have seen, created an integrated theory that persuasively accounted for the musical practice of his time. It is from the physical nature of the fundamental sound, it may be recalled, that Rameau developed the basic concepts of his theory—harmonic generation, harmonic inversion, and the fundamental bass—believing that he had put music on a sound scientific basis. Harmonic tonality, accordingly, operated under the proposition that chordal inversions are but different manifestations of an identical harmony, that is, that the bass note of the root position is invariably conceived as the *reference* for the other notes, regardless of their changed position. Rameau also postulated that the principle that determines the structure of chords also determines their successions, that is, that the interval of the fifth and the third also serve as the most perfect intervals for progression of the fundamental bass. However adequately Rameau may have accounted for the musical practice of his time, harmonic tonality nonetheless came into existence only gradually. As we shall see, it was dismissed in the same gradual way, suspended paradoxically by those who exploited the triadic system to the fullest, to its furthest limits.

Aesthetic preferences invariably affect choices; the latter are mostly fashioned from among the possibilities already in existence. Thus, regardless of the fact that triads and seventh chords, with all their inversions, were already fully employed during the baroque, there was, nonetheless, an increasing predominance of the first, fifth, and fourth degrees—as central chords—as the period progressed, leading to the establishment of the major and minor tonality in all the keys, and an increasing tendency toward modest modulations.[74] Chromatic progressions and altered chords were relatively rare at the time; in vocal music, chromaticism occurred mainly in the form of motifs that accompanied words expressing grief and the like, and chromatic progressions were employed mainly for fugal subjects. Chromatic chords appeared toward the end of the seventeenth century, lending prominence, however, mainly to the diminished seventh chord. Later, in the second half of the eighteenth century and the early part of the nineteenth, there was a considerable reduction of the harmonic vocabulary to its bare essentials—the tonic, dominant, and subdominant—which were used as a vehicle for musical development and the extension of melodies. Modulations, however, were no longer modest, for the music now abounded in distant modulations with or without pivot chords. Chromaticism, on the other hand, was comparatively rare until Beethoven's last works. After Beethoven, a new development took place, which may be characterized by the exploitation of chromatically altered harmony. Yet all of these transformations should not be viewed solely in theoretical terms, for they also reflect aesthetic preferences.

Harmony came to be appreciated, as we have seen, considerably later than counterpoint. Though some intervals were considered to sound better simultaneously than others, it was not until the sixteenth century that musicians also regarded harmonies as primary building materials of music. Yet it was only in the early part of the eighteenth century that harmonies were recognized as structural and compositional elements, despite the seventeenth-century practice of the thoroughbass and the presence of simple chordal progressions even in earlier periods. In fact, not until tonality superseded polyphonic modality could a piece of music be conceived from a harmonic point of view; for only then could the relative importance of chords be determined in relation to a key center or tonic. It is the tonic that both served as a point of departure for the modulations into other keys and provided a designation for their return. Naturally, once chords were conceived as entities they could be enlarged by adding thirds to the initial chord, creating seventh chords, ninth chords, and so forth. For the

74. Among the most common devices of harmonic variety is the change of key within a composition, generally referred to by the term modulation. A modulation is generally effected by means of a "pivot chord," that is, by a chord that is common to both the initial and the new key. For an effective modulation the initial as well as the new key should be established by a cadence.

sake of color it was also possible to raise or lower the various notes of these chords without allowing them to lose their identity and their relationship with the central tonic. Melodic lines, naturally, made apparent the effective arrangement of the harmonies underlying them.

Romantic harmony clearly rested on the triadic system and the logic that attended its use, but it exploited the triadic system to its furthest limits mainly through an abundance of chromatic alterations, unprepared and unresolved chords, and free modulations into distant keys. Obviously, with the increasing boldness of composers in modulating to ever more distant keys and in coloring or altering the notes of their chords more and more, the tonal center became increasingly blurred and its gravitational power consequently weakened. Novel sonorities—engaging unexpected procedures—heightened the attention to the momentary at the expense of an orientation to the overall. The strain to innovate, the need to arouse interest, and the desire to mold one's unique musical identity constituted, no doubt, a major impetus for composers to *explore* the tight system that they had inherited. Since they could add little to the "logic" of the system—which functioned like an organism that adequately accounted for the relationships among its parts and of these, in turn, to the whole—they attempted to remodel its external appearance. Nevertheless, retaining the musical "reasoning" intact, while attempting to remodel its external appearance, constituted a real challenge to the resilience of the system.

Yet the increasing tendency of nineteenth-century composers to fuse the major and minor modes, using chords typical of one mode in the other, and their inclination to avoid strong tonal cadences—substituting all kinds of deceptive cadences that made the contours of phrases less definitive—hardly reaffirmed the habitual ways in which the system functioned. To be sure, procedures of this kind were not new, but whereas they had previously been employed with discretion, they gradually became a routine of the musical unfolding of nineteenth-century music. In the late classical period, the cadence still corresponded to the articulation of the movement and had a constructive value, and modulations took place mostly in connection with cadences and the joining of sections. Tonal regions were, accordingly, placed alongside or in opposition to each other so as to lend interest and flexibility to the movement's course, while deceptive progressions were mainly used as a means of expression, conveying passing shades of disposition. It was primarily structural organization, however, that dictated most of the procedures mentioned. In the Romantic period, by contrast, the treatment of tonalities constituted an end in itself; it was largely meant to contribute to a continuous flow of change. The imperceptible gliding of modulations and deceptive progressions owed much to the harmonic alterations that veiled their contours.

Though harmonic alterations—enriched through the extensive use of chromatic and enharmonic possibilities—were increasingly employed throughout the century, they were still based on the old system whence the novel combinations were extracted. Having reached a peak, however, they seem to have gained a standing of their own. In fact, by the end of the century they became a prerequisite for the shifting harmony of the impressionists, for example, whose music focused mainly on a succession of "colors" rather than on a dynamic development. The latter had a bearing as well on melodic construction, that is, on its potential for motivic and thematic development. In the course of the century, however, melodies had increasingly become a part of those apparent elements through which composers could conspicuously display their originality and inventiveness. No wonder that composers increasingly guarded their thematic originality as a sort of "property right," though they themselves created musical modes of thematic "recollections" in their own compositions—a musical type of *A la recherché du temps perdu*. It is fascinating to note that those who addressed "memory" and "reminiscences" as they did should have been the ones to give rise to a preoccupation with musical "borrowings"— explicit, implicit, intentional, or unintentional—attempting to protect their own originality thereby.[75] The spinning out of songlike melodies, the slow unfolding of their contours led to the building of long compound periods at the expense of a predictably clear formal construction. Thus, while the periodicity of meter and refinement of rhythm still functioned schematically, and the eight-measure period still served as a guideline of construction, the free turn of invention often obscured its own underlying schemes. Given this new state of affairs, it is not at all surprising that music also should have given rise—alongside its concerns with the past of the art—to novel theoretical approaches, which attempted to capture the entirety of musical constructions through more adept "strategies," befitting the composer's *fantasy* (a *Vorstellung*, an envisaged image)—which prompts diverse musical realizations—and the listener's perception of their *appearance (Erscheinung)*.[76]

75. For an interesting article concerning musical borrowings, see Anthony Newcomb, "The Hunt for Reminiscences in Nineteenth-Century Germany," in *Music and the Aesthetics of Modernity* (Cambridge, Mass., 2005), 111–35.

76. These concepts were employed by some German fin-de-siècle musical theorists. I shall discuss them later on.

The Variable Functions of Theory

Although Rameau's music theory encountered criticism at the time as well as subsequently, his "syntactical formulation" provided a basis for later theoretical analyses, whether or not his basic premises were accepted. The nineteenth century, as we have seen, introduced remarkable changes to compositional procedures, yet it availed itself of fundamental musical relationships that Rameau endeavored to summarize (and in a way succeeded in doing so). Theoretical treatises, it must be remembered, are not all of the same kind; over the centuries they addressed varied issues and served diverse purposes. The addressees of these treatises differed as well, covering the entire gamut from philosophers to music students—from those who speculated about music to those who wished to better understand the métier, or sought guidance for actual participation in the making of music. From natural philosophy to tonal relationships, there is much to be learned from these varied investigations and observations, from the thoughts they embrace, the issues they address, and the musical portrayals they contain. In fact, they constitute important source materials for tracing the development of music and the ways in which it was conceived, viewed, and understood.

Theory was not always understood in the way in which it is principally understood today, namely, as the study of the structure of music. As long as music was on the advance toward a tightly defined syntax that would enable it to refer to itself and cohere on its own terms, theory tended to clarify problems as they emerged, or to summarize the state of the art; it seldom suggested novel approaches to musical analysis. The latter were mostly related to significant turns in the overall development of music such as the sanctioning of duple meter alongside triple meter in the *Ars Nova,* or that of the *seconda pratica* alongside the *prima pratica*—a turn that reflected a newly raised consciousness regarding stylistic choice. Indeed, it is impossible to gauge one style with the yardsticks of another unless they hold some elements in common. The expectation that music theory should be in possession of the tools needed to analyze the structure of compositions regardless of their differing styles is altogether inconceivable without a tacit understanding regarding some basic theoretical presuppositions that underlie their different manifestations. It is precisely those theoretical aspects that in the course of music's development built on each other in significant ways—allowing music to refer to itself through ever tighter internal schemes—that granted theory the rudimentary tools for the study of musical structure. If Rameau looms as large as he does, even if he primarily delineated the workings of the music of *his* time, his success may be attributed mainly to the fact that music was already able to "make sense" without recourse to "predications" of various sorts, that is, it was already in the possession of that unique syntax that Rameau summarized and simplified. No wonder then that theory, from Rameau onward, focused primarily on the structure of musical compositions, adding, augmenting, and transforming the tools of musical analysis.

Like music theory, music analysis also embraced diverse activities throughout the development of music. These activities were basically concerned with the ways in which music functions and the manner in which it is perceived. The inquiries ranged from compositional strategies to aesthetic evaluation, from investigations of what music embodies to explorations of its place among the arts. Yet in one way or another, it was invariably concerned with musical structure and its constituent elements. Analysis, as a tool engaged in matters of technique and substance, was already recognized in the early stages of music's development in the West, contributing its share to the study and clarification of the modal systems and their implementations. With the introduction of "musical rhetoric" into musical theory, that is, with the viewing of "musical figures" as analogous to rhetorical figures, the notion of a *formal* analysis of musical works came into being, highlighting their individual modes of construction. This development eventually gave rise to categorizations of various sorts, which attempted to codify *rules* for evaluating "well-developed" compositions and musical genres, as well as providing guidelines for future constructions.

That decisions of this kind should also hinge on *aesthetic* judgment is virtually self-evident. Musical styles, and changes thereof, invariably involve aesthetic considerations, reflecting the people involved, their time and place, and the functions the styles serve. We need to distinguish, therefore, between aesthetic predilections and aesthetic, theoretical contemplation, between stylistic preferences and criteria for the assessments of artistic import, so as to fully grasp the role that musical analysis played. As time went on, musical analysis increasingly ventured to deal not only with the constituent elements of preferred musical structures but also with the aesthetic significance of their configurations. The idea that "Art resides in its *making*" surfaced only gradually; it gained momentum in the seventeenth century, as we have seen, once the relation between Nature and the arts was redefined. Moreover, the idea of allying Beauty to the *ways* in which it is *brought about* and *perceived* gained momentum only in the eighteenth century, concerned as the century was with the "doings" of man, no less than it was with God's Creation. Interestingly, it was *moral* philosophy that awakened the Plotinian notion of 'Beauty'—as an aspiration for the "perfection of form"—which Plotinus thought reflected the striving of man toward a more sublime reality. This development accorded aesthetic contemplation a position divorced from context and social function, and led, as we have seen, to the establishment of aesthetics as one of the major branches of philosophy.

Though Neoplatonic ideas became an essential component of eighteenth- and nineteenth-century aesthetic thought, the relationship between 'form' and 'construction' left a host of issues unresolved. For example, is the construction of a musical work "form specific," that is, does a given form dictate the procedures whereby it is structured? Given that the same form may be realized in a variety of ways, what distinguishes "principal forms" (if such exist) from subordinate ones? Is the number of principal forms limited, while their realization is not? If the number of forms is *un*limited, do they represent the externalization of their content, rather than the other way round? If so, is the content constrained by the musical procedures it follows, or by the state of mind of the composer, whose concept of procedure acquires the shape he is after? How should one explain similarities among pieces if form and content are inseparable entities, intrinsically wedded to each other? What is the definition of 'style,' considering all of the above? Questions of this kind, needless to say, could not have been settled easily in periods governed by a high degree of consensus about musical procedures, and even less so in periods that gave rise to an abundance of musical styles and a profusion of distinct individual modes of expression.

Though much remained unsettled, the separation of beauty from its context diminished the mindfulness that was previously accorded to substance, shifting attention, more and more, toward matters of design— toward the ways in which the "beautiful" is "formed." The ways in which "form is being formed" occupied an increasingly central position in the analysis of the arts in general, and gained special significance for the "temporal arts" and music in particular. The parameter of 'time,' we should remember, is intrinsic to music; it invariably relates to the unfolding process *and* to the experience of its passage. In the West, one might add, it was *consciously* so conceived (see chap. 1, p. 36). However relevant these perceptually based ideas, they entered musical analysis only toward the end of the eighteenth century and, even by then, primarily through the back door—the one more closely annexed to the knowledge of métier than to aesthetic queries. An important theorist such as Heinrich Christoph

Koch,[77] for example, though clearly concerned with issues pertaining to aesthetic import, saw fit to embed them in "instructions for composition," guiding composers in the construction of the units that make up a musical work—melodies, musical phrases, musical periods, and so forth. And, while dealing with these subjects, Koch suggested "layout" schemes that take perceptually based ideas into account. Accordingly, he elaborated on a series of devices whereby the various units may be "extended," "compressed," "interrelated," and "elaborated upon," so as to grant music the desired aesthetic qualities. By the middle of the nineteenth century, the "teachings" of musical composition already confronted all of these issues head-on. Thus Adolf Bernhard Marx,[78] another important theorist, was no longer willing to treat form (any form) as a predictable, habitual structure. Music, he argued, is shaped by composers, whose formal designs convey diverse ideas and reflect variegated states of mind.

Koch and Marx were by no means the only theorists who incorporated aesthetic considerations into their musical analyses; as time went on their numbers steadily increased. Without spelling out their thoughts, this essay can only try to drive home the idea that music analysis as a pursuit in its *own* right only came into being after aesthetic considerations became part and parcel of the study of the construction of music.[79] That this develop-

---

77. Koch's *Versuch einer Anleitung zur Composition* (1782–93) still serves as a major source for the analysis of the music of his time, in which symmetry and proportion were highly regarded. Though Koch was largely concerned with 'symmetry' and 'proportion,' the thrust of his thinking centers on what might be termed "premeditated designs," that is, on compositional "layouts" that take into account the desired aesthetic impressions from the beginning. As such, Koch exerted a marked influence on later musical analysts who struggled with similar questions.

78. In his famous work *Die Lehre von der musikalischen Komposition* (1837–47), a work that was for many decades copiously used as a theory-teaching text, Marx tried to diminish the importance that theorists habitually attached to musical species, stating categorically that the number of forms is "unlimited" and that there are as many forms as there are works of art. The similarities that are apt to occur among works of art, Marx argued, should be attributed to concepts of broader significance, which are related, on the one hand, to "nature," and, on the other, to the "organic" development of music. It is the broader significance, that is, the interaction between the naturally "given" and the historically "developed," that the musical analyst must endeavor to unveil, and certainly make sure not to overlook.

79. In an interesting article about music analysis—its role and function, past and present—Jim Samson makes the following astute observations:

Music analysis was instituted at the turn of the nineteenth and twentieth centuries, its 'historical moment' arriving rather more than a century after the 'historical moment' of aesthetic theory. A consequence of the project of aesthetic

ment should have reached a point of crystallization in the late nineteenth century is, of course, no coincidence. It resulted largely from the music composed by creative individuals who challenged the very system they were using in order to leave an indelible impression through their unique modes of expression. If theory, nowadays, is principally understood as the study of the construction of music, it is causally related to the century that conceived of 'beauty' as a striving toward a sublime reality.

---

autonomy and the rise of the work concept, the institution of analysis formalized the shift towards a work-centered music theory, one which replaced rules with structures. Moreover, the new conceptual world embodied in analytical theory collided with the rebirth of poetics in the other arts, sharing with that development a (heavily ideological) supposition of context in any explanation of the aesthetic. The converse, incidentally, also followed: a structuralist poetics implicitly freed social history, together with cognitive and ethical values, from aesthetic interference. It goes without saying that this separation of specialized categories from each other and from the social world could never be fully realized. The unified musical work, celebrated by the institution of analysis, was a necessary, valuable, and glorious myth, but it was a myth shaped in all essentials by a particular set of social and historical circumstances. Its status was twofold. As product of those dominant processes of rationality from whose repressive influence it sought to escape, the unified work was emblematic of a notionally unified bourgeois culture. On the other hand, as an autonomous aesthetic object seeking to articulate areas of subjectivity excluded by those very processes of rationality, the unified work had the potential to oppose and criticize the social sphere. We are bound to ask if it can retain either meaning today. (Jim Samson, "Analysis in Context," in *Rethinking Music*, ed. Nicholas Cook and Mark Everist [Oxford, 2001], 42.)

PART III

The Retreat from the "Shared Understanding"

FIVE 𝄢

A Shift in Thought and Theory

THE ORGANIC NATURE OF THE THEORETICAL PRESUPPOSITIONS OF MUSIC IN THE WEST

Despite the Romantic attitude to 'Music' and the compositional changes it engendered, it is nonetheless possible to analyze the music created at the time with the tools deriving from the musical syntax that had developed over centuries. This syntax, insofar as internal referential abilities are concerned, reached a peak in the eighteenth century. The organic nature of the system, however, must be attributed to the chain of its cumulative, additive growth. While musical styles kept changing, satisfying momentary needs and aesthetic preferences, the strivings and achievements of composers added systematically to the theoretical presuppositions of music in the West. Though some nineteenth-century composers ingeniously probed the limits of the syntactical system, they did not challenge the system itself.

THE ROMANTIC ERA FROM A BIRD'S-EYE VIEW

It is no coincidence that the century that redefined 'Music,' in the way the nineteenth century did, should be called "Romantic era." Yet within so extended a period and an opulence of styles, even like-minded composers differed from each other in their attitudes to the tradition that they inherited, not to mention their individual temperaments and inclinations. In his attempt to embrace "the commonwealth of art," Curt Sachs suggested, in a lengthy essay bearing this title, that the arts invariably reflect man's emotive reaction to stimuli from without *and* within. The arts display a unity, he argued, in spite of the tendency to address each of the arts separately. The arts "unite in one consistent evolution to mirror man's diversity in space and time and the fate of his soul."[1] It is a kind of dualism rather than progress, Sachs argued, that bestows a consistency on the development of art; art seems to move steadily between two polar tendencies that are best expressed by the words *ethos* and *pathos*. However particular in their configurations, the first term roughly implies moderation, perfection, stylization, and so on, that is, an *idealistic* approach to art, whereas the second term implies the opposite, that is, a *naturalistic* approach, an approach that gives vent to accidental influences such as passion, suffering, and "imperfections" of various kinds. Lest one infer that works of art necessarily belong exclusively to one or the other category, Sachs clarified that the two categories only imply "the courses steered toward one of two poles rather than the poles themselves."[2] The sequence of styles, concluded Sachs, apparently create an "orbit" in which art meanders to-and-fro, safeguarding eternal "motion and balance." Because the cycles evolving from ethos to pathos are embedded in ever larger cycles, it is possible for a composer to reveal a "classical" tendency within what is basically construed as a "Romantic" cycle.

Indeed, the Romantic era had its share of Romantic-classic composers, such as Franz Schubert and Felix Mendelssohn, for example. Even Robert Schumann, who began his career as a Romantic revolutionist, revealed a classical tendency once he turned to symphonic and chamber music, which chronologically came after most of his poetic piano works, his songs, and other vocal compositions. Brahms, for example, reached back further and further, adhering to acceptable strict form from beginning to end, despite his unique sonorities and interesting extensions of the development section of the sonata form, so as to cover the movement as a whole. Liszt, on the other hand, scorned tradition altogether. Though he admired Schubert's songs, in his own songwriting Liszt focused on expressive details to such an extent that the songs lost their form. Berlioz, by contrast, displayed his infatuation with Italy through patently clear melodic lines, but expressed his frenzied and desperate love via a "reminiscence" motive that runs through his entire First Symphony, thereby weakening

1. Curt Sachs, *The Commonwealth of Art* (New York, 1946), 18.
2. See ibid., 199–206.

the accepted symphonic form. As is well known, Wagner used motives as "ground-themes," not only representing recurrent ideas but also characters and typical situations. Although it is easy to create tables of his consistent, so-called leitmotivs, Wagner tended to modify them according to the requirements of the particular situation, guided primarily by the logic of the narrative, rather than by the structural dictates of the music. All of these composers clearly revealed an awareness of the tradition they inherited, though they responded to it in different ways.

Regardless of the differences among them (and among others who were not mentioned), they were all, nonetheless, revolutionaries. All of them, without exception, tried to *innovate*—to bring about change in one aspect or another—each in his own particular way. If Romanticism in music is perceived as a revolutionary movement, there is ample evidence to support the notion. Yet even revolutionaries are not of one shade, and neither is their understanding of the cause they serve necessarily identical. Calls for greater equity in the distribution of wealth, for example, need not imply an overthrow of governing regimes. Likewise, the desire to leave one's imprint on the development of music does not necessarily mean the negation of other such attempts, a fortiori the repudiation of the musical roots that yielded an abundance of blossoming branches with highly coveted fruit.

The Relationship between the Composer and the Public Revisited

In the previous chapter I discussed the relationship between the composer and the public, highlighting their joint predicament. As was suggested, the isolation of the composer from his immediate surroundings was compensated for by his apparent belonging to a larger social entity (an "imagined community" in contemporary terms), whose culture he inadvertently imbibed and uniquely expressed, regardless of his eccentricities. Given the new attitude to psychology in general and emotions in particular, composers also gained special license to give vent to their private states of mind, expecting to enlist sympathetic reverberations in their listeners. They could, of course, also resort to extramusical means—primarily linguistic—so as to prevent misunderstandings of various sorts. It must be remembered, however, that the incorporation of extramusical elements into the musical fabric largely resulted from the redefinition of both 'Music' and the reformulation of the relationships among the arts. Yet the inclination to supply instrumental works with *imaginary* texts had also given way, paradoxically, to the opposite, that is, of listening to vocal music instrumentally. The latter reflects the increased tendency to treat the whole of a composition as a "text" whose meaning is to be deciphered, rather than immediately perceived upon hearing.

As was also pointed out, music was no longer principally written with a specific audience in mind to serve defined functions, as was the custom when composers held permanent positions in one or another institution. In fact, some of the compositions we most admire nowadays might not have been written had their performance not been guaranteed. With all of the changes that have occurred in the interim, it is no wonder that composers steered their courses differently. Interestingly, those who were less concerned with the verdict of history and more concerned with the approval of a specific public, whose aesthetic predilection they respected, continued to write the kind of music that aimed to be intelligible and palatable upon performance. They were even willing to introduce changes into their compositions if the circumstances of the performance so required. These composers were primarily driven by the desire to enliven the musical life that surrounded them; more so, at any rate, than they were driven by an urge to protect the "sanctity" of their musical "text." Their attitude, however, should not be construed as an accommodation, that is, as a sort of willingness to forgo their individual standards and aspirations for the sake of public acclaim. It reflects, rather, a kind of affinity—an appreciation for the tradition that cultivated the composer's own musical taste, as well as that of his public. Respecting both the tradition and its heirs, these composers wished to contribute their share to the musical tradition with which they were familiar, in the hope of being recognized *as such,* regardless of their idiosyncrasies and diverse creative potencies. One need only think of Giuseppe Verdi in order to fully grasp the significance of such an attitude. Verdi was steeped through and through in the musical tradition of his country; he was understood and idolized by the public from beginning to end, though one can hardly claim that he was wanting in inventiveness and originality.

That an attitude of this kind should likely characterize Italian composers is hardly surprising. The Italians have all along preferred discernible designs over concealed, intricate musical structures. This also helps explain their attraction to tuneful melodic contours in preference to sophisticated harmonic developments. This Italian bent toward cantabile, that is, "singable" music, has imbued not only the works of composers actually resident in Italy but also has affected many composers who never reached its shores. In their desire to please the senses, the Italians also made consistent use of freely composed music with popular appeal. Regardless of the function it was intended to serve, the same music was often applied to various texts, mixing the sacred with the profane.[3] Yet one cannot speak of the music as being ill-matched to the content, given that its composers were prone to conceive of the spirit of a prayer addressed to the Madonna in terms similar to that conveyed by a confession addressed to one's beloved. And despite persistent efforts to create a more direct connection between dramatic content and musical expression, for the Italians music remained the major attraction on which the success of an opera depended, not intellectual consistency. That this should hold equally true for most of their other vocal compositions must be related to the Italian love for that performing art that appeals to the senses directly. Since music functions in an integrative fashion—synthesizing separate elements into connected wholes—it can, in fact, forgo the tenacious adherence to textually itemized momentary meanings. The preference for palatable music that directly appeals to the senses upon performance should not be construed, therefore, as a preference for instrumental music. Nor should it be confused with the adoration that instrumental music elicited in Germany. While it suffices to think of the preclassical symphony in order to realize that the Italians also labored in directions that would advance the "coherence" of instrumental music, opera may be viewed as an *essentially* Italian genre.[4] Indeed, opera was nowhere as appreciated as it was, and still is, in Italy, the country that also gave rise to bel canto singing. Music in Italy tried not to be shrouded in mystery; on the contrary, it was invariably perceived as the most genuine expression of Man, who gives vent to his sorrows and delights in the language of gesture.

Compared to this spontaneous down-to-earth approach to music, the German approach seems at once more calculated *and* more mysterious. The redefinition of 'Music' in Germany led, as we have seen, to the treatment

3. The *laude*, for example, the religious popular poetry of the late Middle Ages, were recited and sung by societies, some of which were ascetic in their orientation and others not. Their songs were lifted from the popular tunes of the day, and their mundane subjects were replaced by religious poetry. Alessandro D'Ancona has shown, in his *Origini del teatro italiano* (Turin, 1891), how the *laude* eventually assumed a dramatic form and were called *devozione*. The *devozione*, in turn, gave rise to the *sacra rappresentazione*, which represented the highest point in the development of religious drama in Italy. Music apparently played a decisive part in these dramas. It was an art form, however, primarily of Florence and the Tuscan cities, a significant fact for the future role of Florence in the history of opera. The *sacra rappresentazione*, together with the pastoral drama, constituted the major precursors of the opera as a new musical genre and institution.

4. See Ruth Katz, *Divining the Powers of Music*, 185–89.

of music as a text that elicits exegesis, for it was believed to contain considerably more than "meets the ear." Without repeating what has already been explicated, it is important to remember, however, that the aim of the German Romantics was essentially social and political. They wanted to overcome the alienation created by modernity through a renewed unity with oneself, with others, and with Nature. They advocated an ethics of societal love *coupled* with self-realization. Ethics, politics, and aesthetics, they claimed, should all be seen in the light of a cultural goal, that of making the individual feel at home again in a newly structured solidarity. It is inconceivable to think of a Wagner, for example, without bearing this cultural background and social milieu in mind. Thus, unlike Verdi, Wagner incorporated all of the features that we have come to identify with Romanticism, especially its revolutionary stance.

Although specific composers are not the subject of this essay, a few remarks are in order to justify the attention to Wagner, primarily to his conceptions of the 'music drama.' The novelty of these conceptions, as we shall see, affected not only opera as a music-theatrical genre but aligned the arts in new ways that redefined the role of music in general and the composer's "license" in particular. Like other Romantic composers, Wagner also took the logic of absolute music for granted, yet, unlike the others, he challenged the "absoluteness" of its rational base, that is, the very abstractness of its nature. Although his music was echoed by a goodly number of subsequent composers, the suppleness in which he exploited the *musical* language contributed significantly to its overall reconceptualization. However one relates to Wagner's music and to the ideas he advanced, there is no denying that he was one of those revolutionaries who left a decisive mark on the development of music.

Aesthetic Autonomy—Art for Art's Sake

Though some composers exerted greater influence on subsequent generations than others, this essay has not focused so far on any one of them in particular. Rather, it has tried to examine major ideational and theoretical issues—as they emerged historically—in the attempt to disclose the rationale that underlies the development of music in the West. I have repeatedly stressed that this essay essentially addresses two sets of ideas, one of which pertains to the development of those internal musical references that guided composers and listeners alike, while the other relates to various transformations in the understanding of symbols and the way they function in the arts. It is these two strands of "reasoning" that became inextricably intertwined in the construction of music as a subsystem of culture in the West.

Although different aesthetic predilections came to the fore in the various styles, music theory addressed aesthetic issues—whether directly or indirectly—only sporadically, and even then more in terms of desiderata than as problems subject to theoretical constraints. Indeed, as a bona fide branch of knowledge, aesthetics, as we have seen, came into existence only in the eighteenth century; as such, it was consciously incorporated into the construction and analysis of music only gradually. Though nineteenth-century composers clearly displayed their aesthetic preferences, and a fortiori their drive to innovate, none of them delved into aesthetic-theoretical issues as much as Wagner. He not only theorized, he exemplified his aesthetic theories unambiguously in the music that he composed. Wagner's theories, moreover, sought to establish unequivocally the principle of aesthetic autonomy, granting art, and music in particular, the "stage" he thought it deserved—a cultural role independent of societal constraints and predetermined dictates.

As an ardent admirer of Beethoven, Wagner began his career in a rather conventional way, writing sonatas, variations for the piano, concertos, and songs. He left his mark on the history of music, however, primarily as an opera composer who hoped to inspire his surroundings through his mastery of this realm. He tried to reach a public as large as possible not through music that listeners were already familiar with, but through a novel conception of music that he thought listeners *ought* to become familiar with for their own good! As far as he was concerned, it represented *the* artwork of the future. This future would take into account the ultimate achievements reached in the various arts, in an attempt to surpass their individual attainments through a new union among them—a union that would more compactly and patently wed the ideational and the representational, especially insofar as music and drama are concerned.[5] According

5. See Wagner's essay "Zukunftsmusik" (1860) in which he tried to summarize the contents of his major essays—"Die Kunst und die Revolution" (1849), "Das Kunstwerk der Zukunft" (1850), and "Oper und Drama" (1851–52)—in which he came to terms with the new conception of opera that marked the beginning of his work on the *Ring.* Wagner seems to have written more words than musical notes in the course of his lifetime, in essays, letters, and other writings that reflect the various stages of his life and the development of his thinking. In addition to a host of particular issues he felt compelled to address and the texts he wrote for his own operas, some of his writings disclose the philosophical and political influences under which he labored, while others convey the development of his artistic ideas and his understanding of the arts, primarily those of

to Wagner, music should not only *express* that which it cannot name, but "name"—spell out, as it were—the motivating forces and unconscious associations that underlie seemingly explicit utterances. The *"serva-padrona"* debate,[6] in other words, could be subsumed via a kind of music that lends "visibility" to the drama by unveiling those hidden forces unknown to the role players that propel the action and the dramatic unfolding. The artwork as a whole thus calls the unconscious into consciousness. Such works, moreover, would give vent, according to Wagner, to the "true Germanic spirit." Unlike the Italians, "who use music for love," and the French, who use music "for sociability," the Germans, he asserted categorically, "treat music as a science," or stated simply, "the Italian is a singer, the French a virtuoso, the German—a musician!"[7]

However brazen and presumptuous Wagner might sound, he also sounds like other true revolutionaries who often endorse coercive means to awaken the needy to their needs. Wagner believed that he carried an important uplifting message for his public through the texts he wrote and the music that conveyed them. He made his position quite clear through his extended polemics. Although his *Gesamtkunstwerk* was based on the false assumption that several of the arts had already reached their full potential, he capitalized on the ways in which each of the component arts differs from the others and on the ways in which each can be caused to interact with the others. Indeed, Wagner's dramas achieved new combinations of music and text and a far-reaching metaphorical use of orchestral accompaniment. "He gave the public gigantic original music dramas," says Peter Gay, "which he wanted to be treated as sacred works, not in the hyperbolic or metaphorical sense, but in the literal sense." In his self-appraisal, Wagner "confessed" that his unique achievement was that his work was German: "It was German because it was great and great because it was German."[8]

Setting his beliefs aside, including the voluminous historic-philosophic speculations based on his life, it behooves us, nonetheless, to examine one

---

music and drama. The essays mentioned can be located in the ten volumes entitled *Richard Wagner Dichtungen und Schriften: Jubläumsausgabe* (Frankfurt, 1983), in vols. 8, 5, 6, and 7 (respectively).

6. The history of opera has abounded with debates concerning "who" should serve "whom" in the joint venture between music and drama so as to arrive at satisfactory and persuasive results.

7. See "Über deutsches Musikwese," *Richard Wagner Dichtungen*, vol. 5, 153.

8. See Peter Gay, *Freud, Jews, and Other Germans: Masters and Victims in Modernist Culture* (New York, 1978), 228.

of his major objectives, that is, to fashion music in a way that would lend "visibility" to the drama. Yet it must be remembered that Wagner started his operatic career as a Romantic composer without a distinct stylistic direction. His early works—*Die Feen* (1834), *Das Liebesverbot* (1836), and *Der fliegende Holländer* (1841)—approached the theatrical genre in ways prevalent at the time, in the hope of establishing his own local reputation. Realizing, however, that the way to establish himself in Germany rested on his acceptance in Paris (the European cultural center at the time), he modeled his *Rienzi* (1840) on the grand opera style, that of composers such as Giacomo Meyerbeer and Fromental Halévy. Despite his efforts to accommodate the Parisian public, the Grand Opéra was not receptive. Interestingly, Wagner's fame, one might say, was largely founded on his *theoretical* writings, which he, unlike other theoreticians, applied to his own works. His works exemplified his theories, while his theoretical deliberations helped explicate his works. The public approval that *Tannhäuser* (1845) and *Lohengrin* (1847) earned in the 1850s (both operas were performed throughout Germany during that decade) may be attributed in no small measure to the explications that Wagner himself supplied to his music dramas around that time. Although both operas gradually lost their impact, and *Tristan* (1859) was received as an esoteric music drama, it was ironically *Die Meistersinger* (1868)—the opera that championed the principle of aesthetic autonomy, pleading the cause of "art for art's sake" explicitly—that won Wagner the acclaim he sought. Even those who had failed to endorse his earlier music-theatrical achievements applauded him.

Pleading the cause of art as he did, and eager to lend his music dramas the aesthetic autonomy achieved by Beethoven's symphonies, it is no wonder that Wagner deplored the practice of tracing musical works back to biographical roots.[9] After all, it took quite a while for his ideas to crystallize; he himself asked his readers to treat his writings as stages in his artistic development.[10] It must be remembered that the aesthetic autonomy of the symphony, apart from Beethoven's uniqueness, rested on an already achieved understanding with regard to absolute music, that is, as a musical discourse coherent in and of itself. By what logic, then, could a *Gesamtkunstwerk,* drawing on extramusical factors, turn into a work that, in its

9. See his essay on Beethoven (1870) in *Richard Wagner Dichtungen*, vol. 9, in which he rejected the theses that the Napoleonic association had a major bearing on the *Eroica* Symphony.

10. See his preface to his *Gesammelte Schriften und Dichtung* (Leipzig, 1871–73), which he himself supervised.

entirety, depends primarily on the communicative force of music? Wagner clearly wished to bestow on his music drama the integrity achieved by a Beethoven symphony, yet in what way could a work of this kind also turn into a persuasive theatrical presentation?[11]

True to the musical tradition he admired, Wagner adopted for his music drama the processes characteristic of instrumental music, that of an extended network of relationships established among themes, motives, rhythmical units, and other identifiable constituents, through their repetition, development, transformation, and alterable groupings. Naturally, the quandaries raised by the idea of creating extended forms out of a few elementary units presented problems that not only Wagner had to grapple with. The musical skills that problems of this kind required were quite familiar to the Germans, for they not only grappled with them but also provided some admirable solutions. Wagner's weaving technique, however, was expected to embody more than a symphonic movement; it was expected to "stretch out" so as to be able to embrace an entire opera, and in the case of the *Ring* several of them. Tonal harmony in conjunction with thematic-motivic treatment justified, as we have seen, music's aesthetic claim to be heard for its own sake, not least because the interaction between them could yield diverse compositions and a diversity of musical designs. Wagner, however, wished to add substance to these abstract formulations—a base more natural and mythical at one and the same time. By attaching the rudiments of myth to the metaphysics of music, Wagner hoped to unveil the realm that music—uncontested—could truly master.

It is fair to claim that Wagner took from myth the idea of characters who act under constraints not of their own choosing, while Arthur Schopenhauer's metaphysics lent support to the role music was destined to fulfill in his music dramas. The mythic action, accordingly, is propelled by *hidden* forces, not by the visible acts that take place on the stage. And thus the visual and verbal manifestations only present the tip of the iceberg, while music represents the basic drives, unknown to the role players, though they affect them. Indeed, according to Schopenhauer, these drives

---

11. In his interesting book *Programming the Absolute*, Berthold Hoeckner discusses Wagner's portrayal of his early operas as "inevitable stages in the evolution of his music drama," an evolution that culminated in the *Ring.* Through a fascinating analysis of *Lohengrin* (music and text), Hoeckner reveals the importance of this particular opera in Wagner's claim that Western art has reached a stage in which it may fuse the greatness of Shakespeare's dramas and Beethoven's symphonies via his own conception of the "music drama." See Berthold Hoeckner, *Programming the Absolute: Nineteenth-Century German Music and the Hermeneutics of the Moment* (Princeton, 2002), chap. 3.

may be represented precisely by the art that men are "content to understand directly" although they renounce all claim "to an abstract conception of this direct understanding itself."[12]

Schopenhauer's view of music clearly transcended the Romantic view of 'Music,' for he realized that his explanation of the "inner nature of music" and its "imitative relation to the world" assumed and established a relation between "music as idea" and that which "from its nature can never be idea." Music has therefore to be regarded "as the copy of an original which can never itself be directly presented as idea."[13] Though music, like art in general, is a way of viewing things independent of the principle of sufficient reason, it is "by no means like the other arts the copy of the Ideas, but the *copy of the will itself* whose objectivity the Ideas are." "The effect of music," explained Schopenhauer, "is so much more powerful and penetrating than that of the other arts, for they speak only of shadows, but it speaks of the thing itself."[14]

No wonder that Wagner endorsed Schopenhauer's views; they certainly left ample room for the "composer's voice."[15] Wagner, as is well known, made extensive use of the orchestra in an essentially symphonic way. He expected to render *thereby* the essence concealed behind the visible phenomena. The listener, for his part, Dahlhaus tells us, was expected not only to follow the musical argument but also to grasp its expression, that is, to intuit the substance of the dramatic action, as well as the composer's "self depiction." "The 'orchestral melody,'" he explains, provided "a commentary in sound, giving the composer, as musical narrator, a 'speaking part,' such that the 'sound of his voice' is continually heard."[16] The vocal

---

12. See excerpts from Arthur Schopenhauer's *The World as Will and Idea* in Katz and Dahlhaus, *Contemplating Music,* vol. 1, 149

13. Ibid.

14. Ibid., 150.

15. The term was coined by Edward T. Cone in his insightful essay bearing this very name — *The Composer's Voice* (California, 1974).

16. See § 8, p. 118, in vol. 20 of *The New Grove* (1980). The preoccupation with "voices," whose and how, implicit or explicit, has gained considerable momentum in musicological studies in the last few decades. From a symbolic point of view, the penetration into the hero's psychic life is impossible, argued Edward Cone, without assuming a point of view, that of the composer, what he called "the voice of the composer." Like the narrator in the novel, the composer's persona, claimed Cone, is responsible for everything in the representation; it is his point of view that determines the work. The music, however, that "proceeds entirely and directly from the consciousness of the composer's persona, could be dramatically appropriate and highly expressive" (Cone, ibid., 32).

The greater preoccupation, in recent years, with narratology, its role and function,

style that Wagner employed was singularly suited to the roles the characters enacted on the stage. Wagner, in fact, developed a unique hybrid between declamation and melody, which was based on a newly conceived relationship between voice and orchestra—a merger whereby the declamation assumed a melodic character that it could not have assumed on its own. The vocal parts, in other words, could assimilate what transpired in the orchestra in ways that revealed to the listener what eluded the singers while rendering *their* parts.

Like other Romantic composers, Wagner wished to transport his listeners into spellbinding realms, even while trusting the transported listener not only to recognize the musical motifs that he used in weaving his musical texture but also to honor the meanings that he vested in them, and to fathom the associations that they may incite. By controlling the associations that the music evokes in the mind of the listener, Wagner sought to lend to the drama "visibility." Indeed, the composer was thus able to expose the *hidden* drives that affect the role players—constraints

---

and with the interpretative roles of the narrator, reader, and listener, has given rise to novel approaches to Cone's proposition regarding the composer's voice. Cone's concept of the "musical persona," accordingly, has been viewed as a rhetorical strategy, which aimed to "humanize," says Lawrence Kramer, "the impersonal agency that we hear in music," and the "virtual voice" he addressed is no longer considered by Carolyn Abbate to be that of a single originating speaker. Music cannot narrate in its own right, argues Kramer, since it stands to narrative as critique, performative, or supplement. Music, he suggests, needs to be heard as a cross between rhetoric and history: "When Cone presents his voice as the immanence of the composer's authoritative, monological intelligence in the music, what he fails to recognize is that his supposed immanence is both a rhetorical effect—sometimes urged by the music, sometimes by the protocols of listening—and a historical formation that seeks to exclude other voices: the voices, precisely, of the other." To hear the "unsung voices" that Abbate talks about, argues Kramer, requires "listening through" that voice that has acted historically as the agent of exclusion. See Lawrence Kramer, *Classical Music and Postmodern Knowledge* (California, 1995), 119–21, and Carolyn Abbate, *Unsung Voices: Opera and Musical Narrative in the Nineteenth Century* (Princeton, 1991). These important qualifications give impetus to the investigation of the genealogy of the role of voice in Western music and its various authorial strategies. This involves, however, a different kind of study than the one undertaken in the present essay; a study that would be compelled to deal in depth with the social and ideological forces that underplayed compositional intent and the authority and meaning of musical structures that jointly gave rise to a new relationship between music and the listener. The new musicology, in fact, deals with these issues from a postmodern perspective. Kramer's "listening through" engendered some postmodern concerns with "modes" of listening. To get some insight into the "problematic" that diverse "modes of listening" raised, it pays to read the interesting articles that are included in the edited volume by Andrew Dell'Antonio, *Beyond Structural Listening? Postmodern Modes of Hearing* (California, 2004).

that they themselves are unaware of. By presuming an aesthetic autonomy for the musical drama and by investing it with a quasi-religious aura,
Wagner seriously aspired to transform the public's attitude toward art in
general—turning lay audiences into committed parishioners. Strange as it
may sound, he actually succeeded in converting a goodly number of music
lovers into adamant devotees.

Putting the Wagner cult aside, it cannot be denied that Wagner also attracted many disciples among distinguished composers who stood to gain
new musical insights and much stimulation from the music he wrote. Wagner
paid homage to the Romantic notion of 'infinity,' for example, through what
he coined as "infinite melody." His *Unendlichemelody* was musically obtained
via the avoidance of, or bridging over, caesuras and cadences—preventing
conventional formulae, as it were, from disrupting the continuity and
uniqueness of the thoughts the music was expected to convey—making
it amply clear that it was also possible to sustain the *musical* argument
without recourse to compositional norms that were deemed necessary
for purposes of orientation. Likewise, as is well known, in his method of
composition, primarily in his later operas, Wagner used "basic themes"
(*Grundthemen* was the term he used) for the representation of characters,
situations, and recurrent ideas. These themes, however, were modified,
transformed, taken apart, and merged with each other—in line with dramatic requirements—to constitute an unceasing *musical* development.
Thus was formed an extended symphonic-dramatic structure from a limited number of building blocks, rendered via the changing entanglements
of motivic relationships. Indeed, the "physiognomy" of Wagner's basic
themes changes in the course of the musical unfolding; it is their alterations,
in fact, and their varied interactions that are supposed to impart the true
meanings of the events—meanings not evident to the dramatis personae
whom they involve. These basic building blocks, which are usually referred
to as *leit*motivs, do not function, evidently, as clear-cut identification cards,
though they may "guide" (*leit, leiten* [G]—leading, to lead) the thinking process in desired directions. Thus, the simple listing of leitmotivs as rigidly
fixed melodies does an injustice to their flexible nature, and misrepresents
the ways in which they function. Wagner's themes are obviously of a complexity greater than the word 'motifs' would suggest. Although the latter
invariably constitute a part of the former, they seldom appear on their own,
making it exceedingly difficult to establish their primary forms. Yet even
as such they force the proficient listener to be conscious of the context in
which they appear—not to speak of the diverse musical forms that they
create—so as to be able to follow the dramatic function they serve.

As is well known, many post-Wagnerian operatic composers adopted Wagner's procedures. Richard Strauss even went so far as to proclaim that Wagner's *Oper und Drama* constituted the book of all books on music. Wagner, naturally, had an influence on symphonic music as well, particularly the symphonic poem. Yet even Brahms—whose music was regarded by contemporaries as diametrically opposed to Wagner's—studied the score of *Tristan* with admiration, for it supplied new insights concerning the development of extended forms from musical ideas consisting of only a few notes. It deserves mention, of course, that Brahms's development, instead of being restricted to the middle section of the sonata form, tended to embrace the whole movement, enlisting an intricate web of motivic relationships. Brahms and Wagner clearly shared a technical-aesthetic problem, despite the vastly different overall objectives. Indeed, the compositional liberties that Wagner entertained revealed that formal designs and modes of musical articulation need not follow accepted norms; they can be uniquely manipulated without destroying the technical categories that made absolute music possible. The composer, moreover, may communicate his own emotions to the listeners directly through the novelties he creates in the musical language he employs.

Much has been written about Wagner's harmonic style, from both tonal and atonal perspectives. Whatever the perspective, it cannot be denied that chromaticism acquired a new status with Wagner. The Romantic exploitation of chromaticism, of the kind that no longer impinged on neighboring notes as passing notes, had indeed attained a new degree of independence from its origin in alterations.[17] Root progressions, in Wagner's later works, seem to have given way altogether to a semitonal motion, associating chords in line with their momentary function and the significance they are meant to serve. Without entering into a detailed description of Wagnerian harmony and the new relationships he established between harmony and counterpoint, it is fair to state that Wagner disguised (to say the least) the tonal background by a suspended, floating kind of tonality, while his counterpoint no longer rested on the foundations of harmonic associations. Rather, it rested primarily on motivic combinations, which, in turn, gave rise to his polyphony. Since the motivic material harbors liter-

---

17. Generally speaking, the term alteration applies to the raising or lowering of a note by means of a half note. The Romantic period may be characterized by the extensive exploitation of chromatically altered harmony, that is, of a steady increase of unprepared and—as in Wagner's case—unresolved appoggiatura chords, not to speak of the free modulations into distant keys. All of this led to the eventual disintegration of tonality.

ary inferences, his counterpoint carries poetic intentions as well, creating a multilayered "melody" that is intimately wedded to the text. Such an intricate web carried implications for formal conceptions as well; old formal structures were replaced by new architectonic designs, including novel metrical treatments. In fact, in the musical style associated with Wagner every element can be directly or indirectly derived from every other, making notions of primary versus secondary elements irrelevant. Indeed, Wagner seems to have succeeded, in his own unique way, to accomplish what he set out to accomplish—a music drama the integrity of which does not fall short of the integrity of a Beethoven symphony.

It took Wagner a long time to get to where he finally landed—the complete transformation of opera into a musical drama. His musico-dramatic scenes clearly eliminated opera's succession of separate numbers (e.g., arias, duets, ensembles), lending the melodic writing the freedom to match words and gestures at every moment in the drama. The singing style he employed cannot be characterized either as *cantar recitando* or *recitar cantando*,[18] but as a kind of expressive declamation that resides between aria and recitative, defying operatic conventions. Yet it must be remembered that Wagner's final success rested on his redefinition of the relationship between music and poetry and, for that matter, between music and its supposed meaning. Although the idea that the arts differ from each other in decided ways became blurred in the Romantic period, the sensitivity to the symbolizing functions of each of the arts nonetheless increased. Cognizant of the possibility of effecting metaphorical exchanges, composers were still guided by the distinctions that different modes of reference seem to supply, taking music's hard-earned syntax for granted. The manifold relationships with discursive language heightened the composers' awareness of the ways in which music may enhance the communication of specified meanings. In other words, music still expressed what it denoted, and what it denoted was an acquired property exemplified by "labels." Wagner, by comparison, attempted to wed the ideational with the representational so that each could perform the reverse function for each other. The music and the text illuminate each other in ways that create an inseparable merger between them, in line with the relationship between

---

18. Pirrotta coined these terms in the attempt to describe the difference between the singing style of Peri and Caccini. To Peri—who sought to bring singing nearer to speech—he attributed the term *recitar cantando*. To Caccini—who was committed to words finding expression in music—he attributed the term *cantar recitando*. See Nino Pirrotta, "Early Opera and Aria," in *New Looks at Italian Opera*, ed. Austin, 52.

counterpoint and harmony, which is realized by an orchestration made up of "voices." It is hence difficult to trace separately the function of each of the components that make up the *Gesamtheit* (totality) of the work, for it is precisely their consolidation that renders the structure of the composition and its uniqueness.

Wagner, of course, was not only eager to lend substance to music's abstract harmonic and thematic formulations but was equally determined to create musical dramas, each with its own distinctive character. After all, the aesthetic autonomy he advocated could be justified only through individual works whose outstanding qualities grant them the "entitlement" to stand outside of history, as it were. Evidently, the greatness of such works cannot be fully grasped upon first hearing. Rather than offer the listener what he is familiar with, the full impact of unique works rests on repeated performances that allow the listener to *become* familiar with their singularity. Indeed, as long as musical works were required to make sense upon first hearing (as was the case in earlier times when repeated performances were rare), it was extremely difficult for a composer to deviate from the governing style of his time. Moreover, the uniqueness of an individual composition belonging to a shared style could be grasped more readily than an outstanding composition within a sui generis style. It should not come as a surprise, then, that Wagner should conclude (after all of his polemics) that the meaning of 'music' can be determined only by the listener, who has been introduced to music via "deeds of music made visible," like a child who is introduced through legendary stories to religion.[19]

Nor is it coincidence that Wagner should resort to religion in order to clarify his position. He too, after all, wished to proselytize his audiences to endorse a new "belief." The creed he fostered concerned the aesthetic autonomy of art, and in particular that of the music drama. He spared no effort to exemplify what he advocated. His final conclusion with regard to the *meaning* of music, however, entails a seeming paradox: Why should the listener have to infer the meaning of music on his own, if the architectonic nature of the music drama delivers deeds of music *made visible*? The paradox is indeed only an illusive one for the particular deeds of music do not *define* that "which from its nature can never itself be directly presented as idea." As explicated earlier, Schopenhauer's view of music clearly transcended the Romantic view of Music, since it freed music altogether from formulated principles and preset laws. Although

19. See "Über die Benennung 'Musicdrama,'" in Richard Wagner *Dichtungen und Schriften*, vol. 9, 174

Schopenhauer's views hardly passed unnoticed, it was Wagner—the adamant revolutionary—who fully recognized the compositional license that his philosophy accorded musicians. More than any other Romantic composer, Wagner not only furthered and underlined the autonomy of the individual artist but also, by entrusting the *meaning* of music to hermeneutic activities of various sorts, granted musical interpretation the kind of freedom that it had never enjoyed before.

Much has been said about Wagner as a revolutionary, but the place he accorded to the arts required little speculation; Wagner was quite explicit about the subject in his voluminous writings. Given his overall attitude to the arts, he believed, inter alia, that the grimness of life needed "aesthetization." He was convinced that, by raising reality to the level of his fiction, he had found a formula for doing so. At any rate, he consciously blurred the boundary between the two by blending the ideational with the representational so that each could perform the reverse function for each other. Western music and the interaction among the arts underwent, as we have seen, many changes, yet the "fictive"—the "as if" world of the arts—became solidly grounded in the process. It was embedded in an understanding of the "illusion" it entails and the kinds of metaphors it employs. With this perspective in mind, one may argue that procedures that divest artistic illusion of its suspension of disbelief contribute to the eradication of the borderlines between fiction and reality. Wagner disclosed a way in which it can be done. He also sensitized us to the distinction between attempts that aspire to heighten our aesthetic sensibilities and those that attempt to "aestheticize" life itself. History revealed that the latter may be more deceptive at times than the "illusions" that greatly enhance our lives. It rests, of course, on who exploits what, in what way, and for what purpose. It appears that a distinction between "fiction" and "reality"—however defined—is necessary for the preservation of independent judgment.

'Music': From Closed System to Open Concept

By the time Ferruccio Busoni wrote his *Entwurf einer neuen Ästhwtik der Tonkust* (1907),[20] a proclamation such as "music was born free; and to win freedom is its destiny"[21] could hardly produce the echo it intended; nor did a statement such as "the function of the creative artist consists in making

---

20. See Ferruccio Busoni, "Sketch of a New Esthetic of Music" (trans. Thomas Baker in 1911) in *Three Classics in the Aesthetic of Music* (New York, 1962), 73–102
21. Ibid., 77.

laws, not in following laws ready made"[22] require much persuasion. Yet discussing absolute music as "something very sober, which reminds one of music-desks in orderly rows, of the relation of Tonic to Dominant, of Development and Codas," or the assertion that form "in itself, is the opposite pole of absolute music, on which was bestowed the divine prerogative of buoyancy, of freedom from the limitations of matter"[23] still strikes us as odd. It strikes us this way for it represents a head-on attack on the notion of 'coherence.' Indeed, it attests to the fact that the striving for coherence, which reached a climax in the eighteenth century, must have given way in the course of the nineteenth century to other objectives, important enough so as to forgo what I have called "sense formation *without* predication" (see chap. 3, pp. 150–52).

The move from musical processes to coherence required, as we have seen, modes of construction or representation based on relationships among the particles being processed. Yet coherence, structured as it may be, does not in itself carry meaning; in other words, coherence makes sense but has no meaning. To turn coherence into substantive meaning requires symbolization. That music could be "possessed" by factors extraneous to music has been discussed at length. Such possessions, however, invariably rested on the "sense" that music itself seemed to provide. In fact, deviations from procedural norms could only be detected *as such* because the composer took music's structural presuppositions for granted. Keeping that in mind, let us analyze another statement by Busoni: "What we now call our Tonal System is nothing more than a set of "signs"; an ingenious device to grasp somewhat of that eternal harmony; a meager pocket-edition of that encyclopedic work; artificial light instead of the sun."[24]

Here Busoni is willing to concede that the tonal system that evolved in the West is "an ingenious" communicative device, for it enabled a partial "grasp" of "that eternal harmony." What he seems to challenge are its confines. Naturally, once "eternal harmony" forgoes its metaphoric function and is conceived as some kind of "given" with music as its "conveyor," no music—whatever its confines—can fully live up to such an assignment. Though he can hardly be accused of lacking sufficient knowledge of the métier,[25] Busoni seems to have turned around three major axioms that un-

22. Ibid., 88.
23. Ibid., 78.
24. Ibid., 89.
25. Busoni was not only a world-renowned concert pianist but also a composer of a variety of interesting and celebrated works. He is also well known for his piano transcriptions of Bach's organ works and his edition of Bach's *Well-Tempered Clavichord*.

derlie the present essay. Two of these pertain to music and one of them to art in general.

The reader may recall that this essay began with two reaffirmations, namely (1) that music is *man-made,* and (2) that it is *not* a universal language spontaneously appreciated by every listener irrespective of cultural background or hard-earned understanding. These two axioms, I argued, are interrelated: given that music is man-made and that cultures differ from one another, musical traditions are also bound to differ. Discussing the self-chosen confines of art (see chap. 2), I took the occasion to state that art—as opposed to nature—invariably refers to a *human* skill, to an ability of execution that becomes manifest in the object executed. Thus, without providing a definition of 'Art' or of its objectives, it seems sensible to claim (3) that art, any art, involves a kind of "making" (in the Aristotelian sense of the word), that is, a bringing about of desired artifacts that entail human skills of one kind or another. Without delimitation of various sorts, these essential characteristics clearly turn meaningless. Since the present essay undertook to trace the "making" of Western art music, in an attempt to highlight its uniqueness, it is no wonder that the above three axioms passed unchallenged until now. Indeed, as long as music strove for a coherence of its own, it was necessary to focus on the reasoning that guided its structural organization. This applied no less to all of those attempts to invest music with semantically rooted understandings. Whatever factors different definitions of music chose to emphasize, to the extent that they applied to the audible phenomenon—rather than to the metaphoric uses of the term—they referred to *organized* sounds displaying some kind of order. It is precisely this vantage point that allows us to detect the enormity of the change that had taken place with respect to the *overall* conception of music.

Busoni's ideas aroused much interest in art circles of the time, attracting the attention of such major figures as Arnold Schoenberg and Bernard Shaw. The ideas considered "avant-garde," however, related specifically to music. The aim of the arts, Busoni maintained, is to imitate nature and to interpret man's feelings; each of the arts deals with a different aspect that it separates out from the whole of the reality revealed to man. Music differs from all other arts in that the object it imitates—the music of the universe, or the *Ur-Musik* (primeval music), as he called it—is an entity in itself. Music thus focuses on emotions that long for transcendental worlds in which all conceivable sounds and combinations, and beyond, are in the domain of the *Ur-Musik.* Thus, to construe Busoni's "eternal harmony" as an extension or as reminiscent of the ancient theory of the "harmony of the spheres" is to overlook the essential difference between them. The "harmony of the spheres" rested on an assumed intelligible order of what might be termed a *closed* system, whereas "eternal harmony" was from the start conceived as an *open* concept, challenging the centrality of order as a means for comprehension. Both were deemed to carry significance for terrestrial life, with or without the awareness that both are *cultural* constructs, reflecting their human creators more than the universe of the Creator.[26]

Indeed, despite the many stages that music underwent in the course of its development, music was invariably addressed as an ordered system. The major revolution that occurred in the history of Western music, beginning with Wagner, is not to be sought, therefore, in the excessive use of chromaticism, or in a "floating" kind of tonality that foreshadowed its breakdown, but rather in the *conceptual* alteration of music as a whole. The change was from a closed system to an a priori open concept, thereby granting "freedom" also to its constituent elements, not only to the interpretation of their meaning.

SOME CHARACTERISTICS OF THE "TURN" OF THE CENTURY

The year 1900 serves many historians as a demarcation line signifying a major turn in Western thought symptomatically expressed in the at-

---

26. Objects, explains Lydia Goehr, "do not fall under a given concept simply or just because they share common or essential, exhibited or nonexhibited properties (or, in Goodman's terms, a perfect community of properties). Rather, concepts and their extensions are adaptable according to their role in activities and the theories bound up therewith." Open concepts, Goehr tells us, have most often been described as: "(I) not corresponding to fixed or static essences; (II) not admitting of 'absolutely precise' definitions of the sort traditionally given in terms of necessary and sufficient conditions; (III) intentionally incomplete or 'essentially contestable'—because the possibility of an unforeseen situation arising which would lead us to modify our definition can never be eliminated; (IV) distinct from, though related to, vague concepts."

> By contrast, whenever a concept is treated as closed, it is given exact and complete definition in light of a stipulation made at a given time 'for a special purpose.' This definition stipulates boundary conditions. In closing a concept we decide it is to be used if and only if the relevant objects have certain features. We recognize the stipulation is dependent upon the use to which we want to put the concept. Thus when we want to change the system and thereby the use of the concept, we change the definition. Though we might continue to use the same name, we use a new concept because we give up the old definition and replace it with a new one. (Lydia Goehr, *The Imaginary Museum of Musical Works,* 91–93.)

titude toward the past.[27] The Past—unlike *in* the past—was no longer considered relevant to the Present, that is, it was no longer viewed as a continuous process informing the various intellectual activities of the present. The term "modern," which became the hallmark of the time, so as to distinguish itself from the past, thus ceased to carry the connotation of novelty, whether fad or recent trend. Proclaiming its independence from the past, the term "modern" came to denote the total break from tradition.

The growing indifference to history, however, involved an energetic search for new self-definitions (or the other way round). Indeed, with the authority of history cast aside, the imagination was set free to produce, in rapid succession, a multitude of new constructs. While weakening the *continuity* of history, these activities speeded up its *process*. It is these variegated quasi-concurrent changes that imparted to contemporaries a sense of "history as present."[28] The cultural fragmentation that took place in the so-called modern period defies, however, not only notions such as "historical progress" and "progressive accumulations" but in fact all attempts to establish shared guidelines—based on inferences—that would materialize in what might be viewed as a comprehensive and adequate picture of the period. Attention, thus, has been conferred on each cultural endeavor separately, eliciting appropriate *analytic* tools, rather than pertinent disclosures of historical background.

Yet, dramatic changes—however described—are brought about only gradually. To do justice to the break from tradition, so as to lend credibility to the portrayal delineated above, requires a detailed examination of the transformations that occurred in the diverse branches of knowledge, along with the beliefs that accompanied them.[29] Although the present essay allows no room for such an examination, the transformation that took place around the turn of the century received much scholarly attention. Regardless of the field investigated, and the diversity of phenomena examined, everything points to the collapse of the intellectual

27. The quotation marks around the word "turn" above are obviously deliberate; I wish to emphasize thereby not only the *end* of the century but the *rotation* in thought it brought about.

28. I owe this phrase to Carl E. Schorske. His *Fin-de-Siècle Vienna: Politics and Culture* (New York, 1981) represents one of the classic studies of the period.

29. A concise summary of these transformations may be found in Elisheva Rigbi-Shafrir's doctoral dissertation, "The Modern in Music against the 'Crisis of Historicism' and the Breakdown of the Rational Paradigm: A Critical Analysis of a Style" (Hebrew University of Jerusalem, 2002).

"paradigm"[30] that guided the acquisition of knowledge in the West since the scientific revolution of the late sixteenth and early seventeenth centuries.

The theoretical, methodological, and empirical assumptions that guided scholars since that seminal revolution rested on the belief that it was possible to attain objective knowledge by means of reason. Though Kant—the paradigmatic philosopher of the Enlightenment—had already challenged man's ability to obtain knowledge of the world as it *really* is, he retained "reason" as a primary means to comprehend its "phenomena," that is, its appearances. Exploring the boundaries of knowledge in relation to the world as experienced, Kant treated knowledge as tantamount to "understanding." The latter, he maintained, rests on a priori universal elements, such as 'time' and 'space,' which do not require empirical confirmation. It is these primary elements that constitute, according to Kant, the basis of our cognition of the world. Though the world appears to us only through the basic molds of cognition, and our grasp of it is "subjective," it must be remembered that man is only capable of understanding that which appears in his consciousness. The application of this comprehension to objects that do not belong to the realm of "phenomena" results in postulates or beliefs that cannot be proven.

While insisting on the authority of science, Kant was also eager, as is well known, to preserve the autonomy of morals. In fact, he supplied a model of the subjective origins of the fundamental principles of both science and morality, laying the groundwork for subsequent philosophical reflections, especially insofar as human autonomy is concerned. Of course, the idea that human beings can live up to the principles of knowledge by the use of their own reason—in the broadest sense—is highly attractive. Yet it deserves mention that a century later, the neo-Kantians insisted that everything given is determined by the forms of cognition, or that the object is constituted by the subject's activity.[31] It is striking how close this sounds to current theories concerning "facts" and their representations. Indeed, the fin de siècle shares some interesting features with the "turn of mind" that characterizes what has come to be called *post*modern. How and

30. See chapter 3, note 43, which explains the use of the term "paradigm" in relation to scientific pursuits and their underlying guidelines.

31. See "Neo-Kantianism" (especially Marburg Neo-Kantianism) in *The Encyclopedia of Philosophy* (Macmillan, 1967). Also see Ernst Cassirer, "Neo-Kantianism," in *Encyclopedia Britannica,* 14th ed. (1930), and W. Flach and H. Holzhey, in *Erkenntnistheorie und Logik im Neukantianismus* (Hildesheim, 1980).

in what way shall be discussed later, after we take a closer look at certain aesthetic-theoretical transformations that, apart from Wagner, directly relate to music.

"Aristotelianism" in Musical Aesthetics

Certain fundamental categories that we operate with derive from an Aristotelian tradition. Concepts such as 'form,' 'substance,' 'matter,' 'energy,' 'quality,' and many others, which serve both science and philosophy, owe their coinage to Aristotle. Yet in order to relate the Aristotelian tradition to music, it is necessary to find a standpoint that permits both a specification of the Aristotelian tradition and brings to the fore phenomena that are of significance for the history of music. "Aristotelianism" in musical aesthetics, accordingly, has consisted of an unceasingly progressive process of delimitation, while appealing continuously to sensory perception as the primary decisive authority. Thus, regardless of the diversity among theories across centuries, whenever delimitation was proved to be historically effective one came a step nearer to defining the "essence" of what came to be called music in the West. From this perspective, the Aristoxenian approach to music seems closer to the essence of what we came to understand by music than the speculative Pythagorean approach. By the same token, Kant shares a philosophical disposition with Aristoxenus (though they scarcely belong to the same philosophical tradition) insofar as the evidence produced by sensory perception and the original observation of phenomena shapes the foundation and the actual substance of reflection.

Musical theory, as we have seen, was occupied for a long time with the constituent elements of preferred musical structures, and musical analysis scarcely dealt with the aesthetic significance of their configurations. Naturally, the phenomenon to be observed had to come into being before it could serve as the actual object of reflection. It must be remembered that the idea that "Art resides in its *making*" only gained momentum in the seventeenth century, once the relation between Nature and the arts was redefined. Similarly, the idea of allying Beauty to the ways in which it is *brought about* and *perceived* only gained momentum in the eighteenth century. It was moral philosophy, however, that awakened the Plotinian notion of Beauty as an aspiration for the "perfection of form." It is due to these developments that aesthetic contemplation was accorded a position—divorced from context and social function—that led to the establishment of aesthetics as one of the major branches of philosophy.

From Leibniz, Shaftesbury, and onward, the world came to be viewed, more and more, as a kind of "representation," circumscribed by the "boundaries of cognition," as Kant maintained around the end of the eighteenth century. Interestingly, as the tangible world progressively received a "fictive" status, the fictive status of the arts progressively acquired an ontological standing. Having relegated the arts to the realm of perception, it is no wonder that the eighteenth century should have produced such an abundance of treatises dealing with the correspondences and differences among the arts. While Shaftesbury's preoccupation with Beauty was to reveal the good in man, Adam Smith was ready to state, eighty years later, that man is "pleased" to find that he can comprehend how the effects of the arts are *produced,* pointing to the double experience involved in the comprehension of art—the *cognition* involved in its making, and the *cognizance* of that cognition. Hence the true nature of music is better revealed, according to Smith, in pure instrumental music, since it highlights its "fabrication."

Let us return to Kant, in light of the above developments. Without delving into the details of his critique of aesthetic judgment, one may consider Kant's view of the arts as particular modes of "communication." He divided the arts into three major categories: the "arts of speech," the "formative arts," and the "arts of beautiful sensations." This division allowed for finer distinctions, emphasizing the uniqueness of the domain of their operation. Poetry, for example, operates in the domain of the relationship between imagination and understanding. In the formative arts, imagination only serves as a "bridge" between the aesthetic object and its perfect form, creating a union between the powers of cognition and sensibility. Since the art of "combining tones" does not refer to some free-standing concept, but places its emphasis on *arrangement* in the aesthetic object, it exemplifies, as far as he was concerned, "independent beauty." Although music cannot nourish thought beyond itself, thought is necessary for the *reception* of its "diverse combinations." Music may thus be considered as a language representative of the *thought process,* but not of the thought itself.

In retrospect, one might say that the present essay has tried to trace the development of the "phenomenon" to be observed as well as an understanding of the "essence" that came to be viewed as "music." Before confronting the challenges of this understanding, it was also necessary to trace the transformations that took place in the understanding of symbols and the way they function in the arts. It is these two strands of "reasoning" that became inextricably intertwined in the construction of music, exposing, as it were, their "delimitation" (in the Aristotelian sense). In short, with respect to the music with which this essay has chosen to deal, it is the evidence produced by sensory perception and original observation of the phenomenon that shaped the foundation and the actual substance of reflection.

"Concerning the Musically Beautiful"

The name Eduard Hanslick is known to every student of music history either as a renowned music critic or as the first "musicologist," who delivered university lectures on "music appreciation"—a novel concept at the time—for forty years. As a critic, he dealt primarily with musical works, rather than with their performances. As lecturer, he focused likewise on the music, trying to disclose compositional designs and strategies that elude innocent music listeners. It is also well known that Hanslick received his position at the University of Vienna on the merit of an aesthetic essay he published in 1854—*Vom Musikalisch-Schönen* (literally "Concerning the Musically Beautiful")—which went through ten editions in his own lifetime.

Hanslick, who was born in 1825 and died in 1904, lived through almost the entire Romantic era, as witness to the manifold changes that took place in the course of the century, in both music and in the climate that surrounded it. He knew almost all of the prominent composers personally, having befriended many of them. He was fully aware of their musical struggles and the objectives they aimed to achieve. His judgment of their works, however, was not influenced by factors such as these. Instead, he suffered (figuratively and literally) from a more pertinent "bias," from an aesthetic perspective that exalted *order* and *formal perfection*. Though both order and formal perfection require compositional craftsmanship, Hanslick insisted that it is formal perfection that bestows unity on the work, while order guarantees clarity of communication. In the face of such an aesthetic ideal, a composer such as Wagner could not fare very well. One can readily comprehend, therefore, why Wagner chose to lampoon Hanslick as a "rigid conservative"—a critic who requires music to be "subject to laws," rather than let music "do what it does" with its face to the future.[32]

32. Wagner caricatured Hanslick in the character of Beckmesser in *Die Meistersinger.* In the original draft of the opera's text Beckmesser was still called Hans Lick. Eva, in the opera, is promised by her father to the singer to whom the Mastersingers will award the prize in their summer festival. Yet Eva loves Walther, who seeks admission to the contest in the hope of winning her as his bride. Walther succeeds in participating in the contest, but his song violates the rules to which the Mastersingers adhere. Beckmesser's duty, as

Yet the "Hanslick-Wagner" case is not simply another incident of a composer failing to satisfy a critic, or the other way round, for it engendered a serious debate about music in general, challenging the essence of its definition. Wagner himself knew all too well that his critic was not a backward-looking aesthetician, but a scholar and practitioner who knew music through and through and had helped bring several innovative composers to public attention. Indeed, he chose to debate Hanslick publicly, seizing the opportunity to create yet another "stage" for the airing of his reform theories. Engaging Hanslick in a heated polemic served Wagner in not only furthering his cause but it also was an ingenious way to lend support to his followers, strengthening those who still needed persuasion. For his part, Hanslick never denied Wagner's genius; he thought of him as a great conductor and a highly gifted composer, who unfortunately was led astray by his own exuberance. Moreover, though he admired Verdi and his steadily growing dramatic ability, fending off those who detected a Wagnerian influence in Verdi's late operas,[33] he considered Wagner the greatest living opera composer and, in a historical sense, the only one worth talking about. Indeed, Hanslick's quarrel was not with Wagner alone; he rejected Lizst just as consistently. What he feared in both of them, and in several others, was their "reform" theories. As far as he was concerned, their theories did not represent an extension and enrichment of music, but rather the beginning of the end of that "phenomenon" that was called "music" in the West, including the tacit understanding it embraced.

Hanslick was fully aware that the world of sounds that came to be considered "music" in the West did not come into existence overnight. Viewing his subject in historical and social perspective, he was even willing to concede that the future might well belong to music that lay outside his frame of reference. He believed, however, that the *distinctiveness* that music had achieved—through the cumulative musical and ideational developments that accompanied its structuring and understanding—would continue to guide its future development. This also explains in part why he took little interest in music that predated the seventeenth century, and even then he preferred to deal with music that took the coherence achieved in the

---

the town clerk, was to mark the violations of the rules. Since he himself is interested in winning the hand of Eva, he manages to overlook the beauty of Walther's song. Hans Sachs (the most famous figure of the historical Mastersingers) appreciates its beauty and recognizes in its very freedom from rules a path that leads from a battered tradition toward a more exalted ideal.

33. See his "Verdi's 'Otello'" in Eduard Hanslick, *Music Criticisms 1846–99*, trans. and ed. Henry Pleasants (Baltimore, 1950), 280–87.

classical period into account. It is wrong, however, to think of Hanslick as one who objected to musical genres other than the purely instrumental. He did not oppose the wedding of music with the literary arts; he objected to the introduction of foreign elements in ways that eschewed the "logic" whereby music, in and of itself, made "sense." Treating music as an extraordinary cultural achievement—a feat in a *man-made* world—Hanslick, naturally, did not take kindly to the transcendentalism that characterized the "prophets" of the future. He picked up the glove to duel with Wagner since Wagner seemed the most dangerous of all the prophets. In retrospect, Hanslick can hardly be accused of shortsightedness; he may be charged, instead, for having been overly optimistic, believing, as he did, that the musical path to which he objected would fade away.

Though Wagner could not curb himself from describing Hanslick's *Von Musikalisch-Schönen* as a slander written to further Jewish musical aims,[34] and though Hanslick conceded that he had started writing it as an anti-Wagnerian polemic, the essay is a thoughtful statement about music that future generations could ill afford to ignore. Although the essay appeared at a crucial juncture in the history of music, defending seemingly obsolete ideas, it in fact expressed the latest aesthetic theories of the time. Taking account of both Kant and the new aesthetic insights that preceded him, these theories tried to formulate the relations embodied by the arts through more discernible and distinct systems. In addition to Hanslick's keen awareness of the earlier paths music had taken, it is easy to pinpoint the more immediate philosophical thought that influenced his aesthetic outlook.

As is well known, Hanslick dedicated his essay to Robert Zimmermann—an aesthetician in his own right—who was a disciple of Herbart. Johann Friedrich Herbart (1776–1841) had based his "general practical philosophy" on pre-Kantian and Kantian assumptions. Philosophy, he argued, is not to be characterized by its content, but by the reworking of concepts from which its branches and their interrelations derive. The process of distinguishing and organizing concepts that fix identities, claimed Herbart, contradicts our experience of the constantly changing world. The

---

34. Hanslick's paternal ancestors were Catholics. His father married one of his piano pupils, the daughter of a Jewish banker, who had converted to Catholicism. Wagner's "Das Judentum in der Musik" appeared anonymously in 1850 in the *Neue Zeitschrift für Musik*. In 1869 the essay was reissued under his name with a postscript in which he referred to Hanslick's Jewish origin. Hanslick knew that Wagner could not stand Jews, but he also thought that Wagner developed the habit of regarding as Jewish everything he disapproved of or anyone he did not like.

identity and unity of something is determined, rather, by the specific organization of the relations among things that themselves are constantly
changing. In our thinking, Herbart maintained, we are unable to reach the
substantive essence of the different "reals," since by means of our senses
we come into contact only with their surface features. Our intellectual
comprehension of things is therefore exclusively based on *relationships*.
Aesthetic judgment, hence, focuses on the internal relationships among
the elements that constitute the aesthetic object, and each of the arts
selects a different field of relations: painting selects the relations among
colors, sculpture the relations among outlines, and poetry and ethics (Herbart viewed ethics as part of aesthetics) the relations among thoughts. In
music, where sounds constitute the building blocks, aesthetic judgment
focuses on the relations among them. Since aesthetic judgment concerns
elements that belong to a "field of relations," the intermixing of other elements confounds its very nature. Though the emotional or social dimension may add to the appeal of a work, and historical interpretation may
help to approach it, these are factors that should not be mixed with aesthetics. Aesthetic activity, insisted Herbart, is a cognitive activity. Since
all cognitive activity is based on the clear perception of relations, and
since the essence of human cognition is the organization of the relations
of impressions entering its field, one of the summits of cognition may be
found in a realm in which the internal relationships have crystallized to
the point of demanding awareness. Although the aesthetic experience is
a spontaneous activity, its fullness depends on prior training in the relations special to its field. Since the role of aesthetics is to formulate the
relations embodied by each of the arts into a conceptual system, music is
further advanced than the other arts, given its music-theoretical formulations. It deserves mention that Herbart did not intend to establish an
exhaustive philosophy of art. Excluding emotional and historical aspects
from his aesthetic judgment does not imply that they do not exist in art or
that they are of no importance. Herbart was fully aware of their existence
and significance; so was Hanslick, who was influenced by his philosophical
arguments.

Hanslick's *Von Musikalisch-Schönen* grew out of two divergent tendencies, one that emerged in contemporary musical composition, and the
other that came to the fore in aesthetic criticism. The debate to which
they gave rise, Hanslick thought, stemmed from a misguided conception
of music, upheld, paradoxically, by those who should have known better.
To consider music an art striving for the expression of feelings is a gross
misconception of music's particular "nature," according to Hanslick. Since

all art is conditioned by the sensory realm it addresses, the essence of music—the art of "combining tones"—must be sought in the immanent relations it creates, rather than in the emotions it evokes. "Musical thought" is basically untranslatable; the forging of musical unity is governed by a "logic" that is capable of creating solely "musical ideas." Music, Hanslick tells us, is essentially forms set in motion by sounds (*tönend bewegte Formen*). The process of shaping persuasive forms is brought about, however, by artistically productive minds—by "a spirit that fashions itself from within." The beautiful in music must thus relate to the modes of its construction, not to the content attributed to it by extramusical means. Of course, music may interact with extramusical ideas, including ones related to specific emotions, yet their interaction must be viewed as metaphorical, for music is incapable *by definition* of conveying ideas other than musical ones, a fortiori specified emotions. In short, in the phenomenon called "music" the arrangement of sounds is an end in itself, not a means toward the end of expressing something other than itself, as is the case in language.

Indeed, to consider Hanslick a mere "formalist" diverts attention from his main argument to subjects the importance and significance of which he never denied. Although he had special regard for the music that epitomized the *musically* beautiful, he was fully aware of the ways in which music was employed to convey "meaning," which music, qua music, does not address. Moreover, having emphasized the dynamic aspect of tones, he was even prepared to suggest an analogy between the dynamics of music and that of the course of an emotion—an idea that has been echoed by a number of twentieth-century thinkers and explicated most clearly by Susanne Langer.[35] However, it is Hanslick's emphasis on the *autonomy* of music, lending centrality to the ways in which it is structured, that exerted a major influence on musical analysis. Despite their different theoretical claims, theorists such as Heinrich Schenker, Arnold Schoenberg, Rudolph Reti, and many others were at pains to portray music as "*tönend bewegt*"— as a multifaceted transformation of tones, creating significant and distinct "musical ideas." We must remember, in addition, that Hanslick conceived of the production and comprehension of music as cognitive activities. Had he lived today, he might have reformulated some of his maxims in cognitive terms. Hanslick, clearly, still deserves thinking about. But, most of all, Hanslick merits a special place in this essay because of his premonition (though he hardly trusted his own intuition) that the beginning of the end of what came to be understood as 'music' in the West was in sight.

35. See Langer, *Feeling and Form*, chaps. 3–4.

In Defense of Musicology as Envisioned

This essay has tried to trace—albeit in brash strokes—the ways in which music gradually reached the autonomy Hanslick talked about, emphasizing that music created its own procedures by which it was gauged and understood. These procedures, I claimed, built on each other in an integrative way so as to enable music to include its own full explanation within itself. The compact and organic correlation that *absolute* music exemplified may be said to reveal, in retrospect, the "rationality" that guided the construction of musical knowledge "as a whole." Having reached this point, one can readily understand why individual works were expected to reflect this hard-earned knowledge in their musical representations. In fact, while highlighting style and stylistic change, the histories of Western music invariably take note of the progressive stages of music's theoretical development.

The systematic study of music began, however, at a time when some of its underlying assumptions—those that guided the establishment of musicology—were challenged in domains other than music. The fin de siècle may, in fact, be characterized by the transformation that occurred in the various branches of knowledge, once they relinquished the beliefs that accompanied their scholarly pursuits. Regardless of the field investigated and the diversity of phenomena examined, the turn of the century, as already stated, pointed to the collapse of the intellectual paradigm that had guided the acquisition of knowledge ever since the scientific revolution. Indeed, once it was no longer believed that it was possible to attain *objective* knowledge by means of reason alone, the theoretical, methodological, and empirical assumptions that had guided scholars until then were seriously challenged. The well-established disciplines could, of course, confront the challenge better than a scholarly activity that was making its bid to be recognized as a bona fide discipline.

In the amorphous atmosphere of the period, however, it still made sense to envision the systematic study of music in accord with the "rational paradigm," despite its obvious collapse elsewhere. Although this paradigm lent musicology the recognizable semblance of a *Wissenschaft* (a science), it also reflected the path that music had traversed on its way to autonomy. Unlike the natural sciences, which try to unveil the secrets of a *given* world through "descriptions" formulated by men, music *results* from man-made choices in accordance with cultural desiderata. If musical works are still assessed by theorists via the "musical logic" they display, it is due to the fact that music in the West increasingly strove to integrate its parts into a sensibly unified whole. The unity of the whole is in fact expected to clarify the functions of its parts. The hierarchical setup—within each musical parameter and among the components forming the discernibly different styles—no doubt helped achieve the unity desired. The multiple levels, which interacted with each other in systematic ways, enabled the great variety of complex musical structures, without blurring the logic of their unfolding. In fact, no other music has been able to produce the kind of "long-range directionality"—that is, an extended linear process based on "expectations"—that Western music succeeded in achieving, not to speak of the complexity that it was able to encompass. With a world of sounds so conceived, no wonder that its custodians viewed musical works as "objects" that lend themselves to *objective* analyses. It is likewise no wonder that a composer such as Wolfgang Amadeus Mozart—the paragon of musical coherence—should have constituted *the* standard by which to measure the achievements of subsequent composers.

Though fully aware of some "extraneous" music produced by various contemporary composers who should have known "better," the founding fathers of musicology were in no position to entertain the thought that what Hanslick feared could conceivably happen. Even were they to entertain such thoughts, how could that affect the study of music, the one that developed the way it did? Thus, when Guido Adler[36] proposed his agenda for the systematic study of music, he placed special emphasis on "history" and "style," since the two related to each other in a specific audible manner in the music that guided his thinking. Given that the historical development of music was only partially known and that much still awaited rigorous research, he focused on lacunae that had to be "filled in," on additional source materials that needed unveiling, on treatises that required reexamination, on composers and individual works of historical uniqueness that demanded special attention.[37] All of these still constitute worthy guidelines for much of musicological research (for good reasons, as we have seen), in spite of, or in addition to, some of the trends represented by

36. Adler (1855–1941) was the paramount figure among those associated with the establishment of modern musicology.

37. See Guido Adler, "Umfang, Methode und Ziel der Musikwissenschaft," in *Vierteljahrsschrift für Musikwissenschaft*, vol. 1 (1885), 5–20; "Musik und Musikwissenschaft" (Akademische Antrittsrede), in *Jahrbuch der Musikbibliothek Peters* (1898), 29–39; *Der Stil in der Music* (Leipzig, 1911); *Methode der Musikgeschichte* (Leipzig, 1919); *Handbuch der Musikgeschichte*, ed. Adler (Berlin, 1930).

the "new musicology" and the growing attention that semiotic interpretations seem to command.

Fin-de-siècle musical discourse was likewise saturated with rational values. The leading musical theorists of the time, such as Hugo Riemann,
August Halm, Heinrich Schenker, and Arnold Schoenberg, continued to
struggle—each in his own way—to formulate music in scientific terms,
that is, in accordance with universally valid criteria. Although the attempt
to ground musical knowledge in metatheoretical justifications—whether
physical or metaphysical—was of course not new, now it engaged the musical objects as representations of a naturally "given," against which they
were supposed to be judged. Of course the organic unity that music was
able to display lent support to positivistic approaches, which highlighted
music's *rational* nature. Thus, the development that culminated in absolute
music was now construed as a "revelation"—the consequence of a tireless
process whereby the "secrets" of music were disclosed. Indeed, the shift in
philosophical deliberations, which highlighted the relation between cognitive processes and the phenomena perceived, was itself perceived as fos-
tering such views. Nowadays, however, with the advancement of cognitive
studies, one would no doubt attribute the coherence achieved by absolute
music to so-called *learned* systematic schemata.

The scientific approach to music failed, however, to supply tools for
the stylistic analysis of contemporary music, written by composers who
no longer aspired to bestow the familiar unity on their works or to follow music's presumed "inherent" logic. Modernism implied *true* separation, not disguised uniformity. Distrust in the ability to arrive at objective knowledge diverted attention *away* from universally valid methods,
mobilizing special tools appropriate for the pursuit and analysis of each
cultural domain separately. Though the mimetic tradition concerning the
arts had already been challenged in the eighteenth century, it only now
coincided with a climate ready to forego the '*ut pictura poesis*' dictum altogether. Because of the treatment of 'perception' as a vital field of investigation, the arts now acquired a sovereign position that they previously had
only partially enjoyed. Yet music constituted an anomaly in this context,
since nobody had doubted music's uniqueness to begin with, nor the tools
music devised for its own analysis. What now?

Diverging Trends in Fin-de-Siècle Music and Musical Analysis

The changed conception of music, starting with Wagner, clearly needed
addressing. Wagner, as we have seen, took music's autonomy for granted,

underlining instead the autonomy of the individual artist. By entrusting the *meaning* of music to hermeneutic activities of various sorts, he also granted musical interpretation a sovereignty that it had never enjoyed before. Busoni wished to free music from the "delimitation" exemplified by absolute music, thereby liberating music altogether from the accepted notions about its constitutive character. Wagner and Busoni were, of course, not the only ones who no longer viewed music as a closed predetermined system. Once 'music' had turned into an open concept, musical "objects" were at liberty to become "open works," reflecting the new autonomy of the artist, that is, allowing him to do as he saw fit.

However introspective nineteenth-century composers turned out to be, they wished to leave their mark on history through innovative treatments of music as *traditionally* understood. By contrast, the "open work," though no less subjective, encouraged a kind of heterogeneity, challenging not only Hanslick's "order" and "formal perfection" but the definition of 'style.' Regardless of the factors emphasized, style generally refers to features characteristic of a work or a group of works (by a single artist or a group of artists) that maintain a distinctive constancy. In the open work of the turn of the century old and new styles could be adjoined in one and the same composition, with or without having to lend them an "updated" semblance. It suffices to think of a composer such as Gustav Mahler to realize that his seeming eclecticism was intentional. He avoided the more familiar kind of overall unity, certainly not for want of ability or originality.[38] Mahler's "emancipation," unlike the "emancipation of the dissonance," rested on the freedom to follow his impulse in whatever direction it led. His music, accordingly, exhibits new sound images followed by musical "similes" saturated with associations. Tranquil sections are interrupted by sudden outbursts; "folksy" music is followed by sophisticated musical expressions, creating, in sum, a rich pageant of introspective urgencies and delights. A musical "exhibition" (*Ausstellung*) of this kind naturally rests on prior "mental pictures" (*Vorstellungen*) that induce the musical images created. A state of mind *thus* represented can hardly be bound by a one-sided aesthetic outlook.

38. Mahler, as is well known, was also a great conductor, thus intimately acquainted with the musical styles that figured in the repertoires of concert halls and opera houses. While admired as a knowledgeable and sensitive conductor, he was also highly respected as a composer, despite his "idiosyncrasies." Each of his symphonies was eagerly awaited and their first performances enjoyed extensive coverage by contemporary critics. Yet despite the fame and respect that he enjoyed in his own lifetime, he also suffered from a goodly number of critics who accused him of "eclecticism" and lack of "creative imagination," attributing these characteristics, at times, to his "Semitic" origin.

Yet the idea that prior "mental pictures" guide the execution of works of art was already evident in the revisions composers found necessary to introduce into their completed works. The completed work must have imparted an image of its own; otherwise, how else could one establish whether it does, or does not, correspond to what was anticipated? Now, however, the image of the "whole" was conceived no longer as an organic musical structure affecting the *perception*—not only the function—of its parts but rather as a holistic phase that precedes the mental pictures that it creates. The fact that organically structured compositions may be manifested differently—though they follow the same musical "logic" and aesthetic desiderata—suggests that they, too, must entail some prior "vision" that affects their particularities. In fact, some fin-de-siècle theorists tried to address this issue by advancing new metaphysical claims, or by unveiling primary configurations constitutive of mental musical templates. Even a theorist such as Riemann seems to echo contemporary concerns via his persistent preoccupation with "*Tonvorstellungen*" ("prior sound images"), which he considered from a purely psychological perspective.[39]

The holistic peculiarity of a *Vorstellung* creates a unique tie between the musical image as imagined and its actual appearance, drawing attention to blended surfaces at the expense of deep structures. Holistic mental images may also be conceived as an antecedent phase to the actual tones that represent them. The actual appearance thus requires active listening—not to the tones representing it, but to the materialized images—if one expects to follow the composer's "vision." Furthermore, the antecedent phase that activates the composer may itself be viewed as a kind of "elective fixation" that interrupts, as it were, the primordial fluidity of music. Busoni clearly thought of music in primordial terms, but he was not the only one who thought of music in this way. The idea that a chaotic, primordial movement (*Urbewegung*) underlies music's substantiating process was also entertained by theorists, who otherwise were busy analyzing music in the more familiar manner.[40]

Though most theorists still adhered to "rational" explications of mu-

39. See Hugo Riemann, "Ideen zu einer 'Lehre von den Tonvostellunge,'" in *Jahrbuch der Musikbibliothek Peters* (1914–15) and "Neue Beiträge Zu einer 'Lehre von den Tonvorstellungen,'" ibid., (1916).

40. See, for example, Ernst Kurth, *Musikpsychologie* (Berlin, 1931). In his *Grundlagen des linearen Kontrapunkts: Bach melodische Polyphonie* (Berlin, 1917), Kurth also advanced a theory of melody that is independent of harmony, thereby lending support to some contemporary composers who no longer wished to be constrained by harmonic "dictates."

sic, some also obviously echoed fin-de-siècle concerns that conceived of knowledge as a kind of "making" rather than as a sort of "unveiling." In fact, the illusive character of musical mental images, which allowed the indefinite, indistinct entities to create a continuous musical flow, could be viewed as a representation of a "stream of consciousness"—a mindfulness of life lived, rather than observed. Perceptible analogies to the vitality of existence also came to the fore in the other arts, reflecting in practice as well as theory the preoccupation with "life as experienced"—a major topos of the turn of the century. The focus on "experience" (*Erlebnis*) naturally shifted the emphasis from objective to subjective knowledge.[41]

In her brilliant dissertation concerning fin-de-siècle music,[42] Elisheva Rigbi-Shafrir has persuasively shown how the formal features of knowledge of the period moved away from a focus on discreteness to an enthrallment with continuities marked by unstable identities, ambiguity, and a sort of pluralism. Her survey of the various branches of knowledge traces the breakdown of the rational hierarchy of knowledge, which attempted to provide a unifying locus so that the scientific standing of each of its branches could be gauged separately. The high standing of the exact sciences until that time was due largely to their regard—since the scientific revolution onward—for mathematics and its attendant logic. The status of logic, however, was undermined once objectivism was challenged. The new avenues of knowledge now pointed in the direction of previously acclaimed "peripheries," that is, to the subjective avenues for comprehending the world. The acknowledgment of a subjective element in human understanding seemed obviously more compatible with a "philosophy of life" (*Lebensphilosophie*) based on experience than with philosophies guided by universal abstractions.

It is interesting to note that the kinds of "understanding" (*Verstehen*) that the humanities employed were not considered scientific enough until then, since their "verities" were achieved neither inductively nor deductively, that is, via the major indicators of a bona fide science. Obviously, the multiplicity of variables that the humanities tend to handle—at one and the same time—defy linearity, not to speak of their inability to establish clear-cut causal relationships. But when the very factors that were deemed to impede "unchallenged" truths began to be seen as germane to

41. I frequently use German terms because the major part of the ideational transformations to which they relate happened in the German-speaking orbit.

42. See Rigbi-Shafrir, "Modern in Music."

the acquisition of knowledge, scientific investigations could drop their positivistic attire in favor of a more pragmatic individual garb.[43] Moreover, having lost a unifying locus, the scientific standing of the various branches of knowledge was obscured, challenging their hierarchy and blurring their boundaries. The turn of the century, in fact, gave rise to a kind of pragmatism, which has accompanied the pursuit of knowledge ever since. All of these aspects constitute the background against which Rigbi-Shafrir has examined the music and the discourse about music of the fin de siècle.

The music of the fin de siècle is largely regarded in terms of a transition from nineteenth-century "Romanticism" to twentieth-century "New Music." Though scholars have recognized major landmarks in that music, music historiography—unlike that of other departments of cultural history—did not see fit to consider fin-de-siècle music as an independent period. Yet if one wishes to ally music to the other cultural expressions of a period whose uniqueness has long been established, one must also consider attributing a special place to its music. Such an attempt would not be a mere exercise. After all, music does not happen in a vacuum; it contributes to and reflects the broader context of which it is an integral part no less than do other cultural expressions. In order to fully understand fin-de-siècle music, it is thus necessary to devise "tools" to enable a description that takes into account the art itself *as well as* its wider context.

Rigbi-Shafrir created such a description by identifying first the distinctive formal features of the rational forms of knowledge, so as to be able to show that these were no longer adhered to. The formal features she identified—those that make it possible to contrast the "non-Rational" to the "Rational"—involve "discreteness," "stable identities," and "directionality." Discreteness, accordingly, refers to the dichotomy between object and subject on all levels of articulation. Stable identities submit to the epistemological desiderata of certainty, consistency, and universality. Directionality refers to fixed relations of priority, whether chronological

43. The psychological, sociological, and philosophical investigations of key people such as William James, Emile Durkheim, and Wilhelm Dilthey, respectively, clearly demonstrate a pragmatic shift away from abstract, idealistic approaches. See, for example, William James, *Pragmatism: A New Name for Some Old Ways of Thinking* (1907; Cambridge, 1975), *The Meaning of Truth* (1909; Cambridge, 1975), and *A Pluralistic Universe* (1909; Nebraska, 1996). Also see Emile Durkheim, "Pragmatism and Sociology" (1913–14), in *Essays on Sociology and Philosophy,* ed. Kurt H. Wolff (New York, 1964); Wilhelm Dilthey, "The Construction of the Historical World in the Human Sciences" (1910), in *Selected Writings,* trans. and ed. H. P. Rickman (Cambridge, 1976); *Hermeneutics and the Study of History* (*Selected Works* IV), ed. Rudolf Makkreel and Frithjof Rodi (Princeton, 1996).

or structural, abstract or concrete. "Non-Rational" knowledge can thus be marked by an inherent "connectedness" (instead of discreteness), since no objectification is independent of context; "destabilization of identity" (instead of stable identities) result from the permeability of context; "symmetrical," "holistic," and "circular" structures (instead of directionality), resulting from the symmetrization of the subject/object dichotomy. With these tools at hand, she examined anew the writings of the major musical theorists of the fin de siècle and analyzed a representative body of musical works produced by some of the period's outstanding composers.

Her examination of the theoretical writings revealed musical criteria that were extracted from a seeming "ideal type." These criteria comprise: (1) "meta-theoretical justifications" (claiming a grounding in objectivity); (2) "established norms" (serving as a base for the evaluation of the degree to which the music conforms or deviates from them); (3) "the nature of music" (attributing to music an immanent kind of objectivity); (4) "universal integration" (striving to integrate partial theories into a unified whole); (5) "interdependent aesthetic desiderata" (concretizing the whole of musical knowledge within itself). Given the historical development of music, it does not come as a surprise to find that most of the musical theorists of the time still adhered to analytic modes that had collapsed elsewhere. What is surprising, however, is the tenacity with which those modes were upheld even with regard to musical expressions that clearly deviated from the accepted course that had established the understanding of 'music' in the West. There were also signs, as already mentioned, that pointed to a shift from an objective to a seeming subjective grounding of musical knowledge. The preoccupation with musical *Vorstellungen*—of whatever kind—clearly entailed a psychological dimension that diverted attention from the objects observed to the individuals involved. Yet the preoccupation with holistic mental images served only as a contemplative addendum to a well-entrenched activity that was primarily concerned with music's deep structure and the logic that guided its construction.

Unlike the theoretical discourse, the examination of the music of prominent composers of the period (including Mahler, Strauss, Max Reger, Leoš Janáček, Busoni, Franz Schreker, Alexander von Zemlinsky, Claude Debussy, Igor Stravinsky, and Schoenberg) revealed some or all (depending on the particular composer examined) of the formal features and musical criteria that were identified as "*non*-rational." From a stylistic point of view these comprised undisguised stylistic pluralism; holistic, circular processes, rather than constructive ones; emphasis on gestalt qualities (timbre, texture, atmosphere, and so forth) instead of particles and basic units; constant transitions that create a kind of "musical prose" made up of musical gestures, quotations, associations, and so on, replacing the motivic/thematic domain. All of these aspects, and more, seem compatible with the breakdown of the rational paradigm exhibited in other cultural spheres of the period. Thus, from the perspective of the intellectual climate of the turn of the century, fin-de-siècle music may be regarded, like all the other branches of culture, as constituting an independent period in music history, rather than a transitional one. Moreover, from a broader historical perspective, it seems to have anticipated some features the full significance of which only reached fruition toward the end of the twentieth century. What happened in the interim?

LANDMARKS IN A NEW "TONAL" ENVIRONMENT

One of the most striking changes that occurred in twentieth-century music involves the challenge to tonality as a leading device for musical orientation. Although the means of achieving tonality have greatly varied throughout the development of music in the West, the need for a tonal reference has never been challenged; indeed, the opposite holds true. The history of Western music abounds in treatises that deal with the church modes and the keys of the major and minor modes in relation to both monophonic and polyphonic music. In monophonic music, where the relationships are purely melodic, it was enough to establish a tonal center to which all other tones are related. Modal polyphony, however, went through a number of stages, as we have seen, with regard to modal references and their distribution among the voices that constituted the polyphonic contrapuntal web. Yet from the turn of the seventeenth century onward, harmonized music rested on a system of tonal functions that was based on the establishment of three main chords—the tonic, the dominant, and the subdominant triads—as the carriers of both the harmonic and the melodic movements. The enlargement of the chords and the ample use of modulation and chromatic alterations naturally broadened the ways in which they functioned, but the system of tonal functions prevailed until the twentieth century. Despite the differentiation often made between 'modality' (the use of the church modes) and 'tonality' (the use of major or minor keys), they both clearly reveal a loyalty to a center to which all other tones are related.

The loyalty, however, to one tone to which all other tones are related is not a uniquely Western feature, but a phenomenon that characterizes music throughout its evolution, encompassing non-Western cultures as well. It seems that music the world over has felt the need for some kind of orienting device that would "make sense" of the flow of music. Yet no other culture was as concerned with the structuring of a complex kind of music that could explain itself from within, that is, provide the "logic" of its own coherence. The West, consequently, fully exploited musical expectations based on the "tensions" and "relaxation" that tonality was able to engender, since the tensions *implied* their resolutions, however remote, and relaxation rested on the *stable state* of fundamental tonal relationships. Indeed, no other music was able to create the kind of long-range directionality that characterized Western "absolute music." Nonetheless, though harmonic tonality was dominant from the end of the seventeenth century to the end of the nineteenth century, the music of Wagner and his successors progressively pointed to its breakdown. The tendency was largely manifested in the constant modulations that denied reference to a tonal center, in harmonic structures that defied reductions to cadential schemes, and in chords that dared resolutions of whatever kind. It is sufficient to mention these few aspects to realize that music in the West was undergoing changes that would go far beyond mere technical modifications, for they revealed a readiness to forgo music's major orienting device—a compass, as it were, that had long served listeners and composers alike.

Defying the "Soundness" of the Harmonic System

The abandonment of tonality did not take place overnight, of course. It began with slight deviations that only gradually became more decisive. To free the harmonic concepts from their governing state was no easy matter, for it required no less than a total reconceptualization. Thus from the time that tonality began to be loosened until it was totally abandoned an interesting intermediate phase occurred that aimed to do away with the delimitation of the familiar harmonic system yet wished to retain its form-building force. Indeed, the break from the past was expressed primarily not through the disintegration of traditional tonality but through the challenge of the major and minor tonalities by multiple scalar organizations, new harmonic layers, new orchestral timbres, and so on. These accompanied the stylistic pluralism already mentioned and the predilection for "quotations" of many kinds, musical gestures of various sorts, and so forth.

Debussy provides an ingenious example, one among many, of an attempt to do away with the delimitation of the familiar harmonic system, while wishing to retain the referential function of tonality. Debussy sought to override the dictates of harmonic tonality (which governed also the melodies that were conceived according to a latent idea of a harmonic cadence) via the *re*-introduction of *melodic* tonality into music. In so doing, he hoped to invoke anew the binding force through which musical lines were held together prior to, or in the absence of, harmonic tonality. Such lines are usually held together through apparent relationships among their segments, revolving around each other, or around some focal notes or one central note. The investigation of old tunes, including chant melodies, and a host of melodic lines produced by remote, unfamiliar cultures revealed interesting orienting devices, that is, melodic "tonalities" of various sorts. Debussy, as is well known, spent some time exploring folk tunes and the principles guiding several non-European musical traditions. His search, it seems, affected not only his melodic shapes but also their sounds within a polyphonic web containing harmonies of various types.

Before elaborating further on Debussy's successful attempt to free himself from the delimitation of harmonic tonality while retaining its form-building force, we must return to Wagner, who foreshadowed the future course of music more than did his immediate successors. If Wagner is mostly identified with his *Tristan,* it must be attributed to the harmonic structure of the opera, which harbors the kernel of the change that music was destined to undergo. As we have seen, Wagner challenged not only the seemingly abstract nature of absolute music but also the validity of its harmonic system. Moreover, he changed the entire conception of music in a creative and effective way. His followers attempted likewise to create persuasive musical examples representing a new tonal state. Wagner's "floating" tonality was turned into an expanded type of chromatic harmony by Richard Strauss, who fused several tonalities in a widened orchestral color in his operas and symphonic poems. While still adhering to classical cadence, Strauss's musical texture abounds in unprepared passing chords, harmonic deviations, cumulative unresolved dissonances, and free key relationships between the various groupings, creating a novel splendor of sounds resting on an expanded and drawn-out tonality, as it were.

The same holds true for Mahler in spite of the folk-song style in several of his compositions. Although a singing line also characterizes his polyphonic textures, Mahler's development techniques go even further than those of Strauss, outdoing Anton Bruckner—with whom he studied—in the expansion of the symphonic form. These musicians, and a goodly number of others, were clearly ready to depart from the established norms associated with harmonic tonality. Yet it took some time for tonality to be entirely abandoned. Even Schoenberg, the great liberator of the dissonance, was not completely ready to forgo tonality at the start, although he proceeded farther in the direction initiated by Wagner. At any rate, it is the threshold trespassed by Wagner that eventually led the way to atonality.

Although *Tristan* no doubt reveals dissatisfaction with worn-out elements that had been reduced to mere formulae, it also represents the epitome of an age that valued emotional expression. The Romantic period, as we have seen, evolved new harmonic and melodic techniques that conveyed both intimacy and subtlety of expression. These require that the smallest elements in the individual work be determined, so as to be able to impart the *nuances* of musical expression. Although the preoccupation with minute nuances and their subtle transformations became most evident in the *Lied,* romantic harmony also revealed a similar tendency in vastly enlarged instrumental works. Associating intimacy with vastness did not seem contradictory in an age that had witnessed the effects of the Industrial Revolution as well as the far-reaching implications of the "minutia" with which biological studies were preoccupied. We have already seen how the notion of 'infinity,' for example, fostered a kind of "self-indulgence" that created a bond via assumed shared sentiments between composer and public. Indeed, what may seem contradictory in one age may not seem so in another. Both Strauss and Mahler, despite the differences between them, clearly combined large-scale forms with subtle modes of expression, achieving an emotional intensity through their new techniques of working with small units. These composers owed a great deal to the example set by Wagner, whose expressive style was no less influential than the theories his musical style advanced.

Influenced by Wagner and some of his successors, Alexander Scriabin, to take another example, wished to heighten the expression of music through his own conception of a *Gesamtkunstwerk*. Unlike Wagner, who employed the power of myth in an ingenious way, Scriabin called for the projection of "musical colors"—colors that he listed in a table against given chords—involving the eyes and the ears in an abstract fashion quite different from Wagner's Romantic "realism." His late orchestral pieces and piano works (Scriabin was an outstanding pianist who wrote predominantly for the piano) rejected tonality and supplanted triadic harmony by the use of a six-note chord, consisting of perfect and altered fourths based on the upper partials of the overtone series. In addition to this mysterious chord, of which Scriabin made ample use, his entire aesthetic outlook abounded in new metaphysical notions that provoked a counterreaction in his own homeland, Russia, which in turn inspired subsequent Russian musicians, such as Sergei Prokofiev and Dmitri Shostakovich. Nonetheless, Scriabin's novel ideas were met with enthusiasm among circles outside of Russia. These, no doubt, boosted the well-known collaboration between Wassily Kandinsky and Schoenberg, who also experimented with a kind of synesthesia—relating color to sound. Although Scriabin's experiments had little in common with Wagner's *Gesamtkustwerk,* in retrospect they seem to have foreshadowed what has come to be called "multimedia" in the twentieth century.

Janáček, the well-known Czech composer, advanced another conception of opera. Replacing Wagner's exalted characters by simple human beings, he provided them with a musical language that avoided emotional extremes, allowing them to convey their commonplace stations through a kind of naturalism close to ordinary language. Though his dramatic prosody was influenced by Mussorgsky's ideas of "realistic musical speech," he never imitated the Russian models, but found a way of his own. Yet he too was not only interested in the plight of ordinary people but also attuned to their songs. His interest in folk traditions left a decisive mark on his compositions. He was also attentive to the impressionists' approach to music and admired the ways in which their leading composers made use of folk materials. In sum, his orchestral and choral works steered away from Wagner's hyper-romanticism, though they, too, abounded in new techniques and innovative sound relationships. As far as opera is concerned, mere mention of the Italian verismo composers and Giacomo Puccini—all of whom produced a "palpable" kind of music, readily perceived by the senses and the mind—is sufficient to convey the idea that Wagner's "artwork of the future" had less of a future than did his daring musical language, which challenged long-established norms.

Though Wagner signified the beginning of a new era, not everybody was ready to follow unswervingly the path he chose for himself. Thus Debussy, who at first idolized Wagner, became an anti-Wagnerian, primarily rejecting that aspect of Wagner's musical language that wished to express uncontrollable passion. The musical palette of Debussy and that of his countrymen called for more subdued nuances, for understatements rather than overstated Romantic pathos. Their music sought to express maximum emotion with a minimum of musical upheaval. Debussy's music, as alluded to above, makes use of melodic cells that create a new motivic language, removed from functional harmony. Rather than emphasizing the differences between chords, he sought the affinities among them, rendering a static sort of sound phenomenon that arrests the long-range directionality of tonal harmony. His use of the whole-tone scale, more-

over, dispels the feeling of a tonal center, while his polymetric and polyrhythmic procedures supplant the traditional sense of time and rhythm.
Debussy, clearly, did not simply wish to get rid of tonality; he was after
a finely graded expression, a kind of "introspection" that was diametrically opposed to Wagner's demonstrative, extravagant musical language.
Although chromatic harmony, during the high Romantic period, was able
to increase the intensity of musical expressions, the blatant and excessive
use of chromaticism by Wagner and some of his followers yielded, as far as
Debussy was concerned, "diminishing returns." It *defied,* rather than promoted, subtlety of musical expression. Indeed, Debussy's restricted range
of dynamics, like his discriminating motivic language and the ingenious
ways in which he "arrests" the flow of time, succeed in arousing layers of
consciousness that never before received the attention that he was able to
excite.

Like Debussy, Maurice Ravel was more receptive to non-European music than he was to German music, though he, too, as a young musician was
fascinated by Wagner. Instead of the Romantic pathos expressed by Wagner, Ravel was attracted, more and more, to folk elements, as in the compositions of some Russian composers at the time. In fact, he was attentive
to all kinds of "exotic" flavors, yet he incorporated some of these elements
into his music without forgoing his individuality as a highly imaginative
and innovative composer. Ravel's "impressionistic" orchestration—which
also incorporated the hues of human voices—deserves special mention.
Unlike the heavy orchestration of the German and Austrian composers,
Ravel revealed an overwhelming sensitivity to the varieties of orchestral
tone color, which, thanks to his virtuosity, conveyed a quasi-detached
spell, markedly different from Wagner's seductive magic. Though he, too,
wished to steer away from worn-out formulae, a deliberate assault on tonality was evidently not uppermost in his mind. Like Debussy, he tried to
enrich music by introducing a new palette of sounds—by novel melodic
and harmonic treatments that invite the listener to entertain a new "look."
What held true for Debussy and Ravel holds true for other French composers, who preferred the modal past, folk elements of various sorts, and
even the dance rhythms of the New World, to the romantic Wagnerian
traits by which they were once bewitched. Yet it must be remembered that
composers everywhere, regardless of nationality, were intent on breaking away from those "standardized practices" that had crystallized over
centuries.

It cannot be denied, of course, that the much appreciated coherence
that Western musical expression had attained rested on states of mutual

dependencies—between melody and harmony, rhythm and meter, periods and phrase structures, fixed triadic sequences and musical form—that created a regulative mold that constrained musical ideas. Yet the interesting "violations" of these principles or their concealment—as found in the works of the "great" composers—are most effective when they draw attention to a desired direction by their very deviation from prevailing norms. Given the tight rules of musical construction, it has been suggested that musical ideas were constrained in ways similar to words that are subjected to fixed poetic construction. It is this metaphoric equation that made it possible to view excessive, "uncontrolled," and disorienting chromaticism as having initiated a kind of musical "prose"—an overcoming, as it were, of "poetic" restrictions. Thus, the "realistic musical speech" that Mussorgsky tried to advance in Russia for ideological reasons became more systematized in Germany for music-theoretical reasons. Given the German-Austrian heritage, it embraced all of those mutually dependent musical elements, as one might expect. Reger's conception of "musical prose," for example, displays the release of different musical elements from the constraints of symmetrical organization.

Indeed, the "emancipation of the dissonance," which is often regarded as the key representative of the break from tradition, hardly exhausts the process that music underwent in its attempt to free itself from the shackles of the past. To be sure, once the resolution of a dissonance into a triad was no longer obligatory, and passing harmonies were allowed to stand on their own, the notes became "equal," as it were, with regard to their standing and function. And though it is true that the difference between consonance and dissonance became increasingly blurred, the freeing of musical styles from the integrative procedures that governed the soundness of musical works did not stop with the suspension of tonal ties and the emancipation of dissonance. Wagner notwithstanding, the nineteenth century still adhered to numerous technical devices and the ways in which they can be manipulated in order to impart signification and noteworthy effect, even while encouraging an unprecedented diversity of styles. If history can be defined—among other things—as a selection of details importing signification, the temporal unfolding of music, by analogy, can be defined as tones so organized as to render unique audible experiences. After all, even within a consensual style, composers tried to endow their individual works with "singleness." The unique ways in which they went about it often resulted in what might be viewed as their individual style *within* an overall shared style. However, what previously seemed to have emerged from the compositional manner of individual composers over a span of time turned into *inaugural* stepping-stones for many a composer who followed. By granting autonomy to the art as well as to its practitioners, Wagner no doubt precipitated this process. It must be remembered, however, that he never denied music's axiomatic postulate—that of *organized* sound—though he seriously challenged its procedures. Indeed, "what" should be organized and "how"—so as to be still considered music—became a predominant quest.

The Establishment of a Musical Canon

Given the growing pressure to ensure one's place in the pantheon of history, composers steadily tried to widen the scope that music embraced, and thus to unleash new stylistic possibilities. In the twentieth century this tendency has resulted in so great a variety of musical languages and techniques that it has posed a considerable challenge to the common understanding of what music is, should do, or should sound like.

Though music increasingly departed from shared styles, composers increasingly revealed a shared *concern,* that of leaving individual marks on the historical development of music. Thus, while systematically breaking down accepted norms and procedures, composers sought to address a musically *informed* audience, one that is conscious of *past* achievements. After all, only an audience familiar with the landmarks of the past can be persuaded to consider new attempts and more progressive stages in the continuous development of the music to which these composers aspire to belong. Consequently, as the twentieth century progressed, the break with the past came to be presented as a "logical" outcome *of* the past, and the new compositional experiments were construed, more and more, as contributions to the ongoing development of music. Yet this concern with "historicity" seems to have nonetheless widened the gap between "contemporary" composers and the lay public—the consumers of music as a "performing art."

The desire of composers to secure their place in history arose, as we have seen, in the nineteenth century. Yet the intellectual climate of the century, which intensified the historical awareness of composers, also encouraged an excessive regard for past styles. In fact, concert audiences who were regularly exposed to musical works of the past became increasingly familiar with the music of deceased composers. The works that merited performance were of course chosen from among those written by composers who were thought to have contributed—in one way or another—to the development of music. Thus, works of composers who survived a historical sifting stood more of a chance of being performed than those of contemporary composers who hoped for admission to this exclusive club.

Composers are thought to have acquiesced to this new condition, since most of them no longer wrote music with a special audience in mind, in the hope of winning approval from future generations. It has therefore been suggested that by the twentieth century the concert hall assumed a function similar to that of a museum that displays the works of the "great masters," specifying the highlights of their oeuvre.[44] Museums, naturally, also tend to emphasize the historical dimension by generally aligning art-works according to the periods in which they were produced. The accumulation of such works thus encouraged a separation between the "old masters" and "modern art," giving rise to special museums that house the latter. Yet the dividing line between the two often raises bewilderment, for it is hard to establish whether "modern" implies recentness or a break with past traditions. Indeed, works that are subsumed under the title "modern" are not necessarily recent nor do recent works necessarily shun tradition.

As is well known, even toward the end of the twentieth century much of what was composed in its early decades had not yet secured a safe place in the standard repertoire of public concert halls, nor had much of it been able to overcome the alienation of the average concertgoer. If there is truth in the saying that "taste rests on cultivation," it must also be acknowledged that the audience was not given a fair chance to become acquainted with the new music, since it was rarely performed. It is not hard to surmise that it was rarely performed because it did not seem fruitful from a commercial point of view; the pressure to appeal to as large an audience as possible prevented the undertaking of financial risk. As we have seen, music had undergone many changes since the days in which it served designated functions and was sponsored by institutions that commissioned composers to produce musical works for specified social occasions. Yet once music became a commodity almost totally dependent on the free market, it was also bound to respond to the regulating principle of "supply and demand," a relationship that primarily guides those who are in charge of "marketing," including the marketing of artistic products. It has been suggested, accordingly, that the reverence for the old masters was not only an artistic phenomenon but a commercial one as well, characterized by the growing number of enterprises that had a bearing on music, such as

44. See, for example, J. Peter Burkholder, "Museum Pieces: The Historicist Mainstream in Music of the Last Hundred Years," *Journal of Musicology* 6 (1997).

music publishing houses, firms manufacturing musical instruments, concert management, and many other related industries.[45] All of these factors contributed to *widening* the gap between "contemporary" music and the public, rather than narrowing the rift between them.

Much as twentieth-century composers blamed the public for refusing to lend an attentive ear, they are themselves to be blamed, at least partially. Their overeagerness to leave their individual marks on the historical development of music was in fact counterproductive, even if it seemed sensible in light of the circumstances in which they were caught. History, however, abounds in *un*anticipated consequences. Although music divorced from social functions increasingly attracted more attention to itself, it is equally true that this very process also precipitated the rise of a musical canon—a fixed list of acclaimed composers and musical works—that caused difficulties for those who wished to be included via a kind of historical "*pre*view." The historically minded composers, as we have seen, encouraged the rise of a canon for their own needs and reasons, but the deceased composers gradually gained a lasting status, an unforeseeable permanence that left little room for new experimental works.[46] Having lost communication

45. See, for example, William Weber, "Mass Culture and the Reshaping of European Musical Taste, 1770–1870," *International Review of the Aesthetics and Sociology of Music* 7 (1977): 6.

46. In her notable book *The Imaginary Museum of Musical Works,* Lydia Goehr explains that the concept of musical work attained a centrality at a particular point in history. It attained "a certain kind of status in musical practice, and it acquired this status," argues Goehr, "just because of the particular way in which it emerged. This *institutional centrality* is the foundation for our acquiring at a given time a standard or model by which we choose certain examples as paradigmatic. That we might continue thereafter to use the same paradigm examples is then explained by the further use we make of one and the same standard. Institutionalized centrality is closely related to what in more familiar terms we identify as a mainstream or a canon. The emergence of a mainstream—housing the paradigmatic—depends upon a practice's being standardized with respect to various aspects of its structure." She calls our attention, however, to the fact that institutional centrality "contrasts with a principle according to which our choice is determined by what we like best, or by what is produced contemporaneously or nearest to hand." "We have tended," nonetheless, "and still tend," argues Goehr, "to pick as our examples those works produced at the time when the work-concept acquired a centralized position in musical practice." See Lydia Goehr, *The Imaginary Museum,* 96–97. Tracing the evolution of the canon, William Weber shows that different kinds of canon, performing different tasks, emerged in the history of music. Though they served different aims and function, a deeper examination of the history of the canon reveals four main intellectual bases of the canon: craft, repertory, criticism, and ideology. "The roots of musical canon in craft traditions bound it intimately to the polyphonic tradition," argues Weber. "Repertory has not yet been the subject of much extensive study or analysis." "Criticism" pertains, in

with the audience, musical innovations of all kinds remained the most salient means whereby composers hoped to create their own works of lasting value. Yet it became increasingly difficult to join the composers who were accorded space in the musical pantheon, since the reverence they had acquired (albeit mostly posthumously) continued to function as a driving force for aspiring composers despite its "diminishing returns."

In his suggestive article concerning "the historicist mainstream in music,"[47] J. Peter Burkholder advances an interesting explanation for the emphasis on technical innovations over other aspects of twentieth-century music. Having been admitted into the canon of performed music, the "recognized" works and their "distinguished" composers became differentiated from their contemporaries by their "level of craftsmanship" and by the "strength of their musical personality." Younger composers, thus, tried "to create music in the tradition of art music which would say something new, while incorporating what was best and most useful from the music of the past."[48] Though Burkholder's argument raises the problem of the "chicken and the egg," his point is well taken, the more so because it also provides a basis for understanding those composers who justified their compositional activities in the name of "musical progress." Progress clearly implies some anchorage in the past, if only for the sake of self-assessment. It also imparts a sense of "discovery," rather than some attitudinal change due to idiosyncratic predilections or dispositions. No other musical aspect can better display the combination of these two features—bridging, as it were, the "past" and "future"—than technical innovations. In fact, via compositional craftsmanship one may reveal an awareness of past developments while construing one's own innovations as "progressive" derivations thereof.

Most of the stylistic changes discussed until now (extended forms, mixed styles, heightened dissonance, new treatment of chords, motives, musical sound, and so forth) displayed the unmistakable attention of their creators to the technical procedures that guided their predecessors. In fact, the individual expressions of composers could best be identified against

---

one way or another, to the process of separating "musical wheat from chaff" while "ideology" justifies choices on bases "that command wider, stronger allegiance within society." Looked at from these points of view may unveil "some important continuities," says Weber, "that run through the evolution of musical canon since the sixteenth century." See William Weber, "The History of Canon," in *Rethinking Music,* ed. Cook and Everist, 336–55.

47. Peter Burkholder, *Museum Pieces.*

48. Ibid., 120.

the backdrop of the old masters. Though many composers breached the customary confines that guided the old masters, they launched new compositional ideas with aesthetic, rather than technical, desiderata in mind. Indeed, analysis of their works reveals that technical innovations never constituted ends in themselves. Rather, they wished to convey to the listener the aesthetic import they had succeeded in bringing about. Despite the novelties that they introduced and despite the "permanence" of the "great masters," composers such as Mahler, Strauss, Debussy, Ravel, Janáček, and a host of others managed to penetrate the musical "museum" in their own lifetime. They managed to do so primarily because they never failed to remember that, in the final analysis, music addresses the ear!

The emphasis on technical innovations, which rested on the belief in "progress" and "discovery," also gave rise, in due time, to composers who inadvertently became more interested in persuading their peers than in reaching concertgoers, including those of future generations. Although much of the music they wrote is quite ingenious upon analysis, it was evidently not "communicative" enough upon listening to it; however interrelated the musical particles turned out to be on paper, the work defied the listener who was unable to discern its organizational scheme *audibly*. Though the tendency to treat music as a "text" commenced in the Romantic era, it was vastly intensified in the twentieth century, lending centrality to musical analysis at the expense of many other aspects related to the art.

Technical innovations of various kinds are generally presented as "improvements" in comparison to methods previously employed to achieve certain goals. They may at times solve problems that could not have been solved beforehand. Technical "means," moreover, may suggest new "ends" that were never entertained before. In the twentieth century, however, the technological acceleration has increasingly produced sophisticated means—based on diverse bodies of knowledge—with a standing of their own. However suggestive such accomplishments turn out to be, the idea of putting the cart before the horse rarely leads in directions foreseen or desired. Humanity, apparently, has an agenda of its own, which unfolds at a pace not synchronized with the rate in which man is capable of innovation.

Atonal and Twelve-Tone Music

Although traditional models constrain the artist, constraints are fundamental to art. Of course, artistic conventions may crystallize—via standardized practice—to the point of being regarded as intrinsic to the art involved. In Western music melody and harmony, rhythm and meter, period and phrase structure—and much else—became mutually dependent to a degree that brief passages deviating from these standards came into view only in light of the "rules" that they seemed to break. These rules of construction functioned for a long time as the supposed inherent syntax of that significant "language without a semantic" that we call music. A considerable number of the laws of this syntax were based on a particular conception of tonality and the developments it brought about with regard to tonal harmony. The latter affected not only the relationships among voices but also the various associations between structural procedures and formal designs. Yet it affected, above all, music's unfolding in time, that is, its unidirectional nature. Familiarity with this musical syntax helped guide the listener through simple as well as intricate webs of organized sound, for they were fashioned from individual items or united in identifiable interrelated functions.

The bias toward polyphony, that is, toward independent, simultaneously sounding melodic parts, led however to a decline in the field of rhythm. The classical two- or three-beat bar, and the standardization of chord progressions, constrained the free development of rhythm. In their attempts to rid themselves of the shackles of the past, composers also tried to address anew the rhythmic nature of music's unfolding in time. To reverse the stagnation in the "flow" of music, rhythm and meter had to be reconceptualized so as to be able to yield a greater and more interesting variety. Although emphases on rhythmic qualities also affect formal designs—as did the preoccupation with harmony—they can in themselves be readily perceived even by untrained ears, not just trained ones. At any rate, their saliency does not depend on "detective processes" to unveil their existence. No wonder then that twentieth-century music also witnessed a drastic change with regard to musical rhythms. In fact, many composers became identified with their innovations in this important and long-neglected musical parameter. Apart from the many things that can be said about the music of Béla Bartók and Stravinsky, for example, their use of syncopated displacements of accent, so as to deliberately upset the equilibrium of the bar, became most apparent. From his extended investigations of folk song, Bartók seems to have learned not only that symmetrical rhythmic norms can be "violated" but that asymmetrical accents can be introduced as well within the traditional meters. Clearly, if chords are to be used primarily for their sound value—rather than for their function—they, too, could be effectively employed to heighten rhythmic accents. Those who learned a lesson or two from Bartók and Stravinsky will no doubt agree that these composers brought rhythm and form into a new kind of relationship. The freeing of rhythm and meter from their routine array, like the freeing of phrase and period structure from their "poetic" restrictions, contributed a significant share to what came to be viewed as "musical prose."

Stravinsky and Bartók have an assured place in the list of musical "giants" of the twentieth century. Yet a careful and systematic examination of their musical development reveals that neither of them, despite their greatness, had an easy time in overcoming the alienation of the public. Eventually, however, both succeeded in drawing attention to the eloquence of their musical expression. They succeeded, it seems, in communicating their new "vistas" by making sure that their musical intentions could also be perceived in the concert hall, and not only by their colleagues who may have been better qualified to appreciate their ingenuity. Although it cannot be said that their music eluded public debate, it was hardly of the kind that the so-called Second Viennese School managed to provoke. It is nonetheless the latter that had the strongest impact on the conception of music in the twentieth century. Their composers carry special significance in light of the tradition they inherited and sought to advance.

What came to be known as the Second Viennese School is primarily attributed to three composers: Arnold Schoenberg, Alban Berg, and Anton Webern. Considering that the First Viennese School consisted of Haydn, Mozart, and Beethoven, this is no minor achievement. The name, however, implies both change and continuity. In fact, the members of the school thought of themselves as having taken the inevitable successive step in the progressive development of music. Schoenberg's early music, like that of other composers, revealed a tendency toward freeing music from its customary "molds." His melodies, accordingly, dispensed with symmetrical periodic forms, while the difference between consonance and dissonance became increasingly blurred. Chords were likewise allowed to stand on their own, no longer requiring the resolution of a dissonance into a triad. Schoenberg, however, was not satisfied with mere suspension of tonal relationships and the "emancipation" of dissonances. He also tried to change routine symphonic thematic development by subjecting the musical process to permanent variation, dispensing with the repetition of musical ideas. Dispensing with repetitions carried implications for the dimensions of musical works, tending to reduce their size. But doing away with the mutual dependencies of musical elements, or with the symmetrical patterns to which they gave rise, hardly summarizes Schoenberg's endeavors. While his novelties plus those of his contemporaries reformulated compositional procedures, it was Schoenberg, more than any other composer, who came to symbolize the shift that occurred in twentieth-century musical thought and theory.

Schoenberg started as a tonal composer, employing tonality as a central point of reference. His tonal music, he claimed, was influenced by Brahms (who tried to further music's formal designs) and by Wagner (who tried to vary its utterances). Unlike Wagner, however, he abandoned tonality altogether in 1908 — the first to do so — and continued to explore musical expressions that would bypass tradition in order to reach deeper, less premeditated levels of experience. Like many of the expressionist painters, he tried to convey the prompting of the spirit ever more directly, submitting to impulse and intuition to guide his way. He advised his students to do the same, that is, to disregard academic rules and follow their inclinations and intuitions wherever they led. He was convinced, however, that his own stylistic development, although reached intuitively, was a logical outcome of tradition. Although he took no account of rules, he believed that his musical style observed fundamental laws that would eventually prove definable. His *Harmonielehre*,[49] accordingly, while condemning all academic rules as abstractions from past practice, confined itself within tonality. Its teaching stressed the functional value of the principles of traditional grammar in order to emphasize the logical thinking that accompanied it, suggesting, however, that everything is subject to reinterpretation and change. Nonetheless, the way to impart the "logic" of compositional processes, as well as the ways in which they may lend themselves to change, is best done, he believed, in a context in which theory elucidates practice — remembering, of course, that the former lags behind the latter.

Schoenberg was thoroughly familiar with the music of the past, though he never profited from formal musical education. He discovered much of what he knew on his own. In fact, it was a process of independent discovery that shaped his habit of mind and spiritual life from beginning to end. He believed, like Wagner, that he was destined to fulfill an important mission that would lead music into yet unknown realms. Faith in their mission clearly influenced the development of both men. Indeed, faith was needed in order to pursue the directions they chose, trusting that they

---

49. The *Harmonielehre* (Vienna, 1911) constitutes Schoenberg's first theoretical exposé among his theoretical and pedagogical writings. A revised version of the book appeared in 1922, an abridged English translation appeared in 1948, and a complete version in 1978. The *Harmonielehre* seems to have guided many a student of theory and composition throughout the entire century.

would be vindicated in the long run. Yet the idea of the artist as "priest" or "prophet" is in a way more pronounced in Schoenberg's compositions[50] than it is in Wagner's writings, which elevated the role of art and the artist. Both, however, relied on circles of devotees to disseminate their historical "mission." Wagner changed musical procedures to suit his aims, claiming that he was accommodating the needs of those he tried to serve. As a true revolutionary he preached his cause, identified his objectives, and explicated his compositional deeds. Arrogant though he was, his "vision" was anything but intuitive; it rested on calculated actions that "logically" led to the results he was after. Unlike Wagner, Schoenberg was more prone to experimentation prompted by impulse and intuition, trusting that these were somehow guided by the "invisible hand" of History that affects the development of music according to some fundamental principles. Putting religious overtones aside, Schoenberg experienced a sense of mission reminiscent of Albert Einstein. As is well known, Einstein was convinced that "God is not playing dice." Yet unlike Schoenberg, Einstein was trying to fathom the laws of Creation, not those of a man-made world.

In Schoenberg's music, structural harmony disappeared with the emancipation of the dissonance, along with its need for measured periods and consistent textures, and so did tonality itself as a central point of reference. Motivic work and the tendency to equate the horizontal and vertical dimensions assumed, however, greater responsibility. The disintegration of functional harmony also seems to have destroyed for some time the conditions needed for large-scale forms, while enabling swifter and simultaneous musical transformations. Musical elements that formerly seemed irreconcilable could now create relationships that lent music a novel sound semblance. If so desired, one could even forgo motivic development, relying primarily on texture, dynamics, and other devices that vary the manner of the musical unfolding. With all this license issues concerning music's formal construction—not to mention its coherence as far as the listener is concerned—still needed addressing.

That Schoenberg should resort to texts as a basis for the construction of larger forms does not come as a surprise. The texts he chose clearly made room for changes of mood and musical images, lending meaning to the sequence of the musical unfolding. Conspicuous juxtapositions of

---

50. The works that readily come to mind in this connection are his *Die Jakobsleiter, Moses und Aron, A Survivor from Warsaw, Dreimal tausend Jahre,* and *Modern Psalms.* All of these compositions, as well as some others, have a quasi-meditative quality and convey a feeling of closeness to God.

various sorts—textural contrasts, sudden outbursts, dynamic changes, and so forth—closely followed the unfolding of the textual narrative, which directed the listener's attention to a musical representation that lacked formal coherence unto itself. For his vocal melody, Schoenberg also made use of a kind of voice production—halfway between song and speech—a recitation on pitches that are merely hinted at. Disrupting the musical confines via speech was, of course, not new; it had been employed by music-theatrical genres before. Even the kind of *Sprechgesang* ("sung-speech") that Schoenberg used had been employed before, but unlike Schoenberg's sung-speech it gave the "singer-speaker" some instrumental help in locating the pitches. In the absence of such help, the pitches in Schoenberg's *Sprechgesang* are hard to interpret, as are their dynamic nuances and articulation. They also present some rhythmic problems that are just as difficult to cope with.

A musical web constructed from elements that provide no leads for each other is not only difficult for the listener to comprehend; it is also difficult for performers to perform. It does not come as a surprise, therefore, that Schoenberg should find it necessary to resort to a "soloistic" kind of orchestral writing in his later style, using a strongly differentiated instrumental ensemble. In fact, soloistic orchestral writing characterizes the style of many younger composers who followed his lead. Nor is it surprising that Schoenberg should eventually introduce the method of *serialism,* a method whereby motivic work and the tendency to equate the horizontal and vertical dimensions can be codified so as to assume greater structural responsibility as well as some kind of surveillance. The serial method of composition in fact replaced the old rules with new rules and principles that distribute the structuring of music among all of the elements of musical development. The resultant multiplication of structural characters through their reciprocal relativization was expected to introduce order into what otherwise seemed to be discontinuous concrete sound events lacking in formal organization. Having discarded the traditional rules and conventions that governed music, including tonality, Schoenberg suggested the use of all twelve tones of the chromatic scale in any order the composer desired, provided that the "tone row" he chose remain unchanged throughout the composition. This new limitation, however, allowed for some modifications: the "row" could also appear in inverted and retrograde forms, and in retrograde inversion, while the octave position of any tone of the series could be changed. All forms of the series could be used as well in transposition to any step of the chromatic scale.

Though it imposes formal constraints, serialism is clearly a method of composition that does not dictate style. Indeed, where every motive is transformed, where no pattern establishes itself to enable the listener to gather associations, the idea of musical development—not to speak of its intensification—becomes meaningless. Although the transformations of the series Schoenberg chose cannot be followed by the ear, his themes consist of rhythmic patterns that carry serial derivations so that the interplay of melody and rhythm during the unfolding creates an accumulation of affinities that may more readily be discerned. Yet his evolving relationship to serialism led Schoenberg to return to formal designs—a form of neo-classicism. If Schoenberg's early music can be said to have been influenced by Brahms and Wagner, his later work can be said to have been influenced by earlier composers such as Bach and Mozart. Bach clearly provided the model for contrapuntal treatment, while Mozart stands for thematic contrast and traditional formal patterns. Nonetheless, Schoenberg himself admitted that his atonal style, deprived of the control of harmony, made him rely, among other things, on brevity, exceptional expressiveness, and the use of suitable texts—in order to lend his forms a more readily recognized coherence.[51]

Schoenberg was convinced that the renunciation of the diatonic system—including its consonant norms—constituted a logical stage in the historic tendency that inevitably led (after Wagner) to the emancipation of the dissonance and thereby also of the notion of "chromaticism." Thus the radical novelties he introduced represented, as far as he was concerned, the fulfillment of a "historic mission," which he felt compelled to carry out.[52] Schoenberg, in fact, succeeded in becoming an internationally

51. See the collected essays included in his *Style and Ideas* (New York, 1950), especially "Composition with Twelve Tones" and "Heart and Brain."

52. In *The Rest Is Noise: Listening to the Twentieth Century* (an illuminating book that weaves together musical and cultural history), Alex Ross claims that Schoenberg was most persuasive in justifying his early atonal works when he emphasized their "illogical, irrational dimension," though in public Schoenberg tended to explain his latest works as the logical, rational outcome of a historical process. "All told," concludes Ross, "a Freudian host of urges, emotions, and ideas circled Schoenberg as he put his fateful chords on paper. He endured violent disorder in private life; he felt ostracized by a museum-like concert culture; he experienced the alienation of being a Jew in Vienna; he sensed a historical tendency from consonance to dissonance; he felt disgust for a tonal system grown sickly. But the very multiplicity of possible explanations point up something that cannot be explained. There was no necessity driving atonality; no irreversible current of history made it happen. It was one man's leap into the unknown. It became a movement when

well-known figure, recognized as a composer carrying a significant "message," yet his music encountered widespread incomprehension. More than it was accepted as a new stage in the development of a venerable musical tradition, it was perceived by the lay public—habitual concertgoers—as lacking guidelines to bring its particles into *audibly* discernible relations. His disciples attributed this incomprehension to the "richness" of the music, which, they admitted, required careful study in order to unveil its organizational schemes.[53] Although this does not hold equally true for the vast variety of Schoenberg's compositions, much of his work still requires careful study in order to grasp the ingenuity vested in them.

It should be obvious that this critique is not an argument for "easy listening" of the kind demanded by totalitarian populism. The problem of consuming this kind of music is almost as great for the tutored ears—of those who bring "cultural capital" to their listening—as for the untutored ones. It has even been argued that the "untutored" listeners, who are not burdened by "obsolete" expectations, may be more receptive, in fact, to new trends than the more "learned." At any rate, it may be recalled that in "defense" of the "masses," the Central Committee of the Communist Party in Moscow argued against what they referred to as "formalistic tendencies" represented by composers such as Shostakovich and Prokofiev.[54] These great composers were charged with having replaced "beautiful human music" by an "adulterated" and downright "pathological" music that could not be "comprehended by the masses." As a result of the regime's threats, Prokofiev even confessed that he was guilty of "formalist errors" under the influence of "certain Western trends." He had been "guilty," he claimed, of "atonality" and of failing to realize that atonal structures are "built on sand" whereas the tonal structure of a work is comparable to a "building constructed on solid foundation."[55] Although there is no room in this essay to discuss the uniqueness of these important composers and their outstanding works, this well-known political episode serves to point out that authoritarian ideologies—whether fascist or communist—invariably invoke the "comprehension of the masses" as a criterion for judging artistic

two equally gifted composers jumped in behind him." See Alex Ross, *The Rest Is Noise: Listening to the Twentieth Century* (New York, 2007), 56–61.

53. See Alban Berg, "Warum ist Schoenbergs Musik so schwer verständlich?" in *Musik-blätter des Anbruch* 6 (1924).

54. See Andrei Zhdanov's 1948 speech at the conference of "Soviet Music Workers," in Katz and Dahlhaus, *Contemplating Music*, vol. 4, 129–33.

55. In 1948 Prokofiev saw fit to publish a "confession of guilt." He obviously tried to defend himself via this open confession.

products. Although I clearly wish to dissociate myself from the censorship and control this kind of populism implies,[56] I do believe, nonetheless, that the way in which artistic works cohere, or the ways in which they guide our perception, are relevant to works of art whomever they serve.

Alban Berg and Anton Webern were Schoenberg's students and principal disciples. The former used the twelve-tone technique only intermittently, combining it with methods founded in tonality, whereas the latter carried Schoenberg's ideas even further, developing to the extreme the principle of asymmetry by giving each sound a maximum presence. Despite differences between their musical approaches, they came to be identified—due to the atonal and serial music they composed—with the beginning of a new era in the history of music alongside Schoenberg. Berg, too, discovered in the course of his compositional practice that traditional forms and traditional stylistic elements would restore the coherence of large-scale structures. His *Wozzeck* (one of the two powerful operas he wrote), completed before twelve-note serialism was conceived, suggested that atonal music could benefit, for example, from sectional differentiation. Each act of the opera, accordingly, established a self-contained cyclic form, and each scene a self-contained movement. Leitmotivs play a significant role in the opera, but they do not pervade the music-dramatic texture of the opera as they do in Wagner's operas. Instead, verbal leitmotivs, curtains, changes of lighting, and so forth function structurally, contributing to the overall design of the opera. Berg paid close attention to the production of the opera so as to exercise strict control of its dramatic unfolding. His *Lulu,* which took shape after twelve-note serialism

56. The Soviet approach to the arts, guided by politics and ideology, has antecedents and is neither new nor strictly Russian. Since Lenin, however, art in Russia was expected to contribute to the proletarian cause. The concept of "art *of* and *for* the people," which replaced the so-considered "elitist" view of "art for art's sake," had already been formulated during the French Revolution, whereby the idea of artistic truth became equated with that of social justice. Yet, while in postrevolutionary France the struggle against the dictatorship of the academies led eventually to an emphasis on the uniqueness of individual expression, resulting in unprecedented artistic freedom, artistic expression in postrevolutionary Russia was subjugated to *social realism,* harnessing artistic inspiration for political purposes. Whereas the French Revolution demanded a break with tradition and authority, the Russian Revolution increasingly called for a return to tradition—to an art imbibed and understood by the multitudes. As supervisor in all cultural matters after World War II, Andrei Zhdanov was of the opinion that Culture needed "reinforcement" after the inevitable exposure of millions during the war to Western "morally degenerating" culture. Emphasis on "originality" and "novelty," he thought, were among the foremost signs of a decadent bourgeois society.

was conceived, also reveals Berg's keen preoccupation with formal design. Recapitulative episodes become increasingly intensified in the course of the opera so that they completely dominate the musical material in the final scene.

Webern, unlike Berg, was not only influenced by Schoenberg's technical instruction but by his philosophical tendency as well. He strove to penetrate "prime" musical phenomena—akin to the unspoken levels of thought—through perfection and concentration. Clarity of texture, simplicity of harmony, brevity, silence, and a restrained dynamic range thus characterize his works. Yet he, too, was in need of some organizational schemes that would lend coherence to his compositions, despite their brevity. Aware of the functions that motivic organization and recurrent patterns fulfill, his themes are built from short motifs. It must be remembered that forgoing tonality necessitated the abandonment of traditional thematic working out as well, for their development was linked with tonal modulations. No wonder he endorsed serialism so enthusiastically; serialism enabled him to use the smallest pitch structures related to the same basic ideas so as to bring about motivic coherence. He, too, tried to find support for larger forms in dramatic texts, but quickly turned to brief intimate poems that more readily suited his introverted personality. Unlike Berg, Webern's work made little impression on composers during his lifetime; his music became highly regarded only after World War II. It deserves mentioning, however, that he took a leading part in the organization that Schoenberg created in Vienna (Verein für Musikalische Privataufführungen), which promoted private performances of "novel" works. The members of the organization naturally supported each other, creating a forum in which their compositions could actually be heard. Webern not only played the cello part whenever needed but he directed the performances of compositions written by other composers, often supplying arrangements for their works.

This brief sketch of the Second Viennese School does an injustice to its members, though they have been given greater attention in this essay than other more "reputable" composers. The stylistic diversities they created require, in fact, an analysis of every single composition separately. Indeed, if the great masters of the past and their outstanding works were hardly mentioned individually, it is because their *shared* styles, rather than their differences, enabled us to trace the music-ideational development that this essay has attempted to map. It will also have been noticed that there is an imbalance in the attention given to certain theorists, philosophers, and men of letters, inasmuch as only those whose ideas exerted direct influence on the "thought" that accompanied the development of music in the West became part of the narrative. As music "progressed," it became increasingly difficult, as we have seen, to assign a single encompassing style to a period. Likewise, the uniqueness of a composer could less and less be gauged against the stylistic features he shared with his contemporaries. Eventually it became difficult to gauge a particular work against a distinct style characterizing its composer. While music steadily variegated its productions, the process of increased differentiation also created a differentiation among the consumers of music. No longer could composers assume that they were addressing listeners who shared the same musical language, though some exerted an effort to prove otherwise. Traditions, to be sure, invariably undergo changes, yet they can at times undergo the kind of change that challenges their very foundations. Traditions, it seems, retain their predominance as long as they are taken for granted; they become more self-conscious once their edifices are distraught by doubt. Traditions that are maintained in a self-conscious manner "expose" themselves more for what they are when they are on the defensive.

Developments That Affected Music's External Semblance

Indeed, enrichments in artistic language are often brought about at the expense of its former communicative elements. Thus, for example, the idea of employing speech with notated rhythm and intonation—which grew from Schoenberg's *Sprechstimme*—led to attempts to use a combination of speech-choruses and music of pure noise. Although Darius Milhaud still saw fit to alternate between mixed speech-choruses accompanied by percussion instruments and solo voices accompanied by a traditional orchestra, Henry Cowell's note clusters (a group of adjacent notes struck simultaneously on the piano) eschewed individual notes and intervals altogether in favor of sound impacts produced as wholes. However interesting, such experiments clearly defied the tradition that established the *identities* of musical works based on fixed "immovable" notes that determined the intervals they created among them—their hierarchy, functions, and combinations.

In fact, what secured the European musician against taking "wrong steps" was staff notation, which in the course of its development differentiated among intervals and their direction, steadily clarifying durational relationships with the introduction of smaller note values. As we have seen, it eventually seemed natural for the individual pitch—for the sound event—to carry the time element as well. The various rests thus became

musical events by forgoing their sounds but by retaining their proper duration. The development of counterpoint and harmony upheld the basic understandings that accompanied the development of Western musical notation—which turned, in due time, from a descriptive representation into
a *prescriptive* one—aiming to preserve the identities of musical compositions independent of form and style. Indeed, with a symbol system that
leaves no room for ambiguity, an independent overall language of sounds
was created in the West that could contain many varied, *though congeneric,*
musical utterances. With minor additions, this autonomous symbol system seems to have answered basic musical demands until the twentieth
century, during which it gradually broke down. It was brought down,
however, not by the music-theoretical changes that we already touched
upon, but by a totally new acoustical vision.

European music can hardly be said to have revealed a low tolerance for
simultaneity. In fact, European polyphony disclosed enormous resourcefulness in handling simultaneously audible strands by subjecting them
to overriding principles that the listener could follow. In the twentieth
century, however, simultaneity was applied by some composers to tonality and rhythm in ways that combined more than one tonal plane in the
same composition, while introducing polyrhythmic procedures of a novel
kind. Naturally, the more distantly related the tonalities, the more striking the effect they created; the same holds true for the divergence among
rhythms. Although juxtaposing several rhythmic planes was always part
of advanced polyphony, the use of rhythmic figures that are treated and
developed separately and independently constituted a novel idea. These
new principles of simultaneity—those that were brought to bear in the
fields of melody, harmony, tonality and rhythm—rested, nonetheless, on
a tradition that was historically trained to hear polyphonic music of various kinds. These novelties became perceptible, in fact, over and against
the overriding principles to which the listener was accustomed. The traditional frame of reference became completely irrelevant, however, with
respect to experiments that tried to discover new methods of using acoustical material based on an entirely new conception of music dominated by
timbre and noise.

It was Edgard Varèse who conceived the idea of a musical laboratory in
which experiments could be conducted to discover new methods of using
acoustical material, an idea only later realized by Pierre Schaeffer. His *Ioni-
sation* (a composition for an ensemble of thirteen percussionists) was nonetheless the first work based on a new conception of music to be dominated
by timbre and noise. Scored for forty instruments, it is organized by types

of timbre at each point, following a strict rhythmic and dynamic structure. A polyphony of glissandi of sirens accompanied acoustical "clamors," combining infinite pitches with noise. Although dismissed by music critics and a goodly number of composers, the use of noise-producing instruments became a feature of avant-garde music, which furthered many of Varèse's ideas.

Such new methods of using acoustical material are products of a deliberate search for a novel sound semblance that would make room for hitherto unexplored musical representations that are perceptible on the *immediate* level. The radical innovations in musical language that Schoenberg and his followers introduced clearly produced serious works, but they were thoughtfully entertained primarily by musical experts, leaving most of the lay public behind. By contrast, sounds produced from sources other than musical instruments and the customary use of human voices stood more of a chance to draw wider attention. Yet interest in novelties of this kind wears off fast if the music fails to create *artistic* interest that transcends the medium. Indeed, while all of these remarkable innovations took place, the concert halls upheld their standard repertoires, making little room for "novelties." Traditional rural folk songs, however, were steadily giving way to transient urban hit tunes with popular appeal. The New Music clearly needed a "space" that would make it "visible."

Curiously, the advent of the phonograph went unnoticed by musicians until the introduction, in 1925, of electric recordings that improved the faithfulness of the reproduction by utilizing the microphone that had come into being with radio. The changing speed of the turntable (from 78 revolutions per minute to 33 or 45), which increased the time span of uninterrupted performance, made the recording industry more popular among musicians who wished to reach a wider audience and give permanence to their performances. What started with vocalists and instrumentalists gradually encompassed ensembles of all kinds, including entire orchestras. Exploring the marketing potential of recorded music, the companies also started issuing music that was rarely publicly performed, making it possible for the phonograph owner to come to know a great deal of music he might otherwise never have had a chance to hear. This development, as is well known, contributed to the rebirth of interest in early music and to the unveiling of unknown compositions by renowned composers.

Yet the invention that most affected the recording industry was the development of magnetic-tape recording, introduced commercially in the 1940s. Magnetic-tape recording allowed not only for longer uninterrupted playing time but also made it possible to lower the noise level and to get rid of all kinds of distortions inherent in disc recordings. Most important, however, was the fact that magnetic-tape recording made it possible to *edit* the final product—eliminating mistakes, extraneous noises, and so on—by splicing short sections of tape and replacing them with portions of several separate recordings. Since then, sound recordings have been made on tapes before being transferred to another medium. Though less spontaneous than live musical performance, this fantastic technical superiority made new adventures possible.

Walter Benjamin (1892–1940), in his famous essay "The Work of Art in the Age of Mechanical Reproduction,"[57] also briefly mentions the phonograph record and the changes it brought about in the perception and consumption of music. Since this essay belongs to the basic texts of twentieth-century art criticism it merits some discussion, though the system of categories that Benjamin developed applies primarily to photography and its relationship to painting and to film. Nonetheless, it can easily be applied to music as well and may in fact form the basic precondition of a critique that takes into account current musical culture. To be sure, technical innovations incited cultural transformations all along, but they affected different domains differently. Unlike the letterpress, for example, which elicited rather early a far-reaching transformation of literary culture, the printing of music gained social-historical significance only in the nineteenth century by contributing to the mass circulation of popular musical genres. Nor did the "distracted" perception, which Benjamin attributed to mechanically reproduced works of art, yield everywhere the politicizing effect he expected. Yet the analytical means that his theses supplied were vital for the factual and truth content they conveyed.

Benjamin devised a dichotomous system in which each concept that represents the traditional "auratic" works of art is opposed by a contrasting concept valid for the sphere of mechanical reproduction. Accordingly, "uniqueness," "distance," "permanence," "heterogeneity" and "cult value" are the criteria of a sinking tradition, which he believed were being superseded by "reproducibility," "close range," "transitoriness," "homogeneity" and "exhibition value." Though the prognostic validity of Benjamin's categorical apparatus raises some doubts, it does not affect its analytical value. Thus, for example, the observation that "distance" and "permanence" belong together, just as, conversely, "close range" and "transitoriness" do, is independent—as regards truth content—of the continued existence or demise of the "auratic" work of art. The persistence, however, with which

57. See Walter Benjamin, *Illuminations,* trans. H. Zohn (London, 1973), 219–53.

the difference between serious and popular music asserted itself in the minds of the majority of music consumers challenged the "homogeneity" that mechanical reproduction was expected to promote. Yet the listening habits of the young in recent years prove Benjamin's prognosis, albeit belatedly, to be correct. The observation, moreover, that mechanical reproduction can bring out aspects that elude the "naked eye" though accessible to the lens can be directly transferred to music. Indeed, the impressive revival of some composers, including the reception they have enjoyed, may be attributed in no small measure to the technical apparatus that their mechanical reproduction enjoyed.

The possibility of editing the final product, that is, of manipulating already recorded materials in order to obtain a desired version, allowed Pierre Schaeffer to conceive what came to be known as musique concrète. His vision of a new kind of music in fact derived from experiments he made with recorded sounds in one of the French radio studios, replacing instruments and vocal sounds with sounds obtained from different sources. This material was subjected to various modifications—played backwards, varied in order of occurrence, varied by speed and pitch, cut off wherever desired, amplified, superimposed, and so on—creating a montage of sounds on a final single or multitrack tape. The most interesting aspect of making music directly on tape with real sounds is that it eliminates both the performer and the score. The role of the composer, however, is upheld; clearly, he who "shapes" the sounds that he has selected is the creator of the work. In other words, the composer is not only free to organize his materials as he sees fit but also free to select unprecedented "raw" materials. Compositions of this kind, moreover, do not depend on concert halls to be heard; they are accessible to interested individuals via the "copies" made of the final products, purchasable at a price lower than a regular concert ticket. Unlike concert halls, which cater to *heterogeneous* audiences to avoid financial risks, record companies may better afford to accommodate limited audiences of a more select and monolithic nature. Indeed, to produce a new recording of a familiar symphony—however great the performance—is far more costly, *and* risky, than to issue a limited edition of music that does not involve performers.[58]

58. In their classic study *Performing Arts: The Economic Dilemma,* William Baumol and William Bowen analyzed the economic problems common to theater, opera, music, and dance out of a concern for the future development of the live performing arts in an advanced industrial society. Their study showed that the arts fall within that sector of the economy where productivity cannot be increased at anything like the general rate, and that the costs of live performance, therefore, must inevitably mount. The ultimate

I do not wish to imply that experiments involving new sonic materials were *guided* by the factors I have listed above. Nonetheless, it is fair to claim that Schaeffer was after a kind of music that would constitute an immediately perceptible phenomenon that does not depend on "abstract systems" that either yield to or depend on predetermined compositional methods. If analysis of musique concrète requires no music-theoretical background, it is because it was more concerned with the investigation of an array of sounds as such than with music—any music. Yet music the world over seems to rest on ways in which sounds are *combined* so as to yield desired forms of expression. In fact, what lends different musical traditions their uniqueness is the way in which they *organize* the sounds they see fit to employ. Conscious of theoretical guidelines or not, "abstractions" of various sorts invariably lurk behind the tradition that claims the music as its own.

Unlike musique concrète, electronic music was initially conceived as music made up of sounds created by electronic means rather than recorded sounds, yet it essentially entailed the same three major phases: the generation of sound materials, their transformation, and their final recording on tape. Although inconceivable without the technological strides already mentioned and others that followed, it was *musically* inspired by the objectives that led to serial music and actually engaged some of its composers.[59] Like serial music, electronic music embraced the idea of a unity of thought and musical material. Its main objective was likewise to replace the traditional rules that governed music so as to achieve a multiplication of structural characters through musical elements that would stand in reciprocal relationships to one another. The sounds themselves, like the row in serial music, were to generate the structure of the composition. Electronic music could clearly do more than create specific "scales" for each composition; it could lend timbre, for example, an unprecedented structural role via the various sound spectra it is able to produce. Moreover, it could

---

importance of the study, however, was that it demonstrated that the gap between income and costs was bound to grow over the years and to show deficits of increasing size.
In short, the live performing arts, within the developing economic system, will show mounting deficits. Such findings, of course, have direct implications for the development of these arts and for policymakers, raising questions of values and goals. See William Baumol and William Bowen, *Performing Arts: The Economic Dilemma* (Cambridge [MIT], 1968), part 2, 161–302.

59. Karlheinz Stockhausen, for example, was of the opinion that electronic music shared a theoretical basis with serial composition in that it extended the Schoenbergian twelve-note technique to include aspects of musical sound other than pitch.

render the hitherto employed musical parameters with an unprecedented precision, vary them, and relate them to one another in ways that enabled a variety of new musical forms, endowing as well vocal and instrumental music with fresh inspiration and vitality. The effects produced by different musical works turned out, nonetheless, to be remarkably similar. Indeed, these unlimited possibilities posed anew questions concerning "grammatical arrangements." They engendered a search for "sets of rules" that would govern the musical constructions so as to be able to impart aesthetic significance beyond that of tantalizing the ears. Without elaborating on the psychoacoustic and aesthetic questions raised, or the equipment and the techniques involved, composers of electronic music also found the traditional concert hall inadequate for the performance of their music, for reasons similar to those of musique concrète. With all due respect to acoustical-technical innovations, the music it created affected the course of musical thought less than it affected music's external appearances.

The idea that music entails an *organization* of sounds—with whatever signification—presupposes a relationship between compositional determinacy and aesthetic predictability. These rudimentary understandings regarding music were in fact openly challenged by some twentieth-century composers who introduced a kind of "chance music," generally known as "aleatory music." This kind of music rested, as it were, on "*un*predictability" with regard to either the composition or its performance or both. Accordingly, the pitches that were used, their durations, the degree of their intensities, and so forth, were determined by extramusical procedures that ran the entire gamut from dice throwing through interpretations of abstract designs and certain mathematical laws of chance. Such compositions also made room for the performers' free choice by leaving some musical elements, including the order of their appearance, to the performers' discretion. Aleatory music challenged the stability of form and structure, no longer regarding them as fixed entities that are maintained from one performance to another. In sum, aleatory music gave rise to new musical possibilities at the expense of what had previously been considered artistic necessities.

Having mentioned earlier the inadequacy of the concert hall for certain kinds of music, I intended less to stress the incompatibility between certain artworks and their locale than to raise again the relationship between the work of art and its audience. The relationship between artworks and their audiences is a highly complex one, since it is affected by many factors, such as social conditions, frames of mind, and aesthetic attitudes. The public concert hall, which itself came into being due to the changes that gave rise to new audiences, affected in turn the repertoire, as we have seen, that audiences were offered. Indeed, institutions of all kinds contributed to the general development of music; they were mostly identified by the publics they addressed, the functions they served, the kinds of music they engendered, and so on. It cannot be denied, however, that a permanent rift separates art designed for wide audiences from that which caters to connoisseurs—to those who have accumulated enough "cultural capital" to appreciate what others, the less endowed, or the less fortunate, fail to recognize. Matters of this kind, though self-evident, raise serious questions about the social role of art: Who benefits from artistic achievements and in what way? Although advances in the material elements of music have been taken more or less for granted, the attitude toward "musical progress" has considerably changed in the twentieth century. Art forms that depend on performance for their full realization expose the criteria by which they are to be judged more readily than do the nonperforming arts. Their varying modes of reception also tend to disclose more readily the degree to which their audiences are ready to endorse or to reject what they are offered.

Lending Saliency to the "Social Role of Art"

Though esoteric music repeatedly made a considerable impression at avant-garde music festivals in the twentieth century, its level of sophistication and dwindling audiences induced some of its composers—for intellectual, ideological, or economic reasons—to retreat from the assumptions they had labored under. If music is to serve the needs of the community for which it is written, that is, fulfill its *social* role, it must find new ways and means, some argued, to capture the audience's attention without forgoing artistic respectability. Some composers—even among those who made a considerable impression on avant-garde musicians through their "uncompromising" music—actually steered away from their earlier course in the direction of music with a "lighter touch."[60] Popular music, we must remember, was steadily gaining currency in urban centers among audiences that enjoyed musical stage productions of various kinds

---

60. Between esotericism on the one hand and a desire to make an impact on the public on the other, Ernest Krenek, for example, wrote a jazz opera, *Jonny spielt auf* (1926), that was not only a great success but also "set the stage" for others who wished to merge sophisticated musical technique with popular music—legitimizing, as it were, the former by raising the level of the latter.

and among listeners who could be reached indirectly via diverse media, which became accessible to the periphery as well. Composers could ill afford to overlook the fact that the notion of "entertainment" had undergone changes, no longer necessarily implying low artistic standards. After all, serenades, divertimenti, and a host of other musical genres—written by highly esteemed composers—had served "silly" social functions before they lost their "utilitarian guise." Even composers who believe in artistic autonomy may think about the functions that they perform. In fact, while questions such as "what sort of music represented whom and in what capacity" gained momentum, composers became increasingly aware of the cultural and political implications of their own music.

Though social issues have always exerted influence on the development of music, they rarely came "undisguised." Yet by the twentieth century many of the issues that concerned the public were no longer solely entrusted to the few whose actions passed unchallenged. Without entering into a discussion of the sociopolitical events that brought about changes in matters of governance, it is enough to mention that two centuries of public newspapers—joined by other mass media as they developed—created a sphere that dispelled public "innocence." Those who were formerly affected chiefly by policies advanced by others now felt encouraged to take a more active role in matters concerning their own welfare. Although public opinion increasingly became a factor with which policymakers had to reckon, the public, for its part, increasingly came under the spell of what it read, influencing the issues that became emphasized as well as the ways in which they were understood. Musical perception, even the most impartial kind, is invariably affected by what one has read or "learned" about it; listening to music apparently never involves blank minds.

The history of art, I claimed in the introduction (see introduction, pp. 5–6), chose to focus on styles and their evolution, employing the artifacts *themselves* as evidence that betrays the objectives that guided specific developments. Musicology also based its narrative largely on musical works that exemplify music's unfolding. Nonetheless, though "the highest reality in art is an isolated complete work of art,"[61] those who see in art a "tool" of social change are less concerned with individual works than with their cultural function. Thus, while many of the technical advancements that I discussed above were coupled with a regression in musical hearing,

---

61. The phrase is borrowed from Walter Benjamin; see his "Ursprung des deutsches Trauerspiels" in *Schriften* (Frankfurt, 1955), vol. 1, 172.

it is not altogether clear whether this applies to the compositions or to their reception. Discussing the notion of "progress" in relationship to the avant-garde, Dahlhaus—in his usual erudite and perceptive manner—endeavored to show that the "level" at which attempts were made to determine musical progress changed in the twentieth century.[62] Accordingly, if from the late eighteenth to the early twentieth century "the growing richness of expression" was considered "progressive" (second only to the development of harmony and instrumentation), the emphasis was subsequently placed on "compositional-technical discoveries and hypotheses on methods of musical thinking." Dahlhaus also dismisses the historical delineation of music as a development "from the simple to the complex." The goal of music history, he argues, is subject to change and not all that is "new" is necessarily more complex. In fact, the move from the "old" to the "new' in earlier centuries, insists Dahlhaus, was at times bound up more "with simplification and retrenchment than with complication and emancipation." And while a theorist such as August Halm, for example, saw the goal of music history as a synthesis of "two cultures of music"—represented by the fugue and the sonata[63]—Schoenberg was convinced that there was a developmental tendency toward "music structured in all directions," though he was fully aware of the fact that profit had been paid for—up till then—by loss.[64]

Schoenberg seems to have fully endorsed the compositional means that his predecessors employed to heighten the expressive power of their works. He was convinced, however, that the impact of such means wears off with the passage of time, during which they turn into sentimental banalities.[65] In other words, regardless of the excitement that new musical configurations may induce at their appropriate historical moments, once

62. See Carl Dahlhaus, "Progress and the Avant-Garde," in his *Schoenberg and the New Music,* trans. Derrick Puffet and Alfred Clayton (Cambridge, 1987), 14—22.

63. August Halm (1869–1929) was a German theorist, a contemporary of Heinrich Schenker. Halm also had a keen interest in music education. In his famous essay *Von zwei Kulturen der Musik,* Halm essentially referred to the baroque fugue that culminated in Bach and to the classical sonata that culminated in Beethoven. The fugue, he claimed, represented unity, while the sonata represented conflict. Halm called for historical syntheses of the two, that is, a synthesis that would grant "greater freedom" to the themes and melodic aspects in the classical sonata, which are generally manipulated and limited in terms of their functions within the whole of the form, to the point of losing their own individuality. See *Von zwie Kulturen der Musik* (Munich, 1913), 252–53. Also see Schoenberg's "New Music, Outmoded Music, Style and Idea," in his *Style and Ideas,* 39f–40f.

64. Dahlhaus, "Progress and the Avant-Garde," 21–22.

65. See his *Theory of Harmony,* trans. Roy E. Carter (London, 1978), 238.

they become commonplace their aesthetic "weight" diminishes. Schoenberg's "developmental tendency of music" is propelled, as it were, by a phenomenon of "cyclical exhaustion" that engenders time and again more germane—"up to date"—expressive means. Schoenberg clearly conceived of the *musical material* itself as a cultural artifact that is subject to historical evolution and necessity, rather than being representative of an immutable "natural given." Schoenberg was consequently of the opinion that in order to accommodate the expressive needs of contemporary composers, music *must* go beyond its present stage of development. He was profoundly convinced that the music that he advanced conveyed its immediate sociocultural surroundings, certainly more than the "well-entrenched" music or the popular genres of the day.

Sensitive to the socially conditioned character of both art and its institutions, Theodor Adorno (1903–69)—a social philosopher and sociologist of music—came to the rescue of those who felt hemmed in by an esotericism from which they were trying to escape. Adorno had studied composition under Alban Berg and was intimately acquainted with avantgarde music. In addition to his acquaintance with Schoenberg, Berg, and Webern, he was also in direct contact with Paul Hindemith, Hanns Eisler, Kurt Weill, and Krenek, all of whom were deeply concerned with contemporary compositional issues and with questions pertaining to the social role of art. Like Schoenberg, however, Adorno believed that progress does not apply to the qualities of musical works written at different times, but rather to the grasp of the *musical material* at its most advanced moment in the historical dialectic.[66] He thus strongly rejected Hindemith's attempt to justify his particular system of extended tonality in terms of the "natural laws" of the harmonic series,[67] claiming that Hindemith failed to recognize the historical character of all such theories.[68] Adorno, one should note, was altogether opposed to ontological principles that bestow permanence on what constitutes, as far as he was concerned, a moment in a dynamic historical process. In fact, imposing a static state on what is

66. See Theodor W. Adorno, "Reaktion und Fortschritt," in *Moments musicaux* (Frankfurt, 1964), 153.

67. Hindemith belonged to those composers who wished to bring modern music to a wider audience. Via simplifying his vocal and instrumental compositions, he hoped to reach amateurs as well as children. Anxious to draw up a theoretical foundation for his work—which had crossed the frontiers of tonality and traditional harmony—he sought to reestablish tonal ties through chromatic scales, which he derived from the overtones, enabling him to relate thereby the most distant harmonic phenomena to a root.

68. See Adorno, "Paul Hindemith," in *Neue Blätter für Kunst und Literatur* 4 (1922).

dynamic by nature reflects, according to Adorno, authoritarian regimes that appeal to a mythical collectivity in order to legitimize themselves historically.[69] Unlike the idealized community of the preindustrial world, which allowed for direct communication, modern society, he claimed, is characterized by rapid change, fragmentation, and alienation, which results in *mediated* understandings imposed by industrial capitalism. While seemingly emphasizing individualism, capitalism in fact transforms all reality into "materials" for functional use so that everything, including societal values, becomes "commodified," according to Adorno. Having harnessed Hegelian, Marxist, and Freudian ideologies to the service of avant-garde music, Adorno claimed that serious contemporary music *must be* difficult and disagreeable in order to combat docile consumerism and the use made of serious music by the "culture industry."

In his classic essay on Weimar culture,[70] Peter Gay argued that postwar Germany was in search of roots *and* novelty. Painters, musicians, poets, playwrights, philosophers, architects, psychologists, and many others—who had already been engaged in an international commerce of ideas and were part of a Western community—felt liberated to pursue ideas toward which imperial Germany was hostile. In the quest for national renewal, the hostility of the old regime managed, however, to marginalize the modern trend and its representatives—socialists, democrats, and, above all, Jews—more than ever before.[71] Evidently, the quest for reform—political, social, and economic—that would lead to harmony and unity and a belief in the superiority of German culture did not fare well together. Yet the combination was differently understood by different segments of society, representing not only different social classes but also different fields of intellectual endeavor. Unlike artists and psychologists, the political scientists, argues Gay, were more involved in the life of the republic and sought to influence its course. And while the Deutsche Hochschule für Politik,

69. Adorno's interpretation of the twelve-note technique, which deviates considerably from Schoenberg's own understanding, is not wholly comprehensible without recourse to the dialectic of European rationality in which emancipatory movements repeatedly experience a sudden change into tyranny. Adorno's *Philosophie der neuen Musik* (1949)—in which he summarized some of his key ideas concerning music—was, strictly speaking, an excursus on the *Dialektik der Aufklärung* ("Dialectics of the Enlightenment"), written with Max Horkheimer, which represents a "philosophy in installments" (*Fortsetzungsphilosophie*).

70. Peter Gay, "Weimar Culture: The Outsider as Insider," in *The Intellectual Migration: Europe and America, 1930–1960,* ed. Donald Fleming and Bernard Bailyn (Cambridge, Mass., 1969), 11–93.

71. Ibid., 14–19.

for example, which stood on the ground of bourgeois liberalism, was too radical for most Germans, it was not radical enough for the Institut für Sozialforschung in Frankfurt—the famous Frankfurt School of Social Research.[72]

Adorno was a member of the Institute for Social Research, which had been formed in Frankfurt in 1923. The institute, which was under the directorship of Max Horkheimer (a German social theorist and philosopher) in the early 1930s, succeeded in attracting an impressive group of scholars from different disciplines. Erich Fromm (social psychologist), Friedrich Pollok (economist), Leo Löwenthal (sociologist of literature), and Herbert Marcuse (social philosopher) were among its renowned members. Walter Benjamin was also closely associated with the institute, though he was never a member. The group and those connected with it moved between two positions that well express the relationship between philosophy and the social sciences at the time. The philosophically minded members of the group were critical of the empirical approaches that some of its other members were ready to entertain. Yet the objectives of the institute entailed bridging speculation and empiricism. The group insisted that no isolated phenomenon can be fully comprehended unless viewed from a historical-ideational perspective that also takes into account the component of social structure. The cross-fertilization between theoretical and empirical work was expected to yield a "critical theory" based on a Hegelian-Marxian paradigm, which conceived of history as a process of change over time that interacts with an ostensibly timeless nature, which, unlike in the natural sciences, refers to culture (in the sociological and anthropological sense). The "new" in history, accordingly, does not refer to that which has perpetually been reproduced, but only to that which appears new in it.

Although this essay is hardly the place to elaborate on the extensively studied Frankfurt School of critical theory and its historical significance, it is important to mention that the interdisciplinary approach that characterized its scholars was largely prompted by their shared concern over the rise of fascism and authoritarianism in general. If their empirical studies centered on issues such as popular culture, the mass media, propaganda, and so forth, it is because they wished to better understand their impact on the social life of the *individual* and on the *quality* of his experience—such as the effects of technical reproduction, for example, which we discussed earlier. In sum, the group was essentially concerned with all forms of

72. Ibid., 42–47.

mediation that "manipulate" the behavior and experience of the individual, leaving indelible marks on his perception of self—a "false consciousness," as it were. It should be noted, by the way, that the critique of aesthetic appearance, which Adorno voiced in Schoenberg's name, hinged on Schoenberg's expressionism, which always retained for Adorno the *immediacy* of the initial, overpowering experience. The significance of aesthetic appearance and its critique varies, however, for those for whom expressionism has become history and carries the patina of the past. Adorno spoke of "shocks" and "traumata" (in connection with Schoenberg's *Erwartung*) as symptomatic of "undisguised" tangible stirrings of the unconscious.[73] Yet principles of stylization become invariably apparent in subsequent generations, revealing the seemingly unmediated expression to be, in fact, medi-

---

73. In his profound study *Programming the Absolute,* Berthold Hoeckner discusses Schoenberg's shift from a "successive experience" to a "simultaneous conception" under the influence of the visual arts. Adorno's statement that *Erwartung* "unfolds the eternity of the second in four hundred measures," Hoeckner tells us, echoed Schoenberg's comment that the work's aim had been "to present in *slow motion* everything that occurs during a single second of maximum spiritual excitement." These remarks, argues Hoeckner, "are as evocative as they are contradictory." Adorno, he reminds us, defined Expressionism "as the negation of traditional means." *Erwartung,* accordingly, could not be the "*Augenblick*" of the traditional artwork, which is "the fusion of its particular moments into a whole." Adorno, we are told, had reason to assert that Schoenberg's revolution entailed a "change in function of musical expression. Passions are no longer simulated, but rather embodied emotions of the unconscious; shocks and trauma are registered in the medium of music." Schoenberg's formal innovations are consequently related to the change in the content of expression, and the first atonal works are thus "reports in the sense of psychoanalytical dream transcripts." "Hence," argues Hoeckner, "one might plausibly explain the temporal paradox of *Erwartung* as that of an enacted nightmare." See Berthold Hoeckner, *Programming the Absolute: Nineteenth-Century German Music and the Hermeneutics of the Moment* (Princeton, 2002), 196–97. What drew Adorno to Schoenberg's music, says Rose Subotnik, "was not just its structural idealism, but also the ugliness, by conventional standards, of its sound." Although Adorno valued this ugliness "for its negative capacity to scorn the ideological blandishments of affirmative culture, it is by no means clear," says Subotnik, "that he would have been similarly drawn to the jagged qualities of grunge or punk rock or Laurie Anderson's music, much less that anything could have convinced him to view Leonard Bernstein's choice of the popular route as socially responsible." Adorno was sympathetic to Schoenberg's ugliness, argues Subotnik, because "he understood its cultural significance. And he understood this significance because he operated within the same set of concrete cultural assumptions, expectations, conventions, and values that Schoenberg did. He could listen to Schoenberg's music with the advantage of an insider's knowledge, not of a universal structure, but of a particular style." See Rose Subotnik, *Deconstructive Variations: Music and Reason in Western Society* (Minnesota, 1996), 167.

ated. This pertains not only to "expressionism," but holds equally true for "realism" and "naturalism."

Although Adorno differentiated between history and nature, his concept of nature is itself a historical construct. Viewing nature in historical terms and history in terms of nature, he focused on the *interaction* between the two, attempting to better understand their reciprocal influences. He was not the only one to entertain such thoughts. Though influenced by a number of prominent contemporary thinkers, Adorno's concepts of 'nature' and 'history' seem to have been directly inspired by Georg Lukács—a Marxist philosopher and literary critic. In his *Theorie des Romans* (1916) Lukács discussed the decline of the genre, relating it to the changed relationship of the individual to the world caused by the breakdown of a homogeneous worldview. Unlike the epic, for example, which mirrored the natural unity of the metaphysical sphere to communities in the ancient world, artworks that have become autonomous no longer reflect such totalities, since such totalities, Lukács argued, no longer exist. Most of the social-minded intellectuals of Adorno's generation were, however, primarily influenced by Lukács's *Geschichte und Klassenbewusstsein* (1923)—an essay that is still regarded by scholars as one of the most important works of Marxist philosophy to have appeared in the twentieth century. Unlike Soviet orthodoxy, it became the classic text of Western Marxism owing to Lukács's observation that Marx's theory of history could be read as an application of the Hegelian dialectic. According to Marx, the personal conduct of individuals becomes an alienated independent force once personal interests turn into class interests; it is just such forms of conduct, he tells us, that make up society. Industrial development in the nineteenth century, argued Marx, caused material forces to become saturated with spiritual life, while human existence became a material force. Lukács interpreted Marx to mean that Spirit had become "things" and that things were steeped in spirit. History, thus, was a fabric of meanings that turn into forces. This dialectical relation was best exemplified by the proletariat, which had been reduced by capitalism to labor—a mere economic commodity. The proletariat could however take cognizance of itself as a commodity by acquiring class consciousness. History can thus be conceived as a dialectical totality of knowers and things known and every piece of culture, however affected by class position and historical situation, reflects that totality.

It can be readily understood why theoretical suppositions of this kind should engender seemingly contradictory types of music—high-quality popular music on the one hand, and sophisticated esoteric music on the other. The first, one might argue, empathizes with a social class that has been exploited and shortchanged for far too long, while the second defies the cultural distortions that capitalism brought about. In sum, compassion for the "misled"—regardless of class—calls for serious artistic investments in both. To serve those with whom one empathizes requires compositional adaptations, however, perhaps no less ingenious than the ones brought forth by "progressive" music. Indeed, it is not surprising that some composers should have found it necessary to express their political stance through a divided allegiance, endorsing both "progressive" music and a "proletarian" kind. Concerned with the social function of music, Hanns Eisler, for example, wrote twelve-tone compositions and simple songs for the use of choral ensembles, including choruses for workers and for the Red Army.[74] Close to both Mahler and Schoenberg, Kurt Weill, for example, wrote music in an expressionistic style with interpolations of jazz and popular dance rhythms. His collaboration with Bertolt Brecht, as is well known, produced a series of dramatic works that both exposed societal corruption and betrayal and expressed a deliberate rejection of the complexities of modern music. The music, accordingly, consisted of plain unadorned melodies—accompanied by simple tonal harmonies, jumping from one key to the next without modulating, and simple dance rhythms—sung by actors in charge of delivering the "message" of the text.

In his seminal study of Adorno's aesthetics of music,[75] Max Paddison relates that in 1931 Eisler gave a talk (at a choir's rehearsal of a Brecht play) entitled "The Builders of a New Musical Culture," in which he put forward a dialectical theory of music history from the perspective of the "new music" and the contemporary crisis within music. In his talk, Pad-

---

74. Hanns Eisler was a student of Schoenberg in Vienna. He lived in Berlin until 1932 and migrated to America in 1933. Like some of the Jewish members of the Frankfurt School, who escaped Germany and became associated with the New School for Social Research in New York, he, too, found refuge in America and lectured on music at the New School. Charlie Chaplin engaged him as his musical assistant in 1942 (through 1947); and in 1948 he left the United States under the "voluntary deportation" act because of his "political associations." In addition to the many compositions he wrote that fit the two categories discussed above, he also wrote a book about film music in collaboration with Adorno —*Composing for the Films* (New York, 1947).

75. Max Paddison, *Adorno's Aesthetics of Music* (Cambridge, 1993). For all those who have tried hard to understand Adorno but failed to follow his thoughts, Paddison's book provides a reliable guide through Adorno's intricate maze. It is of course much more than a reliable "guide for the perplexed," since Paddison also endeavored to outline the historical, ideational, and cultural contexts that influenced Adorno's thinking.

dison tells us, he emphasized the *social function* of music, tracing the development of Western music from feudal times to the bourgeois period and its subsequent degeneration in the twentieth century. Diverse social situations, argued Eisler (like Adorno), led to diverse musical techniques that, in turn, made the social situations possible once they were applied in practice. Medieval church music, accordingly, was not directed toward the individual worshiper but to the "religious bearing" of the participants that, in turn, served the class interests of the feudal lords. Eisler explained that the polyphony, which the church nurtured—taking into account its technical devices of *imitation*—presented a static, nonindividualistic point of view. The function of bourgeois music, by comparison, is "entertainment" and "pleasure." It conveys an individualistic point of view by employing *contrast* in ways that enable variety, which also takes into account individual dispositions.[76]

Though much of Eisler's theoretical speculation on the dialectical social function of music is compatible with Adorno's position, Paddison calls to our attention that Eisler, unlike Adorno, wished to use music in "a politically engaged *praxis*, along the lines of Brecht's 'epic theatre.'" Adorno, we are told, feared that such enterprises might degenerate into propaganda and betray "its own 'law of form'—that is, the demands of its material." We are also reminded that Adorno argued that it was "through its form that art opposed coercion, not through direct intervention."[77] Indeed, Eisler's position not only betrays the demands of the "musical material" as defined by Adorno, but also overlooks the interaction between 'history' and 'nature' (as defined above), which circumscribes the newness of the "new." Although it cannot be denied that art also serves social functions conditioned by social situations, it is hard to establish that the development of art is solely prescribed by class interests that fulfill *non*-artistic aims. Moreover, while social consequences are invariably related to human actions, human actions do not necessarily result in anticipated consequences. History, in fact, abounds in *un*anticipated consequences, which in turn promote *re*assessments—theories and conjectures that attempt to explain such "anomalies." It is pointless to point out that "intervention" is tantamount to *mediation* even when enlisted for a venerable cause. Moreover, whoever conceives of Art as a domain that also entails dictates of its own (however understood or employed) is bound to resist "coercions" of all sorts.

76. See ibid., 79–80.
77. Ibid., 80–81.

In sum, no matter how interesting and illuminating a Marxian "reading" of music's history turns out to be, it is unlikely to focus on the issues with which this essay has attempted to deal. On the other hand, this essay—which has limited itself to the structural development of music and the ways in which it was conceived and understood—did not focus on the sociopolitical factors that influenced the various ways in which music was employed. There is, however, a vast difference between these omissions. While the examination of the past via an a priori ideological position results in a reverse kind of "self-fulfilling prophecy"—reaffirming what was assumed to begin with—the examination of the past via the *object* whose development one wishes to trace results in new insights about the "precincts" of the object. Music, of course, developed special stylistic features to suit different social functions and occasions, yet these particular kinds of adaptations abided by a common understanding about the ways in which music qua music functions. Once this common understanding was challenged, the door was open to a host of "interpretations," which could still be addressed—at least for a while—through the music to which they gave rise. Yet by the twentieth century it became increasingly difficult to treat music as the major focal point for the study of music, since music increasingly stopped behaving as a seemingly autonomous cultural subsystem. Indeed, if concerns about the social role of art in the early decades of the century could be related to the defiance of capitalist manipulations and political tyranny, it is possible to claim that by the end of the century—with a few decades in between of "business as usual"—similar concerns can be related to an overall defiance of the "supremacy" of Western culture.

SIX

The Appropriation of Musical Meaning

THE RISE OF A HETERONOMOUS AESTHETIC

Lending saliency to the social role of art also engendered an argument against an autonomous aesthetic in which form takes precedence over content. The preoccupation with content, whether socialist or bourgeois, invariably presupposes a heteronomous aesthetic. Thus the debate between Wagner and Hanslick may be construed as an argument for and against a heteronomous aesthetic. Though Wagner sought to grant art a cultural role independent of societal constraints and predetermined dictates, he challenged the "absoluteness" of what he himself named "absolute music."[1] By attaching the rudiments of myth to the metaphysics of music, he believed that he had unveiled the true realm that music represents. Even while making ample use of the abstract formulations that justified music's claim to be heard for its own sake, Wagner skewed

---

1. Wagner, ironically, is the first to have coined the term "absolute music" in his essay on Beethoven's Ninth Symphony (1846). He subsequently also made use of the term in his "Art Work of the Future" (1849) and in his "Music and Drama" (1851). In his seminal essay *The Idea of Absolute Music*, Carl Dahlhaus has shown that to fully understand what Wagner meant by the term 'absolute,' and the way it was understood by others at the time, the issue must be viewed from the perspective of the development of music, which placed emphasis on music *with* texts since its inception until the nineteenth century. See Carl Dahlhaus, *The Idea of Absolute Music* (Chicago, 1991), chap. 2.

the musical discourse in the direction of a presumed primordial content. In other words, at one and the same time, he both used and denied absolute music.

Wagner's polemical approach to music's autonomous aesthetic implicates sociopolitical interests no less than did those theories that advocated "musical realism" as the true function of art. Without attempting to define it, *social* realism in art invariably contains an element of insurgence. As an instrument of sociopolitical commitment, it highlights that which has either been excluded from the art or not received the attention that it allegedly deserves. Thus, what has been banned for aesthetic reasons may reemerge on the basis of social reasons claiming to represent "reality." Reality, however, is a relative concept, for it depends on the perspective of the viewer. This applies no less to historical perspectives, which are equally dependent on the "viewpoint" of the observer.

Socialist realism, evidently, did not engage only composers who had little knowledge of the métier or composers who were insensible to aesthetic considerations. Some composers even tried to create new compositional methods in the hope of mastering reality by artistic means. Motivated by tactical considerations they promoted strategies for artistic survival, aware that they were tampering with the history of the art they had inherited. To be sure, this history had undergone previous stages in which questions concerning the "true" nature of music were raised. Yet queries of this kind did not deter the development of what came to be considered music in the West. Indeed, for the purpose of art history it is far easier to think of "realism" as a mode of thought that shatters an aesthetic norm than to try to define it as a phenomenon that music is able to reflect or represent in unwavering terms.

THE GENERAL DISTRUST OF CATEGORICAL SYSTEMS

However difficult it may be to deal with subjects that involve a heteronomous aesthetic, there is no denying that "ever since the aesthetics of the beautiful was replaced by the aesthetics of the true, the problem of what true reality really is has plagued compositional practice, as well as theories about music."[2] Discussing these issues, Dahlhaus reminds us that in

2. See Carl Dahlhaus, *Realism in the Nineteenth Century* (Cambridge, 1985), 115. The original essay (Munich, 1982) bore the more telling title *Musikalischer Realismus: Zur Musikgeschichte des 19.Jahrhunderts.* In order to comprehend "musical realism" in the nineteenth century, Dahlhaus first examined the various applications of the notion, so as to reveal the different understandings it entailed from a music-historical point of view.

the second half of the nineteenth century, "inter-subjectivity" formed the main premise in support of a realism that was "propounded as the order of the day in art and art theory." Dahlhaus was of course aware of the fact that this "simple maxim," as he put it, was exposed toward the end of the century to the probing of a theory of knowledge "which aesthetic theory, even when put into practice and documented in works of art, could not ignore indefinitely." The naïve concept of reality, he tells us, was gradually displaced by "a skepticism which spread from the philosophers to infect the public in general." Due to the profound changes that affected epistemology from Kant to Ernst Mach,[3] reality was no longer treated as a "given," but as the composite of "a relationship between the amorphous material received by the senses, and the categorical form contributed by the perceiving consciousness."[4] Comprehending and constructing, we learn, became two aspects of the same process. Without delving further into the paradigmatic shift that took place in the theory of knowledge, it can be claimed that the general distrust of categorical systems affected not only the concepts of 'reality' and 'musical realism' but also the very mechanisms that fostered the Western conception of music.

Musical realism encountered mistrust among composers whose aesthetic orientations had been wrought by the idea of absolute music. Yet it also fostered—at one and the same time—a general distrust of *categorical* systems. Regardless of the rhetoric that enveloped artistic claims in the twentieth century, the dissolution of functional harmony, the disruption of regular tonally based periodic structure, the cessation of familiar thematic-motivic working, and a host of other technical features clearly negated the categorical apparatus pertaining to musical structure. Although change is inevitable during any period in the development of an art, composers of the twentieth century were apparently aware that the developments to which they contributed raised questions of the most fundamental kind, not only questions related to the configurations of their own works but also questions pertaining to the significance and ultimate nature of music itself.[5] Although there had been other periods in which long-established

3. The physicist-philosopher Ernst Mach contributed to the development of a theory that dismissed traditional structures and systems, claiming that these are no more than mental concepts affected by momentary experiences.

4. Dahlhaus, *Realism in the Nineteenth Century,* 117.

5. See, for example, the papers contained in *Problems of Modern Music,* ed. Paul Henry Lang (New York, 1960). These papers were delivered by composers and musical theorists at a Seminar in Advanced Musical Studies, organized by Princeton University in response to a felt need to better understand the upheaval caused by the "new music." Glancing

guidelines had been challenged, the history of music had never encountered a negation of almost everything that had been established before.
As we have seen, habitual stylistic features were regularly replaced by new
ones that seemed more compatible with immediate needs and altered aesthetic desiderata without obliterating music's fundamental premises. In
the twentieth century, however, the search for new musical styles—more
suitable for the "here and now"—became so deliberate an act, imparting
such drastic changes in attitude, frames of mind, and understandings that
it could no longer be reconciled with a tradition that was slow in the making and had only gradually accumulated its defining features.

The statement about the search for musical styles more compatible
with the "here and now" seems to contradict an earlier assertion about
the "future orientation" of composers. It was argued, it may be recalled,
that departure from shared styles increasingly revealed a shared *concern*,
that of leaving individual marks on the historical development of music.
While systematically breaking down accepted norms and procedures,
composers sought to persuade the musically informed that they were engaged in an inevitable advance of the very music with which they were
familiar. Composers also held on to the notion that as long as they have
something original to say they must suffer from not being understood—a
notion they inherited from Romantic musical aesthetics. Failing to be
endorsed by contemporary audiences, composers felt nonetheless in the
right vis-à-vis that audience, trusting that they would be vindicated by future generations. The future, in other words, was expected to reveal their
past contemporariness!

Disregarding contradictions of this sort, there is no denying that the
gap between the creator and consumer of art has widened in the twentieth
century, despite some attempts to narrow the rift. In fact it has become
more and more clear that every attempt to describe the relationship between the conception and perception of musical works seems burdened
by the difficulty of establishing unequivocally which aspects of the conception are supposed to be comprehended in the first place and who determines which features and facts are aesthetically constitutive. Having
abandoned the conviction, still largely accepted in the nineteenth century,

---

through the *Darmstädter Beiträge zur Neuen Musik* and the *Neue Musik in der Bundesre-
publik Deutschland* (the yearbook of the International Society for Contemporary Music)
reveals concerns similar to those expressed in the above papers. The international summer courses for new music that were initiated after World War II (1946) in Darmstadt
encompassed premières of new works, interpretations thereof, and many distinguished
lectures debating the problems to which the new music gave rise.

that the composer's intention is the decisive factor, a *reception* aesthetic ensued that could not escape the unreasonable demands of resolving the aesthetic identity of a work into innumerable modes of perception without laying down certain forms of conception as adequate and rejecting others as inadequate. Yet the notion that the composer fashions only the musical material and not the key to its exegesis could no longer be overlooked. The composer's intention, in other words, was no longer regarded as identical with the "Objectified Spirit" (to use a Hegelian term) of his work, which reveals itself *as it is,* but has to be disclosed through interpretation.[6] In fact, to reject the subjective perceptions of individuals became more and more viewed as a preference for reflective analysis over aesthetic immediacy. Despite the opposition that such a premise provoked, aesthetic immediacy kept gaining ground and eventually conceded equal rights to innumerable modes of perception by diverse listeners. The *"right to differ"*—a claim increasingly legitimized in other arenas—is related to

6. It is worth remembering that Hegel warned against art that retreats into its own medium, that is, art that rids itself of contents that already had gained a standing of their own. He believed that retreats of this kind might lead eventually to a loss of human interest in art. Music, he believed, may not be engaged solely with its own sphere of sounds; it must impart spiritually adequate expressions via its sensuous means if it is to be considered an art. It is this kind of thinking and similar ones that may in fact bring back, albeit through back doors, the dependence of abstract music on language formulations of various sorts or reenact the mimetic paradigm through novel understandings of its function, as Rose Subotnik explains:

> During the twentieth century the contemporary composition has refined the principle of individualization to such an extreme as to shatter social illusions of its own internal necessity. Requiring each element in a work to be structurally necessary, the contemporary composer has come to place a very nearly absolute burden of responsibility on each compositional decision. As a result, in spite of its own essentially abstract structural idea, the contemporary composition has increased to a degree unprecedented in Western history the importance of particularity *as such* to its own conception. Starting with the attempts of such early twentieth-century figures as Debussy, Schoenberg, and Stravinsky to distance themselves in their various ways from romanticism, the contemporary composer has generally avoided presenting his or her composition either as a vision of genius or as an argument that works primarily through stylistic persuasiveness. Attributing a quasi-objective necessity to the demands of their craft, contemporary composers have in fact taken a romantic tendency to its extreme; they have located musical significance not just metaphorically but literally—coextensively and exclusively— in the structure of their works. In so doing, the contemporary composer has demystified the metaphysically evocative romantic artwork into a self-contained piece of craft, with no further claims to a sacred place in society. (Rose Subotnik, *Developing Variations,* 270.)

the sanctioning of diverse perceptions, which contributed directly or indirectly to a relapse of descriptive science into normative thought.

Alternate Perspectives on the Relation between 'Conception' and 'Perception'

Schoenberg, obviously, did not regard tonality and "emancipated dissonances" as ends in themselves, but rather as technical resources bringing unity to the conception and perception of music. Given that tonality came to be experienced as a kind of "objective reality" and atonality as an intellectual exercise devoid of "shared meaning," Schoenberg believed that twelve-tone compositions might replace functional harmony as a new device relating diverse elements to one another. Time and again, he reiterated the importance of "functionality" independent of system. However convincing his argument was in favor of a nonhierarchical organization of tones, it did not succeed in creating compatible perceptual points of view. The difficulty with regard to perception may be related, in part, to the fact that highly sophisticated ways of dealing with sound often result in simple if not primitive contrasts, notwithstanding the elaborate calculations of the composer. In fact, aleatory music—which tried to reduce to a minimum the composer's definition of the musical qualities of his work by emphasizing instead the role of the performer as interpreter—constituted a reaction against serial music, even though it stemmed from the same aesthetic outlook that attempted to deal with the ambiguities as far as perception is concerned.

Though 'perception' surfaced in the eighteenth century as a phenomenon deserving serious investigation, much had to happen to lend it centrality. The arts, especially music, contributed their share to the cognitive turn in epistemology—highlighting aesthetics as a mode of knowing—yet each of the arts tried in its own way to systematize the knowledge of its métier, despite the stylistic changes with which it had to grapple. In this respect, music, more than her sister arts, became regarded as a science. Wedding reason *with* experience, Rameau, as we have seen, tried to prove that chords and their progressions were contained in and were part of the fixed laws of nature. Influenced by Zarlino and Descartes, he sought to deduce unifying principles that would both provide a frame of reference for existing chords and a generating source for their harmonic construction. Having regarded music *as* a science, he was credited with laying the foundations of modern harmonic theory. Rameau's theory naturally failed to provide anchorage for a totally changed conception of music and the manner in which it functions. His theory became more and more deplored as an artificial "superimposition" that does not take into account the un-folding nature of music despite its "generative" claims.

The rejection of this extraneous superimposition engendered theories attentive to the creative processes as manifested in actual compositions. Thus Heinrich Schenker (1868–1935), who is best known for his innovative notions concerning the structure of *tonal* music, declared that his theory emerged organically from the music itself in accordance with aural per-ceptions.[7] Although he produced a method for describing how music be-haves, Schenker was of the opinion that true masterpieces are conceived in a "sweep" of genius and do not result from classroom instruction, since structure and process are organically intertwined in the musical work. The primal compositional material, according to Schenker, is the temporal con-trapuntal projection of the basic harmony—the *ursatz*—which represents the contents of a tonal work at its most basic level, constituting the "back-ground" of the composition. Its transformations create an interaction be-tween "back-ground," "middle-ground," and "foreground"—the structural layers of compositions. This process of *auskomponierung* (prolongation) creates the organic coherence of the musical work, and consequently of the theory. Since Schenker's understanding of music is basically governed by a concept of "hierarchy," the *urlinie*—the melodic diatonic structure that spans the upper voice of a composition—represents as well a mani-festation of the diatonic chord. In fact, each interacting transformative level represents a kind of "repetition" of the basic fundamental harmony governing the work as a whole—"always the same, but not the same way" Schenker liked to say.

As far as Schenker was concerned, "great music" is tonal. Thus, the composition as a whole is ultimately governed by its principal chord—the tonic triad, which he regarded as the "chord of nature," that is, harmony in its natural state. All other harmonic functions are subordinate to the tonic. Analysis, consequently, must distinguish between essential and passing harmonies and the essential and transitional notes of a melody. Given that these distinctions apply to all levels of the composition, what is essential on one level might be transitional on another level. It follows that without entertaining the general it is impossible to comprehend the

7. Although Schenker was of course not the first to have challenged Rameau's theory, he developed his theory of tonal music in the early decades of the twentieth century, aware of atonal music and surrounded by new musical conceptions. His theory, more-over, is still held in high esteem and its influence grew steadily over the course of the twentieth century.

specific, while the exploration of the specific leads to a clear understanding of the general. The analytic procedure, however, is one of reduction: the musical surface—the "foreground" comprising the details—leads to the unveiling of the "middle-ground" and the "back-ground," which contain the deeper and more general compositional patterns. While the layers taken together illuminate the *ursatz,* the basis from which they emanate, they also delineate the uniqueness of the work and expose the creative process of its composer.

Schenker clearly regarded musical structure as a gestalt in which unity and coherence are achieved through organic connections, as opposed to the juxtaposition of chords, motives, themes, and so forth, that are "artificially" molded into preconceived "forms." He was evidently after the kind of analysis that would grow "outward from within," an analysis that would reveal the work as a whole in its particulars and the musical cohesion as self-generated. Yet the totality of a composition, he insisted, could be conceived only spontaneously, through a "sweep" of intuition. Creativity, Schenker believed, is an intuitive power, derived from "Nature and God," a gift possessed by a few. It was the tonal music of the eighteenth and nineteenth centuries that led Schenker to his conviction about the supremacy of German music, a conviction that encountered much criticism considering its metaphysical premise. The theory itself, however, also encountered criticism, less for what it contained and more for what it omitted. It was criticized, for example, for its seeming neglect of *stylistic* differentiations and, paradoxically, for its neglect of temporal organizations, though it addresses the "unfolding" nature of music more profoundly than most other theories.

Though it abounds in regulatory principles and applies to tonal music, Schenker's profound theory turned analysis itself into a creative act by facilitating a closer touch with the work. Schenker, in fact, considered himself an artist, rather than a scientist. His method, moreover, allows considerable latitude in its application, for it engages the individual ears of those who attempt to reveal the "intuitive" processes through which the composer heard. Thus, discussing the "greatness" of the German masters, Schenker claimed to have explained "their daring invention in the realm of hearing, as had previously been experienced only in the realm of the other senses." He also claimed to have "revealed for the first time by verbal communication the realm of hearing, as the masters understood it," and to have thereby "enriched human existence by a new dimension."[8] However

8. *Tonwille,* vol. 5, 55, quoted by William Drabkin in his essay "Heinrich Schenker" in *Western Music Theory,* ed. Thomas Christensen (Cambridge, 2002), 831. To get more

immodest some of his claims might sound, he provided musicians with a powerful tool that enables them not only to delve into the creative process of the composer but also to bring their own perceptions into play. Indeed, Schenkerian analysts have "exercised their right to differ," though they toil hard to persuade one another from within the "community of discourse" to which they belong.

In sum, musical coherence, as far as Schenker was concerned, can be achieved only through a fundamental structure that underlies its transformations, like a kernel that gives rise to a living organism. Since coherence depends on "organic" connections, he placed great emphasis on linear progressions as a primary means of coherence. His theory of tonal language required, in fact, contrapuntal thinking (accompanied, of course, by what he termed "hearing correctly"), since the linear progressions are anchored in polyphony. However insightful Schenker's understanding of music turned out to be, it cannot be transferred easily to nontonal music. Nonetheless, since all music unfolds in time (regardless of the nature of the connections effected between its constituent parts and the aesthetic import achieved thereby), there is much in Schenker's method that may be creatively employed regarding nontonal music, albeit in "reverse" order—that is, to unveil the *overriding lines,* the formal cohesion of diverse musical conceptions, and the creative processes whereby they are obtained.

Physics has clearly occupied an important position in musical thought, but musical aesthetics have been mostly relegated, as we have seen, to the realm of metaphysics. Schenker's occasional metaphysical rhetoric does not overshadow his physiological concerns, however. Indeed, once Hermann Helmholtz summarized his investigation of musical perception,[9] it became necessary to delve further into the scientific basis for artistic processes. Although Helmholtz, too, believed that great works are produced by men of genius, he was of the opinion that music, more than the other arts, deals with perception anchored in pure sensation (similar to Kant), that is, in physiological properties of stimuli and their consequent psycho-

---

insights into Schenker's theory and a broader view of its standing among theories, read Drabkin's essay. In addition to dealing with the theory itself in a concise and intelligible way, Drabkin also traces the origin of some of Schenker's ideas and the influence they exerted on subsequent theories and their applications.

9. Renowned for his achievements in medicine, physiology, and physics, Hermann Helmholtz (1821–94) investigated both the physical and physiological aspects of acoustics in order to establish their role in the construction and perception of musical systems. His seminal work *On the Sensations of Tone* (1863; trans. Alexander J. Ellis, New York, 1948) summarizes years of acoustical research and experiments.

logical perception. The construction of musical systems, he argued, has to take into account the boundary and limits of the variety of tones and their relationships; these, he believed, are directly influenced by the physiological properties of the sensation of hearing and the physical aspects of the tones themselves.[10] The prominence of the octave and the fifth in early music convinced Helmholtz that the tonal relationships in the West rest on the degree of identification among tones. Thus, the repetition of the octave not only constitutes the first partial but also provides the basis for the Western division of the musical scales. The "natural melodic relationship," that is, the diatonic scale, was apparently deduced in similar fashion.

Though melodic relationships were recognized first, harmonic relationships clearly played an important part in the expansion of the musical vocabulary in the West, even if the perception of harmonic relationships—consonant or dissonant—is immediate and does not only depend on partial tones but also on combinational tones. The latter, however, can be connected to the former; in fact, the greater the relationship among the tones that constitute "units," the richer the musical palette, Helmholtz claimed. Moreover, relating chords to one another and to the tonic follows the laws that regulate the relationships of consecutive compound tones. Helmholtz thus suggested a possible connection between the physiology of hearing and some aspects of musical aesthetics. Opposed to metaphysical speculations yet highly interested in human knowledge, Helmholtz wished to better understand the ways in which ideas correspond to reality by unveiling what is "true" in our sense perception and thought. Although the formal aspects of knowledge condition the ways in which scientific knowledge is formulated, scientific knowledge also contributes to our understanding of the forms of intuition and the mental operations involved in *knowing*. All we know about the external world, argued Helmholtz, is brought to consciousness as the result of changes that external causes produce in our sense organs. There is no one-to-one correspondence, however, between a sensation experienced and a specific property of the object causing the sensation. The sensation is but a subjective sign of the object and not an image of it. Indeed, though Helmholtz may be regarded as a late Pythag-

10. His acoustical investigations led to the discovery that music prefers to employ "compound tones," that is, tones that have harmonic upper partial tones, the vibrational numbers of which are integral multiples of the vibrational number of the "prime tone." Compound tones are generated by periodic and uniform motions, producing a uniform and sustained sensation. The physiological construction of the ear, he maintained, influences this preference, since even "simple tones," if sounded with sufficient intensity, excite sensations of harmonic upper partials in the ear.

orean, his conceptions concerning culture and his scientific goals reveal that he was by far more interested in the *process* that knowing entails than in its subject matter. It is to the process, accordingly, to which he ascribed a standing in musical perception, rather than to its acoustical verities.

One of the major figures to have continued Helmholtz's work is Carl Stumpf (1848–1936).[11] Yet, unlike Helmholtz, he approached the subject from a psychological point of view, focusing primarily on the sensory experience of sound and its function, rather than on the organ of hearing. Stumpf was keenly interested in music and knowledgeable about the various modes of its historical and theoretical investigations. Moreover, although he was interested in music as a universal cultural phenomenon, Stumpf saw fit to include non-Western musical traditions in his attempt to differentiate between the "universal" and the "specific"—between natural laws and culturally acquired norms. Thus, in addition to having formulated the concept *'Tonpsychologie'* (1883) and to having treated the subject systematically, he also founded, together with his pupils Erich von Hornbostel and Otto Abraham, the Berlin Phonogrammarchiv (1900).[12] While directing the Beiträge zur Akustik und Musikwissenschaft (1898–1924) he also briefly directed (1922–23) with Hornbostel the Sammelbände für vergleichende Musikwissenschaft. Viewing culture in comparative terms opened up a whole new world of musical investigations, highlighting both cultural determinants and cognitive constraints. While comparative musicology, and later ethnomusicology, sensitized the West to musical traditions other than its own, it also gradually revealed some fundamental principles that underlie seemingly free choices. If cognitive scientists, nowadays, differentiate between "natural" and "learned" schemata, they owe a great deal not only to psychoacoustic studies but also to comparative musicology

11. Known as a psychologist, acoustician, and musicologist, Stumpf had an extensive education both in philosophy and the natural sciences. Stumpf studied music from early childhood, and his writings combine a profound understanding of music with scientific, historical, and philosophical knowledge.

12. Erich von Hornbostel and Otto Abraham applied the concepts and methods of acoustics, psychology, and physiology to the study of non-European musical cultures. It is their scientific rigor that granted the newly established discipline of comparative musicology the recognition it received. Many of Hornbostel's students became leading figures in the discipline that they helped to promote. Indeed, it is hard to imagine the development of comparative musicology without figures such as Hans Hickmann, George Herzog, Heinrich Husmann, Marius Schneider, Robert Lachmann, Mieczyslaw Kolinski, and Walter Wiora, who in turn bequeathed to their followers what they had learned from their highly revered teacher. Hornbostel was the director of the Berlin archive from 1906 until 1933, when he was forced to leave Germany.

as conceived by Stumpf and his followers. Ethnomusicology, however, increasingly emphasized the anthropological aspects in its attempts to delineate the uniqueness of different musical traditions. In fact, the awareness of different cultures—their diverse modes of thought and expression—gained momentum in a world that rapidly turned into a "global village" (to use McLuhan's phrase) due largely to technological innovations.[13]

Psychoacoustics made considerable strides in the course of the twentieth century, but the aesthetic aspects of musical perception remained largely unresolved. In midcentury, two former compatriots of Schenker—Fritz Winckel and Victor Zuckerkandl—advanced novel ideas in an attempt to bridge the "objective" and the "subjective" in music. Interested in the perception of music, Winckel—a leading figure in the field of psychoacoustics—investigated the ways in which structures of music and language constitute forms of communication, using electronic music as a basis for his research. In his *Music, Sound, and Sensation* (1959) Winckel tried to define the relationships among the laws of musical perception (accounting both for the generative mechanism of sound structures and for the mechanism of insight) in a "simple, down to earth way," as he put it, and without recourse to "arbitrary interpretations." Central to his theory are the concepts of perpetual motion and change, which are germane both to sounds and to the mechanism of perception. Music aesthetics, however, is based on a "time-constant" of sound perception. The boundaries of the tone spectrum, as well as its evaluation and the ability to determine the direction of the source of a sound, are dependent on such a constant.[14] Winckel claimed, nonetheless, that nothing is "independent" or "static" in music since consecutive sounds determine the relationships of "intervallic tensions," and given that the affect of one sound complex on another also depends on the changes occurring during the intoning of sound, that is, on the onset process, the modulation and the decay of the sound. Dynamic changes also influence the perception of pitch, Winckel argued, while changes in tempo and rhythm affect tone color. Improvements in methods of measurement, he believed, will greatly refine the description of the per-

13. Since the days of their inception, the standing of musicology and ethnomusicology (their roles and functions) has undergone considerable changes, as did the relationship between the two and the "division of labor" between them. To get an idea of the changes that have taken place and their far-reaching implications, see Bruno Nettl, "The Institutionalization of Musicology: Perspectives of a North American Ethnomusicologist," in *Rethinking Music*, ed. Nicholas Cook and Mark Everist (Oxford, 2001).

14. Acoustical investigations set the integration constant of the ear at 50ms, the time required to become aware of a sensory perception.

ception process of music. He thus drew a sharp distinction between music as heard, music as represented by a score, and the abstract conception of a work. The perception of a musical work is richer than its presentation in the score, and not necessarily identical with the composer's conception. According to Winckel, composers immerse themselves in the functional relationships of a language of notated musical symbols because they are unaware of the importance of the psychoacoustical aspects of sounds. However tempting, one should refrain from attributing to Winckel a special interest in "performance"—a field that has gained systematic study in recent years—since he dealt with the *perception process of music,* not with the diverse ways in which it is interpreted.

Granting that the abstract conception of a work should not be identified with the process of hearing and that the latter should not be confused with the score, there is a greater historical relation between them than Winckel cared to admit. It is precisely the score, one may argue, that largely determined the musical *qualities* to be heard, not the perceptions thereof. This, at any rate, was partially achieved via a notational system that guaranteed the *identity* of musical works, not the way they were performed or interpreted. Along with music's various manifestations, performance practices and musical interpretations were nonetheless constrained. They were constrained, however, by a particular understanding of music and the way it functions, and not by the notational system that music employed. The latter constituted, as we have seen, an integral part of what came to be understood as music in the West. Yet Winckel was utterly convinced that the dependence of subjective musical hearing on natural laws would become *fully* evident in the field of psychoacoustics, which deserved, as he admitted, more rigorous investigation. By suggesting that it is the "subjective" that harbors not only prime perceptions but culturally determined aspects as well, Winckel clearly took a leap beyond his actual findings. Yet based on more advanced psychoacoustic and cognitive studies, one can suggest that diverse musical choices—conveying diverse musical imports—are cognitively constrained in ways that allow diverse aesthetic desiderata to apply, though not at the same time. For example, music that expects the listener to focus on the momentary as it occurs is ipso facto differently structured than music whose "long-range directionality" solicits the listener's attention; the one inevitably excludes the other.[15] Although factors of this kind invariably differentiate musical

---

15. As we have already seen, music had to be differently constructed whenever it intended to draw attention to new aesthetic desiderata. Neurological theory, nowadays,

traditions, they may also occur in differing stylistic features of the same tradition. This seems to suggest that the relationship between cognitive constraints and aesthetic desiderata—the very bond, not its specific nature—is apparently a universal phenomenon.[16]

Schenker's other compatriot—Victor Zuckerkandl (1896–1965)—was, like him, a music theorist and music critic. He, too, taught music theory in Vienna until he left for the United States in 1940. Viewing music as a "miracle," he wished to go beyond the prevailing physical and psychological interpretations of music by introducing what he called the "third stage." Zuckerkandl's "third stage" is a spiritual world that represents the interaction between the inner world of the listener and the outer world from which he receives his stimuli. This merger of worlds is possible, Zuckerkandl argued, because there is a metaphysical component to the material outer world. Furthermore, the merger of the "within" with the "without" is what constitutes the listener's psyche; the psyche, in other words, is not to be viewed as a stage antecedent to that fusion. Music, according to Zuckerkandl, is an important sphere through which philosophical insights into the world are obtained, for in music we both experience the material world and become conscious of ourselves as immaterial beings. Music reveals a concept of space that differs from the physical one; it reveals an audible "placeless space," one of forces, dynamics, tensions, and harmonies—a space experienced. Similarly, time is presented not by the demarcation of successive instances but by their interpretation, whereby the present also contains both the past and the future.

Musical tones, according to Zuckerkandl, are perceived as a play of forces presenting specific dynamic qualities and states of activity. Musical form, the "order of tones," is not a mere juxtaposition of bodies of sound, but a representation of the relations generated by the above forces. We hear energy and relations, not wavelengths and vibrations. The mind perceives these nonphysical occurrences, which the physiological processes neither explain nor exhaust. Hearing music, the listener experiences the "reality" of a placeless space of dynamic forces. Much in Zuckerkandl's

---

takes great interest in aesthetic experiences in an attempt to better understand the neural mechanisms that mediate them. As expected, *attention* looms large in the investigation of consciousness and in the way in which *art and the brain* are being studied. For a start, I recommend reading the much-debated study by V. S. Ramachandran and William Hirstein, "The Science of Art: A Neurological Theory of Aesthetic Experience," *Journal of Consciousness Studies: Controversies in Science and the Humanities* 6 (June–July 1999): 15–51.

16. See Cohen and Katz, *Palestinian Arab Music*, 325–34.

thought is clearly reminiscent of previous theories that suggested, in one way or another, a correspondence between music and the dynamics of an inner life. Nonetheless, his approach is a novel one, for he insists that music *projects* psychological states rather than reflects them. Like linguistic theories that regard language as partaking in the very processes of thought, Zuckerkandl called attention to the cognitive role of music, claiming that real explanations of music cannot be achieved solely through "technical analyses." Musical analysts labor under a false pretense if they believe themselves to have thereby gained an understanding of "the thing itself." Music theory, in the proper sense, must take into account other disciplines, argued Zuckerkandl, so as to better understand the mental processes that accompany the creative act of the composer and of those who try to make sense of what they hear. As a music theorist himself, his arguments should have produced more attention than they did among theorists and professional musicians. Nevertheless, by reexamining the "forces," "dynamics," and "tensions" that music creates, Zuckerkandl became linked not only with a glorious past but also joined all those who tried to unveil the *multidimensional* aspects of music, aiming at a better understanding of the spiritual part music plays in the human psyche. Music *projects* states of mind, rather than reflects them, because the psyche itself already constitutes, according to Zuckerkandl, a fusion between an "inner" and an "outer" world.

Disregarding Zuckerkandl's "metaphysical realm," one may readily accept two of his propositions: (1) given that music does not happen in a vacuum, its explanation must incorporate whatever factors have a bearing on the way in which it is understood; (2) although human beings differ from one another, their psyches invariably represent a fusion between an "inner" and an "outer" world. The two are in fact related to each other, though indirectly: if the psyche already represents a fusion between the inner and outer world, and if some nonmusical factors of the outer world have a bearing on the way we understand music, then the perception of music is not wholly an individual matter, and neither is its "projection." While we knew all along that time, place, ideas, and so forth, circumscribe our understanding of music, Zuckerkandl's assertion that "outer world" factors constitute an integral part of the individual's psyche seems to challenge ideas—regardless of their nature—about the outright autonomy of the individual's perception of music.[17]

17. The systematic studies of music perception and cognition increasingly reveal the mental constraints that affect their processing.

The Relationship between Form
and Formal Function Reexamined

However interesting such theories may be, the idea that music is differently perceived by different individuals continued to persist. And however ardently composers held on to their belief that the listener would eventually "hear" what they tried to communicate, most listeners failed to get "their" message. Though psychoacoustical studies kept gaining momentum thanks to the mushrooming of sophisticated measuring instruments, the "macro" quandaries of aesthetics could hardly be resolved by authoritative answers to some of the "micro" queries about musical perception. Much of the music composed in the twentieth century seems to have raised a more apparent issue, one that challenged a long-held understanding about the relationship between 'matter' and 'form,' between substance and its defining attributes. The relationship between substance and its qualifiers in fact has offered a continuous challenge to philosophers, ever since Aristotle established that the "concrete individual thing" is a substance within which primary and secondary substances are included, that is, species and genus. Though qualities and relations are parasitical to substance, the latter depends on the former. Interestingly, Aristotle's elaborate account of the relationship between 'substance,' 'quality,' and 'essence' gave rise to questions concerning the "truly real" in nature: Is the truly real known by inference or directly, objectively or subjectively, as part of the world of phenomena or of human understanding?

Although the distinction between the thing and its properties also gained serious attention in music, it was increasingly taken for granted—in line with music's historical development—that 'matter' and 'form' are correlative concepts, that is, that the one is empty without the other. (This understanding applies equally to the concept of "material" as propounded by Adorno, for he too was interested in preformed material and not in pure matter.) Indeed, although it is relatively easy to identify music despite the changing appearances it manifests, it is difficult, if at all possible, to identify what underlies or presupposes its many different appearances. Musical appearances are clearly characterized by different qualities and relations. Can the latter also occur without something that has such qualities and relations? Alternately, can music exist without such qualities? Questions of this kind have been historically raised, but less for their search for a substratum capable of independent existence than for the search for a core of essential properties and the relationships between them. In fact, such formal aspects were considered essential to the structuring and comprehension of music, whereas the "*prima materia*" was considered a pure abstraction. The preoccupation with musical materials in the twentieth century, while disqualifying a priori the didactic manifestations of the concept of 'form,' failed to live up to the philosophical truth that nothing exists without having some *identifiable* form, whether by inference or directly.

To clarify the issue, it pays to examine in some detail the debate about 'form' that took place in the Darmstädter Internationale Ferienkurse für Neue Musik (1965) between the composer György Ligeti and Carl Dahlhaus.[18] Ligeti, in fact, is one of those composers who became widely known and appreciated despite, or because of, his unique musical style. What is less known, however, is that Ligeti is a composer who exerted considerable effort to become intimately acquainted not only with the musical styles of earlier periods but also with the thoughts and understandings that underlay their theoretical constructions. His intellectual curiosity does not fall short of his creative capacity. If Ligeti may be considered a composer thoroughly familiar with all that affected the development of music in the West, Dahlhaus may be considered a musicologist whose dazzling intellectual breadth reveals unrivalled familiarity with these developments. Their debate, consequently, displays a great deal of agreement insofar as the development of music is concerned and about the "thinking" that underpinned the way music was understood.

"The historical approach to 'form' is essential," argued Ligeti, "in that there is in music no actual material—in the original sense of the word— that would, in the compositional process, be formed; tones, sonorities, etc., the acoustic substratum, cannot be seen as material for music in the sense that stone and wood are material of sculpture. The process of forming in music refers rather to relations mediated by contexts of tones and sonorities; what is formed in music is, in itself, already form and not material."[19] The "system" of musical form may change, claimed Ligeti, in ways

18. Although Ligeti and Dahlhaus were not the only ones who voiced their views at that seminar, their statements—which also incorporated reactions to other speakers— best exemplify the nature and quality of the discussions that took place.

19. For the full text of the debate, see Katz and Dahlhaus, *Contemplating Music,* vol. 3, 781–814. Although much can be learned from the debate as a whole, I chose to focus primarily on aspects that relate—in one way or another—to musical coherence. I allowed the speakers to use their own wording at times in order not to distort their arguments. I shall not provide references, however, for every formulation of theirs, since they easily can be located in the full text. For Ligeti's wording, see 781–96; and for Dahlhaus's, see 797–814.

that display no continuation with the past. Nevertheless, rifts of this kind turn out to be connected, he argued, to "what has been," once they are viewed from a "distance"—that is, in retrospect. Ligeti listed four main differences between the nature of the form of twentieth-century music and musical form in the earlier tradition: (1) Composers no longer use "established formal schemata," and each individual work displays "a unique overall form adequate only to that work." (2) Rhythmic articulation "became independent of every metrically pulsating basis," a factor that, on the one hand, advanced the possibilities of differentiation in articulation, and, on the other hand, weakened its formally constructive power. (3) There is no longer "a generally valid syntax, one that, despite its variants, nevertheless forms a more or less coherent system." Although there are different possible systems of coherence, they are in fact "partial solutions, comparable to individual forms." (4) The "individualization" of syntax also changed the understanding of "formal function" in that it is "no longer fixed within the formal structure but flexible and relative." These four characteristics developed in close connection with one another, he tells us, and created a process, in which "each individual aspect of the transformation is both cause and effect." Aware that function "is particularly crucial in order for musical form to come into being," Ligeti focused primarily on the question of "to what extent the change in the nature of formal function has affected form itself."

In an attempt to answer his own question, Ligeti claimed that the "coherence-establishing character" remained intact, despite the vanishing of the "vectorial character" of formal function. His answer entailed the observation that "types" of music have emerged—based on "certain color combinations," "fixed layers of sound," "sound objects" (that are "individually deposited into the space of the form"), and so on—that have made an extensive impression, to the point of lending them the appearance of "universal validity." The latter, according to Ligeti, made the "changes in character" observable again. In other words, in the absence of established formal schemata and syntactic systems, it is the "musical types" that become "fixed" historically. The fact that many pieces turn out similar to one another should be attributed, suggested Ligeti, to the disproportion that exists between the great variety of syntax and the smaller variety of musical types, a situation that may well account for the development of a new "academicism" at a rate faster than that of earlier periods.

This paradoxical situation was brought about, Ligeti argued, by the "loosening" of the tie between "compositional process" and the resulting "sensual appearance of music." And while the music displays internal connections, these connections do not necessarily coincide with the "connections that informed the compositional process." Ligeti goes on to show how every kind of general preformation produces connections on the level of "music as sound" that were not intended, creating unanticipated "coherences of meaning" both on the horizontal and on the vertical dimensions of the composition. The interaction between the two gives rise to a "frame of reference" and consequently to "musical form." In short, the equivocal nature of the musical text is not preserved in the appearance of the music. "What is primarily given," concluded Ligeti, "is not the compositional procedure but the conception of the form's totality, the imagination of the music as sound. When applied, the method adapts to the anticipated musical result and is drawn up in concordance with the formal demands of this result."

However adequate Ligeti's description of works exemplifying the "new music" and however persuasive his arguments about retaining the "coherence-establishing factor" in the absence of formal schemata, his insistence that each work display a "unique form adequate to that particular work" (albeit anchored in *unanticipated* syntactic systems) turned formal function into connections unique to each and every composition. If the "form's totality" represents a "conception"—as Ligeti put it—rather than perceptible compositional procedures, then by what means is the listener supposed to follow the *unfolding* of such conceptions, especially when they aspire to differ one from another? These are questions that Ligeti failed to clarify and that Dahlhaus primarily addressed.

Hesitant as Dahlhaus invariably is with regard to definitions, he first called attention to the fact that 'form' is one of those "catchwords" that are defined less by their content than by their function. In literature, for example, "formalism" may represent a critical antithesis of attempts to assert the primacy of content, whereas in music it may be suspected of wanting to imprison music in schematic patterns. However, given that 'matter' and 'form' are correlative concepts in music, the attempt to break out of the "forms of contemplation felt to be a prison" is completely at odds with the "intention of making form perceivable," Dahlhaus argued. Moreover, a theory of form that neglects as indifferent or accidental "the scale on which a formal component is effective," he claimed, "is fancifully misguided." He therefore endeavored to show how the clarity of "statistical formation" and the "stability of formal scale" are mutually supportive, claiming that what is a "detail" and what is a "group" must be as unmistakable "as the difference in earlier music between motif and periods." Even if the special conditions of distinguishing detail from statistical formation are no longer operative, this does not mean, argued Dahlhaus, that the principle is no longer valid.

Dahlhaus suggested that the "new music" may be characterized by the following tendencies: (1) a "fear of things becoming fixed"; (2) a worry that the "real or realized" may constitute a "betrayal of what is possible"; and (3) misguided attempts to eliminate the difference between structure and function, between the composition and the coherence of parts. The idea that music is made up of independent parameters—pitch, duration, dynamics, and timbre—is misleading, Dahlhaus argued, and the reduction of the traditional categories to sound qualities is arbitrary, for melody implies rhythm, and rhythm implies aspects of dynamics and so on. Only what is "complex" is concrete—notes embodied in features and not in "abstract" individual parameters—since music constitutes forms of perception that merge into one another. The description of "interactions" in traditional music is a "retrospective procedure," argued Dahlhaus, an attempt to explain "complexes" that present themselves to our immediate perception as "complete and un-dissected." It was precisely one of the functions of the traditional "categories" to make the compound appear as an "undivided unity." Dahlhaus did not forget, of course, to remind his audience that categories are "forms of contemplation" that regulate perception. Formal concepts are *regulative* concepts; they "mark points of view" from which notes or groups of notes are supposed to be "brought together and related." Moreover, they are not "derivable" from the mere accumulation of "perceptual data." A theory of form remains "unfounded" if it cannot find support in "intermediate categories" that mediate between "blind facts and empty universals." The development of "concepts of form," which transcend definitions of "compositional technique," was hindered, Dahlhaus claimed, by the idea that dodecaphony is incompatible with familiar formal categories. This idea, he said, was based on a "misunderstanding," namely, on the confusion of "abstract relationships" with "concrete forms." Categories such as "theme and continuation," "complement and contrast," are not affected by the "serial principle," argued Dahlhaus, for "dodecaphony neither suggests nor justifies them, neither precludes them nor divests them of meaning." Form is *independent* of the serial principle in the same way that "the syntax of a language is independent of phonological rules."

In his concluding remarks, Dahlhaus endeavored to show that a concept of form that embraces "everything in existence" has no place in music theory; it is only used, he said, "to deny the existence of the problem at hand." He therefore reminds his audience that in the historical develop-

ment of the concept of form, the first principle was the "distinction between content and form," intended not as a "division" but as "a whole," like
the "unity of soul and body." Since the "soul" was consigned to aesthetics,
one can do justice to "the theory of form" only if one recognizes that it
was thought of as a "complement to aesthetics." In fact, a coherent and
unified theory of "the creation of musical forms" did not exist. The theory
of form subsequently embraced the idea that a musical form belonged primarily to a "genre," so that the features *common* to musical works counted
as "essential" and the distinguishing ones as "inessential." Since both the
distinction between "content and form" and the explanation of "forms
as genres" have been abandoned in the twentieth century, Dahlhaus suggested that the "new music" would have to (1) develop "musical poetics
which are not split into a theory of form and aesthetics" and (2) establish
the possibility of appraising musical forms "without invoking concepts of
genre." As for the significance that the word "structure" had acquired in
discussions about the "new music," Dahlhaus explains that 'structure' is
primarily a "technical concept" that suggests the "genesis of a work, the
process of production," whereas 'form' is an aesthetic category that refers
to the "audible shape." A structure need not be perceivable, while the idea
of an "inaudible musical form" would be a contradiction in terms. 'Structure,' for Dahlhaus, is the aspect of the work "directed at the composer,"
'form' that which is "directed at the listener."

The above portrayal of the debate between Ligeti and Dahlhaus only
touches upon the major ideas that were raised. However inclined one may
feel toward Ligeti's explications, one can hardly overlook his defensiveness. And however impressed one may be with Dahlhaus's astute observations one cannot help but sense his detachment. Yet it is precisely Ligeti's
"involved defensiveness" and Dahlhaus's "detached observations" that so
effectively convey both the dilemmas as well as the dialectics that the music of the twentieth century engendered.

THE PLIABILITY OF THE NONREPRESENTATIONAL

Whether autonomous or not and however defined, music is fundamentally nonrepresentational. It can nonetheless be effective since it is able
to reinforce semantic content due to conventions imposed on its forms
and formulae. This goes some way toward explaining why music plays so
central a role in both politics and religion. Indeed, beliefs of all sorts have
exploited music in one form or another to further their aims, aware of its
persuasive powers. By doing so they did not necessarily obfuscate artistic

achievements. For example, the Christian church obviously contributed some of the most significant chapters to the history of Western music, as did many secular institutions that used music in the service of nonreligious aims. The use made of music by governments, politicians, and social movements likewise rests on the conviction that music, if properly employed, can be more effective than the spoken or written word. Thus Weill's highly simplified, aggressive melodies and rhythms created a sophisticated new musical "façade" that came to be identified as "left-wing" music after World War I; so did the quasi return to tonality and simple meters. But not all of the leftist composers adopted this simplified musical language. In fact neither communist nor fascist attempts succeeded in creating a musically defined brand of lasting quality. Yet the belief that music might change the world was kept alive in the century that experienced more than its share of upheavals. It was intensified, paradoxically, in countries whose music was *not* censored, in social regimes where composers were free to express their dismay and protest via musical means of their choosing.

The Function of "Inclusive Symbols"

After World War I political activists of different shades sought to use music to further their political views. Some of the leading avant-garde composers—from among those who were taken in by the promise of the October Revolution—devoted considerable effort in search of "politically correct" musical representations. Yet neither the threat of fascism nor the attraction of communism produced great works. Ideologies, it seems, are not conducive to the creation of such works. Serving a "collective" via works that have "mass appeal" tends to encroach on the free imagination of talented composers. Interestingly, the music of requiem and regret outlived the music of mobilization. Regrets over futile bloodshed seem to engender human sentiments that override ideological differences, thereby enabling reconciliations of various sorts. Such sentiments also seem to create a kind of openness to compositions that represent them, regardless of the way in which the composer sees fit to express them. Indeed, even those who rejected Schoenberg's innovative music could not afford to be inattentive to his *A Survivor from Warsaw,* which powerfully reflected his horror at the inhumanity of which man is capable. And Benjamin Britten's *War Requiem*—written for the rededication of Coventry Cathedral, destroyed in air raids during the war—gained iconic status as a representation of antiwar sentiments. The distinction between "sentiments" and "opinions" is echoed in the works of many composers, who express dismay and protest in their particular ways, backed up by shared sentiments rather than prescribed ideologies.

These sentiments relate to hemmed-in emotions—an accumulation of dissatisfactions in search of an outlet—and should not be confused with our earlier discussions of the relationships between music and the emotions. This whirlpool of feelings seems better served by *compound* representations that create inclusive symbols than by fine-tuned particulars that attempt to convey *specified* emotions via the unfolding of music. The theories that point to the isomorphism between music and the emotions become irrelevant as far as these generalized symbols are concerned. They reinforce, however, the theory that argues that (1) resemblance is not necessary for reference; (2) representation, hence, is not a matter of imitation; and (3) reception and interpretation are interdependent.[20] In short, the success of such "inclusive symbols" is to be sought less in the qualities of the artifacts themselves than it is in the circumstances that lend them so powerful a position. More succinctly, they tend to shift the emphasis from substance to context and from aesthetics to social dynamics.

Appeals to the grassroots rather than the elites, to a diversified public rather than the initiated, and to the community at large rather than individuals have appeared in various guises in the course of music's history. It should be reiterated, however, that intellectual and artistic development in the West was primarily attributed to individuals who were thought to have towered above others in their astuteness and creativity. While the "forward march" was attributed to individuals, it is the world to which they belonged that was assumed to benefit from their strides and achievements. Since there are always individuals or groups who are not conscious of their contributions or fail to be recognized, such oversights are at times rectified in retrospect. Given that what a culture "thinks" of itself constitutes a significant part of its delineation, "corrections" are periodically introduced in its "self-image" via the *un*veiling of social strata or individuals whose cultural input have been overlooked.

Nationalism, as we have seen, celebrated the characteristics that define national entities. Shared languages, political events, and cultural experiences were among the essential factors of a presumed "collective spirit" that emerges from a shared past and influences future developments. Since anthropology was still relatively underdeveloped, those who wished

20. See chapter 4: "A General Theory concerning the Function of Symbol Systems in the Arts."

to "grasp" these unconscious spirits—to recollect, as it were, inherited experiences—searched among the simple folk for clues. The use of folk songs to lend musical compositions a national identity was part of this development. Such uses were markedly different, however, from the later, more sophisticated use of folk materials, which was concerned less with identities and more with changing the accustomed musical language. Thus, the use of prototype scale-structures, found in remote areas untouched by modern civilization, was supposed not only to re-invoke the *melos* of a collective past but also to enrich the musical language of the present. Bartók and Zoltan Kodály, for example, tried to combine the two; they wished to lend importance to the surviving remnants of the "Hungarian spirit" while rejuvenating their own musical language. In fact, the ethnographic materials they gathered from the "voices" of peasants and other simple folk constituted a model for later ethnomusicological investigations that paid more attention to the "unspoiled" carriers of musical traditions than to those who continued to transform them. The study of the uniqueness of diverse groups—inclusive of their particular musical traditions—certainly enriched our understanding of divergences within humankind, but ironically it also gave rise to impoverished shortcuts and stereotypes that shifted attention from the real thing to clichés.

Intended or not, the efforts to turn amorphous spirits into *discernible wholes* resulted—as far as music is concerned—in (1) the creation of group identities via music, and in (2) attempts to lend "primal formulae" a sophisticated appearance in contexts other than their own. The desire to create afresh that which originated in the genius of a people is, of course, a recurrent phenomenon in the history of music. Yet the reasons for its realization were never as bluntly spelled out, and so politically charged, as they were toward the end of the twentieth century. To be sure, the idea of "cumulative progress," which the eighteenth century fervently advanced, had already crumbled by the end of the nineteenth century, but assaults on the naïve trust in progress gained increasing momentum in the twentieth century. Despite the positivistic outlook of some avant-garde composers, the century that knew so many upheavals, such dramatic sociopolitical and technological changes, also produced composers who availed themselves of "ready-made identities." In fact, exploiting readily "identified" wholes, or parts thereof, became an effective means to convey messages of a social and political nature.

Interestingly, like music that has been regularly "possessed" by meanings despite its nonrepresentational nature, twentieth-century philosophy of language managed "to strip" words of their connections to "real things," turning them into arbitrary signifiers that did not necessarily imply what they point to. Language itself, in other words, assumed some of the characteristics of music. This development naturally lent support to existing interpretative theories, while giving rise to new ones as well.[21] Although we have known ever since Kant that our knowledge of the world is limited by man's cognitive delimitations, the notion of *scientific* progress, certainly as far as the natural sciences are concerned, remained unchallenged throughout the nineteenth century and most of the twentieth century. Yet by midcentury even the standing of the natural sciences began to be challenged, despite their involvement with a "given"—rather than a man-made—world. A door was opened that suggested that scientific knowledge, altogether, is a "social construct"—whose set of premises, axioms, and theories reflect and reinforce the perspective of its creators—rather than an objective pursuit of "truth."[22] Clearly, a change of this magnitude does not happen overnight; it was long in the making.

It is hard to overestimate the contribution made by comparative musicology—and somewhat later ethnomusicology—to the *internalization* of the idea that what was understood by 'music' in the West is not shared

21. Interpretative theories such as those of Michel Foucault, Paul Ricoeur, and Jacques Derrida, for example, are inconceivable without the linguistics of Ferdinand de Saussure and the philosophy of Ludwig Wittgenstein and their followers. What is generally referred to as "the linguistic turn" gave semiotics a big boost and aided structuralism as an analytic tool. To get an idea of the kind of musical issues that were affected by the linguistic turn, see, for example, Carl Dahlhaus, "Fragments of a Musical Hermeneutics," *Current Musicology* 50 (1992); Jean-Jacques Nattiez, "Reflections on the Development of Semiology in Music," *Music Analysis* 8 (1989); and Harold Powers, "Language Models and Music Analysis," in *Ethnomusicology* 25 (1980). For a brief comparison between music and language and the challenge of semiotics concerning music as "a language," see Kofi Agawu, "The Challenge of Semiotics," in *Rethinking Music,* ed. Nicholas Cook and Mark Everist (Oxford, 2001).

22. In his highly influential book *The Structure of Scientific Revolutions* (1962) Thomas S. Kuhn argued that scientific knowledge does not progress in ways whereby inaccurate knowledge is steadily replaced by a more accurate one. He suggested instead that the pursuit of knowledge is marked by "revolutions" that replace old premises, axioms, and theories by whole new sets of ideas once the earlier ones are no longer capable of answering the questions asked. The change that takes place is tantamount to "viewing the world differently"—to a "shift in paradigm," to use his terminology. Though Kuhn himself did not claim that scientific knowledge was a social construct, he certainly challenged its neutrality, for he admirably showed that it is constructed by people acting together who share a point of view. Of course, the concept 'paradigm' as defined by Kuhn was subsequently employed in ways he did not anticipate. Cultural studies, for example, makes ample use of the concept in order to delineate or justify behavioral differences among people belonging to different groups or segments of society.

by people the world over. The interest in remote cultures, including their music, has a long history, of course. Missionaries, explorers, colonialists, and numerous others contributed greatly to making Europeans aware of ways of life other than their own. The prominence gained by the Vergleichende Musikwissenschaft around World War I through the Weimar Republic, however, may be attributed to the specific social-political conditions that affected the various empires and to the greater awareness of the changed status of the colonies under their rule. Remote worlds that had previously been ignored or taken for granted were now brought home and widely discussed, gaining the kind of saliency that they had never enjoyed. To this one must add the developments that had taken place in the field of musicology around the turn of the century, turning the field, more and more, into an academic discipline.

The so-called Berlin School of Comparative Musicology was interested in the music of different cultures in order to reveal both commonalities and differences. Comparative musicology sought to uncover the uniqueness of music as a universal human expression no less than to research its different manifestations. Yet the different manifestations were examined more and more closely from the perspective of their creators, rather than from an Olympian point of view. Given that music does not happen in a vacuum, references to social and cultural forces were naturally also incorporated into the study of Western music. But concerns of this kind seemed marginal to the study of music in the West since it emerged as a cultural "subsystem" whose development could be traced *and* understood through its own transformations without having to delve into its immediate social contexts. It must be remembered, however, that music in the West incorporated and reflected, as I tried to show, in its very theoretical guidelines and changed musical manifestations, the major "turns of mind" that the society underwent in the course of its development. Indeed, as long as the "rational paradigm" governed Western art music, as it governed other spheres of knowledge, it was relatively easy to specify its "logic" via an examination of the artifacts alone. However, once the rational paradigm collapsed, the music that "mirrored" this collapse raised new questions that required answers inspired by a "new look"—an altered frame of mind.

The "new music" clearly raised issues that were hardly addressed in our earlier discussions concerning the development of Western music. The new concerns included subjects such as the relationship between 'conception' and 'perception,' between the composer's 'intention' and the 'comprehension' of his work, between 'reception' and 'interpretation,' between works of art and their social role and a host of other issues. Though relevant to Art at all times, these issues only gradually emerged as concerns requiring theoretical formulations of their own; they certainly did not occupy center stage in the past study of music. Indeed, the artistic and social problems that surfaced in the twentieth century gave rise to many theories related to the interpretation of "texts" of all kinds.[23] Although interpretation continued to be viewed as a kind of natural disposition, these theories created an awareness of the various forms it may take, highlighting the different perspectives through which a given work of art may be viewed, including its function. Independent of the answers they gave rise to, these queries contributed greatly to the altered "frame of mind" that made room for multiple conceptions and perceptions of music. Although it is often difficult to establish the causal nexus between artistic expressions and their immediate sociopolitical contexts, or the order in which they affect one another, the twentieth century gave us no choice but to grapple with this nexus, since reception and interpretation have become inextricably intertwined.

The Appropriation of Meaning

The search for progress led Ecclesiastes, the biblical skeptic, to say "There is nothing new under the sun" The "new," he observed, "hath been already, in the ages which were before." The reason he gave for "that which hath been is that which shall be" was based on the insight that "there is no remembrance of them of former times; neither shall there be any remembrance of them of later times."[24] There is much truth in his "circular" theory of progress, however depressing. Nonetheless, his implication that "sameness" prevents "newness" seems to overlook the fact that in *human* life—unlike the natural phenomena that occupied Ecclesiastes—the very same thing may be differently perceived, depending on contexts and points of view. With these preparatory remarks, I wish to reiterate that the establishment of the "modern system of the arts" in the eighteenth century was based on recognition of an epistemological uniqueness of the arts that *defies* the notion of progress. Moreover, the idea that the power of art resides not in the objects it represents but in the

---

23. For a reliable and clear summary of the theories that have made the greatest impact in recent times on the interpretation of "texts" in the humanities, see Wolfgang Iser, *How to Do Theory* (Oxford [Blackwell], 2006). As is well known, literary theory has not only become a branch of learning in its own right, but has been extensively applied to fields other than literature.

24. See *Ecclesiastes* 1:9–11.

modalities that shape its messages assigned the arts to the realm of perception. Indeed, the eighteenth century produced an abundance of treatises
that attempted to clarify and define the "correspondences" and "differences" among the arts. The pursuit of perception led to a separation of the
arts from one another, like the separation of the arts from science somewhat earlier. The long-held notion that the diverse arts were but different
treatments and manifestations of essentially the same subjects yielded,
consequently, to the idea that different artistic media dictated the choice
of compatible subject matter, as claimed by Lessing in his famous *Laocoön*.
What was learned about the differences among the arts naturally guided
the attempts to wed them. Much was of course also learned from works
in which these attempts were actually realized, that is, where each of the
arts successfully took the others into account. Though the interactions
among the arts underwent many changes, the "fictive"—the "as if" world
of the arts—became nonetheless solidly grounded in this process, embedded in an understanding of the "illusion" that it entails and the kinds of
metaphors that it employs.[25]

That these interactions also should have yielded "compact images"—
indivisible wholes, as it were—is hardly surprising. Regardless of the ways
the arts were considered, the interactions between them created "simultaneities" that gained a standing of their own, which only as such could
convey new specified meanings. Communicative "images" of this kind
function to render new meanings similar to deviations from norms. At any
rate, what was learned from the process of relating the individual arts to
one another also revealed that there are things that cannot be "said" without combinatorial entities—compounds of various sorts, whose properties entirely differ from the elements that make up their union.[26] Realizations of this kind challenge not only the distinctions among the arts but

25. Roger Scruton, for example, claims that the understanding of music inevitably
involves metaphorical thinking based on verbal representations of experience. The
descriptive language used by listeners to music, Scruton claims, discloses the categories
and concepts they apply while listening to it. See Roger Scruton, *The Aesthetics of Music*
(Oxford, 1997). Martin Clayton argues that musical discourses "metaphorically link
sound to other domains of experience," but do not represent the musical experience;
experiencing music is not tantamount to what discourse attributes to music. See Martin
Clayton, "Comparing Music, Comparing Musicology," in *The Cultural Study of Music*, ed.
Martin Clayton, Trevor Herbert, and Richard Middleton (New York, 2003). Lawrence
Kramer insists that music does "important cultural work by being spoken of, and would
not be what we call 'music' otherwise." See Lawrence Kramer, "Subjectivity Rampant!
Music, Hermeneutics, and History," in *The Cultural Study of Music*.
26. See Daniel Albright's interesting book: *Untwisting the Serpent: Modernism in Music,*

also the factors that historically highlighted the separation among them. To begin with the arts were divided into "temporal" versus "spatial" arts; while *semantics* differentiated poetry from music within the temporal arts, the *number of dimensions employed* differentiated painting from sculpture and architecture within the spatial arts. Though 'time' and 'space' invariably touch upon each other due to the "illusions" that art is able to create and via the metaphorical exchanges of which it is capable, the history of art nonetheless maintained the distinction between the temporal and the spatial, not least for didactic purposes.[27]

The "cognitive turn" in epistemology did not occur all at once, after all; it resulted from the investigation of many issues, as they emerged, that needed to be looked at more closely. However significant this turn may have been for the history of ideas, the distinction between cognition and epistemology required far more scrutiny. The preoccupation with the mind drew ever more attention to questions concerning the relationship between 'mind' and 'brain' and to the ways they affect or constrain each other. In fact, the "mind-brain" conundrum continues to engage many scholars today in diverse fields, who are still far from having arrived at definitive conclusions.[28] Generally speaking, cognitive studies are concerned with the ways, how and where, the mind processes information and structures coherence. To get from process to coherence, we are told, requires some form of construction or representation, based on relationships

---

Literature, and Other Arts (Chicago, 2000), which abounds with examples illustrating "compounds" of this kind.

27. Mark Johnson, for example, argues that the ultimate grounding of our understanding (including the metaphors we use and the dimensions we apply in art) lies in our body, in its movements and orientations. See Mark Johnson, *The Body in the Mind* (Chicago, 1987).

28. In an interesting short article, Ian Cross calls to our attention that the claim about music as a "universal human behavior," as part of "human nature," does not square with the scholarship that replaces 'music' with musics, holding that the latter "are musics only in their cultural contexts" and that they "can only be approached through culturally situated acts of interpretation." The position that the cultural dynamics of music owe "little or nothing" to the evolutionary processes that underlie our biology, argues Cross, is only tenable "if our biological being can be cleanly dissociated from our cultural lives, and given that our cultural lives are mainly evidenced in material behaviors and their traces, a clean dissociation between culture and biology—or between music and evolution—is infeasible." Today it is generally agreed by cognitive and social scientists that cultural variation is the "effect" of a common cognitive "endowment" that "given different historical and ecological conditions, makes this variability possible." See Ian Cross, "Music and Bio-cultural Evolution," in *The Cultural Study of Music*, ed. Clayton, Herbert, and Middleton, 19–30.

among the particular elements being processed. Although process is influenced by what is being processed, coherence—structured as it may
be—does not, in itself, carry meaning; in other words, coherence "makes
sense" but has no meaning. To turn such meaningful cohesions into cohe-
sive meaning requires symbolization. One can readily see how significant
the contribution of philosophy was to the science of the mind. Debates
concerning the innate versus the learned, and the relations among the
"given worlds" and the "possible worlds," occupied philosophy precisely in
order to differentiate between the inner activities of mental processes and
their interactions with that which is external to them.

Without belaboring the point, one might argue that the mind-brain
"puzzle" has accompanied the development of music in the West since the
genesis of modern science, though it was hardly formulated in these terms.
The present essay has tried to convey the idea that modern thought actually created the conditions whereby the "perception of music" became a
primary route to the understanding of aesthetic experiences. Moreover,
since musical experience came to be viewed as creating its own fictional
world, with its own temporality—a kind of fusion of "narrative time" and
"musical time"—it became, as I have tried to illustrate, "an important
source for several axioms, namely, that experience is *internal,* that its basis
is *temporal,* that it is *narrative,* and that the distinction between truth and
fiction is *dynamic.*"[29] Most important, however, is the fact that music—the
non-representational art—revealed that the antecedents of cognitive science may in fact reside in aesthetics rather than in traditional epistemology. Indeed, although Western art music may have lost its "lofty" standing
among the musics of the world, it no doubt contributed a *lasting* insight to
the workings of the mind.

Ever since Wagner proclaimed that his *Gesamptkunstwerk* makes the
"invisible visible," that music, the nonrepresentational art, functions as
mediator enabling this transfiguration, music has undergone enormous
changes. Though twentieth-century music raised many questions insofar
as coherence is concerned, it has created undeniably recognizable "images" whose "visibility" could not be overlooked, regardless of the interpretations they called forth or the uses that were made of them.[30] The
turn from circumscribed understandings to unbounded interpretations,

29. Quotation from Gabriel Motzkin's comments at a symposium held on *Tuning the
Mind* (Katz and HaCohen) at the Van Leer Foundation, Jerusalem (December 2003).
30. It should be noted that the present interest in images, which is often referred to
as the "iconic turn," supersedes the "linguistic turn" of several decades ago. The latter
superseded the "cognitive turn" of the eighteenth century. These "turns," I believe,

from musical constraints to "emancipated" expressions resulted in a para-digmatic shift in the cultural study of music. It also opened new doors to serious consideration of diverse kinds of music that had hitherto merited little attention. That all of this should call for new criteria of judgment is self-evident. Yet the theories that guided our understanding of music—including that of "remote" cultures—have been challenged in ways that defy a comprehensive overview. What is less obvious is the fact that new understandings are often applied to music that has evidently partaken of and reflects a different social and *intellectual* reality. One would expect those who maintain that a unique connection invariably exists between a given social group and the nature and meaning of its music to apply the same criteria to the music of former days, even if its "complex architec-tonic and harmonic structures" are attributed to those with "power and influence" who "could manipulate" simple frameworks "extensionally."[31] Indeed, those who wish to affect the future often alter the perspectives that informed the past. The unbridled appropriation of meanings, at any rate, became increasingly "visible;" it even reached a point at which it could be fabricated so as to convey what it hypothetically represented.[32]

Cultural studies, as is well known, are thriving nowadays; there is no want of scholars to partake in a genuine effort to redefine their subject matters from allegedly "cultural perspectives." Given the high awareness

---

represent stages—each with its particular emphasis—in the overall attempt to better understand the ways in which the mind processes information and structures coherence.

31. See John Shepherd, "Music and Social Categories," in *The Cultural Study of Music,* ed. Martin Clayton, Trevor Herbert, and Richard Middleton (New York, 2003), 73.

32. Although this sounds like criticism, I do not mean it as such. Richard A. Peterson's brilliant study *Creating Country Music* (Chicago, 1997) reveals how the music industry created and nurtured country music, which was presented as a "reinvention." It has been in the process of "reinventing" itself ever since. The argument that tradi-tions can be "invented"—reflecting thereby the complex interaction between past and present—is poignantly conveyed by the essays that Eric Hobsbawm and Terence Ranger include in their widely read *The Invention of Tradition* (Cambridge, 1983). And Benedict Anderson's famous book *Imagined Communities* ((London, 1983) traced the processes by which nations came to be "imagined as old." The cultural approach to various disciplines is nonetheless relatively new; it was not even part of a field such as sociology, though it investigated many cultural institutions of diverse kinds. Jeffrey C. Alexander in his bril-liant study *The Meaning of Social Life: A Cultural Sociology* (Oxford, 2003) argues that the sociology of culture was not really concerned with "collective meanings" but rather with their "effects" or structural formations. The postmodern period—in which factual state-ments and fictional narratives cannot be separated from each other—calls for a "cultural sociology," Alexander argues, that would address precisely what the "sociology of culture" had overlooked until now, namely, the formations and functions of collective meanings.

of cultural differences and the readiness to withhold value judgments concerning "the other," much of what was once understood by the term 'culture' has thus undergone enormous changes. The term, one might say, has become relativized, dependent on the group or issue under discussion—whether a particular civilization, society, subgroup, gender, age, institution, art form, and so forth.[33] Such subdivisions may of course also partake in attempts to refine and correct histories that represented more "generalized" points of view, supplying as well the reasons for the oversights in the past. The cultural study of music exemplifies all of these changes, but, like cultural studies in general, it has not yet established overall criteria whereby music *as* social practice should be examined.[34]

Every discourse, I still believe, must operate with some implicit appeal to criteria by which claims are justified. Such criteria have implications for conceptions of "reality," even if 'truth' has become suspect, relative, or an empty concept altogether. Indeed, the universal necessity that previously characterized reason and the autonomous rational subject (in the Kantian sense) has been challenged by an irreducible plurality of incommensurable "language games" and forms of life. The a priori character of truth has given way, moreover, to the empirical, to cultural variability, and to fragmentary systems of signs. In short, there seems to be an overall rejection of ultimate foundations, whether transcendental conditions of possibility or metaphysical first principles, suggesting that there is no knowledge without background, and that background cannot be wholly objectified. This does not imply, however, that we need to accept all claims under the pretext of subjectivity or relativism. Precisely because our propositional knowledge of this world is grounded in our dealing with it, and because we are unable to have an objective prior grasp as agents within it, it behooves us to articulate, as best we can, this very background.[35]

33. For the problems that the definition of 'culture' raises, see the introductory chapter by Richard Middleton, "Musical Studies and the Idea of Culture," in *The Cultural Study of Music,* ed. Clayton, Herbert, and Middleton.

34. This is certainly the impression one gets despite the fact that the cultural study of music has produced many interesting and illuminating case studies. Upon a careful reading of the essays included in *The Cultural Study of Music,* one cannot fail but realize that this is indeed the case.

35. The "articulation" of background, however, also requires some kind of "consensus" regarding interpretation. In his critical study of myth as symbol, James Jakób Liszka argues in favor of a critical semiotic that is interested not in the "re-creation of ambivalence" but in attempts to remove it. This can only be achieved, he claims, through dialogue, for "when the latitude of interpretation is diminished by force or direction it fails to be genuine." He persuasively demonstrates how interpretation is effected by *con-*

Evaluating Music: How and in What Way?

It may be too early, perhaps, to fully grasp the momentous changes that have taken place in the last few decades in our thinking in general and with regard to music in particular. The two are naturally intertwined. Many of the theories that guided our understanding of music, including that of "remote" cultures, have clearly been challenged in ways that defy a comprehensive overview.[36] Even cultural relativism is being defied nowadays by globalism, which effects changes not only in the economic and political spheres but also in the production and consumption of cultural artifacts. The ostensible return of relativism in the guise of multiculturalism is clearly not the relativism we once knew. The old relativism was largely based on the supposition of the relative stability and incommensurability of coherent cultures, though it was assumed that steady unswerving cultures hardly exist in the world we live in. The new relativism by comparison is a confusion consisting not only of ethnic, national, or religious groupings but also of newly minded collectives claiming shared identity but porous boundaries and often part-time affiliations. Although mutual respect is demanded and paid, borrowings across group boundaries are not merely common but encouraged. In our "global village" we are allowed not only to borrow from one another but also to toss these borrowings into a new cultural melting pot. If multiculturalism leaves our identities

---

sensus arrived at via genuine *dialogue* rather than by force or direction. Although Liszka's erudite and impressive study is not easy to plow through, it deserves the effort, since he masterfully "creates a dialogue" among various theoretical positions relevant to his topic. See James Jakób Liszka, *The Semiotic of Myth: A Critical Study of the Symbol* (Indiana, 1989). Lest the reader get the impression that what is applicable to myth is unlikely to apply to science, I recommend Mara Beller's outstanding study *Quantum Dialogue: The Making of a Revolution* (Chicago, 1999), which beautifully illustrates how scientific consensus is achieved. She does not simply set up social determinants of scientific belief against the understanding of science in cognitive terms, but persuasively demonstrates that science is primarily rooted in dialogue. This holds true even when it pertains to major scientific breakthroughs such as the quantum revolution.

36. To get an idea of the changes that have taken place and the new issues that they have raised, see Georgina Born and David Hesmondhalgh's "Introduction: On Difference, Representation, and Appropriation in Music" (1–58); Philip V. Bohlman's "Composing the Cantorate: Westernizing Europe's Other Within" (187–212), and Simon Frith's "The Discourse of World Music" (303–22), in Born and Hesmondhalgh, *Western Music and Its Others* (California, 2000). For a short, thoughtful review of the ways in which European intellectual histories set Western music apart from "its others," I highly recommend Gary Tomlinson's article "Musicology, Anthropology, History," in *The Cultural Study of Music,* ed. Clayton, Herbert, and Middleton.

and evaluative criteria relatively intact (in spite of the license we are given to poach on the symbols and artifacts of others), postmodernity and the global perspective invite us to throw our subcultural criteria into the general bonfire, thus rendering systematic evaluations impossible.

In each of these framings, a de-contextualization of cultural artifacts is being legitimated, that is, a de-contextualized space has been created in which they lose their "meaning" even while we are asked to assume and respect the integrity of their cultural origin. We are expected to do so without understanding what they "stand for" in their original settings or the place they hold in the aesthetic systems from which they have been uprooted. How is one to explain, for example, the *reception* of so-called world music? It has been observed by scholars and dilettantes alike that the increased curiosity about the 'Other' and the political correctness implicit therein allows world music to function as an "introduction" to the other. And however curious or sympathetic the audience turns out to be, the music tends in most cases to be "tailored"—delivered in ways attractive to its consumers despite its pretensions to authenticity. It seems that performances of this kind only offer a superficial acquaintance with the music, though perhaps also some indoctrination to the functions it serves in the sociopolitical problems of its society of origin, and perhaps they succeed in enlisting our sympathy. By whose criteria of judgment should such music be analyzed?

The phenomenon of marrying explicitly heretofore unrelated musics to each other, whether in a popular or classical vein, poses an even greater challenge. Much of postmodern music displays aspects of extension as well as of breaks from modernism.[37] In general terms, this music may be characterized by a *negation of boundaries* (between past and present procedures and sonorities), by *challenging distinctions* (between "high" and "low," "elitist" and "populist" values), and by *opposition to categorical systems, structural unity,* and *totalizing forms.* In such composites of sounds, where

---

37. Describing the musical style of John Adams, Alex Ross makes the following observations: "It is a cut-up paradise, a stream of familiar sounds arranged in unfamiliar ways. A glitzy Hollywood fanfare gives way to a trancelike sequence of shifting beats; billowing clouds of Wagnerian harmony are dispersed by a quartet of saxophones. It is present-tense American romanticism, honoring the ghosts of Mahler and Sibelius, plugging into minimalist processes, swiping sounds from jazz and rock, browsing the files of postwar innovation. Sundry sounds are broken down and filtered through an instantly recognizable personal voice, sometimes exuberant and sometimes melancholy, sometimes hip and sometimes noble, winding its way through a fragmentary culture." See Ross, *The Rest Is Noise,* 512–13.

even binary contrasts are suspect, temporalities and meanings become evidently multiplied. Meaning and structure are thus more determined by the listeners than by the musical scores and their performances. Indeed, unlike abstract music, which furthered music's autonomy by a kind of "collapse into itself" (inadvertently distancing itself thereby from the listener), postmodern music not only emphasizes its relevance to cultural, social, and political contexts but it also invites the listener to partake, as it were, in the "structuring" of the music being offered.[38]

Musical critics tend to solve the problem that various musical admixtures nowadays represent by itemizing their "ingredients"—using familiar labels that indicate different styles, genres, times, and places—that make up the whole.[39] Forgoing familiar labels, what would qualify as an appropriate *musical analysis* of compositions that adjoin a variety of recognizable styles—Western and non-Western—into their compositional fabric? Whose "understanding" should be brought to bear on such an analysis, if any at all? Whom does the music represent, and in what way? Should special analytic categories be devised for music *divorced* from its original context? Does the mounting popularity of world music suggest "universals" concerning musical comprehension?[40] Should the relationship between

38. In an interesting article that discusses both postmodern music and musical minimalism, Robert Fink argues that the hierarchical music theory that rested on the "surface-depth" metaphor only seemed relevant to a conception that considered great art as having an organically unified, multileveled integrity. The surface-depth metaphor, argues Fink, is irrelevant to present-day analytical concerns since minimalism and postmodernism have produced music of various kinds of "flatness" that challenge the multileveled conception of art. The new conception, it is argued, suppresses the distance between the music and the listener, enveloping him in ways that make him a part of the "sound-space" that surrounds him. See Robert Fink, "Going Flat: Post-Hierarchical Music Theory and the Musical Surface," in *Rethinking Music*, ed. Cook and Everist.

39. Allen Kozinn (the classical music critic for the *New York Times*) analyzed the works of several composers in the following way: Arvo Pärt's work is described as "antiquity and modernism side by side," Bright Sheng as "East and West meet in contemporary musical language," Henryk Gorecki "can move easily from the classical to the pop shelf," while Gregorio Paniaqua "hops freely through time and space to keep things lively" in the mix of styles in his *La Folia*. By quoting Kozinn, I do not mean to undermine his important contribution to the musical scene, but rather to highlight a theoretical problem that needs to be resolved in a more music-analytical way. For a collection of Kozinn's reviews, see Allen Kozinn, *Classical Music* (New York, 2004).

40. The universals that John Blacking talked about in his famous essay *How Musical Is Man?* (Seattle, 1973) refer to the musical aptitude of man and not to his musical comprehension. He insisted, in fact, that the latter is culture-bound. Nonetheless, Blacking was after "universals" that might shed light on music as a universal phenomenon. John Dewey, we may recall, argued in his *Art and Experience* (New York, 1934) that art—indeed

music and meaning be redefined or be discarded altogether?[41] If music generates a variety of meanings that are not culture-bound, what makes them distinctive? Although there are many more questions one could ask, they all draw attention to the absence of *consensual* theoretical frameworks that would allow scholars to transcend with assuredness that which they may have discarded out of conviction.

CONCLUDING REMARKS

It will have been noticed that I have refrained from discussing the dichotomy between art music and popular music. Despite its present-day prominence, popular music should not be treated as though it were a recent phenomenon. Popular music invariably existed, alongside art music, in all of the cultures that saw fit to differentiate between them. Moreover, art music invariably involved a more restricted audience and designated functions. If art music merited greater scholarly attention, it is largely because art music continually displayed—in one form or another, written or unwritten—a high degree of self-consciousness. To be sure, the dividing lines between popular music and art music kept changing in the development

---

all objects—share universals such as "color, extensity, solidity, movement, rhythm," and that both creator and consumer can apprehend the work in these terms even if their backgrounds do not coincide and even if they have very different references in mind. (Dewey, obviously, was referring to painting. Did he mean to include music in his scheme?) Whether such thinking can be revived and expanded remains a major challenge. Cognitive studies, nowadays, are interested—among many other things—in establishing the "universals" that explain cultural differences and the mental processes that affect different cultural spheres. Altogether, the relationship between 'mind' and 'brain' has received increased attention in recent years. Given this development, it pays to reread Leonard Meyer's astute observations about creation, archetypes, stylistic change, and universals. See the following essays: "Exploiting Limits: Creation, Archetypes, and Style Change" (189–224), "A Pride of Prejudices; or, Delight in Diversity" (262–78), and "A Universe of Universals" (281–303), in his *The Spheres of Music: A Gathering of Essays* (Chicago, 2000). Interestingly, many of the ideas that have been contemplated in the domain of philosophy are being investigated nowadays empirically. Cognitive psychologists, in fact, often consider neuroscience investigations of the mind as a kind of "empirical philosophy." Some of the fundamental issues addressed by neuroscience have a direct bearing on music's role in human evolution and daily life, on the various functions music serves, and, above all, on the complex interrelated circuits in which it is perceived by the human brain. For an introductory overview of the relationship between neuroscience and music, I highly recommend Daniel J. Levitin's reliable ("user friendly") book: *This Is Your Brain on Music: The Science of a Human Obsession* (New York [Dutton], 2006).

41. See Andy Nercessian's enlightening essay on this very subject: *Postmodernism and Globalization in Ethnomusicology: An Epistemological Problem* (London, 2002).

of music in the West, but never before did they raise the social issues and theoretical challenges that such a "dichotomy" presently elicits.[42] Though popular music seems more "natural" than art music, which strikes us as judiciously made, it is precisely that which came into being *un*-naturally, as it were, that this essay has tried to elucidate. Indeed, art music is a kind of thrashed-out activity that, unlike popular music, invariably needs justification, whether from within the art or from the audiences it addresses. Western art music was in fact accompanied by elaborate "reasoning procedures" that were in tune with the intellectual strides and "turns of mind" that Western civilization has undergone over the last millennium. These turns clearly affected not only the ways in which music was structured and understood but also the "semblances" that music created, the institutions it served, the publics it addressed, and the "self-images" of its practitioners. Despite the many changes that Western art music has undergone, it created its distinctiveness precisely through the ways in which it wrestled with continuity and change. Traditions, generally, do not stand still; they endure because of the mechanisms whereby they incorporate novelties and change. Cultural traditions, moreover, represent at all times the collective efforts and understandings of their adherents, even if the contribution of some of their members may loom larger than that of others.

The Romantic turn in the West engendered, as we have seen, a move away from a presumed objective world toward a subjective one that gave vent, more than ever before, to the free imagination and self-expression of artists. While self-expression increasingly exemplified the autonomous spirit of the human subject, it became most apparent in the works of artists that no longer felt obliged to serve some utilitarian purpose. Moreover, this newly conceived "autonomous realm" contributed largely to the trans-

---

42. To get an idea of the problems involved, see John Covach, "Popular Music, Unpopular Musicology," in *Rethinking Music*, ed Cook and Everist. Alex Ross summarizes the present state of the art as follows:

> At the beginning of the twenty-first century, the impulse to pit classical music against pop culture no longer makes intellectual or emotional sense. Young composers have grown up with pop music ringing in their ears, and they make use of it or ignore it as the occasion demands. They are seeking the middle ground between the life of the mind and the noise of the street. Likewise, some of the liveliest reactions to twentieth-century and contemporary classical music have come from the pop arena, roughly defined. The microtonal tuning of Sonic Youth, the opulent harmonic designs of Radiohead, the fractured time signatures of math rock and intelligent dance music . . . all these carry on the long-running conversation between classical and popular traditions. (Ross, *The Rest Is Noise*, 541–42).

formation of 'Art' into a symbolic embodiment of the free spirit of Man and
a channel whereby transcendent metaphysical experiences can be reached.
The emphasis on the autonomous spirit of artists precipitated, in turn, the
need to innovate so as to lend musical compositions their unique "signa-
ture." Composers in the twentieth century furthered the notion of "self-
realization" via an unprecedented degree of technical innovations. However sophisticated and insightful, these innovations gradually led, though
not directly, to a withdrawal of art music not only from its connections
with the "outer world" but also from the spiritual significance that the "inner world" of artists was expected to convey. The interesting transformations that took place eventually resulted in an abstract kind of music whose
technical innovations significantly boosted music theory but failed—with
a few exceptions—to be genuinely endorsed by the public. Despite the
claim that this music represented but a more advanced stage in the uninterrupted development of Western art music, it constituted a break from
a tradition that was deeply embedded in the *signification* of the music that
it produced. The rupture that had taken place should not be confused with
the earlier turn that advocated "art for art's sake." The latter represented a
desire to free art from extraneous controls and demands that curtailed or
seemed to blur the very *spirituality* that Art was thought to suggest.

No other music was as keen to develop its own referential systems as
was Western art music; with the aid of these systems music reached a stage
in which it was able to explain itself from within; it reached a stage of
coherence that "made sense" even without imparting what it was about.
Rather than annul the quest for meaning, it enabled new musical procedures—employing the very coherence music had acquired—that unswervingly conveyed even specified meanings. This seeming "self-sufficiency" of
music also invited, as we have seen, metaphysical speculations as to what
it—as such—represented. The kind of abstract music to which I referred
above challenged both coherence and music's spiritual signification via its
unprecedented "self-absorption." Although it continued to produce works
that left an indelible mark on the development of Western music, it appears nonetheless to have eventually "collapsed into itself" in ways that
defied the audiences for whom it was outwardly intended.[43]

43. In a chapter that deals with "individualism in Western art music and its cultural
costs," Rose Subotnik brings the following to our attention:

> Ours is no longer an age of world-historical figures, at least in art music. Yet we
> continue to define our demands of music in terms of an individualism more suited
> to the ethos of an earlier age, with results that circumscribe the effectiveness of

Once aesthetics became a philosophical discipline concerned with the *cognition* of art in relation to other systems of knowledge, aesthetic representations became indicative of something external to art, yet something that works of art are able to convey. It follows that a sensory expression that does not point to something other than itself is, as it were, "void" of signification. The twentieth century witnessed artistic expressions in each of its branches that seriously challenged long-held theories about the function of Art and its assumed import. In this new state of affairs, music constituted an exception because music, whether autonomous or not and however defined, is fundamentally nonrepresentational. In fact, the "powers" attributed to music since time immemorial were *de*-mystified in the West by revealing the ways in which music acquires meaning. Music in the West, as I tried to show, acquired *its* meaning through the understandings that accompanied its very construction and through an ever growing understanding of symbols and the way they function. Thus, despite its nonrepresentational nature, music displayed its effectiveness through the metaphorical manipulations of its forms, formulae, and unfolding procedures. It became "representational" because it was able to reinforce semantic contents via the manipulations of those understandings that constituted, to begin with, an integral part of its construction. In the twentieth century art music increasingly relinquished not only its defining essences but also detached itself from the metaphysical underpinnings that it previously entertained.

The transformations that came to the fore in twentieth century art explain, in no small measure, the mushrooming of modern theories of art—intellectual tools that try to provide new ways in which works of art, including music, may be conceptualized. Given that the semantic layer of language provides the *connotations* of words—though words, too, may be manipulated so as to lose their original meaning—it is hardly surprising that many of these theories focused at first primarily on literature. Nonetheless, these modern theories suggest that the "self-absorbed" music, to

---

even our most successful composers of art music. For again, once the property of individual expression is idealized beyond the point of any possible counterbalance by collective musical values, musical expression tends to lose its character of expressiveness as well as its corollary capacity for communication. What remains, as we can hear in the large number of formally self-conscious but expressively impotent works produced in our own half-century, is music that constitutes evidence of individualized formal concerns and standards that are no longer expressive in the sense of either individually revelatory or socially effective. (Subotnik, *Developing Variations*, 254.)

which I referred above, does not necessarily represent the end of a venerable musical tradition, but that it must find a way that will allow us to
conceptualize its abstractions as representations.[44] There are interesting
signs that point in this direction. These "signs" require, however, a study
of their own.

I would like to reiterate that my essay attempted to trace the key *ideas*
that affected the advance of music in the West; it should not be construed,
hence, as an "abridged" history of Western music. In fact, the essay intended primarily to highlight the ways in which a particular musical tradition went about creating its uniqueness. Musical traditions clearly differ
from one another not only in their exterior appearances but also in what
they signify to their adherents. They also vary in the processes they undergo that affect their delineations. Consequently, what a certain culture
understands by 'music'—comprising its various functions—may likewise
vary. Now that distinctions between "high" and "low" cultures are no longer tenable and the futility of such arguments has been exposed, there is
all the more reason to examine cultural differences, including their musical
traditions, the better to understand each other and the transformations
that have taken place. In short, my essay neither aimed to extol Western
art music nor to bemoan its fate. It attempted to render the *self-portrait* of
Western art music via the ways in which it constructed itself, conceived of
itself, and aspired to convey signification.

44. In an interesting and sophisticated article that deals with the relationship
between analysis and performance, Nicholas Cook argues that analyses representing
music are fundamentally metaphorical; they are acts "disguised" as statements of facts.
Since our language for music is a language of representation, we cannot get away from
representation, but we must recognize, says Cook, that our language for music is not
monolithic, but that it "draws its signification from any number of alternative representations of music, each of which constitutes sound as a different intentional object." See
Nicholas Cook, "Analyzing Performance and Performing Analysis," in *Rethinking Music*,
ed. Cook and Everist, 258.

Aaron, Pietro. 1516. *Libri tres de institutione harmonica*. Bologna.

Abbate, Carolyn. 1991. *Unsung Voices: Opera and Musical Narrative in the Nineteenth Century*. Princeton.

Abrams, M. H. 1953. *The Mirror and the Lamp: Romantic Theory and the Critical Condition*. Oxford.

Adler, Guido. 1885. "Umfang, Methode und Ziel der Musikwissenschaft," *Vierteljahrsschrift für Musikwissenschaft* 1:5–20.

———. 1898. "Musik und Musikwissenschaft" (Akademische Antrittsrede), *Jahrbuch der Musikbibliothek Peters*, 29–39.

———. 1911. *Der Stil in der Music*. Leipzig.

———. 1919. *Methode der Musikgeschichte*. Leipzig.

———, ed. 1930. *Handbuch der Musikgeschichte*. Berlin.

Adorno, Theodor W. 1922. "Paul Hindemith," *Neue Blätter für Kunst und Literature* 4.

———. 1949. *Philosphie der neuen Musik*. Tubingen.

———. 1964. "Reaktion und Fortschritt," in *Moments musicaux*. Frankfurt.

Adorno, Theodor, and Max Horkheimer. 1981. *Dialektik der Aufklärung: Fortsetzungsphilosophie* [Dialectics of the Enlightenment: Philosophy in Installments]. In *Gesammete Schriften,* edited by Rolf Tiedeman. Frankfurt.

Agawu, Kofi. 2001. "The Challenge of Semiotics." In *Rethinking Music*, edited by Nicholas Cook and Mark Everist. Oxford.

Albright, Daniel. 2000. *Untwisting the Serpent: Modernism in Music, Literature, and Other Arts*. Chicago.

Alexander, Jeffrey C., ed. 1988. *Durkheimian Sociology: Cultural Studies*. New York.

———. 2003. *The Meaning of Social Life: A Cultural Sociology*. Oxford.

Anderson, Benedict. 1983. *Imagined Communities*. London.

Apel, Willi. 1953. *The Notation of Polyphonic Music 900–1600*. Cambridge, Mass.

Aristotle. *Nicomachean Ethics,* book VII.

Arnold, F. Thomas. [1931] 1965. *The Art of Accompaniment from a Thorough-Bass as Practiced in the 17th and 18th Centuries.* Oxford (Dover).

Balzano, G. J. 1980. "The Group Theoretic Description of 12-fold and Microtonal Pitch Systems," *Computer Music Journal* 4:66–84.

Barry, Kevin. 1987. *Language, Music and the Sign: A Study in Aesthetics, Poetics and Poetic Practice.* Cambridge.

Baumgarten, Alexander Gottlieb. [1735]. "Reflections on Poetry." In Ruth Katz and Carl Dahlhaus, *Contemplating,* vol. 2, 571–613.

———. 1750. *Aesthetica.* Frankfurt.

Baumol, William, and William Bowen. 1968. *Performing Arts: The Economic Dilemma.* Cambridge (MIT).

Beller, Mara. 1999. *Quantum Dialogue: The Making of a Revolution.* Chicago.

Benjamin, Walter. 1955. "Ursprung des deutsches Trauerspiels." In *Schriften,* vol. 1, 172. Frankfurt.

———. 1968. "Art in the Age of Mechanical Reproduction." In *Illuminations,* edited by Hannah Arendt, 217–51. New York.

———. 1973. *Illuminations.* Translated by H. Zohn. London.

Berg, Alban. 1924. "Warum ist Schoenbergs Musik so schwer verständlich?" In *Musikblätter des Anbruch* 6.

Berger, Karol. 1987. *Musica Ficta: Theories of Accidental Inflections in Vocal Polyphony from Marchetto Da Padova to Gioseffo Zarlino.* Cambridge.

———. 2000. *A Theory of Art.* Oxford.

———. 2005. "Time's Arrow and the Advent of Musical Modernity." In *Music and the Aesthetics of Modernity,* edited by Karol Berger and Anthony Newcomb. Cambridge, Mass.

Bergson, Henri. [1896] 1911. *Matter and Memory [Matiére et mémoire].* Translated by N. M. Paul and W. S. Palmer. New York.

Berlin, Isaiah. 1956. *The Age of Enlightenment: The Eighteenth-Century Philosophers.* New York.

———. 1976. *Vico and Herder: Two Studies in the History of Ideas.* London.

———. 1981. *Against the Current: Essays in the History of Ideas.* Oxford.

Blacking, John. 1973. *How Musical Is Man?* Seattle.

Boethius. [6th century] 1867. *De institutione musica.* Leipzig.

Bohlman, Philip V. 2000. "Composing the Cantorate: Westernizing Europe's Other Within." In *Western Music and Its Others: Difference, Representation, and Appropriation in Music,* edited by Georgina Born and David Hesmondhalgh, 187–212. California.

———. 2001. "Ontologies of Music." In *Rethinking Music,* edited by Nicholas Cook and Mark Everist. Oxford.

Born, Georgina, and David Hesmondhalgh. 2000. "Introduction: On Difference, Representation, and Appropriation in Music." In *Western Music and Its Others: Difference, Representation, and Appropriation in Music,* edited by Georgina Born and David Hesmondhalgh, 1–58. California.

Bourdieu, Pierre. 1991. "Artists Taste and Cultural Capital." In *Culture and Society,* edited by Jeffrey Alexander and Steven Seidman, 205–15. Cambridge.

Brett, Philip. 1988. "Text, Context, and the Early Music Editor." In *Authenticity and Early Music,* edited by Nicholas Kenyon, 83–114. Oxford.

Brown, Howard M. 1988. "Pedantry or Liberation: A Sketch of the Historical Performance Movement." In *Authenticity and Early Music,* edited by Nicholas Kenyon, 27–56. Oxford.

Brown, Roger W. 1958. *Words and Things.* Glencoe.

Bruner, Jerome S. 1957. "On Perceptual Readiness," *Psychological Review* 64:123–52.

Bukofzer, Manfred F. 1947. *Music in the Baroque Era.* New York.

———. 1950. "The Beginnings of Choral Polyphony." In his *Studies in Medieval and Renaissance Music,* 176–89. New York.

———. 1950. "Caput: A Liturgico-Musical Study." In his *Studies in Medieval and Renaissance Music,* 217–317.

Burkholder, J. Peter. 1997. "Museum Pieces: The Historicist Mainstream in Music of the Last Hundred Years," *Journal of Musicology* 6.

Burnham, Scott. 2005. "On the Beautiful in Mozart." In *Music and the Aesthetics of Modernity,* edited by Karol Berger and Anthony Newcomb, 39–52. Cambridge, Mass.

Busoni, Ferruccio. [1907] 1962. "Sketch of a New Esthetic of Music." In *Three Classics in the Aesthetic of Music,* translated by T. Baker. New York.

Caccini, Giulio. [1602] 1950. *Le nuove musiche.* In Oliver Strunk, *Source Readings in Music History,* 379. New York.

Carlton, Richard. 2000. "Florentine Humanism and the Birth of Opera: The Roots of Operatic 'Conventions,'<ts>" *International Review of the Aesthetics and Sociology of Music* 31:* 67–78.

Cassiodorus. [6th century] 1937. *Institutiones.* Edited by R. A. B. Mynors. Oxford.

Cassirer, Ernst. "Neo-Kantianism." *Encyclopedia Britannica* (14th ed.).

———. 1951. *The Philosophy of the Enlightenment.* Princeton.

———. 1954. *An Essay on Man: An Introduction to a Philosophy of Human Culture.* New York.

———. [1908–29] 1955. *Philosophy of Symbolic Forms.* Translated by Ralph Manheim. 3 vols. New Haven.

———. 1979. *Symbol, Myth, and Culture: Essays and Lectures of Ernst Cassirer, 1935–1945.* Edited by Donald Phillip Verene. New Haven.

Child, Harold. 1921. "Some Thoughts on Opera Libretto." In *Music and Letters,* vol. 2.

Chomsky, Noam. 1957. *Syntactic Structures.* The Hague.

Christensen, Thomas. [1993] 2004. *Rameau and Musical Thought in the Enlightenment.* Cambridge.

Clark, R.C. 1955. *Herder: His Life and Thought.* California.

Clayton, Martin. 2003. "Comparing Music, Comparing Musicology." In *The Cultural Study of Music,* edited by Martin Clayton, Trevor Herbert, and Richard Middleton. New York.

Cochlaeus, Johannes. 1507. *Musica.* Cologne.

Cohen, Dalia. 1971. "Palestrina Counterpoint: A Musical Expression of Unexcited Speech," *Journal of Music Theory* 15:84–110.

Cohen, Dalia, and Ruth Katz. 1979. "The Interdependence of Notation Systems and Musical Information," *Yearbook of the International Folk Music Council,* vol. 2.

———. 1997. "Attitudes to the Time Axis and Cognitive Constraints: The Case of Arabic

Vocal Folk Music." In *Perception and Cognition of Music,* 31–45. East Sussex: Psychology Press.

———. 2006. *Palestinian Arab Music: A Maqām Tradition in Practice.* Chicago.

Condillac, Etienne Bonnot de. 1756. *Essai sur l'origine des connaissances humaines.* Paris.

Cone, Edward. 1974. *The Composer's Voice.* Berkeley.

Cook, Nicholas. 2001. "Analyzing Performance and Performing Analysis." In *Rethinking Music,* edited by Nicholas Cook and Mark Everist. Oxford.

———. 2003. "Music *as* Performance." In *The Cultural Study of Music,* edited by Martin Clayton, Trevor Herbert, and Richard Middleton. New York.

Coser, L. 1965. *Men of Ideas.* New York.

Coussemaker, Charles, Edmond, Henri de. [1864–76] 1963. *Scriptorium.* 4 vols. Hildesheim.

Covach, John. 2001. "Popular Music, Unpopular Musicology." In *Rethinking Music,* edited by Nicholas Cook and Mark Everist. Oxford.

Crane, Diana. 1972. *Invisible College: Diffusion of Knowledge in Scientific Communities.* Chicago.

Crocker, Richard. 1990a. "Liturgical Materials of Roman Chant." In *The New Oxford History of Music,* vol. 2, chap. 4, 111–45.

———. 1990b. "Chants of the Roman Office." In *The New Oxford History of Music,* vol. 2, chap. 5, 146–73.

———. 1990c. "Chants of the Roman Mass." In *The New Oxford History of Music,* vol. 2, chap. 6, 174–224.

———. 1990d. " Medieval Chant." In *The New Oxford History of Music,* vol. 2, chap. 7, 225–309.

Cross, Ian. 2003. "Music and Bio-cultural Evolution." In *The Cultural Study of Music,* edited by Martin Clayton, Trevor Herbert, and Richard Middleton. New York.

Dahlhaus, Carl. 1985. *Realism in the Nineteenth-Century* [*Musikalischer Realismus: Zur Musikgeschichte des 19. Jahrhunderts*]. Cambridge.

———. 1987. "Progress and the Avant-Garde." In *Schoenberg and the New Music,* translated by Derrick Puffet and Alfred Clayton. Cambridge.

———. [1960] 1990. *Studies on the Origin of Harmonic Tonality.* Translated by Robert O. Gjerdingen. Princeton.

———. [1978] 1991. *The Idea of Absolute Music.* Translated by Roger Lustig. Chicago.

———. 1992. "Fragments of Musical Hermeneutics," *Current Musicology* 50.

———. [1967] 1995. *Esthetics of Music.* Translated by William Austin. Cambridge.

———. [1977] 1999. *Foundations of Music History.* Translated by J. B. Robinson. Cambridge.

D'Ancona, Alessandro. 1891. *Origini del teatro italiano.* Turin.

Danuser, Hermann. 2005. "The Textualization of the Context: Comic Strategies in Meta-Operas of the Eighteenth and Twentieth Centuries." In *Music and the Aesthetics of Modernity,* edited by Karol Berger and Anthony Newcomb, 65–97. Cambridge, Mass.

Daston, Lorraine, and Katherine Park. 1998. *Wonders and the Order of Nature.* New York.

Dell'Antonio, Andrew. 2004. *Beyond Structural Listening? Postmodern Modes of Hearing.* California.

Dewey, John. [1934] 1958. *Art and Experience.* New York.

Dilthey, Wilhelm. [1910] 1976. "The Construction of the Historical World in the Human Sciences." In *Selected Writings,* edited and translated by H. P. Rickman. Cambridge.

———. 1996. *Hermeneutics and the Study of History (Selected Works 4).* Edited by Rudolf Makkreel and Frithjof Rodi. Princeton.

Donington, Robert. 1990. *Opera and Its Symbols: The Unity of Words, Music, and Staging.* New Haven.

Drabkin, William. 2002. "Heinrich Schenker." In *Western Music Theory,* edited by Thomas Christensen, 831. Cambridge.

Durkheim, Emile. [1913–14] 1964. "Pragmatism and Sociology." In *Essays on Sociology and Philosophy,* edited by Kurt H. Wolff. New York.

Eaman, William. 1994. *Science and the Secrets of Nature: Books of Secrets in Medieval and Early Modern Culture.* Princeton.

Eco, Umberto. 1981. *The Role of the Reader.* Bloomington.

———. 1990. *The Limits of Interpretation.* Bloomington.

Einstein, Alfred. 1947. *Music in the Romantic Era.* New York.

Eisler, Hanns, and Theodor Adorno. 1947. *Composing for the Films.* New York.

Fink, Robert. 2001. "Going Flat: Post-Hierarchical Music Theory and the Musical Surface." In *Rethinking Music,* edited by Nicholas Cook and Mark Everist. Oxford.

Flach, W., and H. Holzhey. 1980. *Erkenntnistheorie und Logik im Neukantianismus.* Hildesheim.

Franco of Cologne. [ca. 1260] *Ars cantus mensurabilis.* In Oliver Strunk, *Source Readings in Music History.* 1950. New York.

Frith, Simon. 2000. "The Discourse of World Music." In *Western Music and Its Others: Difference, Representation, and Appropriation in Music,* edited by Georgina Born and David Hesmondhalgh, 303–22. California.

Funkenstein, Amos. 1986. *Theology and the Scientific Imagination from the Middle Ages to the Seventeenth Century.* Princeton.

Fux, Johann. [1725] 1949. *Steps to Parnassus, the Study of Counterpoint* [*Gradus ad Parnassum*]. Translated by Alfred Mann. New York.

Gastoué, Amédée. 1930–31. "L'Origine lointaine des huit tons liturgiques," "Chant Juif et Chant Grégorien," and "Les Origines hébraïques de la liturgie et du chant Chrétien," *La Revue du chant gregorien* 34 and 35.

Gay, Peter. 1969. "Weimar Culture: The Outsider as Insider." In *The Intellectual Migration: Europe and America, 1930–1960,* edited by Donald Fleming and Bernard Bailyn, 11–93. Cambridge, Mass.

———. 1978. *Freud, Jews, and Other Germans: Masters and Victims in Modernist Culture.* New York.

Goehr, Lydia. 1992. *The Imaginary Museum of Musical Works: An Essay in the Philosophy of Music.* Oxford.

Gombosi, Otto. 1938–39. "Studien zur Tonartenlehre des frühen Mittelalters," *Acta Musicologia* 10 and 11.

Gombrich, Ernest . [1960] 1977. *Art and Illusion.* New York.

———. [1966] 1985. *Norm and Form.* London.

Goodman, Nelson. 1968. *Languages of Art.* New York.

———. 1975. "The Status of Style," *Critical Inquiry* 1, no. 4: 799–812.

———. 1978. *Ways of World-Making*. Indianapolis.

Goody, Jack. 2006. *The Theft of History*. Cambridge.

Gozzi, Paulo, ed. 2000. *Number to Sound: The Musical Way to the Scientific Revolution*. Boston.

Grover-Friedlander, Michal. 2005. *Vocal Apparitions: The Attraction of Cinema to Opera*. Princeton.

Halm, August. 1913. *Von zwie Kulturen der Musik*. Munich.

Hanslick, Eduard. 1950. "Verdi's 'Otello.'<ts>" In *Music Criticisms 1846–99*, translated and edited by Henry Pleasants, 280–87. Baltimore.

———. [1854] 1957. *The Beautiful in Music*. Translated by Gustav Cohen. New York.

Hauser, Arnold. 1951. *The Social History of Art*. London.

Hegel, Wilhelm Friedrich. [1826] 1955. *The Philosophy of History*. Translated by E. S. Haldane and F. H. Simson. 3 vols. London.

Helmholtz, Hermann. [1863] 1948. *On the Sensation of Tone*. Translated by Alexander J. Ellis. New York.

Henderson, Isobel. 1957. "Ancient Greek Music." In *The New Oxford History of Music*, vol. 1. London.

Herder, Johann Gottfried. [1784–91] 1800. *Outlines of a Philosophy of the History of Man*. Translated by T. O. Churchill. London.

Herskovits, Melville J. 1966. *The Influence of Culture on Visual Perception*. Indianapolis.

Heseltine, Philip. 1920. "The Scope of Opera." In *Music and Letters*, vol. 1.

Hobsbawm, Eric, and Terence Ranger, ed. 1983. *The Invention of Tradition*. Cambridge.

Hoeckner, Berthold. 2002. *Programming the Absolute: Nineteenth-Century German Music and the Hermeneutics of the Moment*. Princeton.

Hoffmann, E. T. A. [1813] 1950a. "Beethoven's Instrumental Music." In Oliver Strunk, *Source Readings in Music History*, 775–76. New York.

———. . [1819–821] 1950b. "The Poet and the Composer." In Oliver Strunk, *Source Readings in Music History*, 787. New York.

Hucke, Helmut. 1954. "Die Einführung des Gregorianischen Gesangs im Frankenreich," *Römische Quartalschrift* 49:172–85.

———. 1955. "Gregorianischer Gesang in alt-römischer und fränkischer Uberlieferung," *Archiv für Musikwissenschaft* 12:74 -87.

———. 1980. "Toward a New Historical View of Gregorian Chant," *Journal of the American Musicological Society* 33, no. 3.

Hume, David. 1739. *A Treatise of Human Nature*. London.

Idelsohn, Abraham Zevi. 1914–32. *Hebräisch-orientalischer Melodienschatz*. 10 vols. Leipzig.

Iser, Wolfgang. 2006. *How to Do Theory*. Oxford (Blackwell).

Izard, Carrol E. 1971. *The Face of Emotion*. New York.

Jakobson, Roman. 1941. *Kindersprache, Aphasie, und allgemeine Lautgesetze*. Uppsala.

James, William. 1907. *Pragmatism: A New Name for Some Old Ways of Thinking*. Cambridge.

———. [1909] 1975. *The Meaning of Truth*. Cambridge.

———. [1909] 1996. *A Pluralistic Universe*. Nebraska.

Jeppersen, Knud. 1939. *Counterpoint, the Polyphonic Vocal Style of the Sixteenth Century*. New York.

Johnson, Mark. 1987. *The Body in the Mind*. Chicago.

Kant, Immanuel. [1790] 1952. *Critique of Judgment.* Translated by J. H. Meredith. Oxford.

Katz, Ruth. 1986a. "Exemplification and the Limits of 'Correctness': The Implicit Methodology of Idelsohn's *Thesaurus,*" *Yuval* (Jerusalem) 5:365–71.

——. 1986b. *Divining the Powers of Music.* New York.

——. 1992. "History as 'Compliance': The Development of Western Musical Notation in the Light of Goodman's Requirements." In *How Classification Works: Nelson Goodman among the Social Sciences,* edited by Mary Douglas and David Hull, 99–128. Edinburgh.

——. 1994. *The Powers of Music, Aesthetic Theory and the Invention of Opera.* Repr. of *Divining the Powers of Music,* rev., new intro. Brunswick, New Jersey.

Katz, Ruth, and Carl Dahlhaus, eds. 1987–93. *Contemplating Music: Source Readings in the Aesthetics of Music.* 4 vols., with extensive introductions and translations by the editors. New York.

Katz, Ruth, and Ruth HaCohen. 2002a. *Tuning the Mind: Connecting Aesthetics to Cognitive Science.* Brunswick, New Jersey.

——. 2002b. *The Arts in Mind.* Brunswick, New Jersey.

Kaufman, Walter. 1967. *Musical Notations of the Orient: Notational Systems of Continental East, South, and Central Asia.* Indiana.

Kenyon, Nicholas, ed. 1988. *Authenticity and Early Music.* Oxford

Kirnberger, Johann Philipp. 1774. 1779. *Die Kunst des reinen Satzes in der Musik aus sicheren Grundsätzen hergeleitet unt mit deutlichen Beispielen versehen.* 2 vols. Berlin.

Koch, Heinrich Christoph. 1782–93. *Versuch einer Anleitung zur Composition.* Rudolstadt.

Kozinn, Allen. 2004. *Classical Music.* New York.

Kramer, Lawrence. 1984. *Music and Poetry: The Nineteenth Century and After.* California.

——. 1995. *Classical Music and Postmodern Knowledge.* California.

——. 2003. "Subjectivity Rampant! Music, Hermeneutics, and History." In *The Cultural Study of Music,* edited by Martin Clayton, Trevor Herbert, and Richard Middleton. New York.

Kristeller, Paul O. 1965. "The Modern System of the Arts." In his *Renaissance Thought and the Arts,* 163–227. Princeton.

Kuhn, Thomas S. [1962] 1970. *The Structure of Scientific Revolution.* Chicago.

Kurth, Ernst. 1917. *Grundlagen des linearen Kontrapunkts: Bach melodische Polyphonie.* Berlin.

——. 1931. *Musikpsychologie.* Berlin.

Lang, Paul Henry. 1960. *Problems of Modern Music.* New York.

Langer, Susanne K. 1953. *Feeling and Form.* New York.

——. 1957. "The Art Symbol and the Symbol in Art." In her *Problems of Art.* New York.

Leibniz, Gottfried Wilhelm. [1686] 1902. *Discourse on Metaphysics.* Translated by G. R. Montgomery. Chicago.

Lessing, Gotthold, Ephraim. [1766] 1957. *Laocoön: An Essay upon the Limits of Painting and Poetry.* Translated by E. Fothinham. New York.

Levitin, Daniel J. 2006. *This Is Your Brain on Music: The Science of a Human Obsession.* New York (Dutton).

Levy, Kenneth. 1990. "On Gregorian Orality," *Journal of the American Musicological Society* 43, no. 2: 185–227.

——. 1998. *Gregorian Chant and the Carolingians.* Princeton.

Lindberg, David, and Robert Westman, eds. 1990. *Re-appraisals of the Scientific Revolution.* Cambridge.

Liszka, James Jakób. 1989. *The Semiotic of Myth: A Critical Study of the Symbol.* Indiana.

Liszt, Franz. 1882. *Gesammelte Schriften.* Leipzig.

Locke, John. . [1690] 1961. *An Essay Concerning Human Understanding.* London.

Loesser, Arthur. 1954. *Men, Women, and Pianos.* New York.

Malinowski, Bronislaw. [1925] 1948. *Magic, Science, and Religion.* New York (Anchor).

Marx, Adolf Bernhard. 1837–47. *Die Lehre von der musikalischen Komposition.* 4 vols. Berlin.

Mattheson, Johann. 1739. *Der Vollkommene Capellmeister.* Kassel.

McClary, Susan. 1992. *Feminine Endings: Music, Gender, and Sexuality.* Minnesota.

———. 2000. *Conventional Wisdom: The Content of Musical Form.* California.

Mersenne, Marin. 1636. *Harmonie universelle.* Paris.

Merton, Robert K. 1973. *The Sociology of Science.* Chicago.

Meyer, Leonard B. 1956. *Emotion and Meaning in Music.* Chicago.

———. 2000a. "Exploiting Limits: Creation, Archetypes, and Style Change." In his *The Spheres of Music: A Gathering of Essays,* 189–225. Chicago

———. 2000b. "A Pride of Prejudices; or, Delight in Diversity." In his *The Spheres of Music: A Gathering of Essays,* 262–78. Chicago.

———. 2000c. "A Universe of Universals." In his *The Spheres of Music: A Gathering of Essays,* 281–303. Chicago.

Miall, David S. 1987. "Metaphor and Affect: The Problem of Creative Thought," *Metaphor and Symbolic Activity* 2.

Middleton, Richard. 2003. "Music Studies and the Idea of Culture." In *The Cultural Study of Music,* edited by Martin Clayton, Trevor Herbert, and Richard Middleton. New York.

Miller, George A. 1962. "Some Psychological Studies of Grammar," *American Psychologist* 17:748–62.

Moravia, Hieronymus de. [ca. 1300]. In Coussemaker, *Scriptorium,* vol. 1.

Morgan, Robert P. 1988. "Tradition, Anxiety, and the Current Musical Scene." In *Authenticity and Early Music,* edited by Nicholas Kenyon, 57–82. Oxford.

Mulkay, M. K. 1972. *The Social Process in Innovation.* London.

Muris, Jean de. [14th century]. *Ars discantus.* In Coussemaker, *Scriptorum de Musica Medii Aevi,* vol. 3.

Nattiez, Jean-Jacques. 1989. "Reflections on the Development of Semiology in Music," *Music Analysis* 8.

"Neo-Kantianism." 1967. In *The Encyclopedia of Philosophy.* New York.

Nercessian, Andy. 2002. *Postmodernism and Globalization in Ethnomusicology: An Epistemological Problem.* London.

Nettl, Bruno. 1972. "Thoughts on Improvisation: A Comparative Approach," *Musical Quarterly* 60.

———. 1982. "Types of Traditions and Transmissions." In *Cross-Cultural Perspectives on Music,* edited by Robert Falck and Timothy Rice. Toronto.

———. 2001. "The Institutionalization of Musicology: Perspectives of a North American Ethnomusicologist." In *Rethinking Music,* edited by Nicholas Cook and Mark Everist. Oxford.

Newcomb, Anthony. 2005. "The Hunt for Reminiscences in Nineteenth-Century Germany." In *Music and the Aesthetics of Modernity*, edited by Karol Berger and Anthony Newcomb, 111–35. Cambridge, Mass.

Newman, William. 1959–66–72. *A History of the Sonata Idea.* 3 vol. North Carolina.

Ossi, Massimo. 2003. *Divining the Oracle: Monteverdi's Seconda Pratica.* Chicago.

Paddison, Max. 1993. *Adorno's Aesthetics of Music.* Cambridge.

Palisca, Claude. 1956. "Vincenzo Galilei's Counterpoint Treatise: A Code for the Seconda Pratica," *Journal of the American Musicological Society* 4:81–96.

——. 1960a. "Vincenzo Galilei and Some Links between 'Pseudo-Monody' and Monody," *Musical Quarterly* 46:347.

——. 1960b. *Mei's Letters on Ancient and Modern Music to Vincenzo and Giovanni Bardi.* Rome.

——. 1961. "Scientific Empiricism in Musical Thought." In his *Seventeenth-Century Science.* Princeton.

——. 1968. "The Alterati of Florence, in *the Theory of Dramatic Music." In *New Looks at Italian Opera*, edited by William Austin. Ithaca.

——. 1972a. "The Camerata Fiorentina: A Reappraisal," *Studi musicali* 1.

——. 1972b. "Musical Asides in the Diplomatic Correspondence of Emilio de' Cavalieri," *Musical Quarterly* 44, no. 3.

——. 1985. *Humanism in Italian Renaissance Musical Thought.* New Haven.

Parrish, Carl. 1957. *The Notation of Medieval Music.* New York.

Pater, Walter. [1893] 1980. *The Renaissance.* Edited by D. L. Hill. California.

Paul, Jean. [1804] 1935. *Vorschule der Ästhetik.* In *Sämtliche Werke*, vol. 1. Weimar.

Peterson, Richard A. 1997. *Creating Country Music.* Chicago.

Pirrotta, Nino. 1954. "Temperaments and Tendencies in the Florentine Camerata," *Musical Quarterly* 40.

——. 1968. "Early Opera and Aria." In *New Looks at Italian Opera: Essays in Honor of Donald J. Grout*, edited by William W. Austin, 52. Ithaca.

Pirrotta, Nino, and Elena Povoledo. [1969] 1982. *Music and Theater from Poliziano to Monteverdi.* Cambridge.

Plutchik, Robert. 1980. "A General Psycho-Evolutionary Theory of Emotion." In *Emotion: Theory, Research, and Experience*, vol. 1 (*Theories of Emotions*), edited by R. Plutchik and H. Kellerman. Orlando.

Powers, Harold. 1980a. "Mode." In *The New Grove Dictionary of Music and Musicians*, vol. 12, 376–450.

——. 1980b. "Language Models and Music Analysis," *Ethnomusicology* 25.

Praz, Mario. 1951. *The Romantic Agony.* Translated by Angus Davidson. 2nd ed. Oxford.

Quine, Willard V. 1973. *The Roots of Reference.* Illinois.

Ramachandran, V. S., and William Hirstein. 1999. "The Science of Art: A Neurological Theory of Aesthetic Experience," *Journal of Consciousness Studied: Controversies in Science and the Humanities* 6:15–51.

Rameau, Jean Philipp. 1722. *Traitè de l'harmonie.* Paris.

Rankin, Susan. 1984. "From Memory to Record: Musical Notations in Manuscripts from Exeter," *Anglo-Saxon England* 13:97–111.

Reese, Gustave. 1940. *Music in the Middle Ages.* New York.

——. 1954. *Music in the Renaissance*. New York.

Reill, Peter Hanns. 1975. *The German Enlightenment and the Rise of Historicism*. California.

Reiss, Timothy. 1997. *Knowledge, Discovery, and Imagination in Early Modern Europe: The Rise of Aesthetic Rationalism*. Cambridge.

Reynolds, L. D., and N. G. Wilson. 1974. *Scribes and Scholars: A Guide to the Transmission of Greek and Latin Literature*. Oxford.

Riemann, Hugo. 1893. *Vereinfachte Harmonielehre oder die Lehre von den tonalen Funktionen der Akkorde*. London.

——. 1907. *Verloren gegangene Selbstverständlichkeiten in der Musik des 15. Bis 16. Jahrhunderts*. Langensalza.

——. 1914–15. "Ideen zu einer 'Lehre von den Tonvostellunge,'" *Jahrbuch der Musikbibliothek Peters*.

——. 1916. "Neue Beiträge Zu einer 'Lehre von den Tonvorstellungen,'" *Jahrbuch der Musikbibliothek Peters*.

Rigbi-Shafrir, Elisheva. 2002. "The Modern in Music against the 'Crisis of Historicism' and the Breakdown of the Rational Paradigm: A Critical Analysis of a Style." PhD diss., Hebrew University, Jerusalem.

Rosen, Charles. 1971. *The Classical Style*. London.

——. 1995. *The Romantic Generation*. Cambridge, Mass.

Rosenberg, B., and N. E. Fliegel. 1965. *The Vanguard Artist*. Chicago.

Ross, Alex. 2007. *The Rest Is Noise: Listening to the Twentieth Century*. New York.

Rowell, Lewis. 2002. "New Temporal Horizons and the Theory of Music." In *Music in the Mirror: Reflections on the History of Music Theory and Literature for the 21st Century*, edited by Andreas Giger and Thomas J. Matheisen. Nebraska.

Sachs, Curt. 1943. *The Rise of Music in the Ancient World*. New York.

——. 1946. *The Commonwealth of Art*. New York.

Samson, Jim. 2001. "Analysis in Context." In *Rethinking Music*, edited by Nicholas Cook and Mark Everist. Oxford.

Schiller, Friedrich. 1795–76. *Über naïve und sentimental Dichtung*. Weimar.

Schoenberg, Arnold. 1911. *Harmonielehre*. (Rev. ed., 1922, 1948, and 1978). Vienna.

——. 1950. *Style and Ideas*. New York.

——. 1978. *Theory of Harmony*. Translated by Roy E. Carter. London.

Schopenhauer, Arthur. [vol. 1, 1818; vol. 2, 1844] 1950. *The World as Will and Idea*. Translated by R. B. Haldane and J. B. Kemp. London.

——. 1987. *The World as Will and Idea*. In Katz and Dahlhaus, *Contemplating Music*, vol. 1.

Schorske, Carl E. 1981. *Fin-de-Siècle Vienna: Politics and Culture*. New York.

Schrade, Leo. 1964. *Tragedy in the Art of Music*. Cambridge.

Schroeder, David P. 1990. *Haydn and the Enlightenment: The Late Symphonies and Their Audiences*. Oxford.

Scruton, Roger. 1997. *The Aesthetics of Music*. Oxford.

Shaftesbury, Anthony Ashley Cooper, Earl of. 1743. *Characteristics*. 3 vols. London.

Shepherd, John. 2003. "Music and Social Categories." In *The Cultural Study of Music*, edited by Martin Clayton, Trevor Herbert, and Richard Middleton. New York.

Smith, Adam. [1759] 1976. *The Theory of Moral Sentiments*. Edited by D. D. Raphael and A. L. Macfie. Oxford.

Sondheimer, R. J. 1925. *Die Theorie der Symphonie.* Leipzig.

Spitzer, Leo. 1963. *Classical and Christian Ideas of World Harmony.* Baltimore.

Spitzer, Michael. 2004. *Metaphor and Musical Thought.* Chicago.

Sternfeld, Frederick. 1988. *The Birth of Opera.* Oxford.

Strunk, Oliver. 1950. *Source Readings in Music History.* New York.

Subotnik, Rose. 1991. *Developing Variations: Style and Ideology in Western Music.* Minnesota.

——. 1996. *Deconstructive Variations: Music and Reason in Western Society.* Minnesota.

Tanay, Dorit. 1999. "Noting Music, Marking Culture: The Intellectual Context of Rhythmic Notation, 1250–1400." American Institute of Musicology, *Musicological Studies and Documents* 46:23–47.

Taruskin, Richard. 1988. "The Pastness of the Present and the Presence of the Past." In *Authenticity and Early Music,* edited by Nicholas Kenyon, 137–207. Oxford.

——. 1995. "Last Thoughts First: Wherein the Author Gently Replies to a Few of His Critics and Takes Tender Leave of the Topic." In his *Text and Act: Essays on Music and Performance,* 3–47. Oxford.

——. 2005. *The Oxford History of Western Music.* Oxford.

Taylor, Charles. 1975. *Hegel.* Cambridge.

——. 1989. *Sources of the Self: The Making of the Modern Identity.* Cambridge, Mass.

Tinctoris, Johannes. 1473. *Terminorum musice diffinitorium.* Naples.

——. 1477. *Liber de arte contrapunti.* Naples.

Tomlinson, Gary. 1993. *Music in Renaissance Magic: Toward a Historiography of Others.* Chicago.

——. 1999. *Metaphysical Song.* Princeton.

——. 2003. "Musicology, Anthropology, History." In *The Cultural Study of Music,* edited by Martin Clayton, Trevor Herbert, and Richard Middleton. New York.

Treitler, Leo. 1974. "Homer and Gregory: The Transmission of Epic Poetry and Plainchant," *Musical Quarterly* 40, no. 3.

——. 1982. "The Early History of Music Writing," *Journal of the Musicological Society* 35, no. 2: 243–44.

——. 1984. "Reading and Singing: On the Genesis of Occidental Music-Writing," *Early Music History* 4:186.

——. 2001. "The Historiography of Music: Issues of Past and Present." In *Rethinking Music,* edited by Nicholas Cook and Mark Everist. Oxford.

Trinkaus, Charles. 1970. *In Our Image and Likeness.* Chicago.

Ursprung, Otto. 1931–33. *Die katholische Kirchenmusik.* Potsdam.

Velten, H. V. 1943. "The Growth of Phonemic and Lexical Patterns in Infant Languages," *Language* 19:281–92.

Verba, Cynthia. 1993. *Music and the French Enlightenment.* Oxford.

Verene, Donald Phillip, ed. 1979. *Symbol, Myth, and Culture: Essays and Lectures of Ernst Cassirer, 1935–1945.* New Haven.

Vico, Giambattista. [1744] 1948. *The New Science.* Translated by T. G. Bergin and M. H. Fisch. Ithaca.

Vygotskii, Lev S. [1934] 1962. *Thought and Language.* Cambridge, Mass.

Wackenroder, W.H. [1797] 1950. "The Remarkable Musical Life of the Musician Joseph

Berlinger," from his *Herzenergiessungen eines kunstliebenden Klosterbruders.* In Oliver
Strunk, *Source Readings in Music History,* 750–763. New York.

Wagner, Peter. 1895. *Einführung in die gregorianischen Melodien.* 3 vols. Leipzig.

———. 1907. *Introduction to the Gregorian Melodies: Part I, Origin and Development of the
Forms of the Liturgical Chant up to the End of the Middle-Ages.*

———. 1929. "Der Gregorianische Gesang." In Guido Adler, *Handbuch der Musikgeschichte.*

Wagner, Richard. 1849. *Die Kunst und die Revolution.*

———. 1850. *Das Kunstwerk der Zukunft.*

———. 1851–52. *Oper und Drama.*

———. 1860. *Zukunftsmusik.*

———. [1850] 1869. "Das Judentum in der Musik." In *Neue Zeitschrift für Musik.*

———. 1871–73. "Preface" to his *Gesammelte Schriften und Dichtung.* Leipzig.

———. 1983. *Richard Wagner Dichtungen und Schriften: Jubläumsausgabe.* Frankfurt.

Waite, William G. 1954. *Twelfth-Century Polyphony, Its Theory and Practice.* New Haven.

Walker, D. P. 1958. *Spiritual and Demonic Magic from Ficino to Campanella.* London.

Warburton, William. 1738–41. *The Divine Legation of Moses Demonstrated from the Principles
of a Deist.* 2 vols. London.

Webb, Daniel. 1760. *An Inquiry into the Beauties of Painting.* London.

———. 1762. *Remarks on the Beauties of Poetry.* London.

———. [1769] 2002. *Observations on the Correspondence between Poetry and Music.* In *The Arts
in Mind,* by Ruth Katz and Ruth HaCohen, vol. 2. Brunswick, New Jersey.

Weber, Max. 1921. *The Rational and Social Foundation of Music.* Munich.

Weber, William. 1977. "Mass Culture and the Reshaping of European Musical Taste,
1770–1870," *International Review of the Aesthetics and Sociology of Music* 7:6.

———. 2001. "The History of Musical Canon." In *Rethinking Music,* edited by Nicholas
Cook and Mark Everist. Oxford.

Wellesz, Egon. 1929. "Die byzantinische und orientalische Kirchenmusik." In Guido
Adler, *Handbuch der Musikgeschichte.*

———. 1932. "Das Alter der Melodien der byzantinischen Kirche." In *Forschungen und
Fortschritte.*

———. 1936. *Der Stand der Forschung auf dem Gebiete der byzantinischen Kirchenmusik.*

Werner, Eric. 1958. *The Sacred Bridge.* London.

White, Harrison, and Cynthia White. 1965. *Canvases and Careers.* New York.

Winckel, Fritz. [1959] 1967. *Music, Sound, and Sensation.* New York.

Wolf, Yohannes. [1913; 1919] 1963. *Handbuch der Notationskunde.* 2 vols. Wiesbaden.

———. [1904] 1965. *Geschichte der Mensural-Notation von 1250–1460.* Wiesbaden.

Wölfflin, Heinrich. [1915] 1929. *Principles of Art History.* Translated (from 7th German ed.)
by M. D. Hottinger. Oxford (Dover).

Yates, Frances A. 1969. *Giordano Bruno and the Hermetic Tradition.* New York.

Yolton, John W. 1985. *Locke—An Introduction.* Oxford.

Zaminer, Frieder. 1959. *Der Vatikanische Organum-Traktat.* Tulzing.

Zarlino, Gioseffe. 1558. *L'Institutioni harmoniche.* Venice.

Zerner, Henri. 2005. "A propos of Buffon's *Discours du style.*" In *Music and the Aesthetics of
Modernity,* edited by Karol Berger and Anthony Newcomb, 53–62. Cambridge, Mass.

Zuckerkandl, Victor. 1956. *Sound and Symbol.* Princeton.